4.95

Learning Theories for Teachers, Second Edition

Morris L. Bigge

Fresno State College

Harper & Row, Publishers
New York, Evanston, San Francisco, London

LEARNING THEORIES FOR TEACHERS, Second Edition
Copyright © 1971 by Morris L. Bigge

Standard Book Number: 06-040671-2
LIBRARY OF CONGRESS CATALOG CARD NUMBER: 78-168349

Contents

Editor's Foreword

This is a scholarly, yet thoroughly down-to-earth study of the aspects of learning theory that have direct bearing upon schoolroom practice. It is a comparative study: each view is followed into the impact it should (if adopted) have upon teaching. This book, therefore, is a highly practical one, especially so because it embodies *the* feature essential to genuine practicality— *theory* that is followed into its logical implications in terms of practice. The points of view treated are those actively influential today, hence those that need to be understood by teachers so they can be discerning in their classroom procedures, as well as in their reading of educational literature or their participation in professional discussions. This is a pertinent, hence important, book.

Few, if any, writers in educational psychology are more lucid than is Dr. Bigge. He intends to communicate, and does. He does not "talk down" to his readers; he simply states things clearly.

Moreover, he is fair, though he makes no pretense of being neutral. He has his own convictions and makes clear what they are, but takes pains to present opposing or alternative views in ways satisfactory to their sponsors. When he presents a view, he furnishes sufficient documentation to demonstrate the validity of his presentation. Nothing is taken out of context. In fact, it is the full context of each learning theory upon which he insists, a context sometimes presented more fully by him than by proponents of a given view. My personal conviction is that few texts now available in educational psychology will be more helpful to teachers than this one.

ERNEST E. BAYLES

Preface

This book is designed for use as a basic text in courses in *learning theory* or a collateral text in *educational psychology* or *psychological foundations of education*. It should also prove useful as a supplementary text in other courses that emphasize the nature of contrasting psychologies of learning. The objective of the volume is to provide prospective and in-service teachers, at all levels, with a comprehensive picture of modern learning theories in as readable style as is possible without oversimplification of the basic tenets, similarities, and differences of most of the important contemporary learning theories.

The book describes learning theories in such a way as to guide readers in critically constructing and evaluating their own outlooks in regard to the nature of the learning process and formulating their optimum roles in its promotion. Thus, it is written with the hope that it will contribute, in some degree, to a long-range sense of direction that will be conducive to more effective teaching.

The author does not claim absolute impartiality; his sympathy lies with the cognitive-field theory of learning. Nevertheless, every effort has been made to provide a balanced treatment of learning theories. Consequently, the book should be equally usable by professors with various theoretical commitments. Each theory is presented much as if the writer were an adherent of that point of view. The volume contains occasional critical comments and evaluations, but they usually are weighted toward supporting the theory then being discussed. In most cases, it is left to readers to discern the weaknesses of each theory in relation to contrasting theories.

Since a truly comparative approach to learning theory is necessarily semihistorical, this volume treats respective learning theories semihistorically as well as comparatively. The historical analysis that is employed is developed in such a way as to help readers grasp and clarify points of confusion in modern education. Many contemporary educational principles and practices are something of a hodgepodge, rooted in premises about the nature of man and his relationships with his physical-social environment that frequently are incompatible with one another. By recounting how psychological assumptions and theories arose and how they evolved over time, the book helps readers see why the theories exist and the directions in which they point. Since some earlier theories of learning, which are seldom advocated now by professional psychologists, continue to influence today's teaching, they too are considered along with contemporary learning theories.

The general plan of the book is as follows: Chapter One lists the theories that are to be treated and introduces readers to various possible assumptions about the basic nature of man. Then Chapter Two presents the more prominent representatives of pre-twentieth century learning theory—mental discipline, natural unfoldment, and apperception—and develops their implications for school practice. Chapter Three introduces the two major contrasting twentieth-century "families" of learning theory—S-R conditioning and Gestalt-field theories. It also provides background by explaining how the families arose and how they relate to mechanistic and relativistic outlooks. Chapter Four focuses on the specific explanation of learning that each contemporary family offers.

Chapters Five, Six, Seven, and Eight are somewhat more technical and specific than are Chapters Three and Four. They are written to give readers a "feel" for how psychologists think and work within their respective points of view. Since space does not permit treatment of all prominent contemporary learning theories, only representative ones are described. Chapters Five and Six describe two systematic versions of S-R conditioning theory or behaviorism—B. F. Skinner's *operant conditioning* and Kenneth W. Spence's *quantitative S-R theory*. Both Skinner and Spence have been greatly interested in the psychology of learning, but their positions in regard to psychologists' contribution to education are quite different. Whereas Professor Skinner represents his psychology as the great hope for improvement of current instructional techniques, Professor Spence has thought that in its present stage of scientific development psychology has little to offer schools. Spence, however, was hopeful for the future of psychology, but he thought that much more research would be needed before this science could make some major contributions to teaching procedures.

Chapter Seven outlines classical "field," or "topological and vector," psychology as it was developed by Kurt Lewin up to the time of his death in 1947. Then Chapter Eight builds upon the concepts developed by Lewin along with those developed by other leading psychologists to structure a cognitive-field theory of learning as a current representative of the Gestalt-field family.

Chapter Nine delineates the respective outlook in regard to *transfer of learning* that harmonizes with each learning theory. Its content grows directly from, and thereby constitutes a summary of, the content of earlier chapters. Chapter Ten, through summarization of some learning principles that are quite generally accepted irrespective of the school of thought to which educational psychologists belong, reminds students of the existence of some areas of common agreement. Finally, Chapters Eleven and Twelve develop the relationships of respective learning theories to classroom practices. Chapter Eleven centers upon four levels of learning and teaching—memory, understanding, autonomous development, and reflection. Then, Chapter Twelve relates different testing procedures to respective levels of teaching and learning.

The author is indebted to so many people for their contributions in making both the first and second editions of this book a reality that any attempt to name them all would be futile. These include his former professors, especially the late Dr. T. L. Collier of Washburn University and Dr. Ernest E. Bayles of the University of Kansas; his former students, both graduate and undergraduate; and his colleagues on the Fresno State College staff who have read parts or all of both manuscripts and have made many valuable criticisms.

Dr. Maurice P. Hunt, Drs. Kenneth W. and Janet J. Spence, Dr. Wayne B. Holder, Mrs. Mabel Hunt, Mrs. Ada Bigge, and Dr. June Lee Bigge have each made unique contributions to the manuscript. My colleague, Dr. Hunt, has granted permission to use materials from *Psychological Foundations of Education* and has ably edited and criticized the new chapters in the manuscript. Dr. and Mrs. Spence both read a late draft of Chapter Six of the first edition and provided marginal notes and suggestions that were inestimably valuable to the writing of the final draft of that chapter. In addition, Mrs. Spence's suggestions were very helpful in preparing the chapter for the second edition. Dr. Holder examined an early draft of Chapter Six and helped the author avoid some pitfalls in describing this rather difficult point of view. Although the author has received great assistance from these individuals, he assumes complete responsibility for the quality of the final manuscript.

Mrs. Mabel Hunt prepared the manuscript of the first edition for the publisher in a masterly fashion. Mrs. Bigge, by manifesting the confidence in the author which only could be held by a good wife, by typing innumerable sections of the manuscript, and by assisting in editing the final proofs of the book, has helped invaluably. Finally our daughter, Dr. June Lee Bigge—earlier an experienced master teacher and now a professor of special education—attended all sessions of a class in which drafts of the manuscript were used as text material and assiduously took notes on all class criticisms and reactions. These notes were of great help in the final refining of the manuscript. More recently, through lengthy conversations, she has sharpened the author's insights in regard to many psychological issues.

MORRIS L. BIGGE

ONE

Why Is Classroom Learning a Problem?

Maturation or learning, or a combination of the two, is the means by which lasting changes in persons occur. Maturation is a developmental process within which a person from time to time manifests different traits, the "blueprints" for which have been carried in his cells from the time of his conception.

Learning, in contrast with maturation, is an enduring change in a living individual that is not heralded by his genetic inheritance. It may be a change in insights, behavior, perception, or motivation, or a combination of these.

"Learning is basic to the development of athletic prowess, of tastes in food and dress, and of the appreciation of art and music. It contributes to ethnic prejudice, to drug addiction, to fear, and to pathological maladjustment. It produces the miser and the philanthropist, the bigot and the patriot. In short, it influences our lives at every turn, accounting in part for the best and worst of human beings and for the best and worst in each of us."[1]

Since teachers can do little to influence the maturational pat-

[1]Ernest R. Hilgard and Donald G. Marquis, *Conditioning and Learning*, 2nd ed., New York: Appleton-Century-Crofts, 1961, p. 10.

terns of students, except perhaps to accelerate or retard them to same degree, their most effectual area of endeavor always centers upon learning. Furthermore, because of man's unique traits and capacities, learning is far more crucial to him than it is to the lower animals.

Man has some distinguishing characteristics that give a unique quality to a study of him. First of all, he talks and he is a timebinding individual—both a past and a future enter into his present perception of things. Also, he is a cultural being; he builds on his past in a peculiarly selective fashion. Then, man has a unique capacity for social interaction with his fellows, which enables him to transcend concrete situations and live in a more or less imaginative realm. And most significantly of all, man, in his perceptual process, may view himself simultaneously as both the subject and the object, as a knower and as a known.

Whereas in the lower animals much behavior supposedly is instinctive, human children, benefiting from their high degree of plasticity, learn their many patterns of human behavior. The relatively long period of children's dependency upon adults, following their complete helplessness at birth, contributes to their acquisition of the culture of their group. Using their relatively high potential for intelligence and their capacity for communication through use of articulate speech and other symbols, members of each generation build upon the achievements—artifacts, ideas, customs, and traditions—of the generation before it. A culture—social heritage—of a society is the result of many generations of cumulative learning.

Man shares with other mammals some primary organic drives such as hunger, thirst, sex, cravings for oxygen, warmth, and rest, and possibly a few primary aversions such as fear and rage. The first expression of these drives and aversions is primarily a maturational process. But, in some way, human beings seem to transcend these hereditary drives and aversions. In large measure, this trancendence is centered in the human capacity to deal with a complex past, present, and future world so as to develop abstractions or generalizations which organize mazes of particulars into sensible patterns. Perhaps a desire to perceive, understand, imagine, and deal with ideas is just as much a part of human nature as are the specific organic drives and aversions. Biologically, *homo sapiens*—man—is a species of mammal characterized by superior knowing and discerning abilities.

There apparently is no group of human beings that has not, through learning, developed some devices for enriching its contacts with the world about it. In the development of these devices, people have attempted to derive satisfactions from understanding and manipulating their world as well as through merely touching, smelling, and tasting its various aspects. Moreover, contrasted with capacities of less advanced animals, man's potential for becoming human lies largely in his capacity for extension of experience to a world of symbolism; to operate on an imaginative level of reality.

Animals seem to derive satisfaction from using whatever abilities they have. Accordingly, man derives satisfaction from using his natural and acquired abilities. Thus, the very process of learning, both concrete and abstract, can become satisfying to him. In his social, aesthetic, economic, religious, and political life he shows a tendency to explore. Not all people develop sophisticated ideological outlooks. However, rarely if ever are there groups of people who subsist solely on a vegetative level with no imaginative or mentalistic endeavors. Even the most primitive cultures have developed some symbolistic folklore and ideology.

WHY THEORIES OF LEARNING?

Not only has man wanted to learn, but often his curiosity has impelled him to try to learn *how* he learns. Since ancient times, at least some members of every civilized society have developed, and to some degree tested, ideas about the nature of the learning process. Since the seventeenth century, more or less systematic theories of learning have emerged periodically to challenge existing theories. Typically, a new theory of learning is not translated into school practice until 25 to 75 years have elapsed. Then, as a new theory eventually comes to affect school policy, it usually does not displace its predecessors; it merly competes with them. Thus, as new theories have been introduced they have been added to the old and the educational scene has become more and more muddled. Probably most teachers, from time to time, have adopted conflicting features from a variety of learning theories without realizing that they are basically contradictory in nature and cannot harmonize with each other.

In most life situations learning is not much of a problem. A (lay) person takes it for granted that we learn from experience and lets it go at that; he sees nothing problematical about learning. Throughout human history people have learned, and in most cases without troubling themselves as to the nature of the process. Parents taught children and master workmen taught apprentices. Children and apprentices both learned, and those who taught felt little need for a grasp of learning theory. Teaching was done by telling and showing how, complimenting the learner when he did well, and scolding or punishing him when he did poorly. A teacher simply taught the way he had been taught when he was a youth.

When schools were developed as special environments to facilitate learning, teaching ceased to be so simple a matter. The subjects taught in school were different from the matters learned as part of routine life in a tribe or society. Mastering school subjects, whether the three R's, foreign languages, geometry, history, or something else, appeared to children as an entirely different sort of learning task from those taken for granted in everyday life. Often their relevance to the problems of daily living seemed unclear. Such subjects, whose immediate usefulness is not obvious, strike a learner as quite different from the crafts and skills needed to carry on day-by-day social, economic, and political life.

Ever since education became formalized in schools, teachers have been aware that learning in school often is highly inefficient. Material to be learned may be presented to students innumerable times without noticeable results. Many students appear uninterested. Many become rebellious and make serious trouble for teachers. Consequently, classrooms often have seemed like battlegrounds in which teachers and students made war against each other. Such a state of affairs may come to be taken for granted by teachers, students, and parents. Consequently, they may consider it "natural" that youngsters dislike school and try to resist school learning. Thus, they may assume that it simply is one of the unpleasant facts of life that many children and youth will learn very little in school.

From the colonial period through the nineteenth century, most people in America probably made such placid assumptions concerning formal education. However, as soon as the professions of psychology and education developed, it was inevitable that professionals would begin asking questions. When teaching moved from the mother's knee to a formalized environment designed to promote learning, it was inescapable that a small group of persons would arise to begin speculating about whether schools were getting the best possible results. Then, professional psychologists and educators who critically analyzed school practices found that development of more or less systematic schools of thought in psychology offered a handy tool for crystallization of their thinking. Each of these schools of thought has contained, explicitly or implicitly, a theory of learning. In turn, a given theory of learning has implied a set of classroom practices. Thus, the way in which an educator builds his curriculum, selects his materials, and chooses his instructional techniques depends, to a large degree, upon how he defines "learning." Hence, a theory of learning may function as an analytical tool; its exponents can use it to judge the quality of a particular classroom situation.

Psychology is not a field of study characterized by a body of theory that is internally consistent and accepted by all psychologists. Rather, it is an area of knowledge characterized by the presence of several schools of thought. In some instances these may supplement one another, but at other times they are in open disagreement. Thus, we may find psychologist X, who is both scholarly and sincere, opposed to many of the crucial ideas of psychologist Y, who is equally scholarly and sincere. Such disagreement among psychologists may be disconcerting to students. But one of the challenges of psychological study lies in theoretical disagreement; only to the degree that a student is willing to think for himself can he emerge from his studies with something worthwhile. Some consolation may be had in the fact that similar disagreement sometimes exists in the physical sciences. One's gaining an understanding and appreciation of the achievements of thinkers in any area is never easy. As stated by Taube, "After all, if the fox twists and turns, so must the hound."[2]

What is learning theory?

Quite often in our scientific age we erroneously think of *theory* as indefinite or indefensible conjecture which existed prior to the use of scientific method and evidence. Consequently, although we might not object to using the term in a description of the historical development of modern concepts of learning, we would expect the word "fact," rather than "theory," to be used in describing the current scene. After all, are we not now on solid enough ground for the term "theory" to be discarded? This, however, is not the case; theory definitely should not be abolished.

Any sharp distinction between theoretical, imaginative knowledge and the action that stems from such knowledge is faulty. Action, whether a part of teaching or any other activity in life,

[2]Mortimer Taube, *Computers and Common Sense*, New York: Columbia University Press, 1961, p. 2.

either is linked with theory or it is blind and purposeless. Consequently, any purposeful action is governed by theory. Everyone who teaches or professes to teach has a theory of learning. A teacher may be able to describe his theory in explicit terms or he may not—in which case we usually can deduce from his actions the theory that he is not yet able to verbalize. The important question, then, is not whether a teacher has a theory of learning, but rather how tenable it is.

Everything a teacher does is colored by the psychological theory he holds. Consequently, a teacher who does not make use of a systematic body of theory in his day-by-day decisions is behaving blindly. Hence, little evidence of long-range rationale, purpose, or plan is observable in his teaching. A teacher without a strong theoretical orientation inescapably makes little more than busy work assignments. True, many teachers operate in this way and use only a hodge-podge of methods without theoretical orientation. However, this muddled kind of teaching undoubtedly is responsible for many of the current adverse criticism of public education.

Yet, a teacher need not base his thinking on tradition and folklore. Instead, he may be quite aware of the most important theories developed by professional psychologists, in which case his own psychological theory is likely to be quite sophisticated. The latter state of affairs is what professional psychologists interested in education of teachers are trying to induce. Teachers who are well grounded in scientific psychology—in contrast to "folklore psychology"—have a basis for making decisions that are much more likely to lead to effectual results in classrooms.

As a student, you may not have a large background either of practical experience or of "book knowledge" to bring to bear on the question of how children and youth learn. Nevertheless, even before reading farther in this book, you do have some resources on which to draw. You have been learning all your life and are continuing to do so. And all your life you have been associating with others who were also learning, often from you. What seems to be the essential nature of the process called learning? What happens within, or to, you when you learn? Does the same thing happen to everyone? It probably would be helpful to you, now, to take paper and pen and write a one- or two-page essay on this subject. (You may not find this an easy assignment!) Repeat the assignment when you have mastered this book and see the difference in your two essays.

Learning theory is a distinct area within theoretical psychology. In recent years, many psychologists have been dedicated to a study of learning theory. Thus, they have concentrated upon developing systematic theories supported by experimentation. Consequently, experimental and theoretical literature on learning has grown to an almost forbidding mass.[3]

This book deliberately presents several competing theories of learning, providing different answers to many of the questions that might be raised, so that students will become increasingly sophisticated about the "schools of thought" that exist in psychology today and understand how differently each attacks respective problems. The "comparative" treatment herein employed requires, among other things, that students do considerable thinking for themselves.

How is learning theory evaluated?

It is one thing to talk about constructive thought and another actually to achieve it. Thinking for oneself is never easy. However, it may be easier for you to do a respectable job of critical thought if you are clearly aware of two competing kinds of criteria for judging the answers to questions; namely, *authoritarian* and *scientific*. Think about any statement that you consider to be true. Do you regard it as true merely because you read it somewhere or heard some teacher or other "authority" say it or because, after you examined all the available pertinent evidence, it seemed to have more factual support than any alternative statement? If you accept the statement "on faith" because someone told it to you, you have used an authoritarian criterion for judging truth. If you accept it because you either have pursued your own careful investigations of it or you have studied the investigations of others, you are operating within a more scientific framework.

Although we recognize the distinction between authoritarian and scientific approaches, the road to inquiry still may not be smooth. Often we are required to reach conclusions before we have had sufficient time either to conduct our own investigation or to study critically the investigations made by those who pose as authorities. In such cases we have no choice except to take someone else's word for it. Whose word do we take? In answering questions in psychology, we might turn to the writings of the most prominent psychologists. But, unfortunately, prominence does not guarantee reliability. Less well-known persons

[3]See Ernest R. Hilgard and Gordon H. Bower, *Theories of Learning*, 3rd ed., New York: Appleton-Century-Crofts, 1966.

may be more nearly right. Furthermore, in the field of psychology it is common for top-ranking authorities, who have spent lifetimes in research, to disagree.

So, there are no final answers to questions concerning learning, and no theory can be found to be absolutely superior to all others. Nevertheless, a teacher can develop a learning theory of his own which, because of its internal harmony and educational adequacy, he can support. Such a theory may turn out to be somewhat of a replica of one introduced in this book, or the reader may benefit by contributions of several theories and derive one of his own. In either event, the quality of his teaching will be enhanced for his having thought through the question of the nature of the learning process that he—a teacher—wants to promote in his students.

Through study of theories of learning and their historical development, teachers should gain insight into the harmonies and conflicts that prevail in present educational theory. Through this insight, they should move toward developing adequate theories of their own. Before attempting to formulate their own learning theory, they would do well to examine carefully and critically the prevalent theories that have been developed by professionals in the area. Furthermore, in order to understand the teaching climate of present-day schools,, it is important to develop some comprehension of learning theories that have emerged in the past and still have prominent places in modern education, even though they are no longer among the theories advocated by present-day theoretical psychologists.

WHAT LEARNING THEORIES ARE REFLECTED IN SCHOOL PRACTICE?

In the remaining section of this chapter, we present an abbreviated sketch of the major lines along which learning theory has developed, and provide an example of teaching nonreaders to read using each. Then, in Chapters 2 to 8 we develop each line of thought in considerable detail. At least ten different theories in regard to the basic nature of the learning process either are prevalent in today's schools or are advocated by leading contemporary psychologists. Table 1.1 lists the ten major theories, groups some of them into families, and outlines the concepts involved in each of the theories. As students pursue study of learning and teaching, they should find it helpful to refer to this table frequently.

Column I of Table 1.1 lists the ten learning theories. The first four of these—the two *mental discipline* theories of the mind substance family, *natural unfoldment*, and *apperception*—were developed prior to the twentieth century, but continue to be highly influential in today's schools. (Chapter 2 is devoted to explanation and evaluation of these first four theories.)

"Mental discipline," of both kinds, means that learning consists of disciplining or training a mind. In teaching nonreaders to read, a teacher who assumes students to be either *bad* or *neutral* and *active* would instruct in a way that would exercise the "sinews" of children's minds. He probably would first list words that he wanted students to be able to recognize, read, and spell. He would use flash cards in teaching them. He would drill his students extensively, test them daily, and have his low achievers return after school for further drill.

There would be "recitations" within which students would be drilled orally and would take turns reading passages of their daily lessons. Those who did poorly would be scolded when they made mistakes, and some of them would be sent to their seats to "study." Students would be driven to stay with their lessons, and thereby perseverance and willpower would be strengthened. Strict discipline would be maintained in order to strengthen the faculty of attention as well as those of memory, will, and perseverance. The teachers would have little hesitation in using various kinds of physical and mental punishment as the situation required.

"Natural unfoldment" is a procedure within which a child unfolds that which Nature or a Creator has enfolded within him. A teacher who adheres to this position would, first of all, wait for each student to express a desire to learn to read before he would make any attempt to teach him. Then, he would be much more concerned with the child's development than with inculcation of any specific skills; he would make sure that each child's learning was a joyous experience.

"Apperception" is a process of new ideas associating themselves with old ones that already constitute a mind. An apperceptionist would teach students to read by starting with the alphabet, making sure that the students could recognize and say each letter. He then would tell them how letters are put together to make words, how letters make sounds, how sounds are telescoped together, and how vowels and consonants worked. In other words, he would give them some rules. He next would talk to them about things that they already knew such as dogs, cats, boys, and girls. Then he would show them *d o g* and explain that it stands for *dog*. He would be concerned primarily with

Table 1.1
Representative Theories of Learning
and Their Implications for Education

	theory of learning I	psychological system or outlook II	conception of man's basic moral and actional nature III
Mental discipline theories of mind substance family	1. Theistic mental discipline	Faculty psychology	*Bad-active* mind substance continues active until curbed
	2. Humanistic mental discipline	Classicism	*Neutral-active* mind substance to be developed through exercise
	3. Natural unfoldment	Romantic naturalism	*Good-active* natural personality to unfold
	4. Apperception or Herbartianism	Structuralism	*Neutral-passive* mind composed of active mental states or ideas
S-R (stimulus-response) conditioning theories of behavioristic family	5. S-R bond	Connectionism	*Neutral-passive* or *reactive* organism with many potential S-R connections
	6. Conditioning (with no reinforcement)	Behaviorism	*Neutral-passive* or *reactive* organism with innate reflexive drives and emotions
	7. Conditioning through reinforcement	Reinforcement	*Neutral-passive* organism with innate reflexes and needs with their drive stimuli
Cognitive theories of Gestalt-field family	8. Insight	Gestalt psychology	*Neutral-active* being whose activity follows psychological laws of organization
	9. Goal-insight	Configurationalism	*Neutral-interactive*, purposive individual in sequential relationships with environment
	10. Cognitive-field	Field psychology or positive relativism	*Neutral-interactive*, purposive person in simultaneous mutual interaction with psychological environment including other persons

basis for transfer of learning IV	emphasis in teaching V	key persons VI	contemporary exponents VII
Exercised faculties, automatic transfer	Exercise of faculties—the "muscles" of the mind	St. Augustine John Calvin J. Edwards	Many Hebraic-Christian fundamentalists
Cultivated mind or intellect	Training of intrinsic mental power	Plato Aristotle	M. J. Adler Robert M. Hutchins
Recapitulation of racial history, no transfer needed	Negative or permissive education	J. J. Rousseau F. Froebel Progressivists	P. Goodman J. Holt A. H. Maslow
Growing apperceptive mass	Addition of new mental states or ideas to a store of old ones in subconscious mind	J. F. Herbart E. B. Titchener	Many teachers and administrators
Identical elements	Promotion of acquisition of desired S-R connections	E. L. Thorndike	A. I. Gates J. M. Stephens
Conditioned responses or reflexes	Promotion of adhesion of desired responses to appropriate stimuli	J. B. Watson	E. R. Guthrie
Reinforced or conditioned responses	Successive, systematic changes in organisms' environment to increase the probability of desired responses	C. L. Hull	B. F. Skinner K. W. Spence
Transposition of insights	Promotion of insightful learning	M. Wertheimer K. Koffka	W. Köhler
Tested insights	Aid students in developing high-quality insights	B. H. Bode R. H. Wheeler	E. E. Bayles
Continuity of life spaces, experience, or insights	Help students restructure their life spaces—gain new insights into their contemporaneous situations	Kurt Lewin E. C. Tolman Gordon W. Allport Adelbert Ames, Jr. J. S. Bruner Hadley Cantril	R. G. Barker M. L. Bigge A. W. Combs H. F. Wright

making reading interesting and being sure that his students got the *right* ideas from their reading.

Twentieth-century theories

Twentieth-century learning theories may be classified into two broad families, namely, S-R *(stimulus-response) conditioning* theories of the behavioristic family and cognitive theories of the Gestalt-field family. Thus, in Table 1.1 entries 5, 6, and 7—S-R bond, conditioning (with no reinforcement), and conditioning through reinforcement—are encompassed by the generalized concepts *S-R conditioning theory and behaviorism*, which may be used interchangeably. Likewise, entries 8, 9, and 10—insight, goal-insight, and cognitive-field theory—are examples of the Gestalt-field family, which emphasizes cognition in learning.

Chapters 3 and 4 discuss the differences between the two families of twentieth-century, scientific learning theories. Next, Chapters 5 and 6 contain descriptions of two popular contemporary psychologies of learning that represent the S-R conditioning family—B. F. Skinner's *operant-conditioning theory* and Kenneth W. Spence's *quantitative S-R theory.* Then, Chapter 7 presents the basic tenets of *field psychology* as they were developed by Kurt Lewin. These provide a background for a leading contemporary representative of the Gestalt-field family— *cognitive field theory,* which is presented in Chapter 8.

For behaviorists or conditioning theorists, learning is a change in behavior. It occurs through stimuli and responses becoming related according to mechanistic principles. Thus, it involved the formation of relations of some sort between series of stimuli and responses. Stimuli—the causes of learning—are environmental agents that act upon an organism so as either to cause it to respond or to increase the probability of a response of a certain class or kind. Responses—effects—are physical reactions of an organism to either external or internal stimulation.

For Gestalt-field theorists, learning is a process of gaining or changing insights, outlooks, or thought patterns. In thinking about the learning processes of students, these theorists prefer the terms *person* to *organism, psychological environment* to *physical* or *biological environment,* and *interaction* to either *action* or *reaction.* Such preference is not merely a whim; there is a conviction that the concepts *person, psychological environment,* and *interaction* are highly advantageous for teachers in describing learning processes. They enable a teacher to see a person, his environment, and his interaction with his environment all occurring at once; this is the meaning of *field.*

To summarize the difference between the two families very briefly, S-R conditioning theorists interpret learning in terms of changes in strength of hypothetical variables called S-R connections, associations, habit strengths, or behavioral tendencies; Gestalt-field theorists define it in terms of reorganization of perceptual or cognitive fields or systems. Consequently, whereas a behavioristic teacher desires to change the behaviors of his students in a significant way, a Gestalt-field oriented teacher aspires to help students change their understandings of significant problems and situations.

A behavioristic teacher, in teaching nonreaders to read, would first develop a list of words that he would want to incorporate into the working vocabularies of his students. Prior to the introduction of specific letter sound relationships, he probably would teach students to read whole words and to express their meanings. Within the S-R conditioning process, students are taught using either one, or a combination, of two procedures, namely, the *stimulus substitution* method of classical conditioning or the *response modification* method of instrumental conditioning.

When using stimulus substitution, the teacher in any way possible would get his students to say each specific word, then he would give them the appropriate stimulus in the form of the written word just prior to their saying that word. Consequently, in the future, upon being stimulated by that written word, students would be likely to say it.

Within response modification, or reinforcement, students would be given a "reward," i.e., their behavior would be reinforced, whenever they either completed a word properly or filled in the proper word in a blank space. There would be "feedback" from the reinforcing "reward," which would increase the probability that, on future occasions, respective students would accurately read or write the completed or filled-in words.

A Gestalt-field oriented teacher, in teaching nonreaders to read, would set out to help them develop a "feel" for sound-symbol relationships.[4] Hence, he would help students get the ideas that surround the use of words. Accordingly, he would spend a greater proportion of teaching time conversing with his students in regard to significant verbal *relationships*. Specifically, he would help his students grasp the relation between individual letters and verbal sounds, blend verbal sounds that are represented by letter groupings, and learn that there are many phonetically

[4]See Siegfried Engelmann, *Preventing Failure in the Primary Grades*, Chicago: Science Research Associates, 1969. Chapter 4, "Reading for the Nonreader."

regular words but also some irregular ones. Students' verbal skills would be in the form of learned insights in regard to such matters as rhyming, telescoping sounds together, and sounding out words that are encountered visually.

WHAT CONCEPTS CHARACTERIZE RESPECTIVE LEARNING THEORIES?

In addition to the ten learning theories, Table 1.1 includes, in six different categories, the concepts that characterize, together with some people who represent, each theory. It is difficult to make a sharp distinction between "key persons" (column VI) and "contemporary exponents" (column VII). However, the criterion for selection of key persons has been their making a major contribution to the theory under consideration and still not being a contemporary adherent of the theory as described. All "key persons" except J. S. Bruner are historical. Bruner is listed in this category and not as a contemporary exponent because he has made a major contribution to the development of cognitive-field theory, yet he does not identify his cognitive approach with field theory, as such. In this chapter, we briefly outline categories II, III, IV, and V under separate headings. Then, they are expanded throughout this book.

Alternative psychological systems or basic outlooks

Each learning theory represents a more or less comprehensive psychological system or basic outlook. Or, to say this in another way, each systematic psychological system or basic outlook has its unique approach to learning. Accordingly, column II of Table 1.1 contains systematic psychologies or basic outlooks which reflect respective theories of learning. We allude to these psychologies or outlooks, from place to place throughout the book as we treat learning, teaching, and related problems.[5]

Presumed innate moral and actional nature of man

Each theory of learning, especially as it is applied in schools, is linked to a conception of the basic, innate nature of man. Consequently, when we seriously consider how learning occurs,

[5]The various systematic psychologies are described in Benjamin B. Wolman, *Contemporary Theories and Systems of Psychology*, New York: Harper & Row, 1960, and J. P. Chaplin and T. S. Krawiec, *Systems and Theories of Psychology*, 2nd ed., New York: Holt, Rinehart and Winston, 1968.

Table 1.2

Conceptions of Man's Basic Moral and Actional Nature
and the Learning Theories They Imply

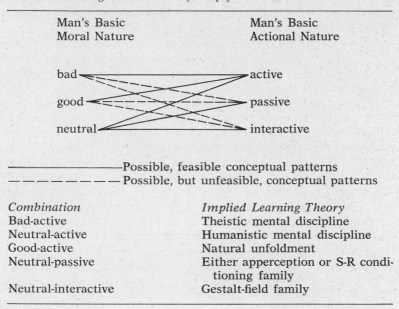

Man's Basic Moral Nature	Man's Basic Actional Nature
bad	active
good	passive
neutral	interactive

—————————————Possible, feasible conceptual patterns
— — — — — — — — Possible, but unfeasible, conceptual patterns

Combination	Implied Learning Theory
Bad-active	Theistic mental discipline
Neutral-active	Humanistic mental discipline
Good-active	Natural unfoldment
Neutral-passive	Either apperception or S-R conditioning family
Neutral-interactive	Gestalt-field family

it is inevitable that we formulate some assumptions about the
essential moral and actional nature of students as human beings. This is the topic of Table 1.1, Column III, Table 1.2, and Figure 1.1. Man's *moral nature* refers to his being basically either bad,
good, or neutral, that is, neither bad nor good. *Actional nature*
involves his being psychologically either active, passive, or interactive. It is essential that we make clear that we are using
the word *man* in a generic sense. It applies collectively to all
members of the human race. Furthermore, as used here, *innate*
and *basic* are synonymous adjectives; both mean *original* or
unlearned. The real question, then, in regard to man's basic
nature is, "What would children and youth be like if each
should be left entirely on his own?"

Consideration of the basic nature of man would be quite
simple were there but one answer. Unfortunately, but interest-
ingly, there are several distinctly different and mutually opposed
answers to this question, each enjoying a good deal of support.
As students read this chapter, they should attempt to define
their own positions in regard to this crucial problem. In basic

moral proclivity, is man naturally *evil?* Or is he naturally *good?* Or is his original, moral nature *neutral*—neither naturally good nor evil? Also, in relationship to his environment, is man naturally *active?* Or is he naturally *passive* or *reactive?* Or is he naturally *interactive?*

Alternate assumptions concerning man's basic moral nature. If we assume man's moral nature to be naturally evil, then we can expect nothing good from him. If left to itself, his evilness will naturally unfold; the person will show no traits other than bad ones. Contrariwise, if we assume that man is innately good, then, unless he is corrupted by some outside force, everything that comes from him will be good. Assumed neutrality in man's basic moral nature simply means that man by nature is neither bad nor good, but merely potential in a way that has no connection with innate badness or goodness.

Alternate assumptions concerning man's actional nature and environmental relationships. If, in actional nature, children and youth are fundamentally *active*, their underlying characteristics are inborn. Hence, their psychological natures come from within them. Environments only serve as locations for their natural unfoldment. Notice that a person's merely moving physically does not mean that he necessarily is being psychologically active. For him to be psychologically active, his personal motive power must be inner-directed and originate entirely from within himself. If persons are basically *passive*, their characteristics are largely a product of environmental influences. Thus, their natures are determined by their environments. If they are *interactive*, their psychological characteristics result from their making sense of their respective physical and social environments. So, their psychological natures arise from their personal-environmental relationships. Hence, each person's reality consists of that which he makes of what he gains through his own unique experience. These three mutually opposed assumptions in regard

Figure 1.1
Models of mutually opposed assumptions in regard
to the basic actional nature of men
and their respective environmental relationships.

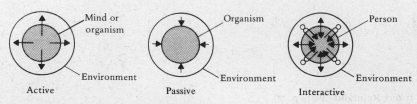

Active   Passive   Interactive

to the nature of human beings and their environmental relationships may be illustrated by three models (Figure 1.1).

Alternate combinations of assumed moral natures with assumed actional natures and their implied environmental relationships. When we consider the possible, feasible combinations of assumptions concerning man's basic moral nature together with those concerning his actional relationship with his environment, we might reasonably assume the innate natures of students to be either bad-active, neutral-active, good-active, neutral-passive, or neutral-interactive (see Table 1.2).

Each of these assumptions in regard to the basic nature of students has definite implications for a theory of the learning process. If we assume students to be either bad-active or neutral-active, we will adhere to some form of *mental discipline*. This learning theory is described in the early part of Chapter 2 (pp. 20–31). If we assume students are good-active, we will think of learning as natural unfoldment (see pp. 31–33).

An assumption of neutral-passivity may take one of several forms: apperception, S-R bond theory, conditioning, or reinforcement. Apperception theory occupies the last section of Chapter 2 (pp. 33–46). The latter three are forms of S-R conditioning theory, which is discussed in Chapters 3 and 4, and specifically represented by Skinner's operant conditioning in Chapter 5 and Spence's quantitative S-R theory in Chapter 6.

Finally, the assumption that students are neutral-interactive is the pivotal thesis of Gestalt-field theories described in Chapters 3, 4, and 7 and specifically represented by cognitive-field theory, treated in detail in Chapter 8.

Quotations from Gordon W. Allport and Rollo May summarize the importance of our assumptions concerning man's basic nature. "Theories of learning (like much else in psychology) rest on the investigator's conception of the nature of man. In other words, every learning theorist is a philosopher, though he may not know it. To put the matter more concretely, psychologists who investigate (and theorize about) learning start with some preconceived view of the nature of human motivation."[6] "The critical battles between approaches to psychology . . . in our culture in the next decades, I propose, will be on the battleground of the image of man—that is to say, on the conceptions of man which underlie the empirical research."[7]

[6]Gordon W. Allport, *Patterns and Growth in Personality*, New York: Holt, Rinehart and Winston, 1961, p. 84.

[7]Rollo May, *Psychology and the Human Dilemma*, New York: Van Nostrand Reinhold, 1967, p. 90.

Basis for transfer of learning

Transfer of learning, the subject of column IV of Table 1.1 (p. 11), is the relationship between a person's learning process and his using his learnings in future learning or life situations; Chapter 9 is devoted to treatment of this subject. This, of course, is the key to the value of learning that occurs in schools. Schools should attempt to teach students in such a way that they not only accumulate many significant learnings applicable to life's situations, but that they also develop a technique for acquiring new insights or understandings independently. These two goals of education constitute the realm of transfer.

Emphasis in teaching

A book on learning theory, to be most meaningful to students, needs to treat, albeit in a theoretical manner, classroom application of psychological outlooks and principles. Such a treatment is the subject of Chapters 11 and 12. However, in the interest of continuity, "emphasis in teaching" also is included in Table 1.1. Thus, column V states the pivotal teaching concept of each learning theory. Although teaching theory, as such, is emphasized only in Chapters 11 and 12, readers will do well to consider it to some degree along with the subject matter of the chapters on learning.

By reading across each entry in Table 1.1, we can get a picture of ten different ways of looking at the problem of how students learn. For example, a person who embraces number (4), apperception, is committed to psychological *structuralism;* he assumes that students basically are of a *neutral-passive, mental* nature; his basis for transfer is the idea of *apperceptive mass;* and, in teaching, he emphasizes addition of new mental states or ideas to a store of old ones "housed" in the subconscious mind. Furthermore, the key historical persons in development of this outlook were J. F. Herbart and E. B. Titchener, and many teachers and administrators are, perhaps unknowingly, its contemporary exponents.

BIBLIOGRAPHY

CANTOR, NATHANIEL, F., *Dynamics of Learning,* Stuart, 1956.
    One of the best books available on how to improve the effectiveness of teaching. The first few theoretical chapters require for

their understanding a rich background in psychology and sociology. Read later chapters which describe in detail how a teacher may conduct a class.

CANTRIL, HADLEY, and CHARLES H. BUMSTEAD, *Reflections on the Human Venture,* New York University Press, 1960.
   Treatment of major issues in psychology from a relativistic view. Draws evidence largely from insights of novelists, poets, and playwrights. Excellent quotations. A profound book, likely to become a classic.

HALL, CALVIN S., and GARDNER LINDZEY, *Theories of Personality,* New York: John Wiley, 1957.
   Description of twelve different "scientific" learning theories, including stimulus-response, Freudian and neo-Freudian, Lewin's, and other relativistic and nonrelativistic theories. Excellent as a reference source.

HILGARD, ERNEST R., ed., *Theories of Learning and Instruction,* The National Society for the Study of Education, Chicago: University of Chicago Press, 1964.
   A modern symposium on learning theory. Professional problems in developing psychological methodologies and educational technologies. Integrating psychologies of learning with technologies of instruction.

KRUTCH, JOSEPH WOOD, *Human Nature and the Human Condition,* New York: Random House, 1959.
   Krutch's attack on relativistic explanations in favor of a belief in an innate human nature. Contrasts with his attack, in his earlier book, on all mechanistic explanations of human nature.

KRUTCH, JOSEPH WOOD, *The Measure of Man,* Indianapolis: Bobbs-Merrill, 1953.
   An extraordinarily stimulating book on issues between mechanistic and nonmechanistic approaches in biology, psychology, and sociology, by a noted humanistic scholar and writer.

MONTAGU, M. F. ASHLEY, *The Direction of Human Development; Biological and Social Bases,* New York: Harper & Row, 1955.
   A book bearing on the question of what man's original nature is and how that nature is influenced to assume a socially functional form. Highly readable, considering the subject matter involved.

MURPHY, GARDNER, *Historical Introduction to Modern Psychology,* New York: Harcourt Brace Jovanovich, 1949.
   A history of psychological thought treating the positions of Locke and the modern scientific psychologists. Perhaps the most readable of the histories of psychology.

SPENCE, KENNETH W., "Theoretical Interpretations of Learning," in S. S. Stevens, ed., *Handbook of Experimental Psychology,* New York: John Wiley, 1951, pp. 690–729.
   A summarization of the task of learning theorists. Classifies kinds of learning theories into perceptual and S-R groups and S-R groups into contiguity, reinforcement, and two-factor subgroups.

TWO

What Early Theories of Learning Are Reflected in Current School Practices?

This chapter is devoted to three conceptions of the learning process that emerged prior to the twentieth century but continue to have great influence in today's schools: (1) *mental discipline*, (2) *natural unfoldment*, and (3) *apperception*. These three theories have one characteristic in common: all were developed as nonexperimental psychologies of learning. That is, their basic orientation is philosophical or speculative. Each may be identified with a particular philosophical system and a corresponding school of psychology. The method used to develop these three conceptions of learning was introspective and subjective; philosopher-psychologists who evolved these ideas tried to analyze their own thought processes and describe in general terms what they thought they found. Since, according to mental-discipline theory, mental training is imparted by the *form* of studies as distinguished from their content, mental discipline also is identified by the expression *formal discipline*. However, throughout this book we use *mental discipline* in discussing this approach to learning.

WHAT IS MENTAL DISCIPLINE?

Mental discipline has roots extending to antiquity. Yet, its manifestations continue to be quite evident in present-day school practices. The theory was somewhat dormant during the first half of the twentieth century. However, the "post-Sputnik age" has led to its revival and revitalization.[1]

According to the doctrine of mental discipline, man is either a bad-active or neutral-active "rational animal" and education is a process of disciplining or training minds. Proponents of the doctrine believe that in this process mental faculties are strengthened through exercise. Just as exercising an arm develops the biceps, exercise of mental faculties makes them more powerful. Choice of learning materials is of some importance but always is secondary to the nature of minds which supposedly undergo the disciplinary process. Within mental discipline, persons are thought to be composed of two kinds of basic substances or realities, namely rational minds and biological organisms. That which is disciplined or trained is *mind substance.*

What is mind substance?

Mind substance is a self-dependent, immaterial essence, which underlies all outward physical manifestations; it is just as real as matter, it has a nature of its own, and it operates in its own distinctive fashion. Furthermore, it usually is assigned the dominant position in a mind-body dualistic conception of man. Physical substance—rocks, buildings, plants, and animals—is characterized by extension; it has length, breadth, thickness, and mass. Mind substance, in contrast, is not extended; it has no length, no breadth, no thickness, and no mass, yet it is as real as anything can be. In a sense, man is considered a mental and physical whole. However, body and mind supposedly are of such nature as to be mutually exclusive of each other; they have no common characteristic.

How did primitive man acquire the idea that he had a substantive mind? We do not know, but it is plausible to suppose that dreaming was partially responsible. Picture warrior A and warrior B lying down together after a hard day's hunting and a heavy feast. Warrior A has eaten too much and as a result is unable to sleep. Having been more moderate in his eating, warrior B sleeps all night but his sleep includes an adventurous dream. Upon awakening in the morning, warrior B relates the experience of finding and stalking game during the night. Warrior A expresses disbelief and insists that warrior B has been on the ground beside him all night. But warrior B is equally insistent

[1]See Walter B. Kolesnik, *Mental Discipline in Modern Education,* Madison: University of Wisconsin Press, 1958.

that he spent the night hunting and describes his dream so convincingly that both men decide that there must be *two* warrior B's. One slept on the ground throughout the night; the other must have come from within the first and carried on his escapades *unhampered by bodily form*. Thus could have been born something like a modern concept of mind substance.

Now, the mind substance concept has been with us a long time. Furthermore, it has grown through the inventive genius of primitive and civilized man, and it has become deeply imbedded in present-day cultures. Consequently, quite often its existence is considered a self-evident truth; the familiar has come to be accepted as the self-evident.

A defensible mind substance theory must take mind out of space completely. As long as one attributes to mind some characteristics of matter, even though they are very thin and elusive, he implies that mind is of essentially the same nature as matter. Thus, in understanding a mind substance theory of learning it is necessary to make a sharp distinction between mind and matter. We must remind ourselves that, if a mind is nonspatial, it cannot be located in the brain or anywhere else; and that, to date, man has devised no way of determining experimentally the way in which spatial and nonspatial entities influence one another.

If one adheres to a mind substance theory, each student's substantive mind is assumed to be active in either an erroneous or an inadequate fashion until it is either curbed or trained. Hence, one sees all learning as basically a process of developing or training minds. Accordingly, learning becomes a process of inner development within which various powers such as imagination, memory, will, and thought are cultivated. Education becomes a process of mental discipline.

How did the mental discipline theory of learning develop?

Plato believed that mental training or discipline in mathematics and philosophy was the best preparation for participation in the conduct of public affairs. Once trained, by having his faculties developed, a philosopher-king was ready to solve problems of all kinds. Aristotle described at least five different faculties, the greatest and the one unique to man being that of reason. According to Aristotle, faculties that man had in common with lower animals were the vegetative, appetitive, sensory, and locomotive.

At the close of the Middle Ages, *Renaissance humanism* was

an endeavor of man to gain more understanding of God, the universe, and himself. Humanism meant that man, rather than the Scriptures, was to be the starting point in satisfying man's urge toward individual development. To gain understanding of the ideal nature of man, humanistic scholars turned to the classics of ancient Greece and Rome. The resulting classicism of the Renaissance was developed on the assumption that a person's direction of growth is to be provided from within, not by yielding to the behest of every chance impulse, but by following principles that an individual himself formulates for guidance of his conduct. Thus, learning was regarded as a process of firm self-discipline; it consisted of harmonious development of all of one's inherent powers so that no one faculty was over-developed at the expense of the others.

Within humanism, the Socratic method was popular as a teaching procedure. A teacher's function was to help students recognize what already was in their minds. Environmental influence was considered of little consequence. "The Socratic method implies that the teacher has no knowledge, or at least professes to impart no information; instead, he seeks to draw the information from his students by means of skillfully directed questions. The method is predicated on the principle that knowledge is inborn but we cannot recall it without expert help."[2]

In the history of education, the nineteenth century could be characterized as the century of mental discipline. Rooted in European traditions of idealistic and rationalistic philosophy, the ideal of mental discipline had some currency in the early part of the century and it gained great popularity in the middle and later decades. A Yale faculty report of 1828 established mental discipline as the supreme aim of education. Study of the classics and mathematics was considered the best means of achieving it. A prominent English scholar, Matthew Arnold, wrote in 1867, "It is vital and formative knowledge to know the most powerful manifestations of the human spirit's activity, for the knowledge of them greatly feeds and quickens our own activity; and they are very imperfectly known without knowing ancient Greece and Rome."[3]

Mental discipline placed little stress upon the acquisition of useful knowledge and information as such. Rather, it emphasized the training of mental faculties and the cultivation of intellectual powers apart from any specific application to prac-

[2]George F. Kneller, *Existentialism and Education*, New York: Philosophical Library, 1958, p. 134.
[3]Matthew Arnold, *School Inquiry*, 6 (1867), 593.

tical problems. Since mental discipline was especially popular in liberal arts colleges, it was advocated for the college preparatory curriculums of academies and high schools.

Reassertion of classicism in the twentieth century. Traditionally, classical humanists have been more interested in perfecting the minds of a few superior individuals than in elevating mankind as a whole. Accordingly, some twentieth-century humanists are attempting to repudiate the intellectual leadership of natural and social scientists in the affairs of life and to revert to the precepts of traditional philosophers as represented by Plato, Aristotle, and the medieval scholastics. These present-day classical humanists believe we should make a sharp distinction between man and the world of nature. Man, being a rational animal, supposedly has certain unique universal and eternal qualities separating him from the lower forms of nature. Thus his education should center upon cultivation of his unique rational faculty. Whereas scientists make great use of other symbols, classicist literary intellectuals center their activity in words. Some leading twentieth-century classical humanists are Robert M. Hutchins, Mortimer J. Adler, and Mark Van Doren.

An example of mental discipline. A brief history of the teaching of Latin and Greek illustrates development of mental discipline as a theory of learning. Throughout the Middle Ages, Latin served a practical purpose. It was the language of scholars throughout the Western world and the vehicle of instruction in schools. Thus it was a living, growing, changing language that today we would call a "tool subject." During the Renaissance, Latin continued to be the language of communication, and both Latin and Greek were used in reading the classics, which contained those ideas considered the best that had been thought by man. To keep up with the thinking of his times, a scholar had to be able to read and use Latin and Greek.

After the Renaissance, modern languages gradually came into more general use. English, German, and French rose to prominence and assumed the role previously played by Latin and Greek. By the end of the sixteenth century, the communicative value of the classical languages was beginning to wane. Supporters of these languages, however, made a determined fight to preserve them. No longer needed for basic communication, Latin and Greek came to be heralded as the best subject matter for mental discipline. Throughout most of the nineteenth century the doctrine of the disciplinary value of these languages was generally accepted in American educational circles. Since, according to the classicists, disciplinary values are intangible and not susceptible to statistical treatment, evaluation of them supposedly was limited to analysis of opinions of recognized authorities on educational matters.

During the early years of the twentieth century, when the mechanistic learning theories opposed to mental discipline—apperception, connectionism, and behaviorism—were on the upsurge in educational circles, Greek practically dropped out of the educational picture and Latin suffered a great decline. However, by the middle of the twentieth century a resurgence of the classical tradition was apparent. With it came its earlier associate, mental discipline, and the teaching of Latin began to be expanded again.

A midtwentieth-century plea for a return to classicism and faculty psychology is expressed in a quotation from an article by James D. Koerner, at one time Executive Secretary of the Council for Basic Education:

> . . . many of us will persist in our notion that the most promising way we have yet found of preparing people to teach is to furnish their minds generously with the best that has been thought and said in the principal fields of man's intellectual activity; to allow them to gain a mastery of, and a delight in, at least one of these fields; to develop in them the power and the habit of thought; and in the process, to awaken their moral faculty and to discipline their will, that they may by example do the same for their students.[4]

What forms may mental discipline take?

The theory of mental discipline has at least two versions—*classicism* and *faculty psychology*. Each is an outgrowth of different cultural traditions. Classicism stems from ancient Greece. It operated on the assumption that the mind of man is an active agent in relation to its environment and also that man is morally neutral at birth.

The psychology known as "faculty psychology" more often is associated with the bad-active principle of human nature than with the earlier Greek neutral-active principle. Because of differences in underlying assumptions concerning the basic nature of man, we find a difference between the kinds of education prescribed by classicists and by faculty psychologists. Let us examine this difference in more detail.

Mental discipline within the classical tradition. Within the

[4]James D. Koerner, "Merely Training in Pedagogy," *NEA Journal* (April 1959), p. 18.

classical tradition a human mind is assumed to be of such nature that, with adequate cultivation, it can know the world as it really is. Man, being a rational animal, is free within limits to act as he chooses in the light of what he understands. Instead of being a creature of instinct, he enjoys a complex and delicate faculty of apprehension whose basic aspect is reason. This capacity resides in every normal human individual. It enables human beings to gain understanding of their needs and their environment, to direct their action in accordance with their understanding, and to communicate this understanding to other members of their group. Thus, it is assumed that the human mind is of such nature that, if it has been properly exercised and it has an opportunity, it will educe truth; it will develop outward manifestations of its innate potential.

Within the classicist frame of reference, knowledge assumes the character of a fixed body of true principles, handed down as a heritage of the race. These principles have been discovered by the great thinkers of human history and have been set down in the great books. Hence, a classicist takes the basic content of the school curriculum from philosophical and literary classics. To him, not only training the mind, but also studying the eternal truths contained in certain great books is of primary importance.

Faculty psychology. Although faculty psychology had been implicit in the classical tradition and in virtually every early scheme of education proposed, it did not appear as an explicit, formalized psychological doctrine until the eighteenth century. Christian Wolff (1679–1754), a German philosopher, is credited with its development. His version was described in his *Rational Psychology*, published in 1734. Wolff's thesis was that the mind, although unitary, has different faculties that are distinct. The mind at times enters into particular activities in much the same way that the whole body at different times takes part in widely different acts. According to Wolff, the basic general faculties are knowing, feeling, and willing. The knowing faculty is divided into several others, which include perception, imagination, memory, and pure reason. The reasoning faculty is the ability to draw distinctions and form judgments.

The belief in a willing faculty is an outgrowth of the notion that human nature may be described in terms of the bad-active principle. If human nature is intrinsically evil, then a strongly developed will is necessary to harness inherent evilness. Without will, a person would be unable to function in human society. Will, in the sense in which it is employed here, refers to ability to implement, or put into effective practice, a decision that has been made. A strongly developed will enables a person to "see a decision through" even though such action violates natural, i.e., evil, impulses. Hence, if one chooses to emancipate himself from his natural impulses, a well-developed will is necessary for success; he must make himself do that which he does not want to do. Faculty psychologists have held that if a person pursues any type of unpleasant work long enough his will is strengthened.

Under faculty psychology, the task of a teacher is to find the kind of mental exercises that will train the various faculties most efficiently. Emphasis is not on acquiring knowledge, but rather on strengthening faculties. A consistent faculty psychologist would not be especially interested in teaching "great truths" or the "heritage of the past" or any other type of subject matter except insofar as it is a good medium for exercising the faculties.

The special attention given by faculty psychology to development of the will has led to the notion that school work is better for a child if it is somewhat distasteful. Consequently, when faculty psychology is a dominant influence in a school, teachers may deliberately keep their assignments both difficult and dull and use force if necessary to insure that students complete them. Also, use of severe punishment, including ridicule and whipping, may be found in frequent use in such a school.

The wedding of classicism and faculty psychology. Faculty psychology, as developed by Wolff and his followers, was at first a challenge to classicism. Logically, faculty psychologists should consider one subject as good as another for exercising a particular faculty; also, knowledge retained by a student was considered much less important than the disciplining effect of learning it. But these conclusions negate the classicist's insistence on the virtues of certain subjects and on learning and retaining the great truths that human experience has unveiled.

However, a rather easy compromise soon became apparent. If it could be established that the best subjects for training the faculties were the classics, then the classical curriculum could be defended. This argument gained strength, and by the late nineteenth century most secondary schools and colleges offered a curriculum limited mainly to the classical liberal arts. These subjects were regarded as valuable for a twofold reason: they were excellent tools for mind training and they incorporated the great truths of human experience.

A curriculum based on traditional philosophy and the liberal arts may not seem very practical to most persons today. However, mental disciplinarians deliberately make a distinction between knowledge of immediate usefulness and practicality and essential matters grounded in eternal standards of truth, goodness, and beauty. Mental disciplinarians are convinced that knowledge of immediate practical value is of little importance. They hold that only the abstract principles of pure theory can free the human mind and promote man's distinctively human capacity for reason.

This emphasis is understandable. Most adherents of mental discipline are mind-body dualists who feel that mind is much the more important member of the partnership. Identification of education with development of minds tends to disparage other aspects of human activity. Thus we are told that "Education, as a whole, can never be a 'science' in the strict sense of the term. It is part of the 'humanities.' "[5]

Scientific attempts to evaluate mental discipline

Mental discipline proponents generally have held that learning theory, curriculum construction, teaching methods, and educational practices cannot be evaluated scientifically; they are derived philosophically, hence they can only be evaluated philosophically. However, by the early twentieth century, an imposing array of psychologists and educators had become captivated by the potentiality of scientific processes, particularly objective and statistical procedures as exemplified in such fields as physics and chemistry.

Whereas on the one hand mental disciplinarians insisted that science could not be applied in such a human enterprise as education, on the other hand scientifically oriented educators and psychologists insisted that science could and must be used in education. Increasingly, scientific-minded persons came to view exponents of mental discipline as conservatives or reactionaries who opposed progress in education.

When the classical curriculum first took form, it represented the point of view of liberals of the time and reflected a desire for progress. Its adherents were sufficiently open-minded to permit changes. However, by the beginning of the twentieth century the classical curriculum had come under such sharp attack that its proponents were placed on the defensive. The more defensive they became, the more rigid and dogmatic their thinking seemed to be. They pleaded for a return to a rigid Renais-

[5]Robert Ulich, *Professional Education as a Humane Study*, New York: Macmillan, 1956, pp. 112–113.

sance ideal, forgetting that the Renaissance ideal itself was an example of change and growth.

Almost to the end of the 1890s public high schools in the United States were loyal to the classical liberal tradition with its psychology of mental discipline. The famous Committee of Ten on Secondary School Studies upheld a doctrine of mental discipline throughout its 1890 report.

In the early 1900s Edward L. Thorndike (1874–1949) and Robert S. Woodworth (1869–1962), in a newer tradition of empirical (scientific) psychology, performed experiments at Columbia University to test the validity of mental discipline as a psychology of learning. Their basic conclusion was that the idea of mental discipline is scientifically untenable. Their experiments showed that drill or training in performing certain tasks did not strengthen the so-called faculties for performing such tasks. Training in estimating the lengths of short lines resulted in no significant improvement in estimating the lengths of longer lines. Development of neatness in one area of activity showed no or very little improvement of students' neatness in other areas; students' arithmetic papers may be noticeably improved in neatness with no parallel improvement in neatness of language and spelling papers.[6]

Thorndike also noted that the results of his experimentation, if corroborated by similar experiments, would prove that the amount of *general* improvement—mental discipline—due to the study of any school subject is small and that the differences in improvement as a result of studying different subjects also are small. Thus, he concluded that the values of subjects must be decided largely by the special learnings that they provide; the languages (or any other liberal arts subjects) have no claims to preeminence as an educational medium. The order of influence, if any, of specific subjects upon the growth of intellect was, first, arithmetic and bookkeeping; second, physical science; third, algebra and geometry; fourth, Latin and French; fifth, physical training; sixth, social science; seventh, history, music, shop, Spanish, English, drawing, and business; and eighth, dramatics, dramatic art, cooking, sewing, stenography, and biological sciences. Thus the so-called disciplinary subjects appear at all levels interwoven with supposedly nondisciplinary sub-

[6]See Edward L. Thorndike and R. S. Woodworth, "The Influence of Improvement in One Mental Function Upon the Efficiency of Other Functions," *Psychological Review*, 8 (May 1901), 247–261; (July 1901), 384–395; (November 1901), 553–564.

jects. Thorndike reported in the *Journal of Educational Psychology:*

> If our inquiry had been carried out by a psychologist from Mars, who knew nothing of theories of mental discipline, and simply tried to answer the question, "What are the amounts of influence of sex, race, age, amounts of ability, and studies taken, upon the gain made during the year in power to think, or intellect, or whatever our stock intelligence tests measure?" he might even dismiss "studies taken" with the comment, "The differences are so small and the unreliabilities are relatively so large that this factor seems unimportant." The one causal factor which he would be sure was at work would be the intellect already existent. Those who have the most to begin with gain the most during the year. Whatever studies they take will seem to produce large gains in intellect.[7]

Thorndike was convinced that the principal reason that good thinkers seemed to have been made good thinkers by certain subjects which they had pursued is that good students tend to take the subjects which people generally identify with good thinking. Good students gain more than do poor students from the study of *any* subject. When good thinkers study Latin and Greek, these subjects seem to cultivate good thinking. However, "If the abler pupils should all study Physical Education and Dramatic Arts, these subjects would seem to make good thinkers."[8]

In 1914 Thorndike disposed of inborn faculties with two sentences:

> [There is] the opinion that attention, memory, reasoning, choice and the like are mystical powers given to man as his birth-right which weigh the dice in favor of thinking or doing one thing rather than another. . . . This opinion is vanishing from the world of expert thought and no more need to be said about it than that it is false and would be useless to human welfare if true.[9]

In 1944 Alexander Wesman made a study following up Thorndike's earlier mental discipline studies. High school students were tested at the start and end of an academic year with a series of general intelligence and achievement tests. Gains on

[7]Edward L. Thorndike, "Mental Discipline in High School Studies," *Journal of Educational Psychology*, No. 2, (February 1924), p. 95.
[8]*Ibid.*, pp. 96–98.
[9]Edward L. Thorndike, *Educational Psychology*, New York: Teachers College Press, Columbia University, 1914, p. 73.

the tests during the year were observed for students taking differing course patterns to see whether some patterns of courses contributed more to intelligence than did others. Wesman's study revealed no superiority of any one school subject over any of the others studied; there was no superior addition to intelligence for any one of the achievement areas measured. Apparently no scientific basis exists for asserting that one high school subject contributes more to students' intelligence than does another.[10]

WHAT IS LEARNING THROUGH UNFOLDMENT?

We come now to the second major position to be treated in this chapter, often called "learning through unfoldment." This outlook on the nature of learning stems logically from the theory that man is naturally good and at the same time active in relation to his environment. All men are assumed to be free, autonomous, and forwardly active persons who are reaching out from themselves to make their worlds. Unless and until they are corrupted by some influences from outside themselves, every act that comes from them will be good. Each student is subjectively free, and his own personal choice and responsibility account for his life. He, and he alone, is the architect and builder of that life.

Early development of this point of view usually is associated with Jean J. Rousseau (1712–1778). Later, the Swiss educational reformer Heinrich Pestalozzi (1746–1827) and the German philosopher, educator, and founder of the kindergarten movement, Friedrich Froebel (1782–1852), used this outlook as a basis for their pedagogical thinking. The over-all philosophical framework of the natural-unfoldment position often is labeled *romantic naturalism*.

Rousseau's position was that everything in nature is basically good. Since man's hereditary nature is good, it need only be permitted to develop in a natural environment free from corruption. Rousseau qualified his interpretation of human nature as an active, self-directing agent by conceding that a bad social environment could make bad human beings; to him social institutions are not natural. Thus, his rejection of environmentalism was not complete. However, his emphasis was on natural, active self-determination.

[10]Alexander Wesman, "A Study of Transfer of Training from High School Subjects to Intelligence," *Teachers College Record*, October 1944, pp. 391–393.

Rousseau urged teachers to permit students to live close to nature so that they might indulge freely in their natural impulses, instincts, and feelings. He emphasized that in rural areas children need practically no schooling or tutoring. An example which he gave related to the learning of speech. A country boy, he said, ordinarily did not need instruction in speech. He called to his parents and playmates from considerable distances and thus practiced making himself heard; consequently, without tutoring, he developed an adequate power of speech. It was only the city boy, growing up in close quarters with no opportunity to exercise his voice in a natural way, who had need for speech instruction. Thus, he recommended that in teaching city boys teachers should, insofar as possible, adopt the method through which country boys learn.

Current subjectivism—natural unfoldment—takes the form of a *psychedelic humanism* within which a person, completely on his own, is sufficient for every situation. His emotional feelings, not his intellectual thoughts, are taken to be the final authority for truth. Hence, he arrives at decisions on all issues in accordance with the way he *feels*, and he is completely confident that he is right.

Since, according to the good-active definition of human nature, a child grows up unfolding that which nature has enfolded within him, devotees of this position tend to place great emphasis on the study of child growth and development and to minimize the study of learning. When they allude to learning, they seem to assume or imply that it, too, is little more than a process of growth and development.

Learning, in the usual sense of the term, generally is conceived as some form of imposition of ideas or standards upon a person or organism. However, within romantic naturalism there is little need for this kind of learning. Instead, a child learns through the promptings of his own interests. There should be no coercion or prescription. A mind and its growth may be considered analogous to an egg in the process of hatching. Its growth is a natural operation, which, without imposition from any outside source, carries its own momentum.

Since romantic naturalists depreciate the value of learning as such, they give a prominent place to the concept of needs. Needs are considered child-centered, as contrasted with environment- or situation-centered. As an organism or mind naturally unfolds through a series of stages, each stage is assumed to have its unique needs. Such child-centered needs have much in common with instincts, they supposedly are innate determining tendencies or permanent trends of human nature which underlie behavior from birth to death under all circumstances in all kinds of societies.

WHAT IS THE BACKGROUND OF APPERCEPTION?

The third major outlook toward learning which we describe— apperception—is far more complicated than either faculty psychology or learning as unfoldment. Apperception is idea-centered. An idea is apperceived when it appears in consciousness and is assimilated to other conscious ideas. Thus, apperception is a process of associating new ideas with old ones.

Adherents of both mental discipline and natural unfoldment assume or imply the existence of an inborn human nature, some aspects of which are common to all men. Although, in their treatment of learning, supporters of both theories sharply differ from one another, they agree that the "furniture of minds" is innate. Whereas romantic naturalists in their emphasis upon natural unfoldment expound instinctive natural development of persons, mental disciplinarians often agree that knowledge is inborn but insist that students need expert help to enable them to recall it.

Apperception, in contrast to both mental discipline and natural unfoldment, is a dynamic mental *associationism* based upon the fundamental premise that there are no innate ideas; everything a person knows comes to him from outside himself. This means that mind is wholly a matter of content—it is a compound of elemental impressions bound together by association, and it is formed when subject matter is presented from without and makes certain associations or connections with prior content.

What is associationist psychology?

An *associationism* is any general psychological theory within which it is assumed that learning starts with irreducible elements and the process of learning is one of combining these. We supposedly connect ideas or actions in memory, thought, or behavior simply because they were connected in our earlier experiences with them. To study human beings within a framework of associationism, the method must be analytic or reductionistic; learnings must be reduced to their component successive parts. Modern associationisms include apperception, S-R bond, and S-R associationistic theories. The basic elements that are associated may be mental, physical, or a combination of both.

Within apperception, the associated elements are completely mental and constitute the structures of minds.

How did associationism develop?

Plato and other ancient philosophers thought that learning really consisted of remembering ideas with which a learner had been endowed before his birth; it was development of innate ideas from within. His student Aristotle perpetuated Plato's mental disciplinary psychology of learning. However, in his psychology, he recognized a role of the senses. The senses performed a subordinate function; they informed the faculties of the mind.

The thinking underlying modern associationism goes back to Aristotle, who observed that recollection of an item of knowledge was facilitated by a person's associating that item or idea with another when he learned it. He maintained that four kinds of connections—associations—would aid or strengthen memory: contiguity of one idea with another, sucession of ideas in a series, similarity of ideas, and contrast of ideas.[11] Contiguity means being together. If a child is told about Eskimos and igloos at the same time, future mention of "Eskimo" will help him recall "igloo." "A tiger is a big kitty" uses the principle of similarity. If a person learns that pleasure is the opposite of pain (contrast), mention of "pain" will aid him in thinking of "pleasure."

John Locke—a sense empiricist.   In the seventeenth century John Locke (1632–1704) challenged the whole notion of innate faculties or ideas and with it the conception of learning as development of innate potentialities or faculties. Locke observed that he could find no common human nature at all. Realizing that he could find no ideas common to all people in any one society or to people in different societies, he developed his *tabula rasa* theory of the human mind. *Tabula rasa*—blank tablet—means that there are no innate ideas. Locke was convinced that, not only was a mind empty at birth, but also any ideas that a person holds must have come to him originally through his senses.

Locke's theory that all of a person's ideas must come to him through his senses is called *empiricism*. His empiricism was directly opposed to the earlier *rationalism* of Plato and Descartes. Whereas these two scholars considered *reason* the source of knowledge, Locke insisted that knowledge was derived from *sense experience.* In his view, perception is synonymous with learning and is a product of experience. A mind is insulated from the world of objects. Thus, any objects that are perceived are only ideas of objects.

For Locke, ideas were the units of a mind, and *associations* consisted of combinations of ideas. Ideas were either simple or complex. One of the operations of a mind was thought to be a compounding of complex ideas from simple ones. This notion of mental combination and analysis was a beginning of the "mental chemistry" which later characterized *apperception.*

To allow for associations within a mind, Locke recognized an "internal sense." He realized that if a mind were only a passive receptacle of sense impressions (which basically he thought it to be), the impressions would accumulate in a disorderly manner. Consequently, he gave mind a means for dealing with passive impressions once they were in. To mind, he attributed the ability to compare impressions, to generalize them, and to discriminate between them. This meant that it could associate ideas through contiguity, continuity, similarity, and contrast.

Locke's writings spearheaded a shift in the conception of education from mental discipline to habit formation. The *tabula rasa* theory implied that the original nature of man was neither good nor bad, nor active. Instead, it was deemed morally neutral and actionally passive. So, a mind was the product of life experiences. Locke's thinking opened the way for psychologists to place their emphasis upon environmental nurture rather than hereditary nature. In school, this meant that teachers were to be the architects and builders of minds of children. They were to develop a systematic instructional program centered in procedures designed to form proper habits in students. Teaching, then, became a matter of training the senses as opposed to training the faculties.

Locke's work constituted a turning point in professional thinking about *learning.* Up to the seventeenth century, most psychological thinking consisted of restatements and reinterpretations of the psychology of antiquity—mental discipline. This trend continued into the seventeenth and eighteenth centuries, but alongside it, Locke, preceded by Hobbes and followed by Hartley and Herbart, spearheaded associationism—a new line of thought in regard to learning.

Whereas Locke and other early associationists had assumed that linkages or associations are passive in nature, Herbart's apperception theory replaced this passivity with *dynamic* ideas.

However, we should remember that, in Herbart's *apperception*, ideas, not persons, are dynamic. Persons are *containers* within which laws of mental chemistry supposedly operate.

WHAT IS APPERCEPTION?

Johann Friedrich Herbart (1776–1841) developed the first modern systematic psychology of learning to harmonize with a *tabula rasa* theory of mind. Herbart was an eminent German philosopher and a skilled teacher. In 1809 he succeeded Immanuel Kant in the world's most distinguished chair of philosophy at Königsberg, Germany and held it until 1833. His speculative thinking developed from his dealing with problems of education. To him, morality was the supreme objective of education; he wanted to make children good. Thus he developed a psychology to achieve this goal.

Herbart's influence on twentieth-century American education has been great. Although his theory was developed early in the nineteenth century, it was not until the 1880s that four young Americans—Charles DeGarmo, Frank McMurry, Charles A. McMurry, and Charles C. Van Liew—studied at the University of Jena and returned to the United States to spread Herbartian doctrine with religious fervor. "Like a tidal wave, interest in this elaborate system swept over American teachers and students of education during the nineties."[12]

From the early years of the twentieth century to the time its tenets were seriously challenged by behaviorism and connectionism, Herbartianism dominated teacher education institutions of the United States. Thus, if one is to comprehend the psychological atmosphere of today's schools, it is essential that one understand the development, principles, and implications of the theory of apperception. Today, one seldom meets an avowed Herbartian; however, much of what takes place in our public schools carries with it the implicit assumption that neutral and passive minds of children are being filled. Although apperceptive teaching seldom is advocated systematically in teacher-education institutions, much actual teaching continues to follow a pattern in harmony with the theory of apperception.

Herbart perpetuated a mind-body dualism which was prevalent in his time. This was a psychophysical parallelism within which the psychic aspect—mind—played the major role, particu-

---

[12]Frederick Eby and C. F. Arrowood, *The Development of Modern Education*, Englewood Cliffs, N.J.: Prentice-Hall, 1934, p. 786.

larly in the learning process. Psychophysical parallelism is a theory of mind and body according to which, for every variation in conscious or mental process, there is a concomitant, parallel neurological or body process. Yet there is no causal relation between body and mind; a person's mind does not affect his body, nor his body his mind.

Through the use of the concepts *presentations, apperception,* and *apperceptive mass* Herbart expanded the notion of mind's neutral passivity into a systematic theory of learning and teaching. He thought minds had no innate natural faculties or talents whatsoever either for receiving or for producing ideas. In them lay not even remote dispositions toward perception, thought, willing, or action. He regarded minds as nothing more than battlegrounds and storehouses of ideas. Ideas, he thought, had an active quality. They could lead a life of their own in minds, which were completely passive. A mind was an aggregate, not of faculties, but of ideas or mental states. John Dewey (1859–1952) described the apperceptionists' view of mind in this way: "The 'furniture' of the mind *is* the mind. Mind is wholly a matter of 'contents.' "[13]

In his metaphysics, Johann Herbart posited a unitary mind or soul for each person, which is part of ultimate reality and consequently exists prior to experience. Such a soul or mind (*Wesen*) really has no spatial or temporal nature. However, as with a mathematical point, in thinking about it we give it space and time dimensions. Furthermore, "The soul has no innate natural talents nor faculties whatever, either for the purpose of receiving or for the purpose of producing. . . . It has originally neither concepts, nor feeling, nor desires."[14] However, since it is no *tabula rasa* but has its own unique receptivity, impressions foreign to it may not be made upon it.

Herbart's ambition was to build a science of human minds that would parallel the physical and biological sciences. He thought that the actual character of a mind consists of an arrangement of ideas, which are very much like the electrons of modern physics—they make up the object that contains them. Accordingly, a mind is an aggregate or group of contents resulting from a person's having certain ideas presented to him. Since he thought of psychology as "mental chemistry," he felt that the chief role of psychology was to study the various blendings and

[13]John Dewey, *Democracy and Education*, New York: Macmillan, 1922, p. 82.

[14]Johann Friedrich Herbart, *A Text-Book in Psychology*, Margaret K. Smith, trans., New York: Appleton-Century-Crofts, 1891, p. 120.

amalgamations of ideas or mental states in minds. Discovery of the principles by which ideas combine and recombine like chemical elements was Herbart's object in psychological investigation.

Although Herbart felt that his psychology was scientific, probably most experimental psychologists today would not agree; he rejected experimentation and the use of physiological data, both of which have been cornerstones of twentieth-century behavioristic psychology. To him, observation and thought were the proper methods for psychological inquiry. Furthermore, the observation he had in mind was self-observation, or introspection. By looking into his own mind, Herbart thought that its "chemistry" could be observed and described. He felt it proper that a science like physics was experimental, but equally appropriate that psychology be metaphysical and introspective.

What are mental states?

Herbart used the German term *Vorstellungen* to name the mental elements which he deemed the constituent parts of a mind. *Vorstellungen* may be translated to mean presentations, mental states, ideas, concepts, or notions, but *presentations* is the English term most often used in connection with Herbartian thought. However, when apperception theory was brought to the United States and subjected to further development, the term *mental states* superseded *presentations*. Consequently, in this country Herbartianism often has been called a "psychology of mental states."

According to Herbartian psychologists, mental states constitute a nonspatial, mental reality that is experienced firsthand. They have three forms: sense impressions, images or copies of previous sense impressions, and affective elements of pleasure and pain. Furthermore, they furnish the only source of mental activity. The derived states, feeling and willing, accompany mental states but are not a source or cause of mental activity.

How does apperception work?

Mind is an aggregate of mental states and a person's stock of mental states at any given time is his "apperceptive mass." Until a first presentation occurs, there is nothing whatever present in a mind; except for its inherent receptivity, it is completely passive. Mental states, the active structure of mind, become associated to produce experience. Thus, new ideas are learned only as they are related to what is already in an apperceptive mass. Hence, it is the addition of new presentations to the old that produces the various types of mental processes. Furthermore, the particular combination of ideas that is predominant at any given time determines what will hold a person's attention at that time.

Within Herbart's system of "mental chemistry" every presentation (mental state) has an inherent quality, giving it an affinity for certain other presentations and an aversion for some others; respective ideas either attract or repel one another. Whereas the ideas of "book" and "school" would have an affinity and attract each other, the ideas of "book" and "fishing rod" probably would have a repugnancy and repel one another.

A Herbartian regards a mind as a battleground of contending ideas. Each idea in the mind of a person has once been in the center of his consciousness and it strives to return; it seeks self-preservation. Furthermore, it tries to enter into relations with other ideas. Having once held the center of consciousness and subsequently lost it, each presentation, like a deposed king, keeps trying to occupy the throne once again. Compatible ideas may operate as teams, helping each other to remain in a conscious mind. But, when two ideas are incompatible, one is likely to be submerged.

To Herbartians, all perception is *apperception;* it is a process of relating new ideas—presentations—to the store of old mental states. A mind is like an iceberg in that most of it is submerged below the level of consciousness. Memories stored in the subconscious enable one to interpret experience of the moment. Without a background of experience, any new sensation would mean almost nothing at all. In picturing a mind, Herbart introduced the idea of threshold of consciousness. Objects occupying consciousness are constantly changing. At any moment, several ideas may occupy the consciousness. However, one will be at the focus of attention, some will be sinking below the threshold, and others will be striving to rise into consciousness. In Figure 2.1, mental state (b) is at the center of consciousness; (a) and (c) are only slightly above the threshold and in the margin of consciousness.

The subconscious aspect of mind contains the store of dynamic perceptions and images that have been accumulated during all past experiences of an individual. Any of these are ready to spring back into consciousness whenever a propitious opportunity occurs. The content of consciousness at any moment is the result of an interplay of many ideas. Apperception is a

Figure 2.1
   Herbart's scheme of psychology. (An adaptation from Frederick Eby,
   The Development of Modern Education, in Theory, Organization,
   and Practice, *2nd Edition,* © *1952, p. 481. Reprinted by permission*
   of Prentice-Hall, Inc., Englewood Cliffs, N.J.

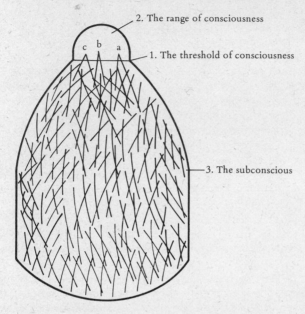

process not only of becoming consciously aware of an idea but
also of assimilating it into a totality of conscious ideas.

Within the apperceptive process Herbart saw the principles
of frequency and association in operation. The principle of frequency means that the more often an idea or concept has been
brought into consciousness, the easier becomes its return. The
principle of association holds that, when a number of presentations or ideas associate or form a mass, the combined powers
of the mass determine the ideas that will enter consciousness.

Herbart recognized three levels or stages of learning. First is
the stage of predominately sense activity. This is followed by
the stage of memory; this second stage is characterized by exact
reproductions of previously formed ideas. The third and highest
level is that of conceptual thinking or understanding. Understanding occurs when the common, or shared, attributes of a
series of ideas make themselves seen. It involves generalization
—deriving rules, principles, or laws from a group of specifics.

What does apperception mean for teaching?

According to apperception, right thinking will produce right action; volition or willing has its roots in thought. If a teacher builds up the right sequence of ideas, the right conduct follows. Hence, the real work of instruction is implantation not only of knowledge but also of inner discipline or will by means of presented ideas. Psychologically, students are made by the world of ideas that is presented to them from without.

Since, in apperception, there is no substantive mind to be trained, it could no longer be said that learning was a matter of disciplining or training a mind; rather learning has to do with the formation of an apperceptive mass. Thus, the task of education is to cause present appropriate experiences to combine with a background. The problem of education, then, is to select the right materials for forming the backgrounds or apperceptive masses of students. The concept of apperceptive mass implied that teachers must start with the experiences that pupils already have had and enlarge and enrich these experiences.

To Herbartians, the art of teaching consists of bringing to the attention of students those ideas that a teacher would like to have dominate their lives. Through controlling experiences of children, an instructor builds up masses of ideas, which develop by assimilation of new ideas to them. Thus, by manipulating ideas he constructs a student's "circle of thought." The goal is a comprehensive circle of thought closely connected or integrated in all its parts. A teacher is the architect and builder of the minds, and hence the characters, of his students.

According to Herbart, at no time should a teacher enter into debate with his students on any matter. "Cases may arise when the impetuosity of the pupil challenges the teacher to a kind of combat. Rather than accept such a challenge, he will usually find it sufficient at first to reprove calmly, to look on quietly, to wait until fatigue sets in."[15]

What are the Herbartian five steps in learning?

Herbart and his followers have been convinced that the learning process proceeds through an ordered series of steps which a teacher should understand and follow. Accordingly, effective teaching requires that, regardless of obstacles, the proper succession of steps be pursued. Herbart's four steps, clearness, asso-

[15]Johann Friedrich Herbart, *Outlines of Educational Doctrine*, New York: Macmillan, 1904, p. 165.

ciation, system, and method, were expanded to five by American Herbartians. Clearness became (1) preparation and (2) presentation; association became (3) comparison and abstraction; system became (4) generalization; and method became (5) application. Use of these steps came to be regarded as the general method to be followed in all teaching. The steps may be demonstrated by the following example, which involves teaching students the generalization that any object will float in liquid or in air if it weighs less than an equal volume of the air or liquid in which it is suspended.

1. *Preparation.* To bring into consciousness relevant ideas, the teacher reminds students of certain experiences they have had with floating objects. The students will recall the floating of boats, balloons, bubbles, and the like.

2. *Presentation.* The teacher presents new facts about floating, perhaps through means of demonstrations. For example, he might demonstrate how oil floats on water, or how a steel ball will float on mercury.

3. *Comparison and abstraction.* If the teacher has performed the first two steps properly, students will see that the new facts have similarities with those already known. Hence, in the students' consciousness, the new and old ideas associate. They are welded together because of their natural affinity for each other. Furthermore, students at this point should see the nature of the common elements that give the two sets of facts their mutual attractiveness. Sorting out this common element is what is meant by abstraction.

4. *Generalization.* In this step, students attempt to name the common elements of the two sets of facts as a principle or generalization. They arrive at the principle of flotation—the stated objective of instruction.

5. *Application.* The newly learned principle then is used to explain further facts or solve problems relating to flotation. This is done through assigned tasks or problems. The teacher might ask students to explain why boats can be made successfully from steel. Or he might give them a problem that requires them to determine whether a certain object would float in a certain medium. For example, he might ask, "Given a freight barge of specified weight and displacement, how much weight could be placed in it without causing it to sink?"

What was the Herbartian doctrine of interest?

The importance of student interest held a prominent place in the theory of apperception. Present-day policy of "making subject matter interesting" probably has strong roots in apperception. Whereas followers of faculty psychology saw little or no point in student interest (some even saw it as a deterrent to developing willpower), Herbartians gave it a central place in their system.

Since, to Herbartians, formation of mind was wholly a matter of presenting the proper educational materials, the task of a teacher was to select the proper subject matter and arrange its presentation on the basis of the current store of ideas in the student's mind. If the new material involved ideas with a natural affinity for those already present, the student would feel interest.

Interest meant "the natural bend or inclination of the mind to find satisfaction in a subject when it is properly presented."[16] Thus, it was an active power residing in the contents of the mind. It depended upon the nature of the apperceptive mass and determined what ideas were to receive attention. A person thinks, feels, and wills in accordance with his dominant presentations. To develop a variety of interests one must acquire a large apperceptive mass. Herbart listed six classes of interests under two major categories—those awakened by the phenomena of nature apart from man and those involving the direct study of human affairs. He then assumed a sort of affinity between the historical development of the race and the stages of mental development of children. He was convinced that the history and great literature of the world, when properly selected and arranged, would make a strong appeal to the interests and understanding of children at their successive periods of growth.

How does apperception influence today's schools?

Ideas developed by Herbartians continue to permeate today's schools. However, some of the terms used to express these ideas have been abandoned or redefined. Some key Herbartian terms were *interest, apperception, apperceptive mass, circle of thought, concentration, correlation, culture epochs, sympathy,* and *formal steps in instruction.* Aspects of these ideas can still be found in textbooks on curriculum and methodology.

Since it was the approach to teaching that was stressed most in a great many of our teacher education institutions from about 1900 to 1920, then much later was used along side conflicting theories of learning and teaching, apperception remains influential even today. Large numbers of persons now teaching or holding administrative posts in schools received their first profes-

[16]Charles A. McMurry, *The Elements of General Method*, New York: Macmillan, 1903, p. 85.

sional education in normal schools or teachers' colleges still strongly under the influence of Herbartianism. Moreover, many present-day teachers of teachers are fundamentally Herbartian in their approach to educational problems.

One area in which Herbartian influence frequently is still seen is that of lesson plans. In the Herbartian system, actual teaching was always preceded by construction of a formal lesson plan, built around the "five steps." Teachers followed these plans, more or less rigidly, on the assumption that the thinking of students could be made to conform to the formal steps. Today, many professors of education continue to insist that there is a fixed order of steps for teaching and learning. They require their students to write lesson plans in which the material to be taught is arranged according to definite steps, and in supervising student teachers they insist that the prepared lesson plans be followed.

Why has Herbartianism ceased to be a moving force in educational theory?

Nowadays, even educators who basically are Herbartian generally no longer think of themselves as such. Herbartian psychology and the teaching to which it led fell under major criticism quite early in the present century. The assumption in regard to the passive character of human nature that is implicit in Herbartian psychology leaves too much to be explained. Herbart recognized that people do think in an active fashion, but he refused to recognize any source or basis for active reflection. Ideas, not the person, carried the burden of thought. How ideas, or mental states, could be active and alive, carrying on a vigorous life of their own within a mind which was essentially passive, simply was not understandable to many people. Furthermore, Herbart's psychology and philosophy could be defended only in terms of psychophysical parallelism, and this philosophical position increasingly has fallen into disrepute.

More important perhaps than criticisms based on the abstruse features of Herbart's philosophy and psychology are criticisms of the teaching practices to which they led. Herbartianism seems to commit teachers to a program of indoctrination. Its approach to teaching requires teachers to determine precisely what their pupils are to be taught. Each lesson plan includes the answers as well as the questions. Students arrive at these answers through a largely mechanical process completely dominated by the teacher. Education is conceived as a process similar to filling a storage container. If learning is the mechanical process that Herbart and Herbartians described, how does reflective, creative thinking enter the educational scene?

Within Herbartianism, a teacher might teach for understanding, but not for reflection.[17] In commenting upon Herbartianism, John Dewey felt constrained to say, "It takes . . . everything educational into account save its essence—vital energy seeking opportunity for effective exercise."[18] Since Herbartian theory at no time suggests that a child is interactive with his environment, when applied in the classroom, it inescapably gives students little or no chance for active participation and constructive thinking.

A third criticism of Herbartianism is theoretical, but nevertheless vitally important. Explanations of the apperceptive process seem to contain no adequate treatment of how the first ideas enter a mind so that apperception—perception upon perception—can take effect. How does the first idea tie up with an old one?

What contributions has Herbartianism made to education?

Herbartianism had its weaknesses; nevertheless it made some important contributions to the development of education. Greatest of all has been its attack upon the doctrine of mental discipline and faculty psychology. In a more positive vein, it has emphasized a psychological approach to teaching and learning that implied a need for sound methods of teaching based upon knowledge of man and his mental functions. Thus, it has directed attention to a need for adequate teachers and an enriched curriculum: preparation of teachers was made an important business. Also, it has made student "interest" a significant idea, and it has emphasized the importance of a background of experience in the process of perception.

Furthermore, Herbart, in developing a scientific though not experimental psychology, pointed the way for the later experimental scientific movement in psychology named *structuralism*. Structuralism was developed in the nineteenth century by Wundt in Germany and Titchener in the United States. Its subject matter was the content of consciousness which was studied only by introspection. Nevertheless, structuralism was highly important in that it helped pave the way for modern psychologies that

[17]See Chapter 11, pp. 305–339, for development of the difference between these processes.
[18]Dewey, *op. cit.* (1916 ed.), p. 84.

have focused on mental processes and at the same time have been experimental in the best scientific sense.

Although apperception preceded the physicalistic S-R conditioning psychologies—behaviorism, connectionism, conditioning, and reinforcement—on the psychological and educational scenes, a case may be made for its equality to, or even superiority over, some of these later psychologies as a foundation for teaching procedures.

BIBLIOGRAPHY

ADLER, MORTIMER J., and MILTON MAYER, *The Revolution in Education*, Chicago, University of Chicago Press, 1958.
Sympathetic criticism of present-day teaching and an attempt to ask the right questions, that is, those questions which might help teachers resolve issues confronting them. The frame of reference is that of a classical scholar but the analysis is impartial. Bibliography covers span from ancient world to 1950s.

BODE, BOYD H., *How We Learn*, Lexington, Mass.: Raytheon/Heath, 1940.
A discussion of four distinct theories of mind—mind substance, mental states, behaviorism, and pragmatism. Excellent for historical background as well as for description of the outlooks.

BRUBACHER, JOHN S., *A History of the Problems of Education*, 2nd ed., New York: McGraw-Hill, 1966.
One of the best overviews of outlooks on learning. Chapter V, "Philosophy of Education," provides theoretical background for learning theory. Chapter VI, "Educational Psychology," summarizes mental discipline, apperception, behaviorism, and Gestalt psychology.

DEWEY, JOHN, *Democracy and Education*, New York: Macmillan, 1916. (Also in paperback, 1961 edition.)
Incisive, enlightening statements concerning natural unfoldment, apperception, and mental (formal) discipline. Pages 130–138 are devoted to Roussellian natural development; 65–68 to Froebelian unfoldment; 70–79 to mental discipline; and 81–84 to Herbartian apperception.

EBY, FREDERICK, *The Development of Modern Education*, Englewood Cliffs, N.J.: Prentice-Hall, 1952.
An excellent account of Herbart and Herbartian education (Chapter 18). Chapter 19 is equally good on Froebel and his system of education through self-activity.

HERBERT, JOHANN FRIEDRICH, *Outlines of Educational Doctrine*, New York: Macmillan, 1904.
The best source in English for Herbart's views upon education. It gives Herbart's psychological orientation, then follows with practical advice for instruction.

KOLESNIK, WALTER B., *Mental Discipline in Modern Education,* Madison: University of Wisconsin Press, 1958.

Review of the historical background and recent evidence on mental discipline. The author traces the changes in the meaning of mental discipline and attempts to give a dispassionate overview of the subject. He sees the viewpoints of the Harvard Committee on General Education, of Robert M. Hutchins, and of John Dewey as three approaches to mental discipline.

MCMURRY, CHARLES A., *The Elements of General Method, Based on the Principles of Herbart,* New York: Macmillan, 1903.

A textbook for teachers presenting Herbartian apperception, with its American modifications, by an early twentieth-century leader in American education.

ROUSSEAU, JEAN JACQUES, *Émile,* Barbara Foxley, trans., New York: Dutton, 1911, in the Everyman's Library.

A complete translation of Rousseau's *Émile.* It is Rousseau's account of his rearing and educating a fictitious boy born to eighteenth-century city dwellers.

ULICH, ROBERT, *History of Educational Thought,* rev. ed., New York: American Book, 1968.

Educational thought followed through lives and thoughts of great thinkers. Separate chapters are devoted to Rousseau, Froebel, Herbart, and so on.

THREE

What Are the Two Major Families of Contemporary Learning Theory?

The two most prominent families of contemporary learning theory are the *behavioristic stimulus-response conditioning theories* and the *Gestalt-field theories*. These have been in process of development throughout the twentieth century and have roots that extend into even earlier periods. In a sense, both families have been protests against the inadequacies and inconsistencies of earlier psychological systems. Their immediate forerunners were mental discipline and apperception. To repeat, items 5, 6, and 7 of Table 1.1 (pp. 10–11) refer to the behavioristic or S-R conditioning theories, and items 8, 9, and 10 to members of the Gestalt-field family.

Although the two psychological approaches contrast in most respects, they also have an area of commonality; they both are scientific approaches to the study of man and they both assume man's basic moral proclivity to be neutral—neither innately bad nor good. In this and the succeeding chapter, we explain the basic differences between the two families of learning theories by showing the respective presuppositions, assumptions, or commitments of adherents of each approach in regard to some specific issues.

This chapter develops the background thinking that underpins the positions of the two families in regard to learning. It first traces their historical development, their philosophical implications, and their chief assumptions about the role of psychology. It next shows how adherents of the two families differ in their interpretations of the perceptive and motivational processes. Then Chapter 4 focuses specifically on the more technical aspects of learning theory that are associated with each family.

During the 1920s and 1930s teachers' colleges moved away from the promotion of Herbartianism as such. But this does not mean that Herbartian ideas were completely abandoned in schools. They were then, and are today, accepted and practiced by many teachers. However, before the twentieth century had been under way very long, a new form of associationism had become popular. This was a nonmentalistic, or physiological, associationism. Its chief exponents during the first third of the century were John B. Watson (1878–1958) and Edward L. Thorndike. Watson's psychology was known as behaviorism. Thorndike's was called connectionism, but it too, in the broadcast sense of the term, was "behavioristic."

Although the psychological systems of Thorndike and Watson no longer are advocated in their original forms, many contemporary psychologists have orientations sufficiently similar to theirs to be termed "neobehaviorists."[1] Some leading contemporary neobehaviorists or S-R conditioning theorists are N. E. Miller, O. H. Mowrer, B. F. Skinner, K. W. Spence (1907–1967), and J. M. Stephens. In its broadest sense the term *behaviorism* encompasses all S-R conditioning theories; these include S-R bond or connectionism, behaviorism, and neobehaviorism. So, we may use the expressions *behaviorism* and *S-R conditioning theory interchangeably.*

The second major family of contemporary learning theories, Gestalt-field psychology, originated in Germany during the early part of the twentieth century. The four leaders in its development were Max Wertheimer (1880–1943), Wolfgang Köhler (1887–1967), Kurt Koffka (1886–1941), and Kurt Lewin (1890–1947). All four of these men migrated to the United States where they devoted their professional lives to development and refinement of their psychological position.

Gestalt-field psychologists consider learning phenomena to be

[1]Neo is a word element meaning "new," "recent," or "modified." When used as a prefix, it refers to a school of thought that is derived from an earlier school of thought but refined in various ways. See T. W. Wann, ed., *Behaviorism and Phenomenology*, Chicago, University of Chicago Press, 1965, pp. 7–21.

closely related to perception. Consequently, they define learning in terms of reorganization of the learner's perceptual or psychological world—his field. Some contemporary leaders whom we may identify with this family are R. G. Barker, E. E. Bayles, A. W. Combs, and H. F. Wright.

Gestalt is a German noun for which there is no equivalent English word, so the term was carried over into English psychological literature. The nearest English translation of *Gestalt* is "configuration" or "pattern." Thus, we refer to related theories which represented or grew out of Gestalt psychology as Gestalt-field or configurational psychology. As configurational psychology evolved, other names such as *organismic, field, phenomenological* and *cognitive-field psychology* became associated with it. Gestalt-field psychology was introduced into the United States in the middle 1920s. It has gathered a large number of exponents and now can be considered the leading rival of the behaviorisms. However, a great many psychologists are eclectic in the sense that they borrow elements from both schools of thought and identify themselves with neither.

Students should be aware of the fact that within each of the two families of psychological theory there is considerable diversity. For example, in the behavioristic family, followers of K. W. Spence and B. F. Skinner would be in disagreement on many points. Likewise, in the Gestalt-field family, followers of Kurt Lewin differ considerably in outlook from followers of Kurt Koffka and proponents of cognitive-field theory differ significantly with both. For example, whereas contemporary representatives of this family consider persons to be neutral-interactive, early Gestaltists often implied that persons were neutral-active. Thus, the situation in psychology is somewhat like that in politics; many persons gravitate toward one or the other of our two political parties, but in spite of some common interests both Democrats and Republicans exhibit a wide range of views. In final analysis, however, behaviorists have certain key ideas in common, just as do Gestalt-field psychologists. Hence, it is proper to consider each category as a definite grouping that can be discussed in terms of the ideas common to its members.

If students are aware that in spite of variance within each family the two families do differ sharply, they will better understand the ensuing chapters on learning. To fundamental issues in psychology the two families provide answers that are often quite incompatible. Thus, in dealing with the following questions, a person oriented toward behaviorism is likely to give a significantly different answer from that given by a Gestalt-field theorist: What is intelligence? What happens when we remember and when we forget? What is perception? What is motivation? What is thinking? What is the role of practice in learning? How does learning transfer to other situations?

Before a student adopts the orientation of one family of psychology or the other, he should recognize that objections may be made to any position one takes in psychology and to any currently available theory of learning. However, although the evidence is not clear enough to warrant dogmatic assertions about learning, one may emerge from a careful study with the feeling that the ideas central to one family of psychological theory are more tenable and have fewer disadvantages than the ideas central to the other.

Although all modern psychologists, irrespective of their orientation, generally accept the methods and results of experimentation, there is wide divergence in interpretation of experimental results and equally wide divergence on how a given interpretation should be applied in solution of a concrete learning problem. These differences appear to stem from disagreement over the fundamental nature of man, the relationship of man to his environment, and the nature of perception and motivation. In spite of disclaimers by some psychologists, it also appears impossible to detach a number of issues in psychology from related issues in philosophy. A psychologist's philosophical leaning may not only determine the kinds of experiments he conducts but also influence the conclusions he draws from experimentation.

WHAT ARE THE ASSOCIATIONIST ORIGINS OF CURRENT BEHAVIORISMS?

We observe in Chapter 2 that early associationists were interested primarily in mental phenomena; their concern was with the association of ideas in minds. In contrast, modern behavioristic associationism tends to be rooted in a different kind of interest—the behavior of bodies.

Nineteenth-century forerunners of modern experimental psychology tended to be philosophical dualists; they considered men to consist of minds and bodies, each genuinely real. There was a good deal of speculation in regard to the nature of the relationship of minds and bodies, but seldom denial of the reality of either. In the transition period between Herbart and Watson, much vacillation took place between emphasis upon the workings of biological organisms and the functions of minds.

During the first half of the nineteenth century, experimental psychology got its start within experimental physiology. The physiologists Bell and Müller became occupied with testing the workings of the nervous system in seeing and hearing. Thus, they became psychologists even though they did not call themselves such.

Wilhelm Wundt (1832–1920) was trained in medicine. He turned from medicine to physiology and from physiology to psychology. In 1879 he established the first psychological laboratory of modern history. His method was introspection; he and his students observed the workings of their respective minds. Students from various parts of the world went to Wundt's laboratory at Leipzig to study introspection. But many became psychological heretics; they turned to study of observable behavior of other persons and animals.

Late in the nineteenth century interest in bodily functioning became apparent among many psychologists. This group of "physiological psychologists" argued that psychology could become a true science only if it switched its focus to bodily processes. In a century that placed ever-increasing emphasis upon experimental science, introspection came more and more to appear a highly unreliable procedure. A person could reflect upon the workings of his own mind, but what did this prove? Scientists were ceasing to be concerned with any kind of evidence that was not "publicly verifiable"—that is, subject to public observation and tests. Thus, they began to focus their attention on objects or events that could be observed with the "five senses," be studied in the same manner by any number of trained investigators, and lead to uniform conclusions.

To a growing number of psychologists, the only logical alternative to the method of introspection was to focus on observable forms of behavior. Such behavior includes not only bodily movement as seen by an observer watching a subject but also the internal physical processes related to overt bodily behavior. Why epinephrine is secreted and how long it takes a person to react to a pinprick are equally proper to a physiological psychologist. Both can be measured objectively, described in terms of definite mechanical sequences or quantities, and reported statistically. Before the twentieth century was very far along, a large number of psychologists had come to feel that psychology, in time, could be made as "scientific" as physics.

We shall name only a few of the persons who contributed to the development of physiological psychology. Marshall Hall (1790–1857) did pioneering work on the neural basis of reflex behavior. Pierre Flourens (1794–1867) demonstrated that different parts of the nervous system have different functions, and he took important steps toward identifying the function of each part. He also proposed that conclusions drawn from animal experimentation should be equally applicable to man. This notion gained wide acceptance and greatly simplified the work of experimental psychologists: after all, it is much cheaper and more convenient to experiment with rats than with human beings.

Some of the most notable animal learning experiments of the late nineteenth and early twentieth centuries were conducted by the Russian physiologist Ivan Petrovich Pavlov (1849–1936). Pavlov put food before a hungry dog and sounded a bell or tuning fork. He found that if this procedure was repeated enough times, the sound alone would cause the dog to salivate. As we shall see, Pavlov's work was extremely influential, and nowhere more so than among the growing group of behaviorists in the United States. Thorndike's animal experiments, making use of chicks, dogs, and cats, were possibly even more comprehensive than Pavlov's and, over the long run, more influential in the United States. His famous "laws of learning" were derived mainly from his interpretation of how cats behave when placed in a cage from which they do not know how to escape—until they learn. Since Thorndike was a dominant figure in the psychology of learning for almost half a century, we describe some of his ideas in detail.

Thorndike's connectionism

Thorndike was an "ecletic" in the sense that he retained in his thinking certain elements of Herbartian "idea associationism," and, at the same time, was strongly influenced by the new physiological psychology (see p. 69 for an explanation of eclecticism). Consequently, he assumed that there are both physical and mental events or units, and that learning is a process of linking the two in various combinations. A mental unit was something sensed or perceived; a physical unit was a stimulus or a response. Specifically, he saw learning as a process of connecting a mental with a physical unit, a physical with a mental unit, a mental with a mental unit, or a physical with a physical unit.

Thorndike's theory of learning is called *S-R bond* theory or *connectionism*. It assumes that, through conditioning, specific responses come to be linked with specific stimuli. These links, bonds, or connections are products of a biological change in a nervous system. Thorndike thought that the principal way in which S-R connections were formed was through random trial and error (or selecting and connecting). It is probably because of Thorndike's influence that the term *trial-and-error* became popularized and found its way into the vocabularies of many Americans.

In a typical trial-and-error experiment, Thorndike would place a "hungry" cat in a cage that could be opened from inside only by striking a latch or button. The cat would claw, bite, and scurry wildly about until it accidentally touched the release and was freed. The experiment would be repeated and the animal would behave the same except that over the course of a number of successive "trials" the total time required by the cat to get out would decrease. Eventually the cat would learn to escape immediately without random activity. Thorndike inferred from the timed behavior of his cats that learning was a process of "stamping in" connections in the nervous system and had nothing to do with insight or "catching on."

Thorndike formulated a number of "laws" of learning and classified them as either primary or secondary. He expressed his primary laws by the terms *readiness, exercise,* and *effect.* His secondary or subordinate laws were identified by the expressions *multiple response, set or attitude, prepotency of elements, response by analogy,* and *associative shifting.*[2] We describe here only his three primary laws:

1. *The law of readiness.* Thorndike termed the neuron (or neurons) and the synapse (or synapses) involved in establishment of a specific bond or connection a *conduction unit.* He assumed that, because of the structure of a nervous system, in a given situation certain conduction units are more predisposed to conduct than others. And *"for a conduction unit ready to conduct to do is satisfying,* and *for it not to do so is annoying."*[3]

2. *The law of exercise or repetition.* According to this law, the more times a stimulus-induced response is repeated, the longer it will be retained. As Thorndike put it, "Other things being equal, *exercise strengthens the bond between situation and response."*[4]

---

[2]See Ernest R. Hilgard and Gordon H. Bower, *Theories of Learning,* 3rd ed., New York: Appleton-Century-Crofts, 1966, pp. 21–22 for descriptions of the subordinate laws.

[3]Edward L. Thorndike, *Educational Psychology,* New York: Teachers College Press, Columbia University, Vol. 1, 1913, p. 127. (Italics in original.)

[4]Edward L. Thorndike, *Education,* New York: Macmillan, 1912, p. 95. (Italics in original.)

3. *The law of effect.* The law of effect stated the famous pleasure-pain principle so frequently associated with Thorndike's name. A response is strengthened if it is followed by pleasure and weakened if followed by displeasure. In Thorndike's words, ". . . [to] a modifiable connection being made . . . between an S and an R and being accompanied or followed by a satisfying state of affairs man responds, other things being equal, by an increase in the strength of that connection. To a connection similar, save that an *annoying* state of affairs goes with or follows it, man responds, other things being equal, by a decrease in the strength of the connection."[5] "By a satisfying state of affairs [positive reinforcer] is meant one that the animal does nothing to avoid, often doing such things as attain and preserve it. By a discomforting or annoying state of affairs is meant one which the animal commonly avoids and abandons."[6]

In his later writings Thorndike disavowed his law of exercise or repetition and one-half—the annoyance aspect—of his law of effect. But he seemed not to have had the courage of his convictions. Through implication, he continued to emphasize repetition in learning. His law of effect shifted its emphasis to pleasure, but the pain aspect was not completely discarded.

Students will readily see that Thorndike's laws of learning are closely related and may operate together. For example, if an organism is ready to respond, then response is pleasurable and this fact in itself will tend to fix the response. Also, the laws appear to be exceedingly mechanical. Furthermore, they seem to leave no room for any sort of thought or insight, and they do not appear to require the assumption of any kind of purposiveness of man or lower animals.

The psychological concept *purposiveness* has no direct relationship to the problem of cosmic or teleological purpose. Within a purposive psychology, as contrasted with a mechanistic one, we assume that each animal or person, whatever his developmental level, is seeking some end or purpose and that we can predict his behavior most accurately when we anticipate what it is he is trying to accomplish.

Watson's behaviorism

Watson, much more strongly than Thorndike, felt the need to base psychology exclusively on the concepts of physics and

[5]Thorndike, *Educational Psychology, op. cit.*, p. 172.
[6]Edward L. Thorndike, *Animal Intelligence*, New York: Macmillan, 1911, p. 245.

chemistry. To his way of thinking, mind and all kinds of mentalistic concepts were not only unsusceptible to scientific inquiry but also irrelevant to the real task of psychology. Watson drew heavily upon Pavlov's work and became convinced that learning was as Pavlov described it, namely, a process of building conditioned reflexes through the substitution of one stimulus for another.

Watson and other "pure behaviorists" came to reject certain of Thorndike's ideas because it seemed impossible to exclude mind and mind-related concepts from them. We already have mentioned that Thorndike talked of "mental units." The pure behaviorists were also bothered by Thorndike's concepts of satisfaction and annoyance. To behaviorists these seemed to be mentalistic concepts which should be disregarded in a truly scientific psychology. Consequently, in the tradition of the earlier physiological psychologists, Watson confined his study to only those aspects of animal life that are sufficiently overt to make possible highly objective observation and measurement of them.

Although Watson rejected some of Thorndike's ideas, he saw great promise in his secondary law, *associative shifting*. The principle enunciated by this law became the keystone for the behavioristic movement of the 1920s. According to this law, we may *"get any response of which a learner is capable* associated with *any situation to which he is sensitive."*[7] In other words, any response that is possible can be linked with any stimulus. An animal's "purposes or thoughts" have nothing to do with such learnings. In fact, purpose and mentalistic thought supposedly are concepts outside the realm of scientific psychology. We may illustrate this law by using an example involving the training of an animal. Suppose we wish to train a dog to sit up at the verbal command "Sit." It is only necessary to induce the dog to sit up repeatedly by dangling a piece of meat or other food above him at the same time the verbal command is issued. Once this procedure has been repeated enough times, the dog should respond properly—without error—whenever the command is given. In this example, as long as the same "adequate stimulus" is used throughout the experiment, it would not matter if the command were replaced by any other accompanying stimulus to which a dog is sensitive—a light, a bell, snapping the fingers, whistling. Furthermore, by using the same basic procedure, it should be possible to teach a dog to perform any other act of which it is

[7]Thorndike, *Educational Psychology, op. cit.,* p. 15. (Italics in original.)

capable—standing on its front legs, rolling over, playing dead, etc. This supposed principle of learning, fundamental to behaviorism, is the principle of stimulus substitution.

Behaviorists defined a living organism as a self-maintaining mechanism. They assumed that the essence of a human machine is a system of receptors (sense organs), conductors (neurons), switching organs (brain and spinal cord), and effectors (muscles) attached to levers (bones)—plus, of course, fueling and controlling organs such as stomach and glands. When an organism is defined in such mechanistic terms, mentalistic concepts can be entirely eliminated. Not only can they be dropped out of the picture but they actually begin to seem rather fanciful. Can one imagine a machine "having tender sentiments" or "soaring on the imagination"? Thus, among behaviorists, there developed an attitude toward the earlier mentalistic psychologists similar to that of a modern physician toward a primitive witch doctor.

The position of a Watsonian behaviorist can be illustrated amusingly in a morning conversation. Ordinarily, a conventional greeting would go as follows: "Good morning, how are you?" "I'm fine, and yourself?" "Just fine." But such a greeting implies introspection. Each person is "looking into himself" in order to decide what kind of shape he is in. Presumably (according to a behaviorist) this is scientifically impossible; instead the two persons would need to inspect each other. The proper salutation of a behaviorist would be, "Good morning, you appear to be fine; how am I?"

The neobehaviorists

There is a large group of American psychologists today who assume that life can be explained in essentially mechanistic terms but who have adopted positions somewhat different from that of the Watsonian behaviorists. It might be said that Watsonian behaviorism, in its pure form, is all but dead. Probably the best term to apply to contemporary S-R conditioning theorists is *neobehaviorists*.

Contemporary S-R conditioning theorists do not place nearly as much emphasis upon the operation of the brain and nervous system as did their predecessors. Watson himself had felt that the precise nature of neural mechanisms was largely irrelevant to an understanding of learning; but Watson's followers, like Thorndike, exhibited a strong interest in neural physiology and the physical mechanics of S-R linkages. Interests of neobehaviorists lie in analyses of behavior per se rather than in the neural mechanism behind it. They still are concerned with how S's and R's become linked, but they are not greatly concerned with the precise operation of the physiological mechanism that lies between the S's and R's.

Neobehaviorists differ from the original behaviorists in another respect. In their experimentation, they have tended to focus attention upon response modification as well as stimulus substitution. Response modification refers to the fate of responses that are made—whether they will be strengthened, weakened or changed by subsequent events. Continual reference is made in the literature of neobehaviorism to *conditioning*. Conditioning means changing a response habit. It is achieved either by stimulus substitution—accompanying an adequate stimulus by a new stimulus—or by response strengthening or modification —following a response with a stimulus which strengthens or changes it. The two kinds of conditioning are explained in Chapter 4.

Since Thorndike's concept of learning as a process of "stamping in" a response that was originally accidental is a form of response modification, one might say that many neobehaviorists have returned to Thorndike's conception of learning. However, most neobehaviorists are better systematizers than Thorndike. Furthermore, they are more consistent, largely by virtue of their building systems that do not at any point require an assumption of conscious behavior. Thorndike tried to be highly mechanical, but the neobehaviorists have developed psychological theories that are even more consistently mechanical than were Thorndike's.

Another feature of neobehaviorism is its attempt to explain behavior that appears to be purposive. Purposiveness has always bothered psychologists who are behavioristically oriented because they have felt that it is difficult to recognize purposiveness without slipping into a mind-body dualism and accompanying mysticism. However, since what seems purposive must be explained in some way, neobehaviorists tend to develop mechanical explanations for apparent purposiveness. So, purposiveness either is regarded as a product of a pattern of stimulation in which certain stimuli are more potent than the rest and thus lead an organism in one way rather than another, or it is interpreted as "drive reduction;" that is, as a relieving reaction to the stimulation induced by organic drives such as hunger or sex. Thus, neobehaviorists remain careful to explain apparent purposiveness in a way that does not require the assumption of conscious behavior or intelligent experience.

We shall mention but one more difference between the contemporary neobehaviorists and old-line pure behaviorists. Historically, behaviorism was "atomistic" in the sense that it focused on the "elements" of a situation. Attempts were made to identify specific stimuli and to describe the behavior of an organism as a product of numerous discrete and isolatable reactions. Today, S-R conditioning theorists are more likely to talk in terms of "stimulus situations," complex configurations of stimulation, and "molar behavior"—the coordinated behavior of a whole act of an organism.

Well-known contemporary neobehaviorists and their followers are greatly interested in the psychology of learning. However, at one extreme Spence has thought that in its present stage of development psychology has little to offer schools, and at the other extreme Skinner represents his psychology as the means of immediately placing education on an efficient basis.[8] In order to give the reader an understanding and appreciation of two systematic neobehavioristic psychologies, Chapter 5 is devoted to an exposition of Skinnerian and Chapter 6 to that of Spencian psychology of learning.

WHAT ARE THE ORIGINS OF GESTALT-FIELD PSYCHOLOGY?

The position of Gestalt psychology was formally stated first by the German philosopher-psychologist Max Wertheimer in 1912. The central idea of Wertheimer's point of view is expressed in the German word *Gestalt,* which, as we have seen, means an organized pattern or configuration, or, more simply, an organized whole in contrast to a collection of parts. The notion that a thing cannot be understood by study of its constituent parts, but only by study of it as a totality, is probably very old. Gardner Murphy suggests that it can be found in the literature of pre-Socratic Greece.[9] Various Greek writers proposed that the universe could best be understood through "laws of arrangement" or "principles of order," rather than through study of its basic building blocks, the elements. In contrast,

[8]See Donald K. Adams *et al., Learning Theory, Personality Theory and Clinical Research,* New York: John Wiley, 1954, p. 2.

[9]Gardner Murphy, *Historical Introduction to Modern Psychology,* New York: Harcourt Brace Jovanovich, 1949, p. 284.

other Greek writers were "atomists," who sought the key to understanding through a study of individual elements. Just as the former might be called the originators of Gestalt idea, so might the latter be called the originators of the atomistic idea that characterized early behaviorism.

Among the nineteenth-century forerunners of Wertheimer we should include Ernst Mach (1838–1916), likewise a German. Although Mach held that the worlds of physics and psychology are essentially the same, he also argued that psychology must take into account those sensations that do not correspond to the physical reality before the viewer. These "nonphysical" sensations are sensations of *relationship*. For example, a person may see three dots on a sheet of paper and think of them as the points of a triangle. There is nothing in individual dots to suggest this; it is their configuration that prompts the relationship.

In the 1890s, following Mach, Christian von Ehrenfels (1859–1932) pursued the same ideas. He stated that, in all perception, qualities appear that represent more than the physical items sensed. A perceiver tends to confer on the physical objects of perception a form, configuration, or meaning; he tries to organize or integrate what he sees. A school of thought began to form along the lines explored by these two men, and a new term came into use—*Gestaltqualitat,* which means approximately "the quality conferred by a pattern."

Wertheimer and his followers went still farther and formulated a series of "laws" of perception—*Prägnanz, similarity, proximity, closure, good continuation,* and *membership character.* According to the *basic law* of *Prägnanz,* if a perceptual field is disorganized when a person first experiences it, he imposes order on the field in a predictable way. The "predictable way" follows the other five laws. *Similarity* means that similar items (dots, for instance) tend to form groups in perception. *Proximity* means that perceptual groups are favored according to the nearness of their respective parts.

Closure means that closed areas are more stable than unclosed ones. Draw a 340° arc and ask a viewer what you have drawn. He very likely will say "a circle." This is an example of closure. Since, to achieve closure is satisfying, it might be considered an alternative to Thorndike's law of effect. *Good continuation* is closely related to closure. It means that, in perception, one tends to continue straight lines as straight lines and curves as curves.

According to the law of *membership character,* a single part of a whole does not have fixed characteristics; it gets its characteristics from the context in which it appears. As Gardner Murphy puts it, "The Gestaltist insists that the attributes or aspects of the component parts, insofar as they can be defined, are defined by their relations to the system as a whole in which they are functioning."[10] For example, a patch of color in a painting derives its quality from its context—the surrounding picture pattern—rather than from anything inherent in itself.

In perception, organization of a field tends to be as simple and clear as the existing conditions allow. A viewer imposes an organization that is characterized by stability, simplicity, regularity, and symmetry. He groups individual items in a field so they will have pattern. He relates similar items required for completeness, and if present patterns are meaningful he tries to maintain them into the future. Imposing a "good" Gestalt, as happens when the foregoing events occur, is a *psychological* task. It does not necessarily involve any change in the physical environment. Rather, it represents a change in how a viewer "sees" his physical environment.

Two of Wertheimer's German colleagues, Wolfgang Köhler and Kurt Koffka were mainly responsible for publicizing Gestalt psychology and establishing it in the United States. Köhler is famous, among other things, for his celebrated study of the learning process in chimpanzees (*The Mentality of Apes*, 1925). He set out to test Thorndike's hypothesis that learning is a matter of trial and error in which correct responses are gradually stamped in. Kohler observed that, in addition to their exhibiting learning that might appear accidental, his apes also displayed a type of learning that appeared insightful. Hence, Köhler concluded that Thorndike's laws of learning were inadequate. Koffka's book *Growth of the Mind* (1924) contained a detailed criticism of trial-and-error learning as conceived by Thorndike. Koffka not only criticized Thorndike; his book also was a critique of the major ideas of behaviorism.

Kurt Lewin, also German-born, took the spirit of Gestalt theory, added to it some new concepts, and coined a new terminology. He developed a field psychology usually referred to as *topological and vector psychology* (deriving these terms from the fields of geometry and mechanics). Lewin spent his later years in the United States, where he acquired a considerable following. Lewin's psychological theory, which is described in Chapter 7, has contributed much to current cognitive-field theory that is developed in Chapter 8.

[10]*Ibid.*, p. 288.

As a result of experimentation by the Gestalt-field psychologists, behaviorists generally are coming to recognize that the earlier atomistic stimulus-response idea, based as it was on the principle of simple reflex arcs, does not explain human behavior or learning adequately. Thus, as previously indicated, there is a tendency among contemporary S-R conditioning theorists to speak of "molar behavior" or behavior of the whole organism in contrast to piecemeal or "molecular" behavior. Accordingly, such psychologists characteristically refer to "total responses to patterns of stimulation." However, because these psychologists continue to think in terms of a mechanical linking of stimuli and responses, they still are within the basic pattern of S-R conditioning theory. In spite of their adoption of the concept of molar behavior, their point of view tends to be fundamentally different from that of Gestalt-field psychologists.

WHAT IS THE PHILOSOPHICAL THINKING BEHIND THE TWO FAMILIES?

It is the purpose of this part of the chapter to explore some of the philosophical implications of the two families of psychology. When a contrast is drawn between their underlying philosophical premises, differences between the two families are made much clearer. Although psychologists have tried during the past century to divorce psychology from philosophy, it is doubtful that this is possible. There is no science so "pure" that it lacks philosophical implications. Even physicists find it helpful to make assumptions about the basic nature of their materials and processes; they too become involved in philosophical formulations.

Since any psychological system rests upon a particular conception of human nature, psychology is deeply involved with philosophy from the very start. The issue among contemporary psychologists is whether man is an active creature of instincts (as exemplified in Freudian or neo-Freudian psychology), an essentially passive or reactive creature in a determining environment (as implied in S-R conditioning theory), or a purposive person interacting with a psychological environment (as currently implied in Gestalt-field psychology). Each of the two latter positions harmonizes with an allied philosophical outlook: S-R conditioning theory with earlier *scientific realism* or contemporary *logical empiricism* and Gestalt-field theory with a systematic *positive relativism*, also called *pragmatism, experi-*

mentalism, or *instrumentalism.* (Logical empiricism is the modern version of scientific realism.)

Scientific realism and S-R conditioning

What is scientific realism? Space permits only the barest treatment. Realists have been convinced that the physical world experienced by human beings is real and essentially what it appears to be when observed through the senses. Furthermore, even if there were no human beings around to observe it, it would exist in the same state. Reality, like existence, is independent of a thing's being known. Realists have assumed that the physical world is governed by natural laws, which operate inexorably and without change. They further have assumed that a basic principle of the universe is sequential cause and effect; every event is determined by events that have gone before. Thus, the universe is a vast mechanism governed by natural laws, which are essentially mechanical in nature.

Contemporary logical empiricists—the current representatives of scientific realism—think that we should abandon dogmatic, other worldly, supernaturalistic, and tender-minded ways of thinking and replace them with critical, worldly, naturalistic, and empirical fact-minded outlooks and procedures. Logical empiricists are likely to assume that there is a kind of hierarchy of the sciences, some being much more objective and reliable than others. They place at the top of the hierarchy physics and chemistry, aided by mathematics. These sciences are regarded as models that other sciences should emulate. For logical empiricists, just as the art of agriculture is based upon biological and chemical scientific knowledge, so education should be based upon the pure sciences of biology and psychology. To a consistent logical empiricist, nothing should be asserted to be real or meaningful unless, through observation, it can be subjected to objective study, using only publicly verifiable data. If anything exists, it supposedly exists in some amount; if it exists in some amount, it can be measured.

Let us trace how this overall point of view has transplanted to psychology. Early in human history, people commonly believed in animism, that is, that all objects, including even rocks, have minds or spirits. Since primitive man had no other way of explaining most types of natural events, animism provided at least some basis for his understanding his surroundings. However, as people learned more about natural causation, animism declined in popularity. In other words, when human beings came to understand something about gravity, a person no longer needed to attribute a mind and will to a rock to know why it fell on his head.

As time went on, mechanical explanations began to be applied to all sorts of physical events involving nonliving objects. Increasingly the nonliving parts of the universe were believed to consist of atoms in motion, each inert by itself, but subject to the push and pull of lawful forces external to itself.

Since living objects, especially human beings, seemed, on the surface at least, to be willful and unpredictable, they did not appear to conform to the mechanical concepts that applied to the world of nature. Thus, some kind of vitalistic mind-force was attributed to them. As we saw in Chapter 2 the belief in a nonmaterial mind-force as applied to human beings led to a distinctive conception of learning as a process of disciplining or training minds. This gave us the classical tradition in education. Although actual teaching under the classical mind-training approach may appear to be highly mechanical, the conception of human nature that underlies it definitely is nonmechanistic in that it assumes the existence of a mind substance, which is capable both of free will and of spontaneous "uncaused" behavior.

Apperception, the first modern associationism, was a mechanistic, albeit mental psychology. Although in developing his learning theory Herbart perpetuated the idea of man's having a mystical aspect, his mechanistic psychology opened the way for rejection of vitalism and accompanying mentalistic concepts, which are inconsistent with a "realistic" interpretation of the universe. Consequently, as the associationistic psychologies developed, psychologists found themselves in increasing sympathy with the tenets of scientific realistic philosophy.

Realistic, mechanistic psychology, then, has been an outgrowth of the attempt of S-R conditioning theorists to make psychology as "scientific" as physics. Thus, S-R theorists have equated *stimulus* and *response* in psychology with *cause* and *effect* in physics. Furthermore, they have made much use of the concepts *reflexes, drives, reactions, objective measurement, quantitative data, sequences of behavior, reinforcement schedules,* and similar expressions in an attempt to be rigidly "scientific."

The issue between mechanistic and nonmechanistic psychology is nowhere stated more clearly than by the contemporary neobehaviorist D. O. Hebb. Hebb says flatly that psychology's only hope of remaining scientific is to assume that man is basically a mechanism. Thus, as far as the basic outlook of a psychologist is concerned, there are for Hebb only two alternatives—mechanism and vitalism.

He writes that behavior is the factual basis of psychology and that we do not include in its definition anything that is not at least potentially observable. He then states, *"Psychology* is . . . the study of the more complex forms of integration or organization in behavior . . . this includes also the study of processes such as learning, emotion or perception that are involved in organizing the behavior. 'Integration' or 'organization' refers to the pattern or combination of different segments of behavior in relation to each other and to external events impinging on the organism."[11]

Furthermore, with respect to the type of study that psychologists can undertake, he says, "All one can know about another's feelings and awareness is an inference from what he *does*—from his muscular contractions and glandular secretions."[12] To a psychologist such as Hebb, Gestalt-field psychology would appear to be nothing more than "confusionism." The philosophical orientation of a behavioristic psychologist is so thoroughly mechanistic that any other outlook seems untenable.

Logical empiricists and their behavioristic psychological counterparts continue to think in terms of stimuli being causes and responses being effects and of there being a time lapse between physical stimuli and organic responses. To quote Hebb further, "Temporarily integrated behavior, extended over a period of time, is treated as a series of reactions to a series of stimulations. . . . Stimulus followed directly by response is the archetype of behavior. . . ."[13] Accordingly, they treat man as basically an extremely well-designed, clever machine, who learns through accumulating memories in an additive process. Human responses are a chance affair and a human being is a biological organism with a history of conditioned behavior. For logical empiricists, words such as foresight, purpose, and desire are literary terms, but not scientific ones.

In his approach to education a logical empiricist, and likewise a behaviorist, is very much an environmentalist and determinist in the sense that he assumes that the surrounding environment

[11]Donald O. Hebb, *A Textbook of Psychology*, 2nd ed., Philadelphia: Saunders, 1966, pp. 7–8.

[12]Donald O. Hebb, *The Organization of Behavior; A Neuro-Psychological Theory*, New York: John Wiley, 1949, p. xiii.

[13]Donald O. Hebb, *A Textbook of Psychology*, Philadelphia: Saunders, 1958, p. 46.

should, and inescapably will, control closely the behavior and learning of students. Thus, teaching practices advocated by S-R psychologists are closely in tune with the logical empiricistic-realistic outlook. Such psychologists tend to recommend that subject matter be selected by qualified adults prior to the teaching act, that it reflect facts and skills useful in contemporary society, and that it be inculcated into students. There is an implicit assumption that, if a given item of subject matter impinges upon a student, there will be a definite and predictable effect. Only secondary, if any, mention is made of such concepts as student goals or problem solving.

Positive relativism and Gestalt-field psychology

Positive relativism has emerged during the past 70 or 80 years and is, in a sense, a reaction against the absolutistic ways that have characterized many facets of man's thinking throughout history; thus, it contrasts sharply with logical empiricism. Logical empiricists assume the existence of an ultimate reality, which consists of fixed natural laws, and they define truth as that which corresponds to natural law and consequently is unchanging. In contrast with logical empiricists, positive relativists neither assert nor deny an absolute existence. Rather, they define psychological reality as that which we "make" of what we gain from our environment. They then deal with reality, so defined, in achieving truth and designing behavior. Thus, whereas for a logical empiricist reality is the same as an objective existence, for a positive relativist reality is psychological and thereby different from any objective existence; it is what people gain through their five-plus senses. This distinction is treated in more detail on pp. 70–71.

The *positive* aspect of positive relativism denotes that such a relativism, to quote Webster, is "logically affirmative" and "capable of being constructively applied" as in "positive proposals for the betterment of society."[14] Accordingly, the philosophy's being affirmative implies that its proponents assert the availability of truth and reality and thereby affirm the feasibility of a body of constructive knowledge. Furthermore, its capability of being constructively applied signifies that it is structured in such a way as to direct its adherents toward promotion of further development, improvement, and advancement of themselves

[14]From *Webster's Third New International Dictionary*, copyright 1966 by G. & C. Merriam Company, Publishers of the Merriam-Webster Dictionaries, p. 1770, definition 4a (1) of *positive*. By permission.

and society. Hence, a person is being positively relativistic in his thinking and action when he harbors no absolutes and simultaneously attempts to strengthen or improve matters or to develop something better to take their place.

The positive-relativistic position often is designated by the one word *relativism*. A central idea of relativism is that a *thing derives its qualities from its relationship to other things*. A person may look at a patch of grass that is in shadow. Compared with grass in the full rays of the sun, the patch appears dark; but compared with grass at night, it appears light. A homely girl, in the company of girls even more homely, appears pretty. Thus, the way we perceive any object or event is colored by the total situation. This principle is actually one with which everyone is familiar. Relativistic philosophy does little more than explore and develop the numerous ramifications and implications of this central idea.

It might appear that if relativism were a valid concept a person could never make a definitive statement about anything, except to say that it "is closer than something else," "is to the left of something else," "is darker than something else," or "is smaller than something else." However, this is not an insurmountable problem. In order to view a thing relativistically, one simply determines a convenient vantage point for reference. A man can say that his automobile has 200 horsepower, and in such an assertion he can be quite confident. The unit of measure, one horsepower, is an arbitrary standard contrived by man and susceptible to future change, yet it has definite usefulness as a point of reference. Such relatively fixed points of reference are *relatively absolute*. The word absolute, so used, is an adjective; it means no more than that the point of reference is one of relative fixity or stability.[15]

If one assumes that objects have to be dealt with relationally, rather than as things-in-themselves, then a distinctive method of defining truth, or knowledge, and an equally distinctive method of arriving at truth are required. A relativist questions the notion that man is able to find and use final or absolute truth. Consequently, he has little interest in "eternal verities." Nevertheless, he is deeply concerned with truths, relativistically defined. Relativists regard knowledge as insights developed and held by human beings using human methods. As Bayles points out, the development of the notion that knowledge is a matter

[15]The present discussion of relativism follows closely that in Ernest E. Bayles, *Democratic Educational Theory*, New York: Harper & Row, 1960; see particularly Chapters 4 and 7.

of human interpretation, and not a literal description of what exists external to man, reflects a shift from an absolutistic to a relativistic view of science.

A scientific law (including a principle of psychology) is a statement that seems true to all or most of those who are competent to study the matter. The relativistic test of truth is anticipatory accuracy, not correspondence to ultimate reality. Thus, in a sense, a scientific law is a generalization about which there is considerable agreement among those scientifically competent in its area; it is in a way a matter of consensus. Its test, however, is not the consensus, but its predictive accuracy. Relativists assume that no scientific law is "sacred"; any law may change, and indeed, over the course of time most will. A significant aspect of the thinking of relativists is their expectancy of change. They are much more likely than are logical empiricists to think of both nature and culture as undergoing continuous modification.

Positive relativists do not mean that truth has no objective standard and that it always varies from person to person, group to group, and time to time. In fact, they recognize that, fortunately, many truths have been so adequately tested that we may safely treat them as if they were certainties. However, their definition of certainty "is something in which I have tremendous faith."[16]

But what grounds does a relativist have for judging anything true? To quote Bayles, an insight is considered true "if, and only if, the deduced behavior pattern, when tested experientially or experimentally, produces the results which were anticipated."[17] Thus, an insight is true if it proves to be reasonably accurate—if what one supposes will follow from its application actually follows. So, for a relativist, truth is not based upon eternal and universal principles. Rather, it is man-made, and man will change it as need be. But, this does not mean that truth is unimportant or ephemeral. It does mean that truth tends to evolve as human experience evolves.

Both logical empiricists and positive relativists assume that the most valid method of inquiry is scientific in nature; it is based on testable evidence. But they define "scientific method" in quite different ways and, as the foregoing discussion has indicated, they seek different ends from it. To a relativist, scien-

---

[16]Hugh Skilling, "An Operational View," *American Scientist*, 52, No. 4 (December 1964), p. 390A.
[17]Bayles, *op. cit.*, p. 113.

tific method is not merely a sequence of steps such as a physicist supposedly uses. Scientific thinking is any form of intellectual pursuit that is based on testable evidence and is productive in relation to the goals of the thinker. To be sure, there are some measuring sticks or criteria of scientific truth; these criteria may be encompassed under the headings of *adequacy* and *harmony* in light of obtainable data. A conclusion, to be properly scientific, must *harmonize* all the data, that is, it must make the data add up. If a single pertinent fact seems to be contradictory, if it remains unexplained, then the conclusion is not to be trusted. According to the principle of *adequacy*, all known pertinent facts must be taken into consideration. None may be ignored—no matter how unpalatable it might seem.

A positive relativist construes science much more broadly than does a logical empiricist. He assumes that the scientific way can be applied in a wide range of situations. A relativist does not think in terms of a hierarchy of sciences, with physics, chemistry, and mathematics at the top. He is also more flexible with respect to the kinds of data he will consider. In psychological research a logical empiricist is likely to admit only data of observable physical objects or substances. Conversely, a positive relativist in psychology will consider all the data of human experience, including that which may seem introspective.

Positive-relativistic Gestalt-field psychology essentially is an emergent synthesis that has developed from an ideological conflict between the psychological tenets of Roussellian "romantic naturalism" and those of "scientific realism."

An *emergent* is something novel that appears in the course of the evolution of ideas. It is not an intermediate position, but a new outlook or concept. When an emergent outlook or concept reflects the results of the interplay of conflicting ideas and arrives at something new, it is a *synthesis*. Whereas one forms an *eclectic compromise* by selecting aspects of opposing theories and taking a position somewhere among a mosaic of them, one achieves an *emergent synthesis* by selecting and modifying knowledge from incompatible positions, adding new thinking as needed, and developing a new position that is internally consistent and still more adequate than any one of its precursors.

Roussellians contend that psychological development is primarily a matter of natural unfoldment. To them, learning is largely equated with unfoldment and is a product of inner urges. Scientific-realistic psychologists, at the other extreme, have considered all development to be a product of biological maturation and learning, and have assumed that learning is a conditioning that occurs through the environment's impinging upon an individual from without.

In bridging the two positions, relativists assume that a child or youth is what he is because of an interaction between himself and his culture. With the emphasis upon interaction, the responsibility for development rests neither with the person alone (as Rousseau would have said) nor with the environment alone (as a scientific-realist would say). Instead, it is in a person and his environment coming together—in a psychological field— that Gestalt-field psychologists find the clue to psychological development and learning.

What has this to do with relativism? Since the number of possible culture patterns is infinite, the possibilities for variety in human development likewise become infinite. Thus, within its biological limits, human nature might become anything. Furthermore, if one accepts the premises of Gestalt-field psychology, one must define reality in a manner different from that of a scientific realist.

HOW DO THE TWO FAMILIES DEFINE REALITY?

Historically, the term *reality* has connoted a transcendental, independent, and absolute existence. Accordingly, behaviorists have tended to treat reality and existence as identical concepts. Thus, for them, the term *reality* refers to physical objects and processes, which exist or are "there" in their own right. The chair on which the reader is sitting may be said to exist, and to a behaviorist the chair is a good example of reality (not one's impression of the chair, but the chair itself). The chair exists in its own right; the way one perceives it is not relevant to its reality.

Gestalt-field theorists make a distinction between reality and existence. Without denying independent existence of objects, or even of other people's ideas, they insist that each person sizes up or interprets his supposed world in such a way that it will form a meaningful pattern for him, and his interpretation is the reality on which he designs his actions. Thus, they think that a person's knowledge of things is always limited by the impossibility of his ever getting completely "outside himself." Consequently, they assume that any perception of a physical-social world will be colored to some degree by the purposes and experiences of the observer, as well as by the procedures used in observing the perceived object. To a relativist, reality consists of the *interpretations* a person makes of himself and his surroundings as he interacts. If reality is to be regarded as interpretations or meanings, rather than as preexistent physical objects as such, it is obvious that reality will be in a constant state of flux. None of these statements, however, should be taken to mean that a person literally makes his world; rather, in any field—science, social relations, morality, even religion—each individual makes, not *the* world, but *his notion of* the world.

To understand fully the way Gestalt-field theorists differ from behaviorists in their meaning of reality, it is necessary to explore in some detail the differences between exponents of the respective outlooks in their definitions of *environment, perception,* and *experience.* We already have suggested some of these differences. We now propose to dig more deeply.

How is environment defined by the two groups of psychologists?

S-R conditioning theorists maintain that a person's psychological and physical environments are identical; his environment consists of all his physical and social surroundings. Because environment is defined in objective, physicalistic terms, presumably anyone can see (or hear, smell, feel, or taste) the environment of anyone else.

In contrast, Gestalt-field psychologists think of a person's environment as psychological; it consists of what he makes of what is around him. It is that portion of a life space or perceptual field that surrounds a person or self. A psychological environment includes impressions of parts of the physical environment but not necessarily all of it. It also extends beyond its physical environment. Sometimes a person's psychological environment includes largely memories or anticipations; in this case he is scarcely aware of the physical world currently around him. Hence, he is operating on a highly imaginative level.[18]

Since each person's perceptual environment is unique, obviously two persons may appear to be in the same location in space and time (or as nearly so as possible) and yet have very different psychological environments. Furthermore, the behaviors of two equally intelligent persons who are confronted with the same "objective facts" may differ drastically because each is different in his purposes and experiential background. Whenever a person has a new experience, he changes his environment and

[18]See Chapter 8, pp. 231–233, for a distinction between imaginative and concrete levels of reality.

will never again be able to recapture the old environment in its identical form. The Gestalt-field conception of environment helps explain why in a particular family one son may become a minister and another turn to crime; their interpretations of their world differ radically, even though to an outsider their social and physical environments would appear quite similar.

How do the two groups define perception?

Behaviorists define perception in such a way as to make it analogous with taking photographs. The sense organs in literal fashion "read" a person's social and physical surroundings and record this "reading" in the nervous system. After sensing something, a person may derive a meaning for it. But note that, according to behaviorists, sensation comes prior to meaning and the two acts, sensing and finding meaning, are regarded as separate. A behaviorist assumes that sensation may be indiscriminate, in that a person tends to "take in" all aspects of the physical world to which his sense organs are sensitive. Such a psychologist defines perception, then, as a two-step process (sensing and deriving meaning), which focuses on particular objects of the environment only insofar as previous conditioning directs.

A Gestalt-field psychologist, on the other hand, does not separate sensation of an object from its meaning. In his view, a person will rarely sense an object unless it has relevance to some purpose of the person. It is this relevance to purpose, this instrumental quality, of an object that constitutes its meaning. Unless a person sees some meaning in an object, he will pay little or no attention to it. Thus, a Gestalt-field psychologist sees perception as a unitary process in which sensation hinges on meaning and meaning on sensation, and sensing and finding meaning occur simultaneously. Perception, to a field psychologist, is highly selective. It always is related to a person's purposes at the time of perception. In his goal-seeking behavior, a person actively seeks out those aspects of his environment that will help or hinder him, and usually it is to these that he is primarily sensitive.

Furthermore, to a Gestalt-field psychologist the meaning of a sensation or perception always is related to the total situation. Relationships, and not a summation of individual elements, determine the quality of any perceptual event. Any psychological event is a result of the interaction of many factors; hence, perception always involves a problem of organization. A thing is perceived as a relationship within a psychological field, which includes the thing, the viewer, and a complex background incorporating the viewer's purposes and previous experience. Considering these notions, it is obvious that, to a Gestalt-field theorist, the senses do not directly mirror physical objects in their geographical environment. The camera analogy, which fits the behavioristic idea of perception, to a field psychologist, seems gross oversimplification.

Is interaction of person and environment alternating or simultaneous and mutual?

The term *interaction* is commonly used in describing the person-environment process through which reality is perceived. Both families of psychology use the term but they define it in sharply different ways. Whereas S-R conditioning theorists mean the *alternating reaction* first of organism, then of environment, Gestalt-field psychologists usually imply that the interaction of a person and his environment is *simultaneous* and *mutual*—both participate at the same time, and the two—person and environment—are not mutually exclusive.

Alternating reaction. Alternating reaction—passive interaction—begins with a reaction of a person to a stimulus. The person is regarded as a passive receiver of stimuli; his habitual pose is one of waiting or repose. When he receives a stimulus he responds in whatever way he must, i.e., in accordance with both the conditioned and the innate behaviors that are called into play. Then, in turn, when he reacts, he is likely to change his physical or social environment in some way. Thus, there is passive interaction. (The environment also is passive, in the sense that it "waits" for him to do something to it.) To a behaviorist, the temporal sequence of the interactive process is stimulus-reaction-stimulus-reaction, and so on. The chain of S-R's may continue indefinitely. Consider an example. A dog bites a man; the man kicks the dog. Let us suppose the kick conditions the dog not to bite. The dog is friendly toward the next man he encounters, and the man reacts by patting him on the head. The dog may then react by licking the man's hand. The man may then buy the dog a steak. And so on, ad infinitum.

Behaviorists tend to think of interaction as involving only physical processes; that is, material objects react to other material objects. So interaction between human beings is analogous to interaction of molecules in a chemical compound. One molecule strikes another, which is deflected against another, which hits another, and so on. Thus, the interactive process is regarded as a chain of causes and effects; stimuli are causes and responses are effects.

Simultaneous mutual interaction. Interaction, when used by Gestalt-field psychologists, refers to a relationship between a person and his environment in which the person in purposeful fashion tries to see meaning in his environment and use objects in his environment in advantageous ways. As he interprets and uses his environment for his own purposes, both are changed. The person's physical environment may, or may not, be changed in ways which others may observe. In any case, its meaning is changed so that it looks different to the person interacting with it. The person also changes in the sense that through interaction he achieves new insights that literally transform him, in however minor ways. Gone from this concept of interaction is the idea of the reaction of a passive organism to a stimulus, and an ensuing chain of S-R's running back and forth from organism to environment. Rather, we now have a simultaneous mutual relation of a person and his *psychological* environment, during which the two are not mutually exclusive, so we do not make a sharp distinction between them. In symbolic terms, this concept is simultaneous mutual interaction—the SMI concept.

Parents and siblings usually constitute important aspects of a child's environment. When a second child arrives in a family, the first child sizes up—perceives—the situation. Whether the first child feels rejected depends, not upon the physical stimuli as such that he receives from his parents and the sibling, but upon what he makes of the relationship of the parents and the second child. The important question is not, Do the parents actually favor child number two? but rather, Does child number one "see" child number two as favored over child number one—himself? In this situation, the parents and the other child are key aspects of each child's and parent's environment. The way child number one perceives the situation has important bearing upon the environments of child number two and the parents. Each person in a situation interacts with the others.

Gestalt-field theorists, in their espousal of the concept of SMI, make a sharp distinction between interaction of physical objects in a physical environment and (the subject of psychology) interaction of psychological realities in a psychological environment. To a field psychologist, it is only what occurs psychologically in a person's life space at that moment, or a longer juncture of time, that is important to that person. A person interacts by relating himself (as he understands himself) to his interpretation of what is around him. Of course, while interacting, he may move his body and manipulate objects in his physical environment in ways conspicuous to observers. But psychological interaction and physical reaction are two different processes. A person can interact within a psychological field while he is seated in an armchair in front of a fireplace. Human experience is synonymous with an interactive event. It does not necessarily require any kind of motion that an observer can detect.

Any idea can be ridden too hard, and the reader has probably already thought of cases in which the concept of SMI does not seem to fit. For example, a man who is not aware of danger may be shot in the back. It seems fairly clear that in such a case the man has been a passive victim of a feature of his environment that was active in relation to him. However, all this example suggests is that there are situations in which a person has no control over what happens to him. Adherents of Gestalt-field psychology and positive-relativistic philosophy do not deny this; instead, they operate on the not inconsistent assumption that, whenever a person can, he seeks to manipulate purposefully all those aspects of his environment that at the time mean anything to him. He may or may not be successful, but whether or not he is, his life space will be different as a result of the attempt.

What is experience?

Gestalt-field psychologists, in general, give their conception of *experience* a major place in their learning theories. But, they define experience in terms of persons purposively interacting with their respective psychological environments. Many behaviorists also employ the term in explaining their learning theories. But, they give it less significance than do Gestalt-field theorists. Other behaviorists, led by B. F. Skinner, espouse *radical behaviorism*, which means that they have little or no place in their learning theory for such concepts as experience, awareness, or consciousness.

A behaviorist may concede that thought appears to occur, but he is likely to insist that, if human beings are to be studied with true scientific objectivity, most kinds of mentalistic concepts must be ruled out of bounds. The well-known neobehaviorist B. F. Skinner expresses this notion clearly:

> . . . the private event [that is, thought or consciousness] is at best no more than a link in a causal chain, and it is usually not even that. We may think before we act in the sense that we may be-

have covertly before we behave overtly, but our action is not an "expression" of the covert response [that is, thought] or the consequence of it. The two are attributable to the same variables.[19]

When behaviorists do use the term *experience*, they interpret it mechanistically. Accordingly, to them, it means the conditioning process by which a human organism either learns new responses or changes old ones as the result of stimuli impinging on its sensory organs. If a child touches a hot stove and if a link is formed between the sight of a stove and a withdrawal response, then it might be said that the child has had an experience. No thought needs to have occurred and no insights need to have been developed.

Gestalt-field psychologists use the term *experience* extensively, but define it in a way consistent with a relativistic outlook. Accordingly, they regard experience as rooted in insightful behavior. From this point of view, experience is a psychological event that involves a person's acting purposefully with anticipation of the probable or possible consequences of such action. So, experience is interaction of a person and his perceived environment. This is what Dewey meant when he said, "An experience is always what it is because of a transaction taking place between an individual and what, *at the time*, constitutes his environment."[20] He further stated, in connection with experience and learning, that "To 'learn from experience' is to make a backward and forward connection between what we do to things and what we enjoy or suffer from things in consequence."[21] Experience includes an active and a passive element, combined in a peculiar fashion: "On the active hand, experience is *trying*. . . . On the passive, it is *undergoing*. When we experience something we act upon it, we do something with it; then we suffer or undergo the consequences. We do something to the things, then it does something to us in return; such is the peculiar combination. The connection of these two phases of experience measures the fruitfulness or value of the experience. Mere activity does not constitute experience."[22]

The SMI concept implies a continuity of experience. Every

[19]B. F. Skinner, *Science and Human Behavior*, New York: Macmillan, 1953, p. 279.

[20]John Dewey, *Experience and Education*, New York: Macmillan, 1938, p. 41. (Our italics.)

[21]John Dewey, *Democracy and Education*, New York: Macmillan, 1916, p. 164.

[22]*Ibid.*, pp. 163–164.

experience both extracts something from experiences that have gone before and modifies in some way experiences that follow. Furthermore, to some degree every experience influences the conditions under which future experiences may be had. Thus, in the case of a reasonably normal person, successive perceptual fields or life spaces tend to be similar to, though not identical with, one another.

WHAT DOES MOTIVATION MEAN TO EACH FAMILY?

Motivation refers to the "mainsprings" or instigative forces of behavior; people do what they do because of motivation. As in the case of concepts treated previously in the chapter, S-R conditioning theorists and Gestalt-field psychologists hold contrasting and seemingly incompatible ideas about the nature of motivation. These differences arise from the contrasting conceptions of the basic nature of man held by the two schools of thought. If one views man mechanistically, he will prefer a theory of motivation compatible with this outlook. Contrariwise, if one views man as a purposeful, reflective, and creative individual, he will have a quite different theory of motivation.

What is motivation to adherents of S-R conditioning?

As we have seen, adherents of S-R conditioning tend to regard man as an intricate machine. Machines operate with induced regularity, according to fixed principles. Even a machine as complicated as an electronic brain does not operate purposefully as we usually use the term. An electronic brain does not know what to do until it has been set by a human being. Even electronic brains that can correct their own errors and do other seemingly fantastic tasks still behave as they do because some person has designed and regulated them. In a sense, a machine has no more purpose than a falling rock; it acts, but it has no thought-out goal. S-R theorists generally attribute this same quality to man's nature.

To an S-R psychologist, all motivation arises either directly from one's organic drives or basic emotions or from a tendency to respond that has been established by prior conditioning of the drives and emotions. Organic drives, such as hunger, thirst, and sexual need, and the emotions–fear, anger, and "love"–supposedly produce behaviors that are both predictable and irresistible. The drives and emotions are "built into" the organism and it can do nothing to resist them. Conditioning produces a series of learned behaviors that spring into action whenever relevant stimuli appear. These conditioned responses and operants operate more or less automatically; a person makes them because he must. Thus, through conditioning, the machine—body —has been regulated to behave in a predictable manner. To an S-R psychologist, then, all behavior is stimulus-directed, whether the stimulus comes from within the organism or without. Motivation is defined as the urge to act that results from a stimulus. Since behavior is stimulus-directed, it is not related to purpose of any kind.

There are certain obvious aspects of the behavior of men or lower animals that do not appear to be adequately explained by the mechanical concepts of S-R theory. One of these is attention. At any given time, a person pays attention to one thing rather than another. At this moment, the reader of this book is "attending" to this page rather than to a television program, a poker game, or a pretty girl. So the fact of attention may seem to demonstrate that human behavior is governed by purpose. However, though S-R theorists concede that a person may often respond selectively to one or a small group of stimuli at a time, they argue that what appears to be selective response can be explained according to S-R principles and that the existence of purpose need not be assumed. According to an adherent of S-R conditioning, a person selects one response rather than another because of the particular combination of prior conditioning and present physiological drives and stimuli that are operating at the moment of perception. To an S-R theorist, to introduce purpose as an explanation of motivation is to risk introducing some kind of metaphysical guiding force and to make impossible a truly scientific approach to the study of behavior.

A behaviorist's theory of motivation has important implications for education. According to his viewpoint, a child does not have to "want" to learn history in order to learn it. He does have to be persuaded to study it, to repeat the verbal responses that we associate with a knowledge of history. Anyone can learn anything of which he is capable if he will only allow himself to be put through the pattern of activity necessary for conditioning to take place. Thus, a behaviorist does not talk much about such things as "psychological involvement" or "helping students see the point of learning." Instead, he engages students in activity and assumes that activity with appropriate conditioning automatically produces learning. A teacher carefully plans which learnings (responses) he wants students to develop.

He then induces these responses and conditions them with stimuli.

What is motivation to Gestalt-field theorists?

Within the Gestalt-field frame of reference, behavior is a function of a total situation—a person interacting within a field of psychological forces, which includes purposes and goals, interpretation of relevant physical objects and events, and memories and anticipations. Accordingly, motivation cannot be described as merely an impulse to act triggered by a stimulus. Rather, it emerges from a dynamic psychological situation, characterized by a person's desire to do something.

A Gestalt-field psychologist regards motivation as a product of disequilibrium within a life space. A life space includes goals and often barriers to the achievement of these goals. A goal may be either positive or negative—something one wants to achieve, or something one wants to avoid. When a barrier, that is, any obstacle to the direct and immediate achievement of a goal, whether physical or psychological, appears, a person feels tension. He tries to relieve tension either by surmounting or circumventing the barrier. The tendency to release tension by proceeding toward a goal, including the overcoming of whatever barriers are in the way, is motivation.

The particular form that motivation takes and its intensity are functions of a field of psychological forces in which no distinction can be made between "inner" and "outer." That is, one cannot identify a category of forces that stems exclusively from physiological drives and another category that stems from the outside environment. Hence, Gestalt-field psychologists object to the manner in which behaviorists attribute motivation to independently acting organic drives and stimuli.

S-R theorists in the Thorndikean tradition make much of pleasure and pain, or satisfaction and annoyance, as instigators of behavior. An organism presumably is so constructed biologically that it seeks to achieve pleasurable states and to avoid painful ones. Contrastingly, Gestalt-field psychologists are more likely to talk about success and failure as motivators, the former truly being the "reward" for completing an act. Success and failure are not merely achievements as such but represent the relationship between a person's ambitions and his achivements. If he has a certain level of aspiration and is able to achieve this level, he feels good about it. If he attains success at one level of aspiration, he is likely to raise the level, and to continue doing so as long as he is able to perform successfully. Thus, goals tend to be more self- than environment-set and to change in dynamic fashion with each new experience.

Another feature of the Gestalt-field theory of motivation, which sets it apart from S-R theory, is the emphasis placed on the present situation. Motivation, to a Gestalt-field theorist, grows out of one's contemporary life space—the psychological forces that are operating right then. In contrast, an S-R theorist tends to think of motivation as emerging from an accumulation of historical events: past conditionings, coupled with currently operating organic drives. Consequently, an S-R theorist looks backward into a person's life to determine why he behaves as he does now. A Gestalt-field psychologist does not ignore the impact of previous experience on a person's contemporary life space, but in explaining the causes of behavior he focuses on the present scene as the person experiences it. For these reasons, it is common to think of S-R psychology as embodying a *historical* approach and Gestalt-field psychology as embodying a *situational* approach to the study of motivation and behavior.[23]

A teacher who accepts the Gestalt-field concept of motivation and a teacher who operates within an S-R framework are likely to approach teaching in fundamentally different ways. For one thing, a teacher with a Gestalt-field orientation is concerned always with the problem of personal involvement, that is, helping students see a need to learn; the personal goals of students will always be relevant. This does not mean that the teacher will cater to students' every whim. Often he will try to help them rethink their goals and discard those that are trivial and whimsical. Much of the time he will attempt to arrange the teaching-learning situation so that students will adopt goals entirely new to them. He will be convinced that, unless a child realizes a need to learn something, the child either will not learn it at all or will learn it only in a transitory and functionally useless way.

BIBLIOGRAPHY

NOTE: References pertaining to Chapters 3 and 4 are at the end of Chapter 4. These two chapters should be studied as a unit.

---

[23]See Chapter 8, p. 214, for development of the situational approach to motivation and learning.

FOUR

How Do the Two Families of Contemporary Learning Theory Describe the Learning Process?

This chapter continues the analysis begun in Chapter 3 but centers on some of the more technical aspects of the learning theories developed by S-R conditioning and Gestalt-field theorists. Some repetition of ideas stated in Chapter 3 is inevitable, but the focus is quite different.

Do animals, including man, learn simply by being conditioned step by step under the tutelage of a teacher or experimenter, or do they learn by surveying their situation and grasping relationships? Let us set up a hypothetical experiment and speculate on how animals will behave. Our subjects will be rats in an elevated maze (see Figure 4.1). The alleys are formed of strips of wood without sidewalls. They are raised high enough from the floor so that the rats will not jump off. The gate in the maze is made so that the weight of a rat will cause it to lower and permit the rat to run through.

In order to accustom the rats to the maze and to develop in them preferential tendencies with reference to the three possible pathways to food, we give them some preliminary training. We deprive them of food for 24 hours, then place them in the starting box and permit them to find their way to the food box. They are given ten such trials per day and soon learn (after

Figure 4.1
  Ground plan of elevated maze used by Tolman and Honzik.
  (From Tolman, E. C. and C. H. Honzik, "Insight in Rats,"
  University of California Publication in Psychology,
  1930, V. 4, p. 223. By permission of University of California Press.)

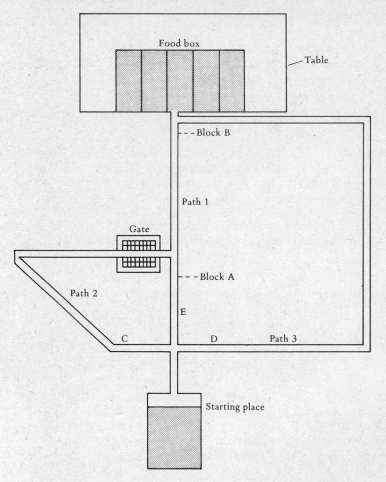

trying the various paths) to take the shortest, path 1, to the food.
We then block path 1 at point A. When this is done, the rats
will turn back to the choice point (fork in the road) and almost
always (about 93 percent of the time) take path 2.

Now, what will the rats do when for the first time the block
is placed in the common section of paths 1 and 2 (at point B)?

They will return toward the starting place on path 1 and turn at the intersection of the three paths. But will they take path 2 or 3? Have they sized up the situation and "seen" that the block is on path 2 as well as path 1? If so, they will take path 3. On the other hand, if the rats are operating mechanistically they will take the second shortest path to the food, path 2, at least half the time.

We will return to our experiment. But first let us consider the significance for man of learning theory based upon experiments with animals. Such experiments occupy a very important place in modern psychological theory.

DO MEN AND OTHER ANIMALS LEARN ALIKE?

Use of results of animal experimentation is governed by the assumptions that the learning process is essentially the same throughout the animal kingdom and that what we discover about animal learning is transferable to human situations. These assumptions would have been thought ridiculous, if not heretical, a few centuries back. Until modern times, philosophers took for granted that there was an unbridgeable gulf between man and the animal kingdom. It was thought that human beings possessed a unique quality: they could reason, whereas animals could not. This quality was believed to arise from the existence of a substantive mind: a mind-force, relatively independent of a body, which only man, among the earth's creatures, possessed.

Chapter 2 describes the manner in which this belief in body-mind dualism led to a distinctive theory of learning and teaching —mental discipline. So long as man was considered fundamentally different from other forms of life, animal biology and human psychology remained two sharply separated disciplines. Until a century or so ago, human psychology relied for its source of knowledge solely upon the study of humans—conducted through inspiration, introspection, and intuition, tempered by reason. However, in the past centuries, there were a few persons who rejected the idea that man and animals are unrelated. Of these, Rousseau was one of the earliest and most striking. In his book *Émile* (1762), Rousseau strongly implied that a human being at birth is a healthy little animal—a creature like, and continuous with, other animals of nature.

During the Romantic period (late eighteenth and early nineteenth centuries) many philosophers and literary figures believed that mind permeated the entire universe, including all living things. Furthermore, this universal mind substance was believed to be unitary—everywhere the same. Man possessed more of it than did lower animals, but the difference between human mind and animal mind was considered one of degree rather than kind. Of course, not all scholars accepted this view. The psychologist Wundt, for example, was convinced that consciousness—a product of mind—was unique to human beings. Now, if men and other animals do learn alike, do men learn like other animals or do other animals learn like men?

Do men learn like other animals?

It was the work of Darwin and other evolutionists of the nineteenth century that most definitely gave man a place in the animal kingdom. Darwin noticed particularly the close similarity of the bodily structure and functions of man and the lower animals. In his *Descent of Man* he also presented much evidence of the existence of psychological, as well as physical, continuity throughout the animal kingdom. Hence, he wrote, "There is no fundamental difference between man and the higher animals in their mental faculties."[1] But in a later section he qualified this opinion by writing, "There can be no doubt that the difference between the mind of the lowest man and that of the highest animal is immense."[2] However, despite this qualification, Darwin appears to have maintained consistently that in their fundamental aspects man and the lower animals exhibit a commonality of both physical and mental characteristics.

Antagonists of the theory of evolution defied Darwin to explain why, if there is a continuity between man and the animal kingdom, man can reason, whereas lower animals seem to be governed by instinct rather than reason. Darwin countered with the explanation that much human action, too, is to be interpreted as instinctive in origin and that animals, on their level, exhibit a capacity for reason.

During the latter part of the nineteenth century the idea that there is a continuity among animal species, and that behavioral tendencies, including learning, are broadly similar throughout the animal world, rapidly gained in popularity among biologists and psychologists. As we noted on p. 52, Pierre Flourens proposed in the nineteenth century that conclusion drawn from animal experimentation should be equally applicable to man.

[1]Charles Darwin, *The Descent of Man*, New York: Appleton-Century-Crofts, 1920, p. 66.
[2]*Ibid.*, p. 125.

Pavlov also made this assumption, as did his American contemporary, Thorndike.

In addition to the advantage of cheapness and convenience in using lower animals rather than humans in a psychological laboratory, obviously experiments that our mores would prevent being tried on people can be performed on animals. Furthermore, many persons have thought that it is easier to isolate simple units of behavior in lower animals than in human beings; although in humans the units may be substantially the same, they are often combined in a manner too complex for ready study. Thus, it has been thought that one might learn more about types of behavior that are fundamental to the animal kingdom by studying the lower animals rather than by studying men. Consequently, animal experimentation has become extremely popular among psychologists.

In Chapter 3 (p. 54) we described briefly the general nature of the animal experimentation undertaken by behaviorists. These psychologists have hoped to formulate laws of human learning by observing overt behavior of laboratory animals placed in various kinds of situations such as puzzle boxes and mazes. By the early 1920s, the manner in which behaviorists conducted their experiments came under the fire of Gestaltists. The nature of the Gestalt-field criticism is developed in the following section.

Do other animals learn like men?

Whereas behaviorists have assumed that men learn like animals, and more specifically like their own experimental animals in their own types of experiments, Gestalt-field psychologists have given the question a reverse twist: Do animals learn like men? Of course, if there is a continuity between man and the lower animals, both ideas should make equal sense and both should be answerable in the affirmative. But Gestalt-field psychologists had something else in mind. While not denying the likelihood of a fundamental similarity in the behavior of man and other animals, Gestalt-field theorists have been interested in raising questions about the whole approach of the behaviorists.

One of the sharpest criticisms that a Gestalt-field theorist can make of the behavioristic conception of learning is directed against the tendency of the latter to deny purpose a central role in learning. Accordingly, Gestalt-field psychologists note that behaviorists usually placed their animals in situations entirely foreign to them and often allowed them only a bare minimum of freedom. Consequently, there was no place for their animals to begin a solution and little opportunity for them really to try various alternatives. Since locks, levers, and mechanical devices used were above the animals' level of comprehension, for them to achieve the correct procedure it was necessary that they stumble upon the key by chance. Because lower animals are less discerning of relationships that seem important to men than are human beings, animals appear, in a humanly contrived "problem," to make completely random movements. Thus, on the surface, the nature of the discovery of the relationship between the release mechanism and escaping from a puzzle box appeared to be completely mechanical. Having set the stage against animals displaying genuinely purposive, problem-solving activity, even if they are capable of such, behaviorists have concluded that learning is a product of a mechanical trial-and-error process.

To Gestalt-field psychologists the tension that motivates an animal to learn is tension *toward a goal.* Thus, to some degree learning always involves purpose. Furthermore, purposiveness in learning is not restricted to man. Abundant experimental evidence indicates that learning is purposive, even among animals quite low on the phylogenetic scale.

An animal behaving purposively does not make random motions—even though on the surface it may appear to do so. Instead, it tries everything at its command, but if the problem is too difficult its trial moves will appear to an observer as random. If one eye of a slug or a honeybee is blinded, the animal at first glance appears to go through meaningless motions. However, more careful observation reveals that it is demonstrating something other than mere random responses. It assumes a posture which orients its body toward the light source; thus it flexes its legs on one side and extends them on the other as if it wanted to move in relationship to the light.

Gestalt-field psychologists further have criticized experimentation of behaviorists on the ground that it has been so arranged that, even if animal learning were insightful, the development of insight would not be noticed. *The real nature of any psychological process can be concealed by the experimenter's designing his experiments in line with adverse predetermined conclusions, and this is precisely what the Gestaltists have insisted that behaviorists have been inclined to do.* In an attempt to refute the contention of behaviorists that learning is mechanical—a mere matter of forming the right connections through chance—the Gestaltists designed entirely different types of animal experiments. Their experiments involved creation of problematic situations that animals might conceivably resolve through development of insight. Such situations were geared in difficulty to the presumed potential intelligence of the animals being studied.

Let us now return to the three-path experiment described at the beginning of the chapter. This actually is a classic experiment performed by Tolman and Honzik at the University of California. When the rats backed out of path 1, they did not take path 2 but path 3—the longest path, but the only one now open to the food box. *Of the 15 rats, 14 behaved in this way.* The rats' backing out of path 1 and taking path 3 was an indication of their having "sized up" the situation—of their having developed insight. Using path 3 was a relatively new and creative solution of what, to the rats, was a real problem.[3]

Köhler's famous experiments with chimpanzees further illustrate the Gestalt-field approach to animal experimentation. Köhler spent four years on the island of Tenerife working with chimpanzees. A typical experiment involved suspending food (usually bananas) from the ceiling of a cage and then providing a chimpanzee with a tool or tools with which to knock down or reach for the fruit. The tool might be a pole of adequate length, a pole in sections that could be joined, or boxes that could be stacked and climbed. Köhler's chimpanzees, rather than gradually acquiring right responses and eliminating wrong ones, seemed at some point in a problem to develop insight into it— to grasp, often rather suddenly, the relationship involved. The chimpanzees seemed to get the idea of "tool use" and to apply it in new situations calling for tool use.[4]

Köhler also experimented with "stupid" chickens and found considerable evidence that even chickens can see relationships and that it is relationships to which they respond rather than specific stimuli. He taught chickens to expect food only from the darker of two papers placed side by side. For the lighter paper he then substituted one even darker than the original dark one. In 70 percent of the trials the chickens switched their preference from the originally preferred dark paper to the paper that was still darker, suggesting that they had achieved an insight: "If I go to the darker of two surfaces, I will get food." The chickens had "generalized," that is, sensed the relationship of darker to lighter *as a general principle* in "food getting."[5]

Two American Gestalt psychologists, Raymond H. Wheeler and

[3]E. C. Tolman and C. H. Honzik, " 'Insight' in Rats," *University of California Publication in Psychology, 4,* No. 14, 215–232.

[4]Wolfgang Köhler, *The Mentality of Apes,* New York: Vintage Books, 1959.

[5]See Henry E. Garrett, *Great Experiments in Psychology,* New York: Appleton-Century-Crofts, 1941, pp. 216–219.

Francis T. Perkins, performed a great deal of animal experimentation in the 1920s and 1930s. Among their most frequently cited experiments was one with goldfish in which the fish received food after responding properly to a configuration of lighting. The fish learned to pick the light of brightest, medium, or dimmest intensity, even though the experimenters kept varying the absolute intensity and the serial arrangement of lights. Wheeler and Perkins also have reported numerous other studies made by themselves and others in which animals ordinarily regarded as not very intelligent learned to respond to relationships in an apparently intelligent way.[6]

The question arises, How far down the phylogenetic scale can an investigator go and still observe animals behaving as if they could generalize, that is, perceive a relationship? To perceive a relationship one must get the feel of how a thing works. At first thought it would seem that to do this an animal must have a certain minimum of sensory and neural equipment—perhaps a brain, even if it is only rudimentary. However, one well-known American biologist, H. S. Jennings (1868–1947) concluded differently. Jennings spent much time observing the behavior of protozoa, such as euglenae, paramecia, and amoebae. He found that the actions of protozoa are not only highly variable but also readily modified, and he decided that their behavior could not be explained merely in terms of simple physiochemical reactions. Jennings thought that, insofar as their observable behavior was revealing, it was as reasonable to infer the presence of purposive behavior among protozoa as among men.[7]

Adolf Portmann, a contemporary biologist supports Jenning's earlier thinking in this regard. He states, "Biological research today must concentrate, therefore, on how things appear to animals, not what they actually are—which is a great change from the days a few decades back when biologists were supposed to reduce everything to physio-chemical laws."[8]

What are we to conclude from all this? One possible conclusion is that an animal experimenter, depending upon his orientation, is likely to arrange his experiment so that animal behavior appears to be either chancelike and mechanical or insightful. A famous philosopher, Bertrand Russell, noted before the end of

[6]Raymond H. Wheeler and Francis T. Perkins, *Principles of Mental Development*, New York: Thomas Y. Crowell, 1932.

[7]H. S. Jennings, *Behavior of the Lower Organisms,* New York: Columbia University Press, 1923, p. 335.

[8]Adolf Portmann, *New Paths in Biology*, New York: Harper & Row, 1964, pp. 91–92.

the 1920s that psychologists could demonstrate two fundamentally different types of response in their animal experiments, depending entirely on how they arranged the experimental situation. Russell commented humorously: ". . . Animals studied by Americans rush about frantically, with an incredible display of hustle and pep, and at last achieve the desired result by chance. Animals observed by Germans sit still and think, and at last evolve the solution out of their inner consciousness."[9] However, the state of affairs with regard to experimentation with lower animals is probably not as indecisive as Russell's comment would lead one to think. Once a student sets his orientation in either a behavioristic or a Gestalt-field direction, he benefits by the broadest possible knowledge of all available experimental, as well as other, evidence.

Behaviorists have clearly shown that animals can be put in experimental situations where they demonstrate overt behavior that seems trial-and-error, chancelike, blind, and mechanical. Furthermore, there seems to be little question but that human experimental subjects can be put in situations causing them to appear to demonstrate the same kind of behavior. The only requirement for such an experiment seems to be that the problem presented the learner be one with which his previous experience has in no way equipped him to cope.

On the other hand, Gestalt-field psychologists have demonstrated the one point they wanted to make, namely, that whether one is dealing with the lower animals or man, situations can be arranged in which learning shows an "Aha!" quality. That is, an experimental subject, in learning something, seems to "catch the point" or get the feel of a confronting situation. If man and the lower animals do seem to learn insightfully in situations which permit it, then serious doubt is cast upon the validity of the behaviorist notion that learning is purposeless, mechanical, and chancelike.

Gestalt-field psychologists insist that, to describe learning throughout the animal kingdom, we do well to begin with human examples. As we examine conscious behavior of ourselves or others, learning often, perhaps always, appears to be a matter of *seeing through things*, of *gaining understanding*. If we start with the assumption that other animals learn in the same way, we devise experiments that enable them to reveal such learning. This does not mean that if we are studying, say, a dog, we dare

[9]Quoted in W. D. Commons and Barry Fagin, *Principles of Educational Psychology*, New York: Ronald Press, 1954, p. 28. Originally in Russell's *Philosophy*, 1927. The Germans referred to obviously are the Gestaltists.

anthropomorphize him—attribute to him human characteristics; it does mean that we must guard against mechanizing him—making a machine of him. The way to study a dog is to "dogize" him, just as in studying a child we should "childize" him. In short, we must consider each animal as well as each human being on its own level. If we always keep this in mind, we can probably make some generalized statements about learning that will hold true with respect to most or even all forms of animal life.

In Chapter 3, we open discussion of the two major contemporary versions of the nature of learning. We now treat them in some detail. As already noted, whereas contemporary S-R conditioning theorists—the neobehaviorists—conceive of learning as *conditioning* or *reinforcement* of behaviors, Gestalt-field psychologists think of it as *development of insights,* which provide a potentiality for behavior.

IS LEARNING S-R CONDITIONING?

Neobehavioristic psychologists construe behavior to be the actions that result from forces or stimuli being exerted upon an organism. Explanation for what organisms—people—do is sought in the environmental circumstances that surround them, the stimuli that impinge upon them, and the actions, including verbalizations, that they emit.

A child or youth is something to be molded in the proper fashion. Learning primarily is a process within which both verbal and nonverbal behaviors are changed. Such behaviors are inculcated by adults telling, showing, directing, guiding, arranging, manipulating, rewarding, punishing, and, at times, coercing the activities of children and youth. Accordingly, teaching is a matter of adults setting behavioristic environmental conditions —stimuli—to make sure that the students accomplish those goals.

So, in the eyes of neobehaviorists, learning is a more or less permanent change of behavior that occurs as a result of practice. Accordingly, the learning process consists of impressions of new reaction patterns on pliable, passive organisms. Since learning arises, in some way, from an interplay of organisms and their environments, the key concepts of neobehaviorists are stimuli—excitement provided by an environment—and *responses*—reactions—made by an organism. Consequently, the problem of the nature of the learning process is centered in a study of the relationships of processions of stimuli and responses and what occurs between them. Since the focus always is upon behavior, in practical application, a neobehavioristically oriented teacher strives to change behaviors of his students in the desired direction by providing the right stimuli at the proper time.

What are the possible kinds of conditioning?

Within S-R neobehaviorism, one thinks of all learning as S-R conditioning and divides conditioning into two basic categories; classical conditioning—that without reinforcement—and instrumental conditioning—that which occurs through reinforcement.[10] Conditioning merely is some sort of stimulus-response sequence that results in either an enduring change in behavior or an increase in the likelihood of a response. Reinforcement is a special type of conditioning of such nature that a reduction of an organic need or a drive stimulus increases the probability of the desired behavior (response) on subsequent occasions. Whereas classical conditioning, that is, conditioning with no reinforcement, is based on an adhesion principle, reinforcement—instrumental or operant conditioning—is based on the feedback principle.

The adhesion principle means merely that a stimulus is attached to a response so that revival of the former evokes the latter. The feedback principle means that the reduction or satisfaction of an *organic need* or *drive stimulus* increases the probability of future responses of the kind that the organism emitted immediately prior to its being fed, watered, satisfied sexually, or otherwise satiated; there is feedback from the satisfaction of some deprivation to the type of behavior that preceded it.

A "need" as used here is an objective, biological requirement of an organism, which must be met if the organism is to survive and grow. Examples of needs are an organism's requirement for food, sex, or escape from pain. A "drive stimulus" is an aroused state of an organism. It is closely related to the need that sets the organism into action, and may be defined as a strong, persistent stimulus that demands an adjustive response. Whenever an organism is deprived of satisfaction of a need, drive stimuli occur.

In addition to the two kinds of positive conditioning—*classical* and *instrumental*—there also is a negative conditioning process

---

[10] See Table 1.1 p. 10, items 5, 6, and 7 for a classification of S-R conditioning learning theories.

—*extinction*. Through classical and instrumental conditioning, an organism *gains* responses or habits; through extinction it *loses* them.

Classical conditioning. Classical conditioning usually is associated with such incidents as Pavlov's teaching a dog to salivate at the ringing of a bell; it is *stimulus substitution*. In Pavlov's conditioning experiment, the sound of a bell occurred prior to, or simultaneously with, the dog's salivation, which was caused by the presence of food. Then in the future the dog salivated at the ringing of the bell, even when the food was not present.

In classical conditioning a new stimulus is presented along with an already adequate, unconditioned stimulus—such as the smell of food—and just prior to the response that is evoked by the unconditioned stimulus. Thus, an organism learns to respond to a new stimulus in the same, or similar, way it responds to the old, unconditioned stimulus—one already adequate to evoke the response. The new stimulus becomes the conditioned one, and the response that follows both stimuli becomes the conditioned response. *A conditioned response*, then, is one that is associated with, or evoked by, a new—conditioned—stimulus. In Pavlov's experiment, the sound of the bell became the new, conditioned stimulus that evoked the old, unconditioned response—salivation. Then, salivation became a conditioned response.

Classical conditioned learning is revealed in the behavior of an organism by the increasing capacity of a previously neutral stimulus, with successive training trials, to evoke a response that originally was evoked by some other stimulus. A "neutral stimulus" is one whose first occurrence does nothing toward either evoking or reinforcing the response that is under study.

Instrumental conditioning. Just as classical conditioning theory derives from the early work of Pavlov, instrumental conditioning theory has emerged from the foundation built by Thorndike. Instrumental conditioning usually is equated with reinforcement; it is response modification or change.[11] An animal first makes a response, then receives a "reward"; the response is instrumental in bringing about its reinforcement. There is a *feedback* from the "rewarding" stimulus which follows the response that the organism is learning; a dog is fed after he "speaks" and, thereby, the likelihood of his "speaking" in the future is increased.

---

[11]Spence's learning theory is an exception to this generalization, it does not treat instrumental conditioning as synonymous with reinforcement.

Extinction. Extinction is the process whereby an organism gradually loses a response or habit through its repeating the response a number of times while no reinforcing stimulus accompanies it. Any habits gained through either classical or instrumental conditioning may be lost through extinction.[12]

How does reinforcement occur?

Neobehaviorists, who emphasize the importance of reinforcement in learning, assume that some psychological conclusions are fairly well established: (1) patterns of action and expectation develop through an organism's responses to repeated stimuli accompanied by "fumble and success" type of trial-and-error learning under conditions of positive or negative reinforcement; (2) reinforcement occurs through satisfaction of either basic biological needs like hunger or sex, or secondary needs such as a need for security, recognition, or aesthetic gratification; and (3) educational encouragement must take the form of positive and negative reinforcers. A positive reinforcer is a stimulus whose presence strengthens a behavior; a negative one is a stimulus whose *withdrawal* strengthens a behavior. Note that negative reinforcement, psychologically, is different from punishment.[13]

Primary reinforcement. Reinforcement may be either *primary* or *secondary.* Primary reinforcement strengthens a certain behavior through the satisfaction of a basic biological need or drive. Secondary reinforcement sometimes is called high-order reinforcement. The reinforcers of secondary or high-order reinforcement have acquired their power of reinforcement indirectly through learning; poker chips for which a chimpanzee will work and money for which man will do almost anything are secondary reinforcers.

The drive-reduction sequence of primary reinforcement proceeds as follows: (1) deprivation of satisfaction of a basic requirement, such as that for food, produces a state of need in an organism; (2) the need expresses itself as a tension state or drive stimulus, which energizes the organism into action (a food-deprived animal shows the restless activity whose manifestation is called the hunger drive); (3) the activity achieves satisfaction

[12]See Chapter 5, pp. 139–140, for a more extensive description of *extinction.*
[13]See Chapter 5, pp. 135–136, for further treatment of positive and negative reinforcement and the differences between negative reinforcement and punishment.

of the need and relieves the tension state; and (4) the form of the activity that immediately preceded the satisfaction of the need or reduction of the drive is reinforced.

Secondary reinforcement. Secondary reinforcement is reinforcement that is brought about by occurrence of an originally neutral stimulus along with a reinforcing stimulus. When a neutral stimulus such as a sound or light is repeatedly paired with food in the presence of a food-deprived (hungry) animal, the formerly neutral stimulus becomes a secondary, conditioned reinforcer. Thus, secondary reinforcement results when originally neutral stimuli become closely associated with primary reinforcing stimuli and thereby become effective in reducing needs. In this way, neutral stimuli acquire the power of acting as reinforcing agents; a chimpanzee learns to accept the poker chips that accompany food as a "reward" just as readily as he accepts food. Consequently, future actions of the chimpanzee are reinforced by his receiving poker chips immediately after he performs them; this is secondary reinforcement.

How may we group S-R conditioning theories?

On the basis of their respective positions in regard to the specific nature of learning, we may divide behaviorists into three groups. One group makes conditioning the heart of the learning process, but holds that reinforcement is not necessary for conditioning to occur. A second group is committed to reinforcement or law-of-effect theories. The third group consists of two-factor theorists who contend that there are two basically different learning processes—conditioning independent of reinforcement and conditioning governed by principles of reinforcement.

Edwin R. Guthrie's *contiguous conditioning* is most representative of the first—conditioning, nonreinforcement—group. The names of Clark L. Hull and B. F. Skinner are most often associated with the *reinforcement* group. However, Hull and Skinner have differed sharply in regard to the nature of the reinforcement process. Three prominent *two-factor psychologies* are those of Kenneth W. Spence, Edward C. Tolman, and O. H. Mowrer. Hence, four representative neobehaviorisms are Guthrie's *contiguous conditioning,* Hull's *deductive behaviorism* or *reinforcement theory,* Skinner's *operant conditioning,* and Spence's *quantitative S-R theory.* All four are alike in their emphasis upon a mechanical treatment of stimuli and responses. Furthermore, they agree that at no time is purposiveness to be assumed; problems of "purposes" must be explained by natural laws or principles whereby organisms mechanically develop "motives." However, they differ rather sharply in their interpretations of stimulus-response relationships in learning procedures. Guthrie was convinced that learning occurs when a stimulus and a response happen simultaneously; Hull centered the essence of learning in what occurs between the stimulus and the response; and Skinner places his emphasis upon the stimulus that follows a response. When we express these serial relationships symbolically, using S for stimulus, R for response, and O for organism, Guthrie holds to an S-R, Hull to an S-O-R, and Skinner to an R-S learning theory. Since Spence incorporates both contiguity and reinforcement into his theory, it cannot be categorized in this way.

We now examine very briefly three representative, systematic behavioristic theories of learning and see how each would color teaching procedures in a school learning situation.

Guthrie's contiguous conditioning. Guthrie's learning theory is classical conditioning, not reinforcement. Furthermore, it is a special kind of conditioning which we may identify as *simultaneous contiguous conditioning. Contiguity* means that stimuli acting *at the time* of a response, on their recurrence, tend to evoke that response. Furthermore, if a stimulus occurs contiguously with a response, the response to that stimulus will continue to occur with it until some other response becomes conditioned to that stimulus.

Guthrie regarded learning as a sudden, not gradual, process and the mechanism of conditioning as stimuli change, not drive reduction. Accordingly, strengthening of individual connections of stimuli and response—the actual conditioning—supposedly takes place with a single simultaneous occurrence of a stimulus and response. This does not mean that repetition has no place in learning, but that within repetition an increasing number of stimuli are made into conditioners; there is no strengthening of individual connections, but there is enlistment of more.

Guthrie thought that, since association can occur with one connection and last for life, there is no need for anything like reward, pleasure, or need reduction to explain learning. Thus, there is no place for reinforcement in his contiguity theory. To Guthrie, scientific laws deal with observable phenomena only. In psychology there are physical stimuli and responses in the form of contractions of muscles and secretions of glands, but there is no place for hypothetical intervening variables between stimuli and responses. We only need to know that ". . . a combination of stimuli which has accompanied a movement will on its recurrence tend to be followed by that movement."[14] We might note that the potential achievement of latent learning, independent learning, and learning under conditions where reward seems irrelevant lends some support to Guthrie's contiguity theory.

A proponent of contiguous conditioning in teaching people first gets them to perform in a certain way, then while they are doing so gives them the stimuli that he wants associated with that behavior. To teach that man is *Homo sapiens,* a Guthriean would induce his student to say *Homo sapiens* and while he was saying it stimulate him with *man* either spelled out, pictured, or both. The more "man" stimuli he could give the student while he was saying *Homo sapiens* the better it would be. In this teaching-learning process *man* is the conditioned stimulus and saying *Homo sapiens* is the conditioned response.

Hull's reinforcement theory. Hull's learning theory also is stimulus-response conditioning, but of a special kind, called *reinforcement.* His theoretical model was a Newtonian mechanism. Accordingly, he employed a unique device to make sure that he maintained a consistently objective approach to psychological study. "This is to regard, from time to time, the behaving organism as a completely self-maintaining robot, constructed of materials as unlike ourselves as may be."[15]

Like Watson, Hull stressed conditioning as the basic learning process. But, in addition, he developed an intricate system of definitions, postulates, and theorems to bridge the gap from simple conditioning to more complex forms of learning. For example, in presenting his theory of learning Hull stated, *"Whenever a reaction* (R) *takes place in temporal contiguity with an afferent receptor impulse* ($\dot{s}$) *resulting from the impact upon a receptor of a stimulus energy* ($\dot{S}$), *and this conjunction is followed closely by the diminution in a need* (*and the associated diminution of the drive, D, and in the drive receptor discharge,* s_D), *there will result an increment* $\triangle$ (s——→R), *in the tendency for that stimulus on subsequent occasions to evoke that reaction."*[16]

Within Hullian reinforcement, the stimulus and the response are not simultaneous; the stimulus precedes the response. Furthermore, learning does not take place with a single trial; it is stamped in through a process of repeated need or drive stimulus

[14]Edwin R. Guthrie, *The Psychology of Learning,* rev. ed., New York: Harper & Row, 1952, p. 23.

[15]Clark L. Hull, *Principles of Behavior,* New York: Appleton-Century-Crofts, 1943, p. 27.

[16]*Ibid.,* p. 71.

reductions. Thus, he thought of learning in terms of receptor-effector connections and of reinforcement in terms of need or drive stimulus reduction.

Imitating Newtonian physics, Hull studied learning in terms of three kinds of variables; namely, independent, intervening, and dependent ones. Independent variables occur first. They include activity, repetition, practice, training, observation, and sensory experience. The principal intervening variable is learning. Dependent variables consist of changes and increments of behavior, modifications of behavior, and trends in behavior.

Hull thought that learning occurs through biological adaptation of an organism to its environment in a way to promote survival. A state of need means that survival of the organism is not being adequately served. Drive is a general condition of organic privation arising from lack of food, water, or air, from unhealthful temperatures, from tissue injury, from sex-linked conditions, or from other deficiencies. When needs or drive stimuli develop, the organism acts and the action often brings reduction in needs or drive stimuli. Actions or responses that lead to reduction of needs or drive stimuli are reinforced; thus reinforcement is centered in adaptation for survival. However, in life situations there are many reinforcers that do not contribute directly to biological adaptation of an organism. Through higher-order conditioning many things and actions come to have value and can serve as reinforcers. Higher-order conditioning is conditioning based upon previous conditioning; it more often is called secondary conditioning (see pp. 93–94).

A child is conditioned to think, i.e., say to himself, "man" when he sees a man or a picture of a man. This conditioning could have been based upon reduction of drive stimuli. Perhaps he wanted a piece of candy and his parents withheld it from him until he said "man." Now, in ninth grade, the stimulus "man" evokes *Homo sapiens*, perhaps through the satisfaction of curiosity, and curiosity is a product of higher-order conditioning; the youth previously had been conditioned to be curious.

Skinner's operant, instrumental conditioning. The unique feature of operant conditioning is that the reinforcing stimulus occurs not simultaneously with or preceding the response but following the response. In operant conditioning, an organism must first make the desired response and then a "reward" is provided. The reward reinforces the response—makes it more likely to recur. The response is instrumental in bringing about its reinforcement. The essence of learning is not stimulus substitution but response modification. In learning, there is a feedback from the reinforcing stimulus to the previous response. To illustrate, in the training of pets a desired response is reinforced after it occurs—a dog is fed after it "speaks," and this increases the likelihood of its "speaking" in the future. (See Chapter 5 for an expansion of this position.)

Note that in operant conditioning the stimulus producing the response in the first place is not centrally involved in the learning process. The original response is a result of a stimulus, but the nature of this stimulation is irrelevant to operant conditioning. It is only necessary that some—any—stimulus elicit the response for operant conditioning to function. Emphasis is on reinforcing agents, not on original causative factors.

An operant-reinforcement approach to teaching a ninth-grader that man is *Homo sapiens* would be to show the student *man* along with several other more complicated words, one of which is *Homo sapiens*. If the student chooses *"non sequitur,"* or any expression other than *Homo sapiens*, nothing happens. If he chooses *"Homo sapiens,"* the teacher says "wonderful." This is reinforcement, and they proceed to a new "problem."[17]

Spence's quantitative S-R theory. Spence's ultimate goal was to attain a high level of exact quantification of behavior theory within an S-R conditioning frame of reference. He foresaw a great need for careful laboratory study of simple behavior prior to any attempt to establish a comprehensive theory of learning. Thus, he thought that the science of psychology is not yet ready to concern itself with actual schoolroom or "real life" situations. (See Chapter 6 for more complete development of the Spencian position.)

For Spence, learning is a nonobservable, hypothetical construct or variable that intervenes between observable independent and dependent variables. Accordingly, like Hull, he thought that learning, in some way, is a relationship of stimuli and responses. However, he accepted only a few of Hull's many definitions and postulates.

Since Spence accepted the reality of both contiguity and reinforcement in conditioning processes, much of his research involved testing to see which type of conditioning prevails in certain kinds of learning situations. For example, several of his research projects were designed to see whether *classical conditioning*—an organism's learning to react defensively to a new stimulus much as it previously had to an unconditioned bothersome stimulus—is governed by reinforcement or merely by

[17]Chapter 5 describes Skinner's learning theory in detail.

contiguity. To accomplish this, air puffs of various strengths, blown in the face of a subject, were accompanied by a disk, at which the subject was looking, being given different degrees of brightness. Learning was revealed by the subject's coming to blink his eye more frequently as the brightness of the disk is increased. The experiment was carefully designed to show whether reinforcement is involved in this kind of learning situation.

Although there are clear-cut psychological theories of learning, neobehaviorists in education tend not to adhere rigidly to any one of the S-R patterns but to intermix them in applying psychology to teaching procedures. In this way they attempt to achieve an integration of the earlier works of Pavlov, Watson, and Thorndike with that of contemporary neobehavioristic psychologists.

Within neobehaviorism, learning is considered nonpurposive habit formation. Habits are formed through conditioning which either attaches desired responses to specific stimuli or increases the probability of desired responses. A stimulus triggers an action or response, which can take only one form because of the nature of the stimulus, the condition of the organism, and the "laws of learning" involved. Teachers who adopt this mechanistic approach to learning decide specifically what behaviors they want their students, when finished products, to manifest, and they proceed to stimulate them in such a way as to evoke and fix those behaviors.

IS LEARNING DEVELOPMENT OF INSIGHT?

The key word of Gestalt-field psychologists in describing learning is *insight*. They regard learning as a process of developing new insights or modifying old ones. Insights occur when an individual, in pursuing his purposes, sees new ways of utilizing elements of his environment, including his own bodily structure. The noun *learning* connotes the new insights or meanings that are acquired.

Gestalt-field theorists attack three weaknesses in the theory that learning is conditioning: (1) the attempt of behaviorists to explain complex interrelated organizations in terms of simpler elements, that is, to insist that learning consists of an accumulation of individual conditioned responses or operants, each relatively simple in itself, but eventuating in a complicated pattern of habits; (2) their tendency to attribute learning to reduction of basic organic drives; and (3) behaviorists' tendency to ignore the apparent purposiveness of much behavior. So, "The chief trouble with behaviorism . . . is that it leaves out so much behavior."[18]

Gestalt-field psychologists view learning as a purposive, explorative, imaginative, and creative enterprise. This conception breaks completely with the idea that learning consists of either linking one thing to another according to certain principles of association or building behaviors in a deterministic, mechanistic fashion. Instead, the learning process is identified with thought or conceptualization; it is a nonmechanical development or change of insight.

Behaviorists also sometimes use the term *insight*, but when they do they mean something quite different from what Gestalt-field theorists mean. When used by behaviorists, the term describes a special and rare kind of learning. To use Woodworth's definition, insight is ". . . some penetration into the [absolutely] true nature of things."[19] But to Woodworth and other behaviorists, the ordinary form that learning takes is S-R conditioning. In fact, the most systematic of the behaviorists deny that there can be two entirely different kinds of learning; therefore they prefer to describe *all* learning as conditioning. Since insight obviously implies something very different from conditioning, many behaviorists do not use the term at all. To them it connotes something intuitive and mystical, something that cannot be described operationally. In contrast, Gestalt-field psychologists do not like to use the term *conditioning;* they regard *development of insight* as the most descriptive phrase available to describe the manner in which learning actually takes place.

The Gestalt-field definition of insight is a sense of, or feeling for, pattern or relationships. To state it differently, insight is the "sensed way through" or "solution" of a problematic situation. Insights often first appear as vague "hunches." We might say that an insight is a kind of "feel" we get about a situation that permits us to continue to strive actively to serve our purposes. When are insights verbalized? Perhaps at once; perhaps never. We probably know many things that we never manage to put into words. This is a problem on which animal experimentation sheds some light. Animals below man cannot talk; they can communicate, but not by placing sounds together in coherent subject-predicate sentences. Yet the evidence indicates

   [18]Rollo May, *Psychology and the Human Dilemma*, New York: Van Nostrand Reinhold 1967, p. 190.
   [19]R. S. Woodworth, *Psychology*, New York: Holt, Rinehart and Winston, 1940, pp. 299–300.

that, when they are confronted with what to them are problems, they insightfully learn.

If we define *hypotheses* broadly, we may refer to insights as hypotheses. However, a hypothesis usually is defined as a special kind of verbalized insight. It is a statement that takes the form of a declarative sentence, or in many cases an "if-then" sentence. For example, one might say, "Most redheaded girls have violent tempers" (a declarative statement), or one might say, "If most redheaded girls reach a certain frustration level, they then display a violent temper" (an if-then statement). Hypotheses, constructed as verbal statements, are the only kind of insights that we can test in a strictly scientific fashion.

This brings us to a crucial question: Are insights necessarily true? Gestalt-field psychologists do not use the term "insights" in a way to imply that they are necessarily true. Granted, the term sometimes is used this way by others. But the relativistic orientation of Gestalt-field theorists necessarily leads them to think of insights as trial answers, which may or may not help a person toward his goal; they may or they may not be true. Truth, relativistically defined, is that quality of an insight that enables its possessor to design behavior that is successful in achievement of what it is designed to achieve.

Insights, then, are to be considered, not literal descriptions of objective physical-social situations, but as interpretations of one's self and one's perceived environment on the basis of which subsequent action may be designed. Although insights are not physicalistic descriptions of objects or processes in the environment, they necessarily take account of the physical environment. Their usability depends in part on how well this is done. Insights may misinterpret a physical environment so badly that they are useless as rules of action, in which case they are to be regarded as false.

It is important to understand that insights are always a learner's own. It is true, of course, that they may become his own through adoption. An insight is usable to a learner only if he can "fit it in." He must understand its significance—for him. A teacher cannot give an insight to a student as we serve a person meat on a platter. He may acquaint students with his insights, but they do not become insights for students until students see their meaning for themselves and adopt them as their own.

One objection frequently raised to the Gestalt-field tendency to construe all learning as insightful is that some learning tasks are performed successfully without apparent development of insight—as, for example, when a child memorizes the multiplication tables. A field psychologist concedes that some learning appears highly mechanical, but he is convinced that it is not necessarily as mechanical as it appears. Accordingly, he contends that even though a child may repeat the multiplication tables until he appears to have memorized them by rote, what the child actually has done is to get the feel of some pattern that is present in the tables. The pattern may lie in the relationship of the numbers or perhaps merely in the order in which the student placed the numbers to "memorize" them.

One's use of the term *insight* does not imply that for a person to learn something he must understand all aspects of its use. Any degree of "feel for a pattern" is sufficient to constitute insightful learning. For example, in learning to extract the square root of a number, one might develop insight as to *why* the method works. Or the insight gained might be much more superficial; it might be merely a "feel" for the method—the pattern of steps—with no real understanding of the basic algebraic formula $(x + y)^2 = x^2 + 2xy + y^2$.

Some examples of insightful learning

Before he can become a sharpshooter, a rifleman must get a "feel" for his rifle. Often a Tennessee squirrel hunter was slow in learning to be an army rifleman. He had an excellent feel for his squirrel gun, but a squirrel gun was not an army rifle. In his army training he had to change old insights as well as develop new ones. On his squirrel gun his sights were fixed immovably to the barrel. To hit a squirrel he had to take wind and distance into consideration and move the rifle away from a line on the target (windward and upward) to give "Tennessee windage" and "Kentucky elevation." He had developed insights to the point that he could behave intelligently without thinking; he could aim his gun and pull the trigger while giving very little attention to what he was doing.

Since his army rifle had movable sights, which prior to aiming were to be adjusted to allow for windage and elevation, he was supposed to set his sights and then line them directly on his target. But under pressure of target practice he used his new insights to adjust his sights correctly, then when he began to fire he gave his rifle Tennessee windage and Kentucky elevation and missed the target completely. He had used two sets of incompatible insights. He could learn to shoot his army rifle accurately only by getting complete feel for his army rifle and leaving most of his squirrel-gun-aiming insights out of the picture.

What is the answer to $\sqrt{(\text{dog})^2} = ?$ How did you know it was "dog"? Had you ever before worked with square root and dog at the same time? If you knew the answer was "dog," you had an insight into the problem. Perhaps you had never put the insight into words, but you know that[20] $\sqrt{x^2} = x$ and $\sqrt{4^2} = 4$. Your insight, when verbalized, would run something like, "The square root of anything squared is that thing." Conversely, you may have "learned"—memorized—"The square root of a quantity squared is that quantity" and still not know the answer to $\sqrt{(\text{dog})^2} = ?$.

Teaching for development of insight has definite implication for methods of teaching and learning spelling. Groups or families of words might be studied in such a way that students would develop a feeling for a certain spelling pattern. Once a pattern is discovered, other words can be sought that conform to it. *Cat, fat,* and *bat* are "at" words. Now what about *hat, mat, pat, rat,* and *sat*? As students, working cooperatively with their teacher, find other word families, they soon will encounter words that apparently should, but do not, fit a certain family— they find some limitations to an insight. They then seek other words with the same divergence from the "rule" and make a family of them. Or, in case there is only one divergent word, they think of it as an exception. As the insights into patterns of spelling are put into words, a class can formulate rules. But now rules will be verbalizations of student's insight as contrasted with meaningless statements memorized at the beginning of study.[21]

Insight, understanding, and generalization

Often when an insight is first "caught" it applies to a single case. Even so, a person is likely to assume that the insight may work in similar situations. Suppose, for example, that, after studying a particular situation, we hypothesize, "Mary became a shoplifter because she felt unwanted by her parents." The natural next step is to think, "Boys and girls who feel unwanted at home tend to become thieves." Of course, this generalization is only *suggested*. It is not *warranted* by evidence from a single

[20]This holds true when x is equal to or greater than zero.
[21]Chapter 11 pp. 305–339 continues the discussion of the nature of insightful learning and teaching.

case. Before generalizations become reliable; that is, before they become understandings, it is usually necessary that they rest on a number of specific insights, all suggesting the same conclusion. In short, dependable generalizations, i.e., understandings, usually are products of considerable experience. Furthermore, they are prone to change in the course of experience, evolving continuously in the direction of greater usefulness as tools of thought.

An *understanding* of a thing or process is its generalized meaning, i.e., it is a tested generalized insight. Thus, it entails one's ability to use an object, fact, process, or idea in several or even many somewhat different situations. It is one's understandings that enables one to behave intelligently, that is, with foresight of consequences. A tested generalization or understanding is assumed to be valid in any future situation similar to the situations in which it was tested. Tested generalizations have the character of *rules, principles,* or *laws*. Syntactically, generalizations are frequently if-then statements: if we take a given action, then the probability is high that a given consequence will follow. We emphasize that tested generalizations should be regarded as *probabilities*, not absolute certainties. Although, to behave with foresight, we must assume that our generalizations have predictive value, the predictions are always, to some degree, based on probability.

As suggested earlier, if-then statements usually also may be expressed in present-tense declarative sentences. For example, when a person says, "An increase in the quantity of money is likely to produce a rise in prices," he may mean exactly the same as if he said, "If the quantity of money in circulation is increased, then prices are likely to rise." In using generalizations as hypotheses in scientific procedure, the if-then form often is preferable. It is more likely than is a simple declarative sentence to suggest operations to be performed, and therefore throw emphasis upon experimental tests.

HOW IS OBSERVABLE BEHAVIOR CHANGE RELATED TO LEARNING?

Gestalt-field theories contrast sharply with the S-R conditioning theories or behaviorisms in regard to the manner in which adherents of the two respective positions use observable behavior of persons as psychological data. Behaviorists use observable behavior and only observable behavior as data. Consequently, they restrict learning objectives to those expressible in terms of observable behaviors. In contrast, Gestalt-field psychologists also study observable behaviors, but they infer from them the changing personalities, environments, and insights of the persons being studied. So, whereas for behaviorists one's physical behavior also is one's psychological behavior, for Gestalt-field theorists psychological behavior is something quite different from mere physical movement; it is change in the way a person perceives both himself and his psychological environment.

Learning and change in observable behavior often occur side by side and seem to be interrelated. So, behaviorists contend that any change of behavior is learning, and conversely that any learning is a change of behavior. Thus, the current practice among many educators of defining learning as "change in behavior" usually reflects a behavioristic psychology.

For behaviorists, *"behavior,* as a technical psychological term, may be defined as the publicly observable activity of muscles or glands of external secretion as manifested for example in movements of parts of the body or the appearance of tears, sweat, saliva and so forth."[22] But, Gestalt-field psychologists give *behavior* a quite different meaning. For them, it is any change in a person, his perceived environment, or the relation between the two that is subject to *psychological* principles or laws. *Psychological,* as used here, means their involving purpose and intelligence. Hence, psychological behavior is not identified with physical movement. Such behavior is not directly observable, but must be inferred from actions and demeanors that are observable.[23]

Gestalt-field theorists think that behaviorists err in making the observable results of learning synonymous with the learning itself. For them, a change of observable behavior may be evidence that learning has occurred or is occurring, but such behavioral change is not the learning. So, a change in biological behavior does not necessarily mean that learning has occurred. A person who is in a dark alley and is struck from behind and knocked down may gain from this experience a healthy respect for dark alleys, but the change in behavior—falling down—is not equivalent to any change in insight that may have occurred. Furthermore, a person may use insights that he has

22Donald O. Hebb, *A Textbook of Psychology,* 2nd ed., Philadelphia: Saunders, 1966, p. 7.
23See "Field Theory in Social Psychology," in Gardner Lindzey and Elliot Aronson, eds., *The Handbook of Social Psychology,* 2nd ed., Vol. 1, Boston: Addison-Wesley, 1968.

gained through an earlier experience as the basis for a change in his present behavior. For example, a writer may know that too much coffee is not good for him but persist in drinking coffee until he completes a manuscript, then reduce the amount of coffee he drinks.

Many changes in the behavior of school children probably do not reflect their teachers' desired changes in student insights. Johnny may start saying "please" and "thank you" without an insightful grasp of the implications of his so doing, or he may labor hours every night over homework without having his work produce any change of mind about matters implicit in the homework itself. (Of course, the assignment may cause changes in his attitude toward teachers and school.)

Gestalt-field psychologists maintain that not only may a change in behavior occur without learning, but also learning may occur without any *observable*, related changes in behavior. This is true in innumerable situations. There may be an insight but no opportunity or occasion for a change in behavior, as when one decides it would be nice to give more to charity but does not have the money to do so. Also, when new insights compete with older ones that have a strong hold on a person, the new insights may fail to change the person's behavior. For example, one may decide that racial discrimination is bad, but continue to practice it.

Because of their emphasis on behavioral change, many people with a behavioristic orientation think that doing something a number of times will necessarily affect one's future behavior. Thus, if one smokes a pack of cigarettes a day for several weeks he will become a habitual smoker. Gestalt-field theorists deny that this is the case. Doing a thing either once or many times will affect subsequent behavior only to the degree in which doing it gives the doer a feeling for the act or insight into the consequences of its performance. It is the perceptual process, not the action as such that is crucial. For this reason, Gestalt-field psychologists emphasize experience rather than behavior, with experience defined as an interactive event within which a person, through acting and seeing what happens, comes to see and feel the consequences of a given course of action. When a person learns something, his behavior usually changes; but it does not follow that, for learning to take place, a change in observable behavior must occur at the same time, or that from a change in overt behavior we always can accurately infer the full nature of the insight related to it.

The emphasis of behaviorists upon overt behavior has led to

school practices designed to produce a desired kind of behavior and to methods of evaluation that measure overt behavior— and nothing else. Teachers, or other school authorities, decide which specific behaviors they want students to display. They then stimulate the students in such a way as to evoke the desired behaviors. The success of the process is judged by how dependably the behavior can be invoked in the future (usually on tests). Field psychologists protest this approach to education; they think that a student may learn little more from it than the insights he gains about teachers and schools and about how to play the memory-work game successfully.

For Gestalt-field psychologists, learning is a persistent change in knowledge, skills, attitudes, values, or beliefs. It may, or it may not, be reflected in changes in overt behavior. One does not "learn by doing" except insofar as one's doing contributes to a change in one's cognitive structure. For learning to result, doing must be accompanied by the doer's realization of the consequences of the act. Thus learning occurs through, and results from, experience; and, "Mere activity does not constitute experience."[24] For an activity to be included in experience, it must be interrelated with a realization of the consequences that accompany it.

HOW DO ADHERENTS OF THE TWO LEARNING FAMILIES DESCRIBE THE THINKING PROCESS?

In its broadest meaning, the term *thinking* may embrace simple association or recall, reverie, fantasy, dreams, autism, and animism as well as creative ideational activity. However, in the more restricted sense in which we use the term herein, it is a directed, goal-oriented activity of an individual; in other words, it is a creative, problem-solving process.

Thinking, then, is goal-related problem solving. It is an attempt to work through an obstacle in order to find the means to achieve an end. For the purpose of analysis, we may distinguish two levels of problem solving, but any line drawn between them is necessarily arbitrary. One level may be termed *simple problem solving*. Simple problem solving does not involve weighty decisions. Examples of problems on this level are expressed in the following questions: Shall I wear a red or green tie today? Shall I have eggs or cereal for breakfast?

24John Dewey, *Democracy and Education*, New York: Macmillan, 1916, p. 163.

Shall I drive or walk to work? Shall I spend the evening reading a book or watching a motion picture? During the solution
of problems of this kind, our tension level remains relatively
low, and we usually solve these problems without lengthy de-
liberation. Once we have made a decision, we are unlikely to
worry about it later.

The other level of thinking may be termed *complex problem
solving*. It is on this level that we face problems not so easy
to settle—that is, unless we decide to ignore them. This level
of problem solving usually requires much effort and time and
is accompanied by relatively high tension. The distinguishing
characteristic of this level is that each problem presents the
person involved with something new. Although many elements
of the problem may be familiar, some are unfamiliar. Consequently, each act of complex problem solving requires some
degree of originality or creativity. Examples of problems on this
level are suggested by questions such as: Shall I encourage
my son to go to college? Shall I seek a divorce? Shall I change
my registration from Democrat to Republican? Shall I switch
my church affiliation? Of course, not all complex problem solving involves questions as weighty as these. Deciding which in-
secticide to use or which service station to patronize might also
require complex problem-solving procedures.

How is thinking associated with learning?

Since our principal tools of thought—concepts—are learned, people generally associate learning and thinking quite closely. Furthermore, one objective of education upon which persons of
various shades of opinion *seem* to agree is that, "students should
be taught to think." However, when people attempt to define
"thinking" and to specify the proper procedure for its promotion, the apparent agreement soon fades away. Let us now take
the question, "should students be required to think as part of
their activity in school?"

One group of educators seems to feel that school should prepare students to think, but that during the period of preparation thinking is not necessary. Proponents of this position usually argue that the purpose of education is to give students background—the factual equipment with which to think at some later
time. But often they do not make themselves clear as to just
when thinking should start. Apparently, some of them feel that
this should be some time after people reach the age 21.

There are others who seem to believe that it is good for students to think part, but not all, of the time that they are in school. People of this persuasion often associate thinking with certain courses, like higher mathematics. Accordingly, they classify subjects into two categories: background "fact courses" and courses in which students need to think. Usually they consider the former just as important as the latter.

A third group, exemplified by Gestalt-field psychologists, thinks that learning and thought are closely allied; one does not occur without some degree of the other, thus they are convinced that change of insight invariably is accompanied by thought of some kind, and thought of any kind always produces some change of insight, however small.

Both S-R conditioning and Gestalt-field psychologists construe thinking within a scientific frame of reference, albeit in their respective manners. In the next sections we outline in some detail the psychological thinking of the two scientific approaches.

Within behaviorism, what is thinking?

For most behaviorists, an "idea" or "thought" consists of a symbolic movement that constitutes an intermediate step between overt stimuli and responses. *Symbols* are events that represent something beyond themselves. They may be either substitute stimuli or substitute responses. Whenever an organism is responding in a certain way and the stimulus which originally was adequate to evoke the response is absent, it is responding to a symbolic stimulus. A symbolic response is an incipient—partial—movement that takes the place of a completely expressed pattern of behavior. It may take the form of a shrug of the shoulders, a facial expression, a nod of the head, or a change in posture. In thinking, symbolic movements may be so slight that the individual may be aware of only a "thought" divorced from any movement. Nevertheless, when one thinks some slight muscular or neural action supposedly occurs.

Man's thinking, then, is his behaving symbolically or incipiently in a random trial-and-error fashion. Thought is not some mysterious mentalistic process that is the cause of behavior, but the behavior itself. Thus, thinking is symbolic or incipient trial-and-error behavior that culminates in learning. Like all other instances of an organism's behavior, it is a function or result of a set of antecedent or preceding conditions.

In thinking, an organism makes symbolic, miniature responses that sample the feedbacks that would occur if the action represented symbolically or incipiently were really carried out. Thus, to S-R conditioning theorists, thought consists of very small preparatory responses. These can be observed in the incipient or miniature trial-and-error movements of a rat at a "choice point" in a maze. Here, small movements, this way and that, often precede the rat's actually moving down a pathway. In human beings, this process is more subtle and elaborated but no different in kind from that of rats and other lower animals.

In its broadest sense, thinking behavior is both verbal and nonverbal and both overt and covert. However, any nonverbal or covert aspects are considered to function much like the observable ones; they too are segments of stimulus-response sequences. Accordingly, behaviorists assume that, once natural laws governing the relationship of observable stimuli and responses are identified and established, internal processes likewise can be described in terms of stimulus-response sequences that conform to the same laws. Thus, ideational thought, a variable that intervenes between observable stimuli and responses, likewise consist of stimuli and responses, albeit covert ones.

Although B. F. Skinner and some other contemporary neobehaviorists consider the study of any private, internal events irrelevant to a functional analysis of behavior, many others follow John B. Watson's earlier leadership in considering thinking basically to be implicit speech—talking to oneself. Thus, they associate thought very closely with language, which is a rich collection of symbols. So considered, thought basically is laryngeal activity. However, it is closely aligned with gestures, frowns, shrugs, and grimaces which stand for more overt actions or behaviors.

In the thinking process, words, other symbols, and incipient movements become *cues* for behavior. Cues are stimuli of faint intensity that evoke or guide an organism's movements. Any uniqueness man may have involves his "better" use of cues. Thus, three principal factors make man's thinking processes "higher" than those of other animals. (1) Man has greater capacity to respond selectively to more subtle aspects of the environment as cues. (2) He also is able to make a greater variety of distinctive responses that constitute cues for his actions; he is more able to stimulate himself. (3) He can emit a greater number of cue-responses simultaneously. Thus, he can elicit many more of his own future responses based on patterns of cues, which represent, or result from, several different earlier patterns of stimulation.[25]

[25]See Sigmund Koch, ed., *Psychology: A Study of a Science, Vol. 2, General Systematic Formulations, Learning, and Special Processes*, New York: McGraw-Hill, 1959, p. 247.

Gestalt-field psychology and reflective thinking

Gestalt-field psychologists interpret thinking to be a reflective process within which persons develop new or changed tested, generalized insights—understanding—or, in lay language, undergo a change of mind. So construed, reflective thinking combines both inductive—fact gathering—and deductive processes in such way as to find, elaborate, and test hypotheses. Thus, there is no essential difference between reflective thinking and scientific processes, broadly defined. However, the term *scientific* does carry a connotation that is less suited to our purposes than does the term *reflective*.

In the thinking of many persons *science* implies white-gowned technicians, microscopes and telescopes, chemical tables, and cyclotrons. Furthermore, it suggests precise measurement, use of mathematics, a large amount of rather esoteric wizardry, and neglect of moral values. However, *scientific* in its broadest sense covers not only a special kind of gadgetry and techniques but also a unique outlook, attitude, and method of inquiry.

Reflection refers to the essential but nongadgetlike features of scientific method—to an attitude of mind and a generalized set of operations with which we may approach all problems, whether physical, social, or psychological. John Dewey gave us a classic definition of reflection when he called it the "active, persistent, and careful consideration of any belief or supposed form of knowledge in the light of the grounds that support it and the further conclusions to which it tends. . . ."[26] Thus, Dewey conceived of reflection as the kind of thought that embodies the scientific method, defined in its broadest sense. To him, all thinking that is worthwhile is reflection, as we have defined it. Furthermore, reflection leads to generalizations of a kind that are understood by learners and that have maximum transfer value to new situations.

Components of reflective thinking. Five rather definite aspects are present in each completed act of reflection. However, no one should suppose that a person goes through them in the consecutive, orderly fashion in which they may be listed on paper. Any or even all of the aspects may develop concurrently. Moreover, reflection normally is characterized by confusion, hesitation, backtracking, and "going around in circles." In many cases it appears to a thinker that he will never reach a solution at all. And once reached, a conclusion often must be abandoned and the process started all over again. Reflection is seldom

[26]John Dewey, *How We Think*, Lexington Mass.: Raytheon/Heath, 1933, p. 9.

easy; at best it is exhilarating and exciting, and at worst it is painfully hard work beset with many frustrating moments.

The principal aspects of reflective thinking are as follows.[27]

1. *Recognition and definition of a problem.* This occurs when one becomes aware either of conflicting goals or of a goal and an intervening obstacle to its achievement. Often a problem consists of a newly sensed discrepancy in known data.

2. *Formulation of hypotheses.* Hypotheses are invented generalizations—possible answers—which, to be used most successfully, must be verified by human experience. In a relativistic sense, all scientific generalizations are hypotheses in which greater or lesser degrees of assurance can be placed. They range from hunches based on minimum data to laws which reflect a very high degree of factual verification.

3. *Elaboration of logical implications of hypotheses.* This includes deducing the implications or consequences whose observations already have been made so that hypotheses may be checked against present knowledge, and deducing implications or consequences whose observations have not yet been made so that hypotheses may be tested through experiments yet to be designed.

4. *Testing of hypotheses.* This involves attempts to verify implications or consequences deduced under the third aspect, in terms of both the data of previous experience—*scrutiny-explanation*—and data procured in experimental tests—*prediction-verification.*

5. *Drawing conclusions.* This consists of either acceptance, modification, or rejection of hypotheses, or concluding that as of now the available pertinent evidence does not warrant taking any stand at all.

Characteristic principles of reflective thinking. There is a great deal more to understanding the reflective process than merely listing its basic aspects. Experience of the past few centuries has led to certain conventions concerning how a reflective or scientific process is to be pursued. We use the term *conventions* because there is nothing absolutistic about the rules that govern testing hypotheses. The purpose of rules associated with a reflective approach is to make for "good thinking," which, in the final test, may be judged *only against its results.* The presumed purpose of any act of thought is to provide a person with tested generalized insights that are worth more than the

[27]The formulation presented here is somewhat standard, and its essential form appears in many writings; the specific way in which the aspects appear here was suggested to the author by Ernest E. Bayles.

ones formerly held. Currently accepted rules of reflection lead to more productive results than any alternative rules that yet have been devised. But there is no reason to suppose that these rules will not continue to evolve as mankind gains more experience.

We now list some of the more important principles that characterize reflective thinking, together with some needed qualifications. However, there is no implication that this is a complete listing of rules governing such a process.

1. Whenever one insight or conclusion is accepted in preference to another, it is presumed that *reasons exist for its acceptance.* The grounds for its acceptance may be scant, but as long as they are better than the grounds any competing insight can offer, they justify its tentative acceptance. What we regard as true does not need to be proved in any final sense. But it does require some supporting evidence.

2. Insights always are *provisional.* That is, all knowledge is assumed to be a product of human experience and hence subject to change. No question is closed to reexamination, provided a reason to reexamine it develops. This does not mean that one may not establish principles or laws, which are assumed to be valid for a very long period of time. Such principles or laws do not become absolutes so long as people remain willing to re-examine them at any time questions arise involving them.

3. Insights are consistent with each other. *We assume that two contradictory insights can never be true at the same time, for the same purpose, and under the same conditions.* This does not mean that one may not switch from one idea to another that is incompatible with it. Changing one's mind is not an example of inconsistency; in fact, a reflective person is known for his flexibility. A person is inconsistent only when he holds two opposite insights at once and under the same assumed conditions. Ernest Bayles states this "principle of harmony" in this way: ". . . The process of testing hypotheses by the use of data is one of asking whether the data agree with the hypothesis. [Or] which hypothesis, if any, causes the data to fall into a thoroughly harmonious pattern? A problem can be considered solved *beyond reasonable doubt* when and only when (1) one proposed solution presents a pattern which harmonizes all the data which have been obtained . . . and (2) there are no data which are incompatible with that proposal."[28]

[28]Ernest E. Bayles, *The Theory and Practice of Teaching*, New York: Harper & Row, 1950, pp. 108–109.

4. All pertinent, available evidence is examined before conclusions are drawn. An investigator looks at all facts then available, no matter how unpalatable some of them may seem. There is never a slanting, ignoring, or distorting of data to prove a point. Unrestrained taboos and prejudices do not mix with a reflective approach. Bayles refers to this principle as that of "adequacy," the data must be adequate, i.e., as complete as possible.

5. The ultimate authority for any scientific conclusion is to be found in perceivable phenomena, as acquired through observation and experiment. The crucial test, of course, is the actual predicated functioning of a hypothesis in new situations. If it "works" in this manner, this is the best thing that can be said for it. Yet, a person who is relativistically oriented does not like arbitrarily to rule out *any* kind of evidence; he prefers the idea of an "open universe" in which anything is possible.

All operations in a reflective act must be performed openly and in a fashion that will enable other competent persons to repeat them. Each act of reflection must be able to supply its own recipe, so to speak; or, stated in another way, it must be subject to operational description. A mechanic overhauling a carburetor can describe each step along the way, and, if he does so and one is bright enough, one can repeat the operation. Scientific reflection is a *public* rather than a private road to truth. Although the foregoing rules have been described separately, it should be obvious that they are closely interrelated; each hinges to some degree upon the others.

BIBLIOGRAPHY

CHAPLIN, JAMES P., and T. S. KRAWIEC, *Systems and Theories of Psychology*, 2nd ed., New York: Holt, Rinehart and Winston, 1968.
A treatment of the evolution of psychological thought, which is traced from classical scholars to the major contemporary theories. Shows the continuity of thought from philosophy and physiology to psychology. Contains a good list of biographical sketches of contributors to psychological thought. Chapters 6–10 are especially pertinent to learning.
CONANT, JAMES B., *Modern Science and Modern Man*, Garden City, N.Y.: Doubleday, 1953.
An explanation of how every phase of our lives is becoming involved with scientific procedures, and how this revolution in living has carried with it a revolution in scientific outlook. Man, as a scientist, no longer is seeking absolute, but rather, workable, truth; he is becoming relativistic.
Contemporary Approaches to Cognition. A symposium held at the Uni-

versity of Colorado, Cambridge, Mass.: Harvard University Press, 1957.
For the advanced student. Includes a range of positions all of which focus on psychological, rather than behavioral, facts.

DESSE, JAMES, and Stewart H. Hulse, *The Psychology of Learning.* 3rd ed., New York: McGraw-Hill, 1967.
A scholarly but difficult presentation of neobehavioristic theory of learning. Includes an extensive list of references on learning.

FRANK, PHILIPP, *Relativity—A Richer Truth,* Boston: Beacon Press, 1950.
An examination and evaluation of the relativistic outlook, with a foreword by Albert Einstein. A key chapter, Chapter 22, is "How Can an Anti-Metaphysical View of Science Help Democracy?"

FULLAGAR, WILLIAM A., *et al., Readings for Educational Psychology,* 2nd ed., New York: Thomas Y. Crowell, 1964.
An excellent selection of readings with major emphasis upon learning. Especially recommended are No. 1, "The Nature of Learning Theories," by Hilgard; No. 5, "The Idea of Learning as Development of Insights," by Bayles; and No. 7, "Counseling as a Learning Process," by Combs.

GEIGER, GEORGE RAYMOND, *John Dewey in Perspective,* New York: Oxford University Press, 1958.
By an astute student of Dewey and the "relativistic" position which Dewey helped develop. This book is somewhat easier reading than most of Dewey's works, yet it gives an accurate picture of Dewey's thoughts.

HARRIS, THEODORE L., and Wilson E. Schwahn, *The Learning Process,* New York: Oxford University Press, 1961.
An exceptionally good book of readings on learning. Emphasizes experimental studies of learning and developmental and evaluational problems related to the learning process.

HEBB, DONALD O., *A Textbook of Psychology,* 2nd ed., Philadelphia: Saunders, 1966.
A textbook in general psychology which treats psychology as a biological, not a social, science. Mechanisms of behavior in learning, perception, and emotion are discussed in a thoroughly S-R associationistic manner.

HENRY, NELSON B., ed., *The Psychology of Learning,* Part II, *The Forty-first Yearbook of the National Society for the Study of Education.* Chicago, University of Chicago Press, 1942.
In Section 1: contemporary theories of learning; in Section 2: the implications of learning theories for education. Chapter 7, by T. R. McConnell, is an attempt to reconcile conditioning, connectionism, and field theory to form a synthesis of learning theories.

HILGARD, ERNEST R., and Gordon H. Bower, *Theories of Learning,* 3rd ed., New York: Appleton-Century-Crofts, 1966.
A systematic, critical presentation of the most prominent learning theories current among contemporary psychologists.

HOOK, SIDNEY, ed., *Dimensions of Mind*, New York University Press, 1960.
A symposium of 29 papers on the mind-body, mind-brain problem. Papers are grouped under "The Mind-Body Problem," "The Brain and the Machine," and "Concept Formation." Three major kinds of considerations undergird the papers —nature of experience or "raw feel," traditional dualistic language habits, and results of modern psychology and brain physiology.

KOCH, SIGMUND, *Psychology: A Study of a Science*, Vol. 2, *General Systematic Formulations, Learning, and Special Processes*, New York: McGraw-Hill, 1959.
A technical but highly informative volume, concerned with the general conceptual formulations of current psychologies. Each approach or theory is represented by a distinguished psychologist.

KÖHLER, WOLFGANG, *The Mentality of Apes*, New York: Vintage Books, 1959. Especially Chapter VII.
An extensive report of Köhler's experiments with animal learning during the period of World War I, at Tenerife.

LINZEY, GARDNER, and ELLIOT ARONSON, eds., *The Handbook of Social Psychology*, 2nd ed., Vol. 1, *Historical Introduction and Systematic Positions*, Reading, Mass.: Addison-Wesley, 1968.
Contains excellent presentations of seven systematic psychological approaches which have definite implications for learning as well as for social psychology. Stimulus-Response mathematical, cognitive, psycholo-analytic, field, role, and organization positions are presented.

LOGAN, FRANK A., *Fundamentals of Learning and Motivation*, Boston: Little Brown, 1970.
Presents various constructs of behavioristic psychology. Includes a glossary of terms.

MAY, ROLLO, *Psychology and the Human Dilemma*, New York: Van Nostrand Reinhold, 1967.
A psychiatrist's presentation of views that harmonize with Gestalt-field learning theory.

MELTON, ARTHUR W., ed., *Categories of Human Learning*, New York: Academic, 1964.
A symposium in the psychology of human learning. Concentrates upon definition and classification of learning theories. Difficult.

SAHAKIAN, WILLIAM S., *Psychology of Learning: Systems, Models, and Theories*, Chicago: Markham Publishing Company, 1970.
A contemporary summary of scientific learning systems. Somewhat encyclopaedic, but a good reference source.

SCHULTZ, DUANE P., *A History of Modern Psychology*, New York: Academic, 1969.
Traces 100 years of psychological thought including the rise and outcome of each system or school.

THORNDIKE, EDWARD L., *Selected Writings from a Connectionist's Psychology*, New York: Appleton-Century-Crofts, 1949.

A collection of Thorndike's papers to give students a firsthand knowledge of connectionist psychology. His autobiography gives the reader a picture of how educational psychology has developed.

WATSON, JOHN B., *Psychology from the Standpoint of a Behaviorist,* 2nd ed., Philadelphia: Lippincott, 1924.
An introductory psychology textbook written strictly from a mechanistic, behavoristic point of view.

WATSON, JOHN B., *The Ways of Behaviorism,* New York: Harper & Row, 1928.
An explanation of the what and why of behaviorism (which had been growing some 15 years) and why it opposes mentalistic concepts like instinct and unconscious.

WATSON, JOHN B., and WILLIAM McDOUGALL, *The Battle of Behaviorism,* New York: Norton, 1929.
A debate between McDougall, the eminent psychologist of instinct theory, and Watson, the upsurging behaviorist. The sharp conflict between mentalistic and physicalistic psychology becomes clear.

WERTHEIMER, MAX, *Productive Thinking,* enlarged ed., edited by Michael Wertheimer, New York: Harper & Row, 1959.
An analysis of the thinking process, by one of the three leading Gestalt psychologists. He developed the differences between associationistic and field study of thinking and showed how Gestalt psychology and reflective thinking are closely related.

WOLMAN, BENJAMIN B., *Contemporary Theories and Systems in Psychology,* New York: Harper & Row, 1960.
A comprehensive picture of contemporary psychological theory. It emphasizes concept formation, relationship of psychology to other sciences, and methods of research. Chapters 1–4 present S-R conditioning theories, and Chapters 10–13 Gestalt-field theories.

FIVE

How Does Skinner's Operant Conditioning Work?

Let the reader picture himself as a fourth grader, Dale Cooper, in a possible classroom of the future. At the first bell students enter the room; at the second bell they become silent. When opening exercises have been completed, the teacher says, "Arithmetic." Dale has been conditioned at this signal to place his arithmetic cylinder on his teaching machine, find where he left off yesterday, and proceed with conditioning himself to solve arithmetic problems. After 20 minutes the teacher says, "Reading," and in another 20 minutes, "Spelling." Each word is the appropriate stimulus for Dale to change cylinders on his machine. Then comes recess. At the sound of a bell with a different tone from that of the one which brought students into the room, they go out to the playground. Here, playground equipment has been adequately mechanized and sequenced so that there is little need for a teacher or any other supervisory personnel. The teacher uses the recess period to check, repair, and lubricate the machines.

The psychology that would support the emphasis on teaching machines for Dale's education has been developed by B. F. Skinner. Skinner has found *operant conditioning* highly effective in training lower animals, and he is confident that it promises equal success when used with children and youth. In operant conditioning, teachers are considered architects and builders of students' behavior. Learning objectives are divided in a large number of very small tasks and reinforced one by one. Operants —sets of acts—are reinforced or strengthened so as to increase the probability of their recurrence in the future. In this process it is of prime importance that teachers employ properly timed and spaced schedules of reinforcement.

Professor Skinner considers it the purpose of psychology to predict and control *behavior* of individual organisms. He insists upon limiting scientific psychological study to observable behavior of organism; his only data are those acquired by sensory observation. Since such terms as "will power," "sensation," "image," "drive," or "instinct" imply supposedly nonphysical events, he opposes their use by psychologists or teachers in any connection with their thinking scientifically about people. Behavior is ". . . the movement of an organism or of its parts in a frame of reference provided by the organism itself or by various external objects or fields of force."[1]

Skinner's psychology is a strictly engineering type of science which supposedly is devoid of theory in any usual sense. He insists that psychology is a science of overt behavior and only overt behavior. Accordingly, he defines learning as a change in probability of response. In most cases this change is brought about by operant conditioning.

Operant conditioning is the learning process whereby a response is made more probable or more frequent; an *operant* is strengthened—reinforced. Reinforcement was explained in Chapter 4, p. 93. An operant is a set of acts which constitutes an organism's doing something—raising its head, pushing a lever, saying "horse." It is so-called because behavior operates upon the environment and generates consequences. In the process of operant conditioning, operant responses are modified or changed. Reinforcement means that the probability of the repetition of certain classes of responses is increased.

Skinner thinks that nearly all human behavior is a product of operant reinforcement. He notes that in everyday life, in various fields including education, people constantly change the probabilities of responses of others by arranging reinforcing consequences. Furthermore, through their being operantly reinforced, people learn to keep their balance, walk, talk, play games,

[1]B. F. Skinner, *The Behavior of Organisms*, New York: Appleton-Century-Crofts, 1938, p. 6.

and handle tools and instruments; they perform a set of motions, reinforcement occurs, and the likelihood of their repeating the motions is increased. Thus, operant reinforcement improves the efficiency of behavior.

Whenever something reinforces a particular form of behavior, the chances are better that that behavior will be repeated. The task of psychologists is to gain more understanding of conditions under which reinforcement works best, and thereby open the way for cultural control through social engineering. To the many "natural" reinforcers of behavior, a host of artificial reinforcers may be added. "Any list of values is a list of reinforcers —conditioned or otherwise. We are so constituted that under certain circumstances food, water, sexual contact, and so on, will make any behavior which produces them more likely to occur again. Other things may acquire this power. . . . An organism can be reinforced by—can be made to 'choose'—almost any given state of affairs."[2]

HOW HAS SKINNER USED ANIMALS TO STUDY OPERANT REINFORCEMENT?

In general, experimental psychologists have tended not to relate their laws and theories to instances of learning in real life.[3] However, Professor Skinner and his associates have experienced remarkable success in training animals. It is probable that even professional animal trainers, through study of the procedures used in operant conditioning, could improve their techniques. In one college class period, by presenting food to a hungry pigeon at the right time, Skinner has implanted in the bird three or four well-defined responses such as turning around, pacing the floor in a figure-eight pattern, stretching the neck, and stamping the foot.

Skinner's basic thesis is that, since an organism tends in the future to do what it was doing at the time of reinforcement, one can, by baiting each step of the way, lead it to do very much what the experimenter wishes it to do. Using this thesis as a basis for his procedure, he has taught rats to use a marble to obtain food from a vending machine, pigeons to play a modified game of tennis, and dogs to operate the pedal of a refuse can so as to retrieve a bone.

[2]B. F. Skinner, *Cumulative Record*, New York: Appleton-Century-Crofts, 1959, p. 33. (This and other excerpts from *Cumulative Record* are reprinted by permission of Appleton-Century-Crofts.)

[3]See Donald K. Adams *et al.*, *Learning Theory, Personality Theory, and Clinical Research*, New York: John Wiley, 1954, p. 2.

Skinner has centered his study on lower animals because their behavior is simpler, conditions surrounding them may be controlled better, basic processes are revealed more readily and can be recorded over longer periods of time, and observations are not complicated by social relations between subjects and the psychologist.[4] However, more recently he has conducted research on learning using human beings of various ages and abilities.

The "Skinner box" is a simple box that contains a rat, a lever, and a device for delivering a pellet of food each time the rat presses the lever. Recording devices are set outside the box so that the experimenter can go home at night and see in the morning what the rat has been doing. There also are Skinner boxes for the study of pigeons and other animals. A rat or pigeon learns rapidly in a Skinner box because in the box there is little else for him to do. Skinner says, "The barest possible statement of the process is this: we make a given consequence contingent [dependent] upon certain physical properties of behavior (the upward movement of the head), and the behavior is then observed to increase in frequency."[5]

A pigeon's behavior can be reinforced in such a way that neck stretching will become habitual. The pigeon is placed in a cage so that the experimenter can sight across its head at a scale pinned on the far wall of the cage. The height at which the head is normally held is established on the scale; then some line, which is reached only infrequently, is selected. The experimenter, keeping his eye on the scale, quickly opens the food tray whenever the bird's head rises above the established line. As a result, learning occurs; ". . . we observe an immediate change in the frequency with which the head crosses the line. We also observe, and this is of some importance theoretically, that higher lines are now being crossed. We may advance almost immediately to a higher line in determining when food is to be presented. In a minute or two, the bird's posture has changed so that the top of the head seldom falls below the line which we first chose."[6]

By training two pigeons separately to do their parts in a total performance, Skinner has constructed a social scene within which competition is exemplified by two pigeons playing a modified game of ping-pong. He accomplished the training through

[4]B. F. Skinner, *Science and Human Behavior*, New York: Macmillan, 1953, p. 38.
[5]*Ibid.*, p. 64. (This and other excerpts from *Science and Human Behavior* are reprinted by permission of The Macmillan Company.)
[6]*Ibid.*, pp. 63–64.

operant reinforcement. First, the pigeons were reinforced when they merely pushed the ball. Then, when the ball got by one pigeon, the other was reinforced. He also has trained pigeons to coordinate their behavior in dancing in a cooperative manner which rivals the skills of human dancers.

Reinforcement procedures may vary according to intervals of time and the number of responses between reinforcements. A schedule of reinforcement is a pattern of "rewarding" behavior based upon a fixed time interval and a fixed number of responses between "rewards." In a laboratory, Skinner and Ferster have obtained performances appropriate to each of nine different ratio-interval schedules.[7] When a stimulus is presented, the pigeon executes the performance appropriate to its reinforcement schedule. Then, when another stimulus is presented, the pigeon executes the performance appropriate to its specific schedule. Skinner thinks that this achievement makes more plausible the extension of laboratory results to daily human life. To him learning, in the everyday life of people, is more complicated but nevertheless of the same basic nature as a lower animal's learning through operant conditioning.

In operant conditioning experiments, the species of organism studied has made surprisingly little difference. "Comparable results have been obtained with pigeons, rats, dogs, monkeys, human children, and most recently, . . . human psychotic subjects. In spite of great phylogenetic differences, all these organisms show amazingly similar properties of the learning process."[8]

WHAT PSYCHOLOGICAL THEORY UNDERLIES SKINNER'S TEACHING PROCEDURES?

Throughout his study and writings, Professor Skinner has adhered rigorously to a basic conviction that psychologists should restrict their study to the correlations between stimuli and responses and not meddle with any "make-believe" psychology which constructs intervening physiological or mental links between stimuli and responses. He considers only past events to be relevant to prediction of behavior. Accordingly he states, "Even if we could discover a spider's felt intention or sense of purpose, we could not offer it as a cause of the behavior."[9] So,

[7]See C. B. Ferster and B. F. Skinner, *Schedules of Reinforcement*, New York: Appleton-Century-Crofts, 1957.

[8]See Skinner, *Cumulative Record*, *op. cit.*, p. 148.

[9]B. F. Skinner, *Contingencies of Reinforcement*, New York: Appleton-Century-Crofts, 1969, p. 194.

any mentalistic description of behavior offers no real explanation of it. Instead, it only impedes its more effective analysis. The study of either physiological or mentalistic intervening variables between stimuli and responses constitutes a dummy physiology or psychology doing duty for truth when facts are missing.

In a sense Skinner's psychology, operant behaviorism, is a modern extension of the earlier mechanistic stimulus-response psychologies—connectionism as developed by Thorndike and behaviorism as developed by Watson. A *mechanistic* psychology presupposes that all human actions are sequential *reactions* to external or internal stimuli. Thus, it strives to reduce all psychological phenomena to physical elements.[10] Thorndike dealt with both physical and mental elements but was always mechanistic in his study of man. Watson, too, was mechanistic; however, he limited his study to the behavior of biological organisms. Skinner, like both Thorndike and Watson, assumes that man is neutral and passive and that all behavior can be described in sequential mechanistic terms. In his study of man and animals, he constantly is mechanistic and elementistic; to him, psychology is the *science of behavior.*

What is the meaning of the "science of behavior"?

Skinner sees a great and crucial future for a science of behavior. In his view, since a science of behavior is concerned with demonstrating the consequences of cultural practices, there is reason to believe that presence of such a science will be an essential mark of the culture or cultures that will survive in the future, and that the culture most likely to survive is the one in which the methods of science are most effectively applied to the problems of human behavior.[11] Consequently, throughout his work he has striven constantly to be scientific to the nth degree. He sees "science" as ". . . more than a set of attitudes. It is a search for order, for uniformities, for lawful relations among the events in nature. It begins, as we all begin, by observing single episodes, but it quickly passes on to the general rule, to scientific law."[12] Thus, he places himself in line as a contemporary representative of inductive, atomistic science following the earlier pattern of Francis Bacon and John Stuart

[10]See Chapter 4, pp. 64–65 for further descriptions of the meaning of "mechanistic" as the term is used here.
[11]Skinner, *Science and Human Behavior, op. cit.,* p. 446.
[12]*Ibid.,* p. 13.

Mill. One can get the "flavor" of Skinner's work only through reading his books and papers. His frequent usage of the definite article *the* as contrasted with his infrequent usage of the indefinite articles *a* or *an* is quickly apparent. Like other scientific-realistic scientists, he assumes that this practice adds to objectivity and makes reports of studies more "scientific."

A scientific-realistic definition of science. Skinner works on the basic assumption that there is order in nature, including human behavior, and that it is the function of science to *discover* the order; this is the commitment of a scientific realistic, as opposed to that of a positive-relativistic scientist.[13] Within Skinner's scientific-realistic outlook, science is concerned with discovery of preexistent laws, which govern the world about us. Knowledge of these laws enhances predictability, and thereby control, of the variables that cause events to occur. This supposedly is as true in psychology as in physics or chemistry. Thus, man, through discovery of laws and organization of them into systems, enables himself to deal effectively with aspects of the naturalistic world. "Science is in large part a direct analysis of reinforcing systems found in nature; it is concerned with facilitating the behavior which is reinforced by them."[14]

Skinner recognizes that ". . . it is time to insist that science does not progress by carefully designed steps called 'experiments' each of which has a well-defined beginning and end. Science is a continuous and often a disorderly and accidental process."[15] Nevertheless, he leaves unrecognized the relativistic principle that "reality" consists of that which we make of what we gain from our environment through the use of our senses and is ". . . definable as something which might, should, or does make a difference to someone or something."[16]

Man, a subject of science. According to Skinner, it is not to be assumed that human behavior has any peculiar properties that require a unique method or special kind of knowledge. "An experimental analysis [of behavior] describes stimuli in the language of physics."[17] So, the variables of psychology, like the variables of any other science, must be described in physical terms. In Skinner's psychology, the dependent variable in a situa-

13Skinner, *Cumulative Record, op. cit.,* pp. 88–89.
14Skinner, *Contingencies of Reinforcement, op. cit.,* p. 143.
15Skinner, *Cumulative Record, op. cit.,* p. 98.
16Ernest E. Bayles, *Democratic Educational Theory,* New York: Harper & Row, 1960, p. 94.
17Skinner, *Contingencies of Reinforcement, op. cit.,* pp. 78–79.

tion is the behavior of an individual organism. The independent variable consists of external conditions of which the behavior is a function. This means that behavior operates upon the environment to generate consequences; *it* behaves.

The laws of the science of psychology are as definite as those of any other science. Skinner says, "It is decidedly not true that a horse may be led to water but cannot be made to drink."[18] He thinks that, through applying the laws of psychology and arranging a history of severe deprivation, it could be made absolutely sure that drinking would occur; likewise, a desired behavior can be caused in a human being.

Skinner's goal in psychology is to achieve the degree of prediction and control in regard to human behavior that has been achieved by the physical sciences. The scientist of behavior evaluates probability of behavior and explores conditions that determine it. Through gathering data in regard to the frequencies of responses that have already occurred, he is able to make accurate statements about the likelihood of occurrence of a single future response of the same kind; frequency of response indicates probability of response. "We are concerned, then, with the causes of human behavior. We want to know why men behave as they do. Any condition or event which can be shown to have an effect upon behavior must be taken into account. By discovering and analyzing these causes, we can predict behavior; to the extent that we can manipulate them, we can control behavior."[19]

The problem of predicting whether a man will commit suicide is of the same nature as the problem of predicting the probability of explosion of the first atomic bomb. The basic datum in scientific analysis of behavior is probability. However, the actual observed dependent variable is frequency of response. Since much important human behavior occurs only once, it cannot be studied in terms of frequencies. A man may marry only once, he may engage in a business deal only once, or he will commit suicide only once. So, like the probability of the first atomic bomb explosion, some behavior cannot be stated in terms of frequency. Nevertheless, it can be evaluated in terms of probabilities of many of the component events which can be based upon data in the form of frequencies, and any behavior may be studied in terms of its component parts.[20]

[18]Skinner, *Science and Human Behavior, op. cit.,* p. 32.
[19]*Ibid.,* p. 23.
[20]Skinner, *Cumulative Record, op. cit.,* p. 76.

How is the science of behavior related to determinism?

Skinner's psychology implies a strictly naturalistic determinism. He notes that a scientific conception of human behavior dictates one practice and a philosophy of personal freedom another; and that a scientific conception of human behavior entails the acceptance of an assumption of determinism. Determinism means that behavior is caused, and that the behavior which appears is the only kind which could have appeared. Skinner emphasizes that the same type of determinism that is commonly accepted as applying to machines applies equally to human beings. Accordingly he states: "Man is a machine, but he is a very complex one. At present he is far beyond the powers of men to construct —except, of course, in the usual biological way."[21]

As machines have become more lifelike, living organisms have been found to be more like machines. Today, many machines are deliberately designed to operate in ways which resemble "human behavior." "Man has, in short, created the machine in his own image."[22] Since mechanical calculators now solve equations too difficult or too time-consuming even for human mathematicians, human beings have lost much of their uniqueness.

Determinism carries with it the implication that environment determines an individual even when he alters his own environment. "It does not matter that the individual may take it upon himself to control the variables of which his own behavior is a function or, in a broad sense, to engage in the design of his own culture. He does this only because he is the product of a culture which generates self-control or cultural design as a mode of behavior."[23] "All human behavior, including the behavior of machines which man builds to behave in his place, is ultimately to be accounted for in terms of the phylogenic contingencies of survival which have produced man as a species and the ontogenic contingencies of reinforcement which have produced him as an individual."[24]

Skinner says, "The scientist, like any organism, is the product of a unique history."[25] He considers science of major importance in human affairs, but recognizes that even scientists and science are not free. Science, too, is a part of a naturally determined course of events, and it cannot interfere with that course. Thus,

[21]Skinner, *Contingencies of Reinforcement, op. cit.,* p. 294.
[22]Skinner, *Science and Human Behavior, op. cit.,* p. 46.
[23]*Ibid.,* p. 448.
[24]Skinner, *Contingencies of Reinforcement, op. cit.,* p. 297.
[25]Skinner, *Cumulative Record, op. cit.,* p. 99.

the actions of scientists also must be included in any adequate account of processes of which it itself is an example.[26]

HOW IS OPERANT CONDITIONING NONPHYSIOLOGICAL AND NONPHENOMENOLOGICAL?

A system of operant conditioning has no place for study of either physiological or phenomenological psychology. *Physiological psychology* is devoted to study of physiological, neurological, and biological functions within an organism. *Phenomenological psychology* centers upon what events mean to the persons involved. In a sense it is similar to physiological psychology in that it, too, is centered upon what takes place within a person. However, it differs sharply from physiological psychology in that major emphasis is placed upon the process of conscious experiencing. Because Skinner rejects the use of the intervening variables of both physiological and phenomenological psychology, his friends sometimes speak of his dealing with the "empty organism."

Nonphysiological psychology

Skinner is convinced that the practice of looking inside an organism for an explanation of behavior has tended to obscure the variables that lie outside the organism and are immediately available for scientific analysis. These variables outside the organism are in its environmental history and its immediate environment. Their study permits behavior to be explained scientifically just as behavior of nonliving objects is explained scientifically by physicists. These independent variables are of many sorts and their relation to behavior often is subtle and complex; nevertheless, according to Skinner, it is only through analyzing them that we may hope to reach an adequate account of behavior.

Since statements about operations of the nervous system are not expressed in the same terms and cannot be confirmed by the same method of observation as the facts for which they are supposed to account, they are theories. Thus, Skinner feels that they can make little contribution to a scientific psychology. In the present stage of science an adequate neurological explanation of behavior is impossible. However, this fact in no way implies that a scientific psychology of learning cannot be established separate from any neurological theory.

[26]Skinner, *Science and Human Behavior, op. cit.,* p. 446.

Nonphenomenological psychology

Statements about mental events, like neurological statements, also are theoretical. Thus, Skinner belittles attempts of psychologists to infer what a physical situation *means* to an organism or to distinguish between the physical world and the psychological world of experience. He constantly emphasizes that events affecting an organism must be capable of being described in the language of physical science.[27] To him, the "free inner man," who is held responsible for the behavior of the external biological organism, is only a prescientific substitute for the external causes of behavior which are susceptible to scientific analysis. Hence there is no place in scientific psychology for study of the inner personal experience of man as such.

Skinner sees the practice of some scientists who indicate that they are describing only half the universe and that there is another half—a world of self, mind, or consciousness—as a part of the cultural heritage from which science has emerged but which now stands in the way of a unified scientific account of nature. Even in discussing the higher human function, thinking, Skinner sees little need for the concept *self*. He recognizes that behavior is a function of the environment, that environment presumably means any event in the universe capable of affecting the organism, and that a very small part of this universe is private, that is, it is enclosed within the organism's own skin. Thus, some independent variables, for example, an aching tooth, may be related to behavior in a unique way. However, he sees no reason to suppose that the stimulating effect of an inflamed tooth is essentially different from that of a hot stove.[28]

Since the self is not identical with the physical organism, such a concept is not essential in any analysis of behavior. The concept may have had an early advantage in representing a relatively coherent response system, but it is hazardous in that it may lead us to expect consistencies and functional integrities which do not exist. "The alternative to the use of the concept [self] is simply to deal with demonstrated covariations in the strength of responses."[29]

Private events. Skinner thinks that students of a science of behavior should face the problem of privacy, but that they should do so without abandoning the basic position of "radical behaviorism." Radical behaviorists, including professor Skinner,

[27]*Ibid.*, p. 36.
[28]*Ibid.*, p. 258.
[29]*Ibid.*, p. 286.

think that: "An adequate science of behavior must consider events taking place within the skin of the organism, not as physiological mediators of behavior, but as part of behavior itself."[30] Both private and public events have the same kind of physical dimensions. Thus, contingencies that involve private stimuli also follow from simple mechanical relations between stimuli, responses, and reinforcing consequences.

Private stimuli are either interoceptive or proprioceptive ones. Interoceptive stimuli are those received by nerve endings in the internal organs, for example, the stimuli provided by hunger pangs or a full bladder. Proprioceptive stimuli are received through afferent nerve endings in the muscles of the body, for example, the stimuli provided by lame or sore muscles.

It is because a person's community cannot reinforce his self-descriptive responses consistently that he cannot describe or otherwise know events occurring within his own skin as subtly and precisely as he knows events in the outside world.[31] Nevertheless, "So far as behavior is concerned, both sensation and perception may be analyzed as forms of stimulus control."[32] All of the ways of changing a man's mind consist of either verbal or nonverbal manipulation of his environment.

Conscious experience and feelings. Persons learn to see that they are seeing only because a verbal community arranges for them to do so. Even when the thing being seen is not present, as in a dream, contingencies produced by the verbal environment may set up self-descriptive responses that describe the behavior of seeing. "The heart of the behavioristic position on conscious experience may be summed up in this way: seeing does not imply something seen. We acquire the behavior of seeing under stimulation from actual objects, but it may occur in the absence of these objects under the control of other variables. . . . We also acquire the behavior of seeing-that-we-are-seeing when we are seeing actual objects, but it may also occur in their absence."[33]

Any personal feelings, at their best, are accompaniments, not causes, of behavior. Furthermore, covert responses are not the causes of related overt ones; both are the products of common independent variables. Consequently, the *conditions* that one feels, not one's feelings as such, are the important factors in a study of behavior. "A radical behaviorism denies the existence

[30]Skinner, *Contingencies of Reinforcement, op. cit.,* p. 228.
[31]*Ibid.,* p. 230.
[32]*Ibid.,* p. 235.
[33]*Ibid.,* pp. 234–235.

of a mental world, not because it is contentious or jealous of a rival, but because those who claim to be studying the other world necessarily talk about the world of behavior in ways which conflict with an experimental analysis."[34]

In opposing the "inner man" concept of human behavior, Skinner notes the similarity of the inner man concept to a "God within" who does not occupy space and thus may be multiplied at will, as is done in the Freudian pattern. He points out that as more of the behavior of organisms have come to be explained in terms of responses to stimuli through the scientific development of psychology, some part of the control of the organism has passed from a hypothetical inner entity to the external environment. "The 'will' has retreated up the spinal cord, through the lower and then the higher parts of the brain, and finally, with the conditioned reflex, has escaped through the front of the head."[35]

In Skinner's system there is no place for the statement that behavior is under the control of an incentive or goal. A scientific psychology, as Skinner defines it, replaces statements that might use such words as "incentive," "goal," or "purpose" with statements about conditioning. Instead of saying that a man behaves because of the consequences that are to follow his behavior, we simply state that he behaves thus and so because of the consequences that have followed similar behavior in the past. When one is "looking for something" he is emitting responses that in the past produced something as a consequence. When one says, "I am looking for my glasses," what he really means is ". . . 'I have lost my glasses,' 'I shall stop what I am doing when I find my glasses,' or 'When I have done this in the past, I have found my glasses.' "[36]

Professor Skinner uses the analogy that astronomers may speak of the sun rising and setting, but they do not do so when they are performing the role of scientists. Likewise, psychologists and teachers properly may use such literary descriptions of human activity as the person *expected, hoped, observed, felt, knew, remembered, feared, was hungry,* or *was anxious.* But as behavioral scientists they should report only observed facts such as the *organism was reinforced when it pushed the lever,* the *intake of food was so much,* or *aversive stimuli or preaversive stimuli were present.*[37]

Since the terms *pleasant* and *satisfying* do not refer to any

[34]*Ibid.,* p. 267.
[35]Skinner, *Science and Human Behavior, op. cit.,* pp. 48–49.
[36]*Ibid.,* p. 90
[37]Skinner, *Contingencies of Reinforcement, op. cit.,* pp. 236–240.

physical property of reinforcing events, and physical sciences use neither of these terms nor their equivalents, they, too, should be deleted from the language of a science of psychology. Furthermore, since behavior is always the behavior of an individual, a science of behavior that concerns only the behavior of groups is not likely to be of help in understanding particular cases. Thus, "A 'social force' is no more useful in manipulating behavior than an inner state of hunger, anxiety, or skepticism."[38]

WHAT IS THE NATURE OF OPERANT CONDITIONING OR REINFORCEMENT?

In the pigeon experiment, the process of *operant conditioning* is the change in frequency with which the head is lifted to a given height, the *reinforcer* is food, and the *reinforcement* is food presentation when the response is emitted. The *operant* is the behavior upon which the reinforcement is contingent—the height to which the head must be raised.

In operant conditioning, the important stimulus is the one immediately following the response, not the one preceding it. Any emitted response that leads to reinforcement is thereby strengthened. However, it is not the specific response (R) that is strengthened, but rather the *general tendency* to make the response. Hence, carefully stated, an operant is a class of responses of which a specific response is an instance or member. A rat presses a lever and gets food. Because of this, the rat will be more likely to press the lever again. "What is changed is the future probability of response in the same *class*."[39] The operant as a class of behavior, rather than the response as a particular instance, is reinforced. It is not correct to say that an operant reinforcement strengthened the response which preceded it; the response has already occurred and cannot be changed. What has been changed is that the probability that that class of responses will occur in the future has been increased. Since each reinforcement builds up a reserve of responses, a pigeon may continue to raise its head or a rat to press the lever several, or even many, times after food has ceased to appear.

The law of operant conditioning is that, if the occurrence of an operant is followed by presentation of a reinforcing stimulus, the strength—probability—is increased. What is strengthened is not a stimulus-response connection; the operant requires no specific eliciting stimulus. Insofar as the organism is concerned,

[38]Skinner, *Science and Human Behavior, op. cit.,* p. 36.
[39]*Ibid.,* p. 87.

the only important property of the operant contingency is time; the reinforcer follows the response. How this is brought about does not matter. The process of operant conditioning may be described adequately without any mention of a stimulus that acts before the response is made. In reinforcing a pigeon's neck stretching, it is necessary only for one to wait for neck stretching to occur. It is not necessary for the experimenter to elicit it.

In operant conditioning, the subject's seeing a connection is in no way essential. Skinner considers Thorndike's expression "trial-and-error learning" to be superfluous and out of place. As he has observed the behavior of pigeons and other animals, he has seen no reason to call the movements being taught "trials" and any movements that did not achieve a specified consequence "errors." "The statement that the bird 'learns that it will get food by stretching its neck' is an inaccurate report of what has happened."[40] A Gestalt-field explanation of how the bird learns, of course, would be just this.

Skinner observes that behavior that is more likely to be reinforced is the more likely to occur. Presence of a cat is the occasion upon which the response "cat" is likely to be reinforced. However, a stimulus-eliciting "cat" is in no way an essential part of the operant-conditioning process. Operant reinforcement of a behavior is contingent—dependent—upon a response, not the stimulus that gave rise to that response. The stimulus that preceded the response—the presence of a cat—is a discriminative, not an eliciting, one. "The discriminative stimulus does not elicit a response, it simply alters a probability of occurrence."[41]

Skinner revised Thorndike's law of effect. "Instead of saying that a man behaves because of the consequences which *are* to follow his behavior, we simply say that he behaves because of the consequences which *have* followed similar behavior in the past. This is, of course, the Law of Effect or operant conditioning."[42] The law of effect exemplified in operant conditioning simply specifies a procedure for altering the probability of a chosen response. By progressively changing the *contingencies of reinforcement* in the direction of the desired behavior, one can see learning occur.

What is a contingency of reinforcement?

A contingency of reinforcement is a sequence within which a response is followed by a reinforcing stimulus. The ordered

---

40*Ibid.*, p. 64.
41*Ibid.*, p. 110.
42Skinner, *Science and Human Behavior, op. cit.*, p. 87.

interrelations between three terms or variables compose such a contingency. These variables are (1) a discriminative stimulus (S^D), (2) the behavior or response itself (R), and (3) the reinforcing stimulus (S^{rein}). A descriminative stimulus (S^D) occurs prior to the response (R) being reinforced. It is any stimulus that arises from the nature of the space within which the organism is placed, the apparatus used to sense occurrences of the response, or any special stimulating devices that may be used. Thus, it sets the conditions under which a behavior occurs. The reinforcing stimulus (S^{rein}) follows the discriminative stimulus and the response and renders consequences to the organism.[43]

Operant reinforcement, then, not only strengthens a given response; it also may bring the response under the control of a discriminative stimulus. But the discriminative or controlling stimulus does not elicit the response, it merely sets the occasion upon which the response is more likely to occur.[44] So, when a response occurs and is reinforced the probability that it will occur again in the presence of similar stimuli is increased.

In a contingency the occurrence of an operant—response—is *followed* by presentation of a reinforcing stimulus, and the strength—probability—of recurrence of the operant is increased. The three-term contingency of operant reinforcement occurs when a child is taught to read; a given response is reinforced with "Right" or "Wrong" according to how the student responds to the appropriate visual stimulus—word or sentence.

The key to successful teaching or training is to analyze the effect of reinforcement and design techniques that manipulate the process with considerable precision—to set up specific reinforcing contingencies. In this way the behavior of an individual organism may be brought under precise control. Implicit in operant behaviorism is the conviction that "When all relevant variables have been arranged, an organism will or will not respond. If it does not, it cannot. If it can, it will."[45]

How does operant differ from respondent or reflexive conditioning?

Reflexive learning involves such situations as are described in the Pavlovian dog studies. Essentially it is a process of stimulus substitution. An organism supposedly responds reflexively to a natural or unconditioned stimulus. A new stimulus is presented

[43]Skinner, *Contingencies of Reinforcement, op. cit.,* p. 23.
[44]*Ibid.,* p. 175.
[45]Skinner, *Science and Human Behavior, op. cit.,* p. 112.

along with the original stimulus and the organism comes to respond to the new stimulus in the same way it formerly did to the original one. The new stimulus becomes a conditioned stimulus; the organism has learned. In reflexive or respondent conditioning the key stimulus is the one that precedes the response. Whereas reflexive learning is an S-R process, operant learning is an R-S one.

In operant learning, the most significant stimulus is that which immediately follows the response. Any modification of the environment constitutes a stimulus. Operant behavior is that behavior which operates upon the environment to generate consequences. Notice that in this process not the person or the environment but it—behavior—behaves; behavior is a phenomenon of nature. Just as wind blows, behavior behaves.

Although Skinner acknowledges two kinds of learning—operant and reflexive—he places far greater emphasis upon operant learning, which is under the control of its consequences. He sees most human behavior and consequently nearly all human conditioning or learning as operant. He feels that, if all the behavior which falls into the pattern of simple reflexes were assembled, it would represent only a very small fraction of the total behavior of an organism. He is convinced that early investigators overworked the principle of reflexive conditioning and made exaggerated claims for it. However, he warns that the area of reflex behavior should not be overlooked. To ignore completely the principle of the conditioned reflex would be unwarranted. But "It is neither plausible nor expedient to conceive of the organism as a complicated jack-in-the-box with a long list of tricks, each of which may be evoked by pressing the proper button. The greater part of the behavior of the intact organism is not under this primitive sort of stimulus control. The environment affects the organism in many ways which are not conveniently classed as 'stimuli,' and even in the field of stimulation only a small part of the forces acting upon the organism elicit responses in the invariable manner of reflex action."[46] The environment is so constructed that certain things tend to happen together. Respondent conditioning is the effect of this phenomenon upon behavior. When certain events like the color and taste of ripe fruit occur together, an organism responds in the same manner to either stimulus, color, or taste. It has learned this through respondent conditioning. However, the importance of this kind of learning has been emphasized far too much. Behavior such as eating a meal or driving

[46]*Ibid.*, pp. 49–50.

a car shows but little respondent character; most of it is operant in nature.

WHAT ARE THE PROCESSES OF OPERANT REINFORCEMENT AND EXTINCTION?

In operant conditioning, an operant is strengthened through its *reinforcement* or weakened through its *extinction*. The psychologist's task is simply to account for probability of responses in terms of a history of reinforcement and extinction. The effect of *reinforcement* always is to increase the probability of response. Extinction is the reverse of reinforcement. When a reinforcing stimulus no longer occurs following a response, the response becomes less and less frequent; this is operant *extinction*. "Conditioning builds up a predisposition to respond—a 'reserve'— which extinction exhausts."[47] We will discuss *extinction* on pp. 139–140 but first we describe the kinds of reinforcers and types of reinforcement.

What are the two kinds of reinforcers?

Any stimulus whose presentation or removal increases the probability of a response is a reinforcer. Consequently, there are two kinds of reinforcers or reinforcing events—positive and negative. A positive reinforcer is any stimulus the *presentation* of which strengthens the behavior upon which it is made contingent; a negative reinforcer is any stimulus the *withdrawal* of which strengthens that behavior. Since in both cases responses are strengthened, reinforcement is taking place. A positive reinforcement consists of presenting a stimulus, of adding something— food, water, or a teacher's smile—to an organism's environment. A negative reinforcement consists of removing something—a loud noise, an electric shock, or a teacher's frown—from the situation. In both of these cases the probability that the response will recur is increased.

Although in lay usage both positive and negative reinforcers are "rewards," Skinner warns against defining a positive reinforcer as pleasant or satisfying and a negative reinforcer as annoying. "It would be as difficult to show that the reinforcing power of an aversion stimulus is due to its unpleasantness as to show that the reinforcing power of a positive reinforcer is due to its pleasantness."[48] When a person reports that an event

47Skinner, *Cumulative Record, op. cit.,* p. 53.
48Skinner, *Science and Human Behavior, op. cit.,* p. 173.

is pleasant, this simply means that the event is of such kind that it reinforces him. Physical science uses no such terms as "pleasant" and "unpleasant" or their equivalents. The terms in no way refer to physical properties of reinforcing agents.

Is punishment reinforcement?

Punishment is a basically different process from reinforcement. Whereas reinforcement involves presentation of a positive reinforcer or removal of a negative one, punishment consists of presentation of a negative stimulus or removal of a positive one. Again, whereas reinforcement is defined in terms of strengthening of a response, punishment supposedly is a process which weakens a response. Putting it succinctly, when a stimulus is involved in *strengthening* a response there is reinforcement; when a stimulus is presented or withdrawn in an attempt to *weaken* a response, there is punishment.

Results of experiments indicate that punishment does not permanently reduce a tendency to respond. Thorndike's experiments with human subjects indicated that a reward strengthened the behavior that preceded it but that punishment did not weaken it. Through reward, behavior may be stamped in; but the converse, that through punishment it can be stamped out, does not hold. Whereas reinforcement can be used to good advantage in controlling other organisms, in the long run punishment works to the disadvantage of both the punished organism and the punishing agency. Its results are neither predictable nor dependable. Extinction—permitting a behavior to die out by not reinforcing it—and not punishment is the appropriate process for breaking habits.

What are the types of operant reinforcement?

There are two rather distinct types of operant reinforcements—stimulus discrimination and response differentiation. Nearly all human learning can be classified under these two. However, the process of respondent (reflexive) conditioning must not be completely ignored.

Through operant reinforcement a relatively complete new unit of behavior may be learned or an existing unit of behavior may be refined. In general, reinforcement that leads to behavior acquirement is a process of discrimination of stimuli, whereas behavior refinement or skill development is a process of differentiation of responses.

Discrimination of stimuli. Operant discrimination is the establishment of a certain type of behavior that occurs as the result of a given stimulus either preceding or accompanying that behavior and the behavior's then being reinforced. If an operant behavior is reinforced by S^{rein} when a discriminative stimulus S^D is present but is not reinforced when the S^D is not present, the tendency for the organism to respond with that operant behavior when the S^D is present gradually becomes strengthened, and the tendency for it to respond in like manner when not the S^D but other stimuli are present is gradually extinguished. As stated on p. 133, S^{rein} symbolizes the reinforcing stimulus, which follows the operant response (R), and S^D—discriminative stimulus—indicates the stimulus that either precedes or accompanies the operant response or behavior (R).

Through the use of a discriminative stimulus followed by reinforcement, by giving a pigeon pellets when it stretches its neck and a light is on, it can be made to be more likely to respond by stretching its neck at times when a light is on. Imitative behavior is an example of the result of discriminative operant reinforcement. Such behavior does not arise because of any inherent reflexive or mentalistic mechanism but develops in the history of the individual as a result of discriminative reinforcements. The visual stimulation of someone's waving a hand is the occasion upon which waving a hand probably received reinforcement. The reinforcement, not the stimulation from the other person's waving his hand, is the cause of future hand waving in similar situations. Because objects in shop windows into which other people are looking are likely to reinforce looking into such windows, when a person sees other people looking into a shop window he too is likely to look. The expressions "taking an interest" or "attending" are commonly used to describe the consequence of discriminative operant reinforcement. "Attention is a controlling *relation*—the relation between a response and a discriminative stimulus. When someone is paying attention he is under special control of a stimulus.[49]

Operant discrimination of a stimulus causes an organism readily to respond in a given manner when the occasion is appropriate for it to do so. In an elementary school room a teacher says "yellow"; the student points to yellow on a color chart; he then is reinforced for doing so, but only on those occasions when the teacher first has said "yellow." In this way the student is conditioned to point to yellow only after the teacher, or someone similar to the teacher, has said "yellow."

[49] *Ibid.*, p. 123.

In a secondary school mathematics class the teacher says $(x + y)^2$, the student says $(x^2 + 2xy + y^2)$, and the behavior is reinforced by the teacher's saying "correct." However, should the student say $(x^2 + 2xy + y^2)$ after the teacher had said $(x - y)^2$, the teacher would say nothing.

Rules, laws, and maxims constitute a special category of discriminative stimuli; as well as specifying the occasions upon which a behavior will occur, they also often describe the behavior itself, and its reinforcing consequences. Thus, each rule, law, or maxim is effective as the first part of a set of contingencies of reinforcement.[50] Whereas behavior that is reinforced is under the control of *succeeding* stimuli; rules, laws, and maxims are under the control of *prior* ones.

Differentiation of responses.   Skills are improved through differentiating reinforcements of varying responses. Many differentiating reinforcements may be supplied automatically by mechanical exigencies of the environment of an organism. To throw a ball skillfully, a person must release it at the proper moment; instances in which release comes before or after the proper moment are not reinforced. However, in more complex skill learning, reinforcement must be supplied by a teacher. In this process, any reinforcement that develops skill must be immediate. "By reinforcing a series of successive approximations, we bring a rare response to a very high probability in a short time."[51]

Through the procedure of operant conditioning, within which differentiation of responses is reinforced, a hungry pigeon that is well adapted to the experimental situation and the food tray usually can be brought to respond by pecking a specific spot, in two or three minutes. To get the pigeon to peck a specific spot as quickly as possible, the bird first is given food when it turns slightly in the direction of the spot. This increases the frequency of turning toward the spot. Reinforcement is then withheld until the bird makes a slight movement toward the spot. Then positions that are successively closer to the spot are reinforced. Then reinforcement is given only when the head is moved slightly forward, and finally only when the beak actually makes contact with the spot.

In target practice a rifleman needs a report of the accuracy of the shot from time to time to maintain the reinforcing power of feedback. However, after some practice he eventually knows before the target is hit whether the shot was good or bad. His own behavior generates a stimulating feedback. Hits and misses

---

[50]Skinner, *Contingencies of Reinforcement, op. cit.,* pp. 160–170.
[51]Skinner, *Science and Human Behavior, op. cit.,* p. 92.

generate different forms of this feedback. Likewise, good form in bowling is reinforced by feedback from the bowler's body.

What is extinction?

We know that, in general, when we engage in behavior which no longer "pays off," we find ourselves less inclined to behave in that way again. If we get no answers to telephone calls, we eventually stop telephoning. In operant behaviorism this phenomenon would be described by saying that when reinforcement is no longer forthcoming, a response becomes less and less frequent. This is the process of operant extinction.

Operant extinction takes place much more slowly than does operant reinforcement. However, as an organism responds less and less, a uniform process of extinction may be detected. Since behavior during extinction is a result of the conditioning which had preceded it, extinction occurs quickly when only a few incidents of a given response have been reinforced and is greatly protracted when there has been a long history of reinforcement.

The extinction process includes the interesting phenomenon of spontaneous recovery. Even after prolonged extinction, an organism, at the beginning of another session of an activity in which it had been trained but now is no longer being reinforced, often will respond at higher rate for at least a few moments.

Sometimes an extinction curve is disturbed by an emotional effect. Failure of a response to be reinforced not only leads to operant extinction but also may be accompanied by a reaction commonly called frustration or rage. A pigeon that has failed to receive reinforcement flaps its wings and engages in other emotional behavior. A mechanic, who is in the habit of having bolts unscrew when he turns his wrench, vents his spleen when one breaks off instead. However, after exercising his vocabulary, he turns back to the next bolt. Likewise a pigeon or rat will turn again to the operating key of the box when the emotional response has subsided. Extinction curves often show cyclic oscillation as the emotional response builds up, disappears, and builds up again.

Whereas the mere passage of time after reinforcement has surprisingly little effect upon loss of an act or habit, extinction is an effective way of removing an operant from the habit repertoire of an organism. When unaccompanied by extinction, forgetting takes place very slowly if at all. Note the key difference here: Whereas mere forgetting is the losing of a habit through the passage of time, extinction requires that the response be emitted without reinforcement. "In human behavior skilled responses generated by relatively precise contingencies frequently survive unused for as much as half a life-time."[52] The commonly heard assertion that early experiences of a child determine the personality of the mature person implies that the effect of operant reinforcement is very durable and that in human beings operant extinction is unlikely to occur on a large scale.

The resistance to extinction generated by intermittent reinforcement of a response is much greater than that achieved by the same number of reinforcements being given for consecutive responses. If we only occasionally reinforce a child's good behavior, the behavior survives after reinforcement is discontinued much longer than if we had reinforced every instance up to the same total number of reinforcements. Since intermittent reinforcement generates longer extinction curves than does continuous reinforcement, there is no simple relation between the number of reinforcements and the number of unreinforced responses necessary for extinction.

HOW MAY OPERANT CONDITIONING BE APPLIED TO SCHOOLROOM PRACTICES?

For Professor Skinner, "Teaching is the arrangement of contingencies of reinforcement which expedite learning."[53] He is convinced that operant conditioning, so effectual when applied to animal training, promises equal success when used in schools. Furthermore, he thinks that the most effective control of human learning requires instrumental aid. He is appalled at the present ineffiecient practices in schools and recommends a procedure whereby they can be corrected. He thinks that, when teachers have taught successfully, they always have arranged effective contingencies of reinforcement, but that they are more likely to do this if they understand what it is that they are doing.

He recognizes the *first* task of teachers to be to shape proper responses, to get children to pronounce and write responses properly. But he sees their *principal* task as bringing proper behavior under many sorts of stimulus control. "Teaching spelling is mainly a process of shaping complex forms of behavior. In other subjects—for example, arithmetic—responses must be brought under the control of appropriate stimuli."[54] To achieve this task, Skinner recommends the use of programmed learning.

Programmed instruction is a system of teaching and learning within which pre-established subject matter is broken down into

[52]*Ibid.*, p. 71.
[53]Skinner, *Contingencies of Reinforcement, op. cit.*, p. 15.
[54]Skinner, *Cumulative Record, op. cit.*, p. 165.

small, discrete steps and carefully organized into a logical sequence in which it can be learned readily by the students. Each step builds deliberately upon the preceding one. The learner can progress through the sequence of steps at his own rate and he is reinforced immediately after each step. Reinforcement consists of his either being given the correct response immediately after his registering his response or his being permitted to proceed to the next step only after he has registered the correct response. Programmed instruction may be accomplished with or without the use of teaching machines. (A teaching machine is described on p. 145.)

What are the shortcomings of current educational practice?

Skinner believes that it is in bringing correct responses under stimulus control that the greatest inefficiency of current teaching procedures occurs. "In education we design and re-design our curricula in a desperate attempt to provide a liberal education while steadfastly refusing to employ available engineering techniques which would efficiently build the interests and instill the knowledge which are the goals of education."[55] Consequently he notes some current weaknesses in educational practices: (1) behavior is dominated by aversion (escape) stimulation; (2) too great a lapse of time exists between behavior and its reinforcement; (3) a skillful program of reinforcement that moves forward through a series of progressive approximations to the final complex behavior desired is lacking; and (4) reinforcement of desired behavior occurs much too infrequently.

Behavior dominated by aversion stimulation. Although the type of threatened displeasure or pain has been changed in the past fifty years, behavior in the lower grades is still dominated by aversive stimulation—a child is trying to escape or keep away from something. Fifty years ago a child read numbers, copied numbers, and memorized tables to escape the birch rod or cane, that is, as far as the child was concerned, he did these things to avoid or escape punishment. Today a school child behaves the way he does primarily to escape the threat of a series of minor distasteful events—the teacher's displeasure, criticism or ridicule by his classmates, a poor showing in competition, low marks, or a trip to the principal's office. When children are dominated by this atmosphere, getting the right answer is in itself a rather insignificant event. Thus, the emphasis in teaching and learning is not centered where it should be—in operant conditioning.

[55]*Ibid.*, p. 228.

Excessive time lapse between behavior and reinforcement. Unless explicit mediating behavior has been set up, the lapse of only a few seconds between a response and its reinforcement destroys most of the effect. A grade on a test taken near the end of the week is too far away from the behaviors the students emitted—sent out—in studying the subject matter earlier in the week. Reinforcing stimuli should follow responses immediately.

Through use of the generalized reinforcer—approval—schools and society reinforce acquisition of the type of behavior learned in school. This is done by awarding grades, promotions, keys, diplomas, degrees, and medals. Skinner notes that these reinforcers do reinforce students' going to school and gaining a diploma or degree; their shortcoming is that they seldom if ever reinforce the subject matter elements themselves.

Absence of a program of serial reinforcement. A carefully planned program of teaching supposedly should move forward step by step by reinforcing a series of progressive approximations to the final behavior that is desired. To bring a human organism into possession of mathematical, or any other systematic, behavior most efficiently, a long series of reinforcement contingencies is necessary. Since a teacher has only so much time, he cannot deal with a student's responses one at a time and it is usually necessary for him to reinforce the desired behavior only in blocks of responses.

Infrequency of reinforcement. Perhaps the most serious criticism of current classroom procedures is the relative infrequency of reinforcement of the desired acts of students. It is just not humanly possible for one teacher to provide an adequate number of reinforcement contingencies for a class of thirty or forty children. Skinner estimates that, although adequate efficient mathematical behavior at the level of the first four grades requires somewhere between 25,000 and 50,000 reinforcement contingencies, a teacher at best could provide only a few thousand. Thus, even our best schools may be criticized for their inefficiency in teaching drill subjects such as arithmetic. Skinner believes that advances recently made in techniques for control of the learning process suggest that classroom practices should be thoroughly revised.

*What are the relevant considerations
in conditioning (teaching) a child?*

In order to plan a procedure for inculcating certain desired behavior in a child some specific questions need to be answered: (1) What behavior is to be established? (2) What reinforcers are

available? (3) What responses are available? (4) How can reinforcements be most efficiently scheduled?[56]

Behavior to be established. To teach efficiently, the first job
of a teacher who is an adherent of operant conditioning is to
determine carefully just what it is he plans to teach at a specific
time; he is the builder of behaviors. He must decide what he
wants to teach, then teach it. His objectives are specific, and
they are defined in terms of desired behaviors. Thus, operant
behaviorism requires a teacher-centered classroom.

Reinforcers available. What does a school have in its possession that will reinforce a child? Since the sheer control of nature in itself is reinforcing, the material to be learned may provide considerable automatic reinforcement. Children play for
hours with mechanical toys, paints, and puzzles. These feed back
significant changes in the environment and are reasonably free
of aversive properties. Automatic reinforcement from manipulation of the environment is probably rather mild. However, in
teaching, the net amount of reinforcement in each contingency
is of little significance. When properly and carefully used, a
series of very slight reinforcements may be tremendous effective in controlling behavior.

In addition to automatic reinforcement arising from manipulation of the environment, some other reinforcers are available
and often used. A child behaves in a certain way and the behavior is reinforced by its immediate consequences. Reinforcement may follow from a child's excelling others. However, when
he is competitively "rewarded," the reinforcement of one child
is, of necessity, aversive—"punishing"—to others. The goodwill
and affection of the teacher also may be reinforcing. A positive
"reward" or "consequence" (stimulus) strengthens the behavior
that is part of the contingency including that stimulus; it supposedly has nothing to do with satisfying organismic purpose.

Responses available. In planning a program of progressive
approximations that will lead to the desired final form of behavior a teacher must have at hand an inventory of the responses
that are available throughout the conditioning process.

Most efficient scheduling of reinforcements. To schedule reinforcements efficiently means to make them contingent upon the
desired behavior. Here two considerations are involved: (1) gradual elaboration of extremely complex patterns of behavior into
small units or stages, and (2) maintenance of the behavior in
strength at each stage. "The whole process of becoming competent in any field must be divided into a very large number of

[56]*Ibid.*, pp. 152–153.

very small steps, and reinforcement must be contingent upon the accomplishment of each step. . . . By making each successive step as small as possible, the frequency of reinforcement can be raised to a maximum, while the possibly aversive consequences of being wrong are reduced to a minimum."[57] This is the purpose of programmed instruction.

According to operant conditioning, ". . . learning a subject like fundamentals of electricity is largely a matter of learning (or giving) a large number of correct responses to logically related sequences of questions that constitute the subject. . . . Once a subject has been carefully divided ('programmed') into a series of many small bits of information ('steps') a student has only to learn by repetition and reward ('rapid and frequent reinforcement') the correct answer to a series of questions about the small bits of information."[58]

Skinner contends that the necessary requirements for adequate reinforcement are not excessive, but they probably are incompatible with current realities of present-day classrooms. Experimental studies of learning have indicated that, in order to arrange the contingencies of reinforcement that are most efficient in controlling learning in an organism, mechanical and electrical devices must be used. As a mere reinforcing mechanism, a teacher is out of date—and would be so even if he devoted all his time to a single child. Only through mechanical devices can the necessarily large number of contingencies be provided. "We have every reason to expect, therefore, that the most effective control of human learning will require instrumental aid."[59]

How do teaching machines work?

In Skinner's view, education must become more efficient to a degree that cannot be accomplished merely by our building more schools and preparing more teachers; adequate systems of labor-saving capital equipment, that is, teaching machines, must be developed. He is critical, too, of traditional education which makes students more and more the passive receivers of instruction. Teaching machines, he feels, encourage students to take an "active" role in the instructional process—they must develop the answers before they are reinforced.

[57]*Ibid.*, p. 153.
[58]H. T. Fitzgerald, "Teaching Machines: a Demurrer," *The School Review*, Autumn, 1962, pp. 248–249.
[59]*Ibid.*, p. 154.

Requirements of an appropriate teaching machine. Skinner thinks that, in light of modern psychological knowledge, an appropriate teaching machine has two basic requirements: First, a student must compose his response rather than select it from a set of alternatives.[60] Second, in acquiring complex behavior, a student must pass through a carefully designed sequence of steps; each step must be so small that it always can be taken, yet in taking it the student must move somewhat closer to fully competent behavior, and the machine must operate so as to make sure that steps are taken in a carefully prescribed order.[61]

Operation of a teaching machine. Skinner has anticipated no particular difficulty in producing workable teaching machines. The necessary contingencies may be arranged either mechanically or electrically. Let's see how he describes a teaching device.

The device consists of a box about the size of a small record player. On the top surface is a glazed window through which a question or problem printed on a paper tape may be seen. The child answers the question by moving one or more sliders upon which the digits 0 through 9 are printed. The answer appears in square holes punched in the paper upon which the question is printed. When the answer has been set, the child turns a knob. The operation is as simple as adjusting a television set. If the answer is right, the knob turns freely and can be made to ring a bell or provide some other conditioned reinforcement. If the answer is wrong, the knob will not turn. A counter may be added to tally wrong answers. The knob must then be reversed slightly and a second attempt at a right answer made. (Unlike the flash card, the device reports a wrong answer without giving the right answer.) When the answer is right, a further turn of the knob engages a clutch which moves the next problem into place in the window. This movement cannot be completed, however, until the sliders have been returned to zero.[62]

What are the advantages of the use of mechanical teaching devices?

Skinner claims a long list of advantages available through use of mechanical teaching devices[63] in present-day classrooms. (1)

[60]In the 1920s Sidney L. Pressey developed a teaching machine which students used in taking and scoring multiple-choice tests; they selected, but did not formulate, the answers.

[61]Skinner, *Cumulative Record, op. cit.,* p. 161.

[62]*Ibid.,* p. 154.

[63]B. F. Skinner, *The Technology of Teaching,* New York: Appleton-Century-Crofts, 1968, p. 24.

Reinforcement for the right answer is immediate. (2) Provided traces of earlier aversive control can be erased, mere manipulation of the device probably will be reinforcing enough to keep an average pupil at work for a suitable period each day. (3) All at one time, a teacher may supervise an entire class at work on such devices; yet each child may complete as many problems as possible in the class period and progress at his own rate. (4) Any child who is forced to leave school for a period may return at any time and continue from where he left off. (5) Each child may advance at his own rate and when he gets too far ahead of the class may be assigned to other tasks. (6) Through carefully designing materials, teachers may arrange problems in a serial order in the direction of an immensely complex repertoire. (7) Since the machines record the number of mistakes, tapes can be modified to enhance their effectiveness. (8) Knowing just what each student has done, a teacher can apply necessary supplementary reinforcement at the greatest vantage point.

In building a case for teaching machines, Skinner states ". . . the effect upon each student is surprisingly like that of a private tutor."[64] He then elaborates the nature of this similarity with the following points: (1) there is a constant interchange between programs and students; thus, the machine induces sustained activity; (2) the machine insists that a given point be thoroughly understood before the student moves on; (3) it presents that material for which the student is ready; (4) partly through its constructed program and partly through its techniques of prompting or hinting, the machine helps the student to come up with the right answer; and (5) like a private tutor, it reinforces the student for every correct response.

Can machines teach a child to think?

Professor Skinner recognizes that: "It is quite possible that the behavior of a man thinking is the most subtle and complex phenomenon ever submitted to scientific analysis."[65] But, he also emphasizes that thinking or originality is not absence of lawfulness and it should never be considered a spontaneous process. He points out that as long as thinking is identified with spontaneity or lawlessness it is a hopeless task to attempt systematically to influence a child's thinking in any way. Thinking, like the rest of the behavior of an organism, is a lawful process.

[64]B. F. Skinner, "Teaching Machines," *Science*, October 24, 1958, p. 971.
[65]Skinner, *The Technology of Teaching, op. cit.*, p. 140.

Thus, verbal behavior, in terms of which human thinking eventually must be defined, should be treated in its own right as a substantial goal of education. In inculcating this behavior, learning devices can teach verbal thinking—establish the large and important repertoire of verbal relationships encountered in science and logic.

Skinner thinks it is of critical importance for us to realize that, in operant behaviorism, thought is not some mysterious process which is the cause of behavior, but the behavior itself. Man thinking is man behaving, and human thought is operant, not reflexive, behavior. "Shakespeare's thought was his behavior *with respect to his extremely complex environment.*"[66] "In the broadest possible sense, the thought of Julius Caesar was simply the sum total of his responses to the complex world in which he lived."[67]

Skinner observes that study of what traditionally has been called the human mind is more appropriately a study of concepts and methods which have emerged from an analysis of behavior. Thinking behavior is verbal or nonverbal, overt or covert. It is primarily the verbal behavior of men which has survived in recorded form, but from this and other records we can know something about their nonverbal behavior. When we say that Caesar thought Brutus could be trusted we do not necessarily mean that he ever said as much. Rather he behaved verbally and otherwise as if Brutus could be trusted. The rest of his behavior, his nonverbal plans and achievements, were also part of his thoughts.

Although in earlier behavioristic analyses thinking was identified with subaudible talking, Skinner feels that nothing is gained by so doing. There are difficulties in assuming that covert behavior is always executed by the muscular apparatus responsible for the overt form. Furthermore, the data that give rise to the notion of covert speech can be treated, as such, with a high degree of rigor. Rather than identifying thinking with *talking*, a better case can be made for identifying it with a special kind of *behaving*, that which automatically affects behavior and is reinforcing because it does.

"It is important that the student should learn without being taught, solve problems by himself, explore the unknown, make decisions, and behave in original ways, and these activities

[66]B. F. Skinner, *Verbal Behavior*, New York: Appleton-Century-Crofts, 1957, p. 450.
[67]*Ibid.*, pp. 451–452.

should, if possible, be taught."[68] But we should not attempt to teach thinking while teaching subject matter. "If thinking can be analyzed and taught separately, the already-known can be transmitted with maximal efficiency."[69] "It is as important to define the terminal behavior in teaching thinking as in teaching knowledge."[70]

Thinking is more productive when verbal responses lead to specific consequences and are reinforced because they do so. Just as a musician plays or composes what reinforces him audibly or an artist paints what reinforces him visually, a speaker or writer, engaged in verbal fantasy, says that which is reinforced by hearing it, or writes that which is reinforced by reading it. However, it must be recognized that in any case the solution to a problem is simply a response which alters the situation so that another strong response can be emitted. "Reinforcing contingencies shape the behavior of the individual, and novel contingencies generate novel forms of behavior."[71] Thus, man's present better control of the world could be described and expressed just as well by saying that the environment now is in better control of man.

The key to effective teaching of thinking, as well as any other behavior, is immediate feedback. To teach thinking, we should ". . . analyze the behavior called 'thinking' and produce it according to specifications. A program specifically concerned with such behavior could be composed of material already available in logic, mathematics, scientific method, and psychology."[72]

BIBLIOGRAPHY

FERSTER, C. B., and B. F. Skinner, *Schedules of Reinforcement*, New York: Appleton-Century-Crofts, 1957.
A report of scientific study of various reinforcement schedules.
FITZGERALD, H. T., "Teaching Machines: A Demurrer," *The School Review*, Autumn 1962, pp. 247–256.
A well-written, sobering critique of machine teaching written by a director of education and training for an automotive parts plant. He considers mechanical reinforcement theory ". . . an intrinsically undemocratic—worse, an anti-intellectual—theory of learning," and and concludes with the statement, "Teaching machines only teach (condition) machines."

[68]Skinner, *The Technology of Teaching*, op. cit., p. 116.
[69]*Ibid.*, p. 116.
[70]*Ibid.*, p. 117.
[71]Skinner, *Verbal Behavior*, op. cit., p. 255.
[72]Skinner, *Cumulative Record*, op. cit., p. 173.

GALANTER, EUGENE, *Automatic Teaching: The State of the Art*, New York: John Wiley, 1959.
A collection of papers, one by B. F. Skinner, which treat the experimentation, analysis, and programming related to machine teaching. Chapter 15, "Teaching Machines and Psychological Theory," by Howard H. Kindler, is an excellent critique on the teaching machine movement.

HILGARD, ERNEST R., and GORDON H. BOWER, *Theories of Learning*, 3rd ed., New York: Appleton-Century-Crofts, 1966.
In Chapter 5, "Skinner's Operant Conditioning": a descriptive interpretation of Skinner's operant conditioning theory of learning.

HOLLAND, JAMES G., and B. F. SKINNER, *The Analysis of Behavior*, New York: McGraw-Hill, 1961.
A programmed textbook for an introductory course in psychology to be used as a substitute for a teaching machine. A student supposedly is to learn the basic terms and principles of behavioristic conditioning; he writes the correct answer to a question, then is reinforced by finding it on the next page.

LUMSDAINE, A. A., "Educational Technology, Programmed Learning, and Instructional Science," in Ernest R. Hilgard, *Theories of Learning and Instruction*, National Society for the Study of Education, Chicago: University of Chicago Press, 1964.
A comprehensive treatment of applications of programming to instructional procedures.

PRYOR, KAREN, "Behavior Modification: The Porpoise Caper," *Psychology Today*, December 1969, pp. 46–49, 64.
Porpoises, in having their behaviors modified, seem to get the idea in regard to the "pay-off" and behave beyond the expectations of their trainers, i.e., to show creative behavior. "Some of Malia's spontaneous stunts were so unusual that the trainers couldn't imagine achieving them with the shaping system."

SKINNER, B. F., *The Behavior of Organisms*, New York: Appleton-Century-Crofts, 1938.
Skinner's early systematic statement of operant behavior and conditioning.

SKINNER, B. F., "A Case History in Scientific Method," in Sigmund Koch, *Psychology: A Study of Science*, Vol. 2, *General Systematic Formulations, Learning, and Special Processes*, New York: McGraw-Hill, 1959.
Skinner's own personal history illustrating his philosophy of science and psychology of behavior. He relates how he was operant-conditioned to perform in certain ways as he studied the conditioning of animals. The chapter is interesting reading. See pp. 359–379.

SKINNER, B. F., *Contingencies of Reinforcement*, New York: Appleton-Century-Crofts, 1969.
Professor Skinner's theoretical analysis of his psychological system and its comparison with other systems.

SKINNER, B. F., *Cumulative Record*, New York: Appleton-Century-Crofts, 1959.
A series of Skinner's papers which reflects the implications of his position, Part III, "The Science of Learning and the Art of Teaching" and "Teaching Machines," is particularly pertinent to this chapter.

Skinner, B. F., "The Machine That Is Man," *Psychology Today*, April 1969, 22–25, 60–64.
Disposes of "inner man" by replacing him with genetic and environmental variables. "In pigeon and Indian alike, adventitious reinforcements generate ritualistic behavior."

SKINNER, B. F., "Teaching Machines," *Science*, October 24, 1958, pp. 969–977.
Professor Skinner's strongest presentation of the case for teaching machines.

SKINNER, B. F., *The Technology of Teaching*, New York: Appleton-Century-Crofts, 1968.
An expansion of the concept that teaching consists of arranging contingencies of reinforcement. Provides psychological rationale for making teaching a process of changing the behaviors of organisms.

SKINNER B. F., *Science and Human Behavior*, New York: Macmillan, 1953.
An application of "realistic" scientific method to a study of human behavior centered around operant conditioning. "Scientific Analysis" is extended to the behavior of people in groups and the operation of controlling agencies such as government and religion. Its final section analyzes education as a process of control of human behavior.

SKINNER, B. F., *Verbal Behavior*, New York: Appleton-Century-Crofts, 1957.
An explanation of how verbal behavior, including thinking, takes its place in the larger field of human behavior; it too is learned through operant conditioning. Ways of manipulating verbal behavior of individuals are tested.

SKINNER, B. F., *Walden Two*, New York: Macmillan, 1948.
A novel proposing and describing a community within which maximum use is made of conditioning to control human welfare. It deals with the educational and social implications of behaviorism.

SIX

How Does Spence's Quantitative S-R Theory Treat Learning?

Kenneth W. Spence (1907–1967), an eminent contemporary research psychologist, centered his professional efforts on an experimental study of learning. After receiving his doctorate from Yale in 1933, he served on the Yale staff from 1933 to 1937. Spence spent one year at the University of Virginia, then went to the State University of Iowa where he served as head of the department of psychology until 1964 when he went to the University of Texas.

The ultimate goal of Spence's psychological research was to attain a high level of exact quantification of behavior theory, and to achieve this within an S-R conditioning frame of reference. Thus, the system that he developed and that is being extended by his associates and students is a *quantitative S-R theory*. In his study, he extended and refined Hull's psychological system;[1] however, his approach is somewhat different from Hull's. His first commitment, like Hull's, was to the proposition that learning, in some way, is a process of relating stimuli and responses. Thus, he built his thinking upon a stimulus-response

[1]See Chapter 4, p. 96–97, for a brief description of Hullian Psychology. Neo-Hullian means a new, contemporary version of Hull's psychology.

type of theoretical analysis such as Hull earlier led in establishing. However, Spence accepted only a small number of Hull's many definitions and postulates, and he pursued a much more rigorous and exacting program of research.

This psychologist was interested in securing, through experimental procedures, the same kind of precise, quantitative knowledge about behavior that scientists in physics, chemistry, and biology had developed in their respective areas. For him, the science of psychology, in principle, had neither a unique set of methods nor a unique subject matter. Hence, the subject matter of psychology, i.e., the behavior of living organisms, methodologically, was of the same kind as the subject matter of the other sciences. Through usage of pure, as contrasted with applied, research he was interested in development of a comprehensive theory of behavior and learning that would explain the different laws manifested in various behavioral situations.

Spence carefully divorced his research results from immediate applicability to current school situations. Yet, when we look at matters from a long-range point of view, his learning theory and research may make a greater contribution to learning and teaching practices than some approaches which seem to promise much in terms of immediate results. His attempt to discover lawful relations in "pure" laboratory situations may eventually provide a better and more comprehensive understanding of effective learning in complex school situations.

WHAT IS THE NATURE OF SPENCE'S EXPERIMENTATION?

An examination of one of Spence's experiments should help us acquire some feeling for the flavor of his purposes, methods, and achievements. He performed an extensive series of experiments, some of which tested whether, in classical aversive conditioning, the magnitude of reinforcement determines how much is learned or whether it influences performance in some other way (it earlier had been established that the magnitude of a reinforcer influenced performance of an organism, the question was how).

In classical aversive conditioning an organism learns to respond avertively—protect itself—when it is stimulated by a signal that previously had been inadequate to evoke the protective behavior. Spence assumed that, if habit strength—learning—is found to vary with changes in the intensity of the unconditioned —adequate—stimulus, then the learning that occurs is governed

Figure 6.1
Classical Aversive Conditioning.

UCS: loud noise, *"NO!"* ────▶ Response: startled reaction

CS: Word "no"

QUESTION: Does the loudness of the noise affect the child's
learning to respond to the noise?

by reinforcement. The experiment which we now examine involves classical aversive eyelid conditioning.[2]

In *classical conditioning,* a new, conditioned, stimulus (CS) is
substituted for an already adequate, unconditioned, stimulus
(UCS). In classical aversive conditioning, when the new stimulus
is present, the organism learns to defend itself—reacts—in much
the same way as it had in the presence of the earlier, unconditioned stimulus. (Classical aversive conditioning is described in
more detail on pp. 166–167.)

Since Spence defined learning as *habit formation,* he specified
it in terms of increments—increases—of habit strength (H).[3] His
problem was to discover, in the case of a defense or aversive
conditioned response, whether habit strength—learning—depends
upon the intensity of the unconditioned—originally adequate—
stimulus that is active in the learning situation; that is, whether
the strength of the unconditioned stimulus is related to the
strengh of the learning.

This problem, when applied to "educational engineering," is
exemplified by the following: in the presence of a loud noise,
a child reflexively draws up into a startled posture. In a classical
learning situation, a teacher makes a loud noise, *"NO!";* simultaneously a child hears the word "no." Does the degree of the
noise, "NO!" have any bearing upon the child's learning to "hold
everything" at the sound of the word "no"? The *loud noise,*
"NO!" is the unconditioned stimulus, the word "no" is the conditioned stimulus. This problem is illustrated in Figure 6.1.

In the classical aversive eyelid-conditioning experiment under
consideration, the UCS was a puff of air in the right eye of a
subject. The response was an eyeblink. The CS was an increase
in brightness of a circular disc. Learning—increase in habit
strength—is revealed by a subject's coming to blink his eye
more often when the brightness of the disc is increased.

[2]See Kenneth W. Spence, *Behavior Theory and Learning,* Englewood
Cliffs, N.J.: Prentice-Hall, 1960, pp. 164–168.
[3]In keeping with his scientific orientation, Spence has developed abbreviated symbols for most of his principal concepts.

Subjects for the experiment were three groups of college students in an introductory psychology course. Each group contained 25 men and 25 women. Group 1 was a high reinforcement and high drive group; Group 2 a low reinforcement and high drive group; and Group 3 a low reinforcement and low drive group. *Drive* is a strong, persistent, internal state of an organism, which is closely related to a need that activates the organism. In this experiment, drive was the aroused state of the organism, which increased as air puffs were made stronger.

The subjects, in turn, were seated in a dental chair in a semidarkened room. Each received 100 trials. In 50 trials, the conditioning ones, each subject was presented with the CS—increase in disc brightness—paired with the UCS—air puff—and in 50, the reflexive ones, he was presented with only the UCS—air puff. Paired and unpaired trials were prearranged in an irregular order.

Drive level was controlled for each group by the strength of the air puffs which were experienced. The experiment was conducted so that the drive level (D) in terms of intensities of the UCS was equated for Groups 1 and 2 and was much lower for Group 3; Groups 1 and 2 received strong puffs on 50 trials, Group 3 received no strong puffs.

It is essential that we discern how meticulously Spence measures the strength and duration of pertinent stimuli and responses. Each CS—an increase in brightness of the circular disc from .004 to .506 foot-candles—lasted for 500 milliseconds (a millisecond is a thousandth of a second). Each UCS—air puff applied to the right eye—occurred 450 milliseconds after the onset of the CS. The duration of the UCS was 50 milliseconds. Weak puffs were .33 and strong puffs 2.0 pounds per square inch.

In the case of the high reinforcement and high drive group (Group 1), the strong puff—UCS—was always paired with the CS—increased brightness of the disc—and the weak puff was always presented without the CS. In the case of the low reinforcement and high drive group (Group 2), the reverse occurred; the weak puff was paired with the CS and the strong puff was presented alone. In the case of the low reinforcement and low drive group (Group 3), a weak puff was both paired with the CS and presented alone. Bear in mind that, on the same group of subjects, a drive level which is increased in the noncondition-ing trials is still present to influence reinforcement in the conditioning trials. See Figure 6.2 for a condensed representation of the experimental design.

A conditioned response (CR) was recorded whenever a sub-

Figure 6.2
Three Experimental Groups.

Gp. 1—high reinforcement and high drive	50 trials	Strong puff—UCS—paired with CS—increased brightness.
	* 50 trials	Weak puff presented without increased brightness.
Gp. 2—low reinforcement and high drive	50 trials	Weak puff — UCS—paired with CS—increased brightness.
	* 50 trials	Strong puff presented without increased brightness.
Gp. 3—low reinforcement and low drive	50 trials	Weak puff — UCS — paired with CS—increased brightness.
	* 50 trials	Weak puff presented without increased brightness.

* indicates nonconditioning trials; they influence drive only.

ject's eyelid showed a deflection of 1 millimeter or more in the interval 200 to 450 milliseconds following the onset of the CS. See Figure 6.3.

Figure 6.4 presents frequency curves of conditioning for the three groups. Frequency of conditioned responses is high in both Groups 1 and 2 because subjects in both groups were exposed to 50 strong puffs—drive producing stimuli. The significant difference in the performance levels of Groups 1 and 2 presumably reflects a difference in habit strength (H) which is related to the different intensities of the puff strengths—reinforcement levels—on the paired—conditioning trials. Furthermore, since Groups 2 and 3 had equated puff strengths on the conditioning—H-producing—trials, differences in the performance level of these groups presumably reflect a difference in the level of drive (D) which was controlled in the nonconditioning trials.

Figure 6.3
Duration of Each CS, UCS, and CR.

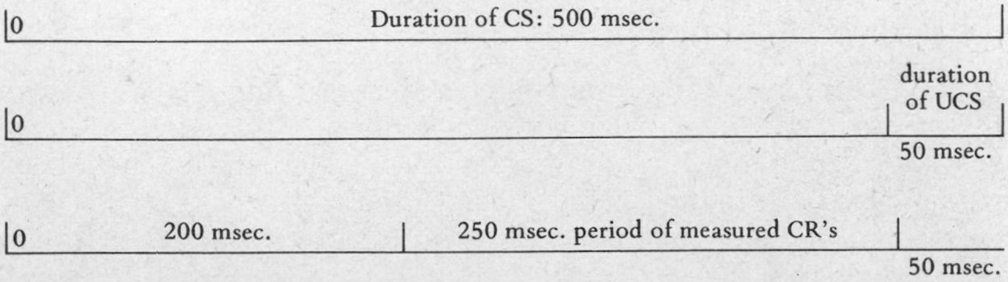

| 0 | Duration of CS: 500 msec. | |

		duration of UCS
0		
		50 msec.

| 0 | 200 msec. | 250 msec. period of measured CR's | |
| | | | 50 msec. |

Figure 6.4
Frequency Curves of Conditioning for Three Groups,
An Adaptation from Kenneth W. Spence, Behavior Theory
and Learning, Englewood Cliffs, N.J., *Prentice-Hall, 1960, p. 166.*

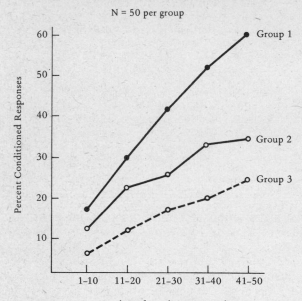

N = 50 per group

Number of Conditioning Trials

The differences in the levels of habit strength (H) acquired by the three groups in the same number of trials indicates that the learning factor in *classical aversive conditioning is influenced by* the magnitude of *reinforcement;* it is a function of the intensity of the UCS. This finding suggests that, in case of the problem described on p. 153, the habit strength of "holding everything" at the word "no," will depend upon the loudness of the word *"NO!"* during the learning—conditioning—procedure.

WHY DOES SPENCE'S PSYCHOLOGY OFFER LITTLE IMMEDIATE, BUT MUCH EVENTUAL, HELP FOR TEACHERS?

Spence recognized that many reputable psychologists concern themselves with human learning behavior as it occurs in everyday life situations, including schools. Such behavior has been studied by child, educational, social, and clinical psychologists. However, Spence concluded that studies conducted through more or less uncontrolled observation by these psychologists have not gone very far in attainment of precise psychological laws. Thus, he saw a great need for careful laboratory analysis of simple behavior in order to establish a comprehensive theory of learning. He observed that the history of other sciences has repeatedly shown that the adequacy of any engineering program depends upon the development of an adequate, basic foundation of scientific laws. Consequently, he thought that an adequate educational technology likewise must rest upon a precise psychological science.

Spence believed that too much time and energy of too many psychologists was being devoted to practical human engineering rather than basic, purely scientific problems. He thought that if psychologists are ever to bring their science "of age" they, like other scientists, must formulate an adequate system of abstract laws and comprehensive theories, and that such an achievement requires extensive use of artificial, nonlifelike, experimental conditions. Consequently Spence emphasized that everyday, familiar instances of behavior do not, and should not, constitute the data with which a learning psychologist is concerned. Spence, as a learning psychologist, deliberately chose *not* to concern himself with "real-life" situations. He stated, "The fact of the matter is that we so-called learning theorists, particularly those of us whose research has been conducted mostly with animal subjects, have not been interested in the practical aspects of learning for many years."[4]

For Professor Spence, and those who continue his work, defensible psychological laws and theories are most likely to have their origin in data obtained from highly controlled laboratory situations. Such laboratory arrangements have included study of the lever-pressing behavior and running speed of rats, the salivary responses of dogs, and the blinking of human eyelids. Seldom, if ever, have these studies been related to instances of workaday learning.

There are definite reasons why Spence, and other learning psychologists of his disposition, have chosen to concentrate their efforts on rats, dogs, monkeys, and eyelids rather than gross human activity. They have emphasized that the first objective of a scientist is to discover the low-order, empirical, and lawful relationships that prevail among the particular variables specified by his field of study and measuring technique, and that

[4]Kenneth W. Spence, "The Relation of Learning Theory to the Technology of Education," *Harvard Educational Review*, Spring 1959, p. 85.

scientific progress is more likely when psychologists study relatively simple organisms in relatively simple situations. They have further noted that research scientists in various areas of knowledge have never hesitated to arrange "unreal" situations in order to achieve their goals. For example, physicists have questioned the possibility of achievement of a perfect vacuum. Nevertheless, they have in no way avoided theorizing about a vacuum and experimentally approximating one. Furthermore, biologists have devoted much time and energy to the study of isolated tissues in test tubes, yet a tissue is a far cry from a total organism. The point is that, in scientific research, artificial arrangements help discover laws, which in time provide explanations of events of "real" life.[5]

According to Spence, a scientifically oriented psychologist, as such, should never concern himself with the question of whether any particular realm of behavioral study is close to "real" life. The only criterion for priority in investigation, other than the personal curiosity of the psychologist, is whether an area of study lends itself to the degree of scientific control and analysis necessary for formulation of pertinent abstract laws and comprehensive theories. "Being guided by such purely scientific objectives, and not having any special interests, humanitarian, religious, social betterment or otherwise, no particular area of human or animal behavior is seen as more important than another."[6]

WHAT IS THE NATURE OF SPENCE'S PSYCHOLOGICAL THEORY?

Spence took it for granted that things around him that he perceived—his world—were independently real, and that they could be investigated by observation. Thus, he may be identified as a scientific realist or logical empiricist. For him, science is concerned only with knowledge that reliably can be made a matter of public record and thus be taken out of the realm of private experience.

Spence's basic assumption was that behavior has sufficient order and regularity so that lawful descriptions of it may be

[5]See Kenneth W. Spence, "Current Interpretation of Learning Data and Some Recent Developments in Stimulus-Response Theory," in Donald K. Adams *et al.*, *Learning Theory, Personality Theory, and Clinical Research*, New York: John Wiley, 1954, p. 2.

[6]Kenneth W. Spence, *Behavior Theory and Learning*, Englewood Cliffs, N.J.: Prentice-Hall, 1960, pp. 79–80.

found. Such lawful descriptions are to be achieved in the same manner that scientists in other disciplines supposedly find their laws. Since behavior is assumed to be, at least in part, a function of the forces *exerted upon* organisms, explanation of what people, or other organisms, do is sought in their general organic condition and the physical and social circumstances that surround them.

As a scientist, Spence preferred to keep as far away as possible from metaphysical or supernatural issues. He was not concerned with analysis of the various philosophical definitions of knowledge and its attainment. Neither did he use data based on introspection or empathic projection. *Empathic projection* means that one experiences a situation from another person's point of view or places himself in "another's shoes." Spence, like other behaviorists, considered scientific data to be only observable public events about which observers could agree. Hence, he thought that introspective or empathic knowledge, if there is such, does not meet the criteria for pertinent data of the natural sciences. However, he acknowledged that introspection could be accepted as verbal behavior and given the same status as any other behavior as long as it is not asserted to be isomorphic—of like form—to a private, internal "world" of a subject.

There is no place in Spence's psychological system for concepts such as perceptual interaction or life space. However, he did not object to other persons developing introspective or empathic knowledge about human personality, provided such knowledge is not called "scientific." His only criterion for selection of items or aspects of experiential data for scientific study is a high degree of agreement among competent observers concerning a particular observable datum.[7]

According to Spence, scientific psychology today is at about the same point of development that physics was at the time of Kepler and Galileo—the seventeenth century. He wanted psychologists to have the same opportunity to develop a scientific account of their discipline as their colleagues in the physical and biological sciences have had. Accordingly, he stated,

As scientists we are interested in discovering and formulating a body of knowledge concerning the behavior of living organisms that is continuous with and has the same properties, empirical and logical, as the knowledge sought in the other natural sciences. Since the attainment of such knowledge requires methods of ob-

[7]*Ibid.*, pp. 74–75.

servation that assure publicly verifiable concepts, we have naturally insisted on the use of such techniques.[8]

Why did Spence study "molar" behavior?

Spence distinguished between "molar" and "physiological" descriptions of behavior.[9] Molar behavior as he defined it, consists of an organism's performance of some task or function, such as pressing a bar, running down an alley, or choosing between two alternative actions. In contrast, a physiological description of behavior would be in terms of organic functions, sensory and motor impulses, and muscular contractions. In light of this distinction, he considered his task as a psychologist that of studying molar behavior in a way that would yield general laws concerning it.[10]

Spence recognized that all molar behavior probably has physiological aspects. However, at the present—mid-twentieth century—stage of development of psychology, he saw little value in employment of physiological concepts. Yet, by maintenance of a neutral position in regard to physiological descriptions of learning, he left the way open for future, effective physiological concepts in psychology.

How are psychological laws discovered?

Spence thought that psychologists, as scientists, should first attempt to discover generalized laws that interrelate the observable events of behavior with one another. Then, the next step was to formulate theories, each of which would be a generalization representing a number of laws.

In the process of discovery of laws, Spence and his students have isolated and described various aspects of learning situations to see what interrelations are involved. They have thought that a study of simple behavioral changes would contribute most to their discovery of underlying laws. In the process of study, they have manipulated or controlled various aspects of an organism's environment, which elicit and follow its responses. At the same time, they have manipulated motivational or drive factors in their subjects. The experiment reported on pp. 154–156 is an example of this type of scientific procedure.

[8]*Ibid.*, p. 79.
[9]*Ibid.*, p. 36.
[10]See Chapter 3, pp. 59–60, for Gestalt-field psychologists' somewhat different use of the concept *molar*. To them, the opposite of molar is "molecular" or "atomistic," not "physiological."

Professor Spence anticipated that eventually much of the behavior of living organisms would be described in terms of the same types of quantitative "pointer readings" as are now employed in physics. He stated that practically all of the observations of psychologists who employ animals as subjects in their studies are of this quantitative type. Examples of significant data are the time required to run down an alley, the rate of depressing a lever, or the amplitude of a conditioned leg flexion.

How are constructs used?

To accomplish their respective tasks, scientists in all fields employ the most effectual constructs they can devise. A *construct* is a created, usable concept. According to Spence's view, constructs are either empirical or theoretical. The principal *empirical constructs* are *independent* (stimulus) and *dependent* (response) variables in the form of behaviors that are open to public inspection. *Theoretical constructs*, in contrast, are *intermediate* or *intervening* variables such as motivation, drive, and learning, which are not physically observable.

A *variable* is a pertinent, changing factor in a situation. It is a quantity that may be increased or decreased without an essential change in the nature of the element that has the quality with which we are concerned. The amount of snow on the ground is a variable; there can be more or less of it. In an experiment, a condition—independent variable—is altered, and the result—dependent variable—is observed and, if possible, measured.

The *dependent* variable is the consequence to be observed; it depends upon the conditions of the experiment. The conditions of the experiment constitute the *independent* variables. In the experiment reported on pp. 154–156, the independent variable was the manipulated intensity of the air puff. The dependent variable was the organisms' blinking their eyes more often. Intervening variables were the controlled variations in reinforcement and drive, and the increase in habit strength—learning.

What is the purpose of psychological theory?

According to Spence, a theory is a broad generalization that is based on known laws. It should reflect correctly both the known and the unknown laws of behavior. Spence's primary concern was to build a theoretical model with which we could derive and interrelate the specific laws found in different learning situations. He began his endeavor with experimental findings from the two simplest kinds of learning situations—classical and instrumental conditioning. Based on data acquired in these situations he proposed, and later tested for, a system of laws involving both intervening and experimental variables. His theoretical models were tested in terms of the degree to which they were able to predict the lawful relations that would appear in new, pertinent data.

Through experimentation, Spence had collected a variety of learning curves involving different organisms, apparatuses, and response measures. He, then, showed that they all may be considered special instances of a few hypothetical equations. Hence, he stated, "As yet only a start has been made toward the development of the type of higher-order generalizations (i.e., theories) that serve to integrate or unify the laws specific to each experimental situation."[11]

Spence implored psychologists to make more effective, positive use of theories and not to take the negativistic attitude that theories are something to be proved wrong. He reminded them that:

A theory in science serves to bring order and meaning into a particular realm of events. The task of ordering a set of events consists in discovering relations among them, or as we say, in finding empirical laws. In the initial phases of this search we employ the process of inductive generalization from observation and experiment. In the physical sciences this process is straightforward enough, for the scientist in this area is able to arrange for simple systems of observation that permit the isolation and control of a relatively small number of variables. Unfortunately the behavior of living organisms does not yield so readily to simplification and control. The greater complexity of psychological phenomena makes difficult, if not impossible, the experimental isolation and measurement of the relevant variables. Consequently psychologists have found it necessary to guess or theorize much more than physicists had to at this stage of development in their field of knowledge.[12]

Spence and his associates strived to develop a system of psychological theories—high-order generalizations—that would enable them to derive the different "empirical functions"—observed relationships—between the empirical variables that are

[11]Kenneth W. Spence, "Current Interpretations of Learning Data and Some Recent Developments in Stimulus-Response Theory," *op. cit.*, p. 3.
[12]Kenneth W. Spence, "Theoretical Interpretations of Learning," in S. S. Stevens, ed., *Handbook of Experimental Psychology*, New York: John Wiley, 1951, p. 690.

to be found in various types of conditioning experiments. They hoped and believed that such a theoretical psychological structure would permit them to account for more complex learning phenomena in addition to that upon which their studies were based. These psychologists have considered *the business of psychological science that of ascertaining which objective factors in the past and present conditions of organisms and their environments account for their differences in response.* Then, when psychologists attain this objective, they can predict behavior instead of merely attributing it, after it has happened, to some difference in the environment; they will have formulated general laws and theories which have a wide range of application to particular instances of behavior.

HOW DID SPENCE STUDY LEARNING?

For Spence, learning phenomena consisted of ". . . behavioral changes that occur with repeated experience [trial occasions] in the same or essentially similar situations. . . ."[13] He attributed the progressive changes in behavior that occur in a learning experiment to changes in a theoretical "learning state" which result from previous experiences in a situation. *Learning, then, is a nonobservable, hypothetical construct; it intervenes between observable independent and dependent variables.* When learning is defined this way, there is a difference between performance and learning. Performance refers to an observable, measurable response. Learning, a postulated, hypothetical factor, is less tangible; it ". . . is assumed, on the one hand, to be the product of the past interactions of the individual with his environment, and, on the other, to be one of the conditions that determines his performance at any moment."[14]

Learning, while nonobservable in itself, is inferred from the changes that occur in the behavior of a subject on successive trial occasions. Spence, an S-R conditioning psychologist, recorded and measured these changes in the properties of observable behavior and attempted to ascertain the factors or variables that are related to them. Whereas he was primarily concerned with laws of learning, which relate changing responses to suc-

13Kenneth W. Spence, "The Relation of Learning Theory to the Technology of Education," *Harvard Educational Review*, Spring, 1959, p. 85.

14Spence, "Theoretical Interpretations of Learning," p. 691. "Interaction" as used in this quotation means alternating reaction, not simultaneous, mutual interaction, of person and environment as in field psychology. See Chapter 3, pp. 73–75.

cessive trial occurrences; he also was interested in all of the variables that determine behavior in learning situations.[15]

What variables determine behavior?

A two-fold task confronts an S-R conditioning learning theorist: (1) specification of the experimental variables, both organic and environmental, that determine the observed behavior changes which occur during an organism's activity, and (2) formulation of the functional interrelations—laws—which hold in regard to "sets of variables"—behavioral situations. The second of these two tasks requires extensive use of intervening variables.

In keeping with the purposes of an S-R psychologist, Spence performed observations and experimentation to lead to discovery and formulation of a body of low-order laws of behavior. He then postulated an intermediate or intervening intangible variable-learning. In his experiments, he changed or controlled independent variables, then measured the dependent variable which ensued, and thereby inferred the intervening variable. *Independent and dependent variables are in the form of stimuli and responses; intervening variables are not.* (See p. 97 for definitions of independent and dependent variables.)

Stimulus, or *input,* variables are qualitative descriptions or measurements of events or properties of the physical and social environment in which the organism behaves. They consist of everything that impinges upon an organism, either internally or externally, prior to and, at the time of, the behavior being studied. However, as Spence noted, ". . . the presence of a particular situational stimulus does not guarantee that it will also be a stimulus for the organism at the moment of responding."[16]

We should not give stimulus variables too narrow a definition; they may be situational, effective, or intraorganic. Situational stimuli arise from physical objects or events in the environment; they may be specified quite independently of the responding organism, and are under the direct control of the experimenter. Effective stimuli refer to the particular situational stimuli that are acting upon and exciting the organism's receptors at the time of a response. These, to a considerable extent, are dependent upon the organism's receptor-orienting behavior. Both situational and effective stimuli are received through exteroceptors—sense organs stimulated directly by energy changes out-

[15]See Kenneth W. Spence, *Behavior Theory and Conditioning,* New Haven, Conn.: Yale University Press, 1956, pp. 51–52.
[16]*Ibid.,* pp. 30–40.

side the body. Intraorganic stimuli are those stimuli whose properties are specified on the basis of known physiological laws or hypothesized organic internal relations; they are received through interoceptors—sense organs located in the viscera of a body—or proprioceptors—sense organs excited by activities of parts of a body, such as the muscles.[17]

Response, or *output*, variables are qualitative descriptions or measurements of the behavioral properties of living organisms. Each response involves a chain or sequence of acts. It is described in "molar," not "physiological," terms.

Intervening variables are mediating links in learning; they intervene—psychologically occur—between independent stimulus variables on one hand and dependent response variables on the other. They are introduced into psychology ". . . either when we do not know all the important variables entering into a set of experimental events, or the precise nature of the interrelating function is not known."[18] Thus, the intervening variables of learning theory serve as general or abstract terms applicable to a variety of situations. Consequently, ". . . learning is to be conceived in terms of alterations in the strengths of hypothetical intervening variables, variously referred to as S-R connections, associations, habits, or tendencies."[19]

Psychologists use the independent and intervening variables in a situation such as stimuli, practice, drive, and reward to predict responsive behavior—the dependent variable. Such a prediction is in terms of whether the response will occur, how quickly it will occur, and what its amplitude—amount of change—will be. Often this was stated by Spence in terms of a "terminal" construct—"excitatory potential" (E). *Excitatory potential* means the likelihood, speed, and change of a response, which is the result of a conditioning process and which correlates with the quantitative characteristics of a response. Independent variables feed into excitatory potential, and dependent variables are determined from it.

HOW DID SPENCE EXPERIMENT WITH LEARNING?

A conditioning process may, or may not, include reinforcement.[20] Spence suggested that his learning theory might be called an

---

[17]*Ibid.*, p. 41.

[18]Spence, *Behavior Theory and Learning*, *op. cit.*, pp. 28–29.

[19]Spence, "Theoretical Interpretations of Learning," *op. cit.*, p. 692.

[20]See Chapter 4, pp. 90–94, for general definitions and treatment of *conditioning* and *reinforcement*.

S-R expectancy—half reinforcement and half contiguity theory.[21] In classical aversive conditioning, involving escape motivation, he proposed a reinforcement principle. However, in instrumental reward conditioning, which involves some form of appetitional motivation, he preferred a contiguity—nonreinforcement—principle.

Spence's experiments with learning involved classical conditioning, instrumental conditioning, and selective learning. *Classical* conditioning may be either reward or aversive conditioning, and *instrumental* conditioning may take the form of either reward or escape conditioning. However, Spence concentrated his study on classical aversive and instrumental reward conditioning. *Classical aversive conditioning* occurs when an organism learns to react defensively to a new, conditioned stimulus much as it previously had to an originally noxious unconditioned stimulus. *Instrumental reward conditioning* occurs when an animal learns to behave in a given manner because it is "rewarded" when it manifests the given behavior. *Selective learning* may be either spatial trial-and-error or discrimination learning.

Spence treated the study of classical conditioning, instrumental conditioning, and selective learning each in detail as if they necessitate three completely different kinds of experimentation. However, he explained that classical conditioning really is an inherent part of instrumental conditioning, and that instrumental conditioning situations are special cases of trial-and-error selective learning. We now discuss Spence's experiments with each type of learning in some detail.

How does classical conditioning work?

As we explain on p. 92, in classical conditioning a new, conditioned stimulus is substituted for an already adequate, unconditioned stimulus, as was the case when Pavlov trained his dogs to secrete saliva at the sound of a bell. Spence suggested that reinforcement plays a decisive role in acquisition of habit strength—learning—in classical aversive, but not in instrumental reward, conditioning.[22]

In classical aversive conditioning, the excitatory potential (E) —likelihood, speed, and change—of a classical conditioned response is increased by two intervening variables, habit and

[21]See Chapter 4, pp. 94–97, for summaries of Hull's reinforcement and Guthrie's contiguity theories of learning.

[22]Experiments such as the one reported on pp. 154–156, support this thesis.

drive. Habit (H) links a response to a stimulus and is acquired gradually as a function of reinforced trials—pairing of conditioned and unconditioned stimuli along with the response.

Drive (D) is the basic intervening variable. *General drive* arises from all the needs of the organism that are present at any one time and activate habits; it reflects both the primary and the secondary needs that are present. *Primary needs* depend upon deprivation of necessities such as food, water, and sex objects, and upon intensity of any noxious stimulation such as shock. This latter represents aversive drive. *Secondary needs* depend upon the presence of stimuli that previously have been paired with achievement of satisfying stimulation or escape from noxious stimuli. We have a secondary need for money because it has been paired with both our receipt of satisfying stimuli and our escape from noxious, undesirable stimuli.

An example of classical aversive conditioning occurs when a subject closes his eyelid as a puff of air strikes the cornea; he concurrently hears a tone, and eventually he comes to close his eyelid at the sound of the tone even in the absence of the noxious stimulus—the puff of air. The experimenter limits the response to a single, brief act—closing the eyelid—by having the noxious, unconditioned stimulus and the tone to be conditioned occur together for only a brief time. The tone becomes a conditioned stimulus.

In classical reward conditioning, the response is elicited by the reinforcing object—food, in the case of Pavlov's dogs. Thus, this object serves a dual function; it elicits the unconditioned reflex and provides the reinforcing event which brings about the conditioning of a substitute stimulus—the bell.[23]

What is the nature of instrumental conditioning?

In both classical and instrumental conditioning experiments, the experimenter aims to arrange for the occurrence of but a single response or response chain, which is followed by reinforcement, conditioning, or extinction of the S-R relation. In instrumental reward conditioning, the experimenter attempts to choose the strongest—most likely—response as the one to be conditioned. He then limits his investigation to a study of the strengthening of this single response. Thus, "Most instances of instrumental conditioning are really limiting cases of trial-and-

[23]Spence, *Behavior Theory and Conditioning, op. cit.,* pp. 46–49.

error learning in which competing responses, while minimized, still play a more or less important role."[24]

In a type of study of instrumental reward conditioning that was conducted by Spence, an animal was deprived of food for a specific length of time. He then was placed at one end of a "straight-ahead" alley, and his behavior was rewarded when he reached the other end of the alley; he received food. Then, the times that it took him to go down the alley in succeeding trials were recorded. Of course, the animal usually developed some competing responses other than merely going straight down the alley; for instance, it might turn its head or attempt to go up the side of the alley. But, only its arrival at the end of the alley would be rewarded, and only record made would be of the times the animal required to travel down the alley.[25]

Spence's special thesis was that, just as reinforcement is crucial to the occurrence of learning in classical conditioning, it is not essential to instrumental conditioning. Remember that classical conditioning is stimulus substitution, and instrumental conditioning is response modification. In instrumental conditioning, as Spence saw it, stimuli and responses are associated merely because they occur together; this is the law of contiguity.

Spence's key terms in his treatment of instrumental reward conditioning are *fractional anticipatory goal responses,* and a companion concept, *incentive motivational factors.* A fractional anticipatory goal response is an *acquired* incentive motivational factor.

In a chain of activity that transpires prior to an organism's reaching a goal, instrumental responses are strengthened merely because they occur, not because of their being reinforced through some act at the end of the chain of activity—reaching the goal. Reinforcement does occur at the end of the chain, e.g., the animal eats the food he finds in the goal box. By a process of classical conditioning, the sight of the goal box begins to elicit eating responses—salivating, chewing, etc. But, fractional anticipatory goal responses (r_g's), which also have motivational properties, tend to be elicited earlier in the chain of responses. Thus, respective r_g's affect earlier links of the chain of activity as incentive motivational factors, not as reinforcers. Spence stated, ". . . the evidence strongly suggests that the habit strength of instrumental reward responses is not a function of the level of appetitional needs during acquisition."[26] Thus, the

[24]Spence, *Behavior Theory and Learning, op. cit.,* p. 122.
[25]See Spence, *Behavior Theory and Conditioning, op. cit.,* pp. 37–39.
[26]*Ibid.,* p. 168.

habit strength of an instrumental response is not dependent upon the properties of its "reinforcer."

As previously stated, in instrumental learning involving reward, classical conditioning also is taking place. For conditioning to occur, a subject must respond to a goal object either by consuming it or by perceiving it. Thus, events at the goal are important. Such a reinforcing act produces the conditioning of fractional goal responses to stimulus cues throughout the response chain of the activity prior to the goal. These conditioned responses (r_g's) and the stimuli they produce (s_g's) serve as important integrators of behavior; they are incentive motivational factors (K).[27] The strength of the incentive motivational factor at any stage of instrumental reward learning depends upon the conditions of reinforcement at the end of the chain of activity—the magnitude and delay of reinforcement at the end of the chain—and on the stage of training—the number of previously reinforced trials.

Whereas needs and drives are organism-centered, r_g's are "goal-oriented." The longer the behavior chain from the initial action to reinforcement at the end, the less similar are the stimulus cues at the beginning to those at the end of the chain, and hence the weaker are the fractional anticipatory goal responses at the beginning of the sequence. The ". . . differences in reaction potential (E) of responses at different distances from the reinforcement end of the behavior chain are due to differences in the [incentive motivational] K factor rather than to differences in [habit strength] H."[28]

How did Spence study selective learning?

Selective learning consists of spatial trial-and-error and discrimination learning. It is an extension of instrumental conditioning to experimental situations designed so that two or more equally strong chains of responses are possible, or several stimuli "compete" for evocation of a response. Whereas in trial-and-error learning the subject selects a response from among competing responses, in discrimination learning the subject selects a stimulus from among competing stimuli.

In studying spatial trial-and-error learning Spence experimented with a single choice point type of maze that had two or more

[27]See Ernest R. Hilgard, *Theories of Learning*, 2nd ed., New York: Appleton-Century-Crofts, 1956, p. 416.
[28]Spence, *Behavior Theory and Conditioning*, op. cit., p. 151.

Figure 6.5
Ground Plan of the Single Choice Point Maze. An Adaptation
from Kenneth W. Spence, Behavior Theory and Conditioning,
Yale University Press, 1956, p. 28.

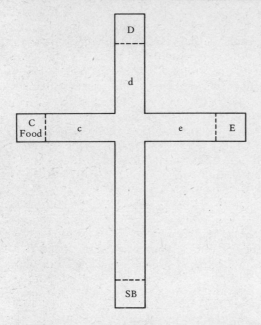

choices at the choice point. The subject learned to turn and
proceed in one direction consistently.

Figure 6.5 shows the ground plan for a single choice point
maze. An animal is placed in the starting box (SB) and he is to
learn upon reaching the choice point to enter and run down
alley c to reach the goal object (a piece of food) in end box C
and not to enter alleys d or e which lead to empty end boxes D
and E.

What are the components of trial-and-error learning?

A spatial trial-and-error type of experiment has four major components: (1) a motivated organism, (2) an environmental choice
situation which offers several alternate response possibilities, (3)
the behavior possibilities of the organism, and (4) the situation
or stimulus events consequent to the several responses.[29]

[29]*Ibid.*, pp. 28–34.

A motivated organism. An organism is motivated when it is deprived of some appetitional need such as food or provided some discomfort such as shock. Motivation is achieved by manipulating the organism's past or present environment so that tension within the organism is either created or increased.

An environmental choice situation. Such a situation offers a number of discriminable aspects or objects which may serve as potential stimuli to which the animal may respond in several different ways. In the maze pictured in Figure 6.5, potential stimuli to which the organism may respond are the three alternative pathways, the wire top of the apparatus, the door leading from the starting box, corners of the choice chamber, and others. The environmental choice situation, as such, contains no reinforcing agent, for example, food or escape from shock. Furthermore, any relation of the various points of the maze to a reinforcing event is not immediately apparent without occurrence of the appropriate response; the animal is not trying to do anything and is not "sizing up" the situation in which it is involved.

Behavior possibilities. An organism brings to a new situation a variety of innate and acquired response tendencies which differ in relative strengths or likelihood of occurrence. A combination of the motivating state and the environmental situation impels the animals to respond to various aspects of the situation until either a reinforcer is reached or the animal is removed from the situation. Each response consists of a chain of movements or skills involving sensory-motor integrations of varying complexity that have been acquired prior to the experiment. Trial-and-error learning is a process of elimination of erroneous responses, and establishment of the correct response to the point that it occurs promptly on each trial. The course of simple trial-and-error selective learning is marked by gradual decrease in frequency of occurrence of incorrect, nonreinforced response chains and gradual increase in the frequency of occurrence of the correct, reinforced response sequence.

Consequent stimulus events. A selective trial-and-error type of experiment is designed so that one potential response, the *correct* one, leads to a reinforcing event, while all other responses do not bring reinforcement. Now, what are reinforcers?

Spence developed the meaning of reinforcers by describing how reinforcement occurs. Thus, he noted that in simple selective learning situations, psychologists have observed that, when certain types of environmental events accompany or follow a particular response, the response is more likely to occur on subsequent occasions. Moreover, omission of such events following a response may be observed to lead to a lessened likelihood of its occurrence. *Reinforcers* or *reinforcing events* are environmental events which exhibit the property of increasing the probability of occurrence of responses that they accompany. All environmental events that do not exhibit this property fall into a different class called *nonreinforcers*. By means of these two classes of events—reinforcers and nonreinforcers—it becomes possible to formulate the following law: "Responses accompanied or followed by certain kinds of events (namely, reinforcers) are more likely to occur on subsequent occasions, whereas responses followed by certain other kinds of events (namely, nonreinforcers) do not subsequently show a greater likelihood of occurrence."[30] In the experimental design depicted in Figure 6.5, food is a reinforcer.

How does discrimination differ from spatial trial-and-error selective learning?

As stated on p. 169, in discrimination selective learning a subject selects a stimulus from among competing stimuli. In a discrimination maze, the subject must learn to enter a certain colored arm regardless of its position; one may be white and the other black, but their relative positions are changed repeatedly throughout the learning period. The organism must select—respond to—the right stimulus. Thus, the two types of selective learning experiments, trial-and-error and discrimination, have much in common.

Spence confined his discrimination learning experiments to relatively simple situations in which ". . . the stimulus configuration contained two discriminanda [alternatives] differing in a single attribute or dimension such as brightness, size, form, etc."[31] However, he anticipated extension of his study to more complicated types of discrimination learning, which involve the principle of patterning. In testing a theory of discrimination he preferred to employ simple types of stimulus cues such as brightness, rather than more complex ones such as form and size.

WHAT MAY QUANTITATIVE S-R THEORY OFFER SCHOOLS OF THE FUTURE?

To psychologists of a logical-empiricistic bend, such as Spence, there is a science of learning and a technology of education, and

[30]*Ibid.*, p. 33.
[31]Spence, *Behavior Theory and Learning, op. cit.*, p. 390.

we should distinguish sharply between the two. Teaching and education are related to psychology and the other behavioral sciences in the same way that engineering is related to the physical sciences and medicine to the biological sciences. Just as engineers use scientific knowledge to design and shape hardware, educators likewise should use scientific knowledge to design and shape human "software."

Spence confined his experimentation to simple learning situations involving classical and instrumental conditioning and selective learning. However, he anticipated that, in time and with the addition of some new variables, the basic principles and theories derived from study of simple learning situations would be applicable to behavior such as children display in school. He and his associates chose to investigate simpler phenomena first because of their conviction that it is in this area that formulation of psychological laws and principles would be most rapid.

Although Spence's psychological study was not applied to school situations as such, teachers may assume that his findings in experiments with simple phenomena will apply, perhaps with adaptations, to complex learning situations. However, in applying these principles, teachers, too, should adopt an experimental attitude; they should take careful note of the educational outcomes of their application. They should bear in mind that "The laws that the experimental learning psychologist has discovered and the theories that he has formulated with respect to them grew out of these laboratory phenomena and as yet have not been related to instances of learning in real life.' "[32]

Spence thought that, insofar as the variables operating in simple behavior are also present in complex behavior, the same psychological laws would hold. However, he recognized that, in more complex situations, there would be additional variables and that lawful relations of the new variables to the more basic ones would need to be taken into account. He felt that we are at least beginning to attain the knowledge necessary to predict and hence control behavior in new situations. He stated,

> Twenty-five years of experimentation with classical and instrumental conditioning have led to the discovery and formulation of a quite extensive body of fairly precise quantitative laws descriptive of the manner in which the stimulus, motivational, and incentive variables interact with each other and with various practice variables to determine performance in these situations.[33]

[32]Kenneth W. Spence, "Current Interpretations of Learning Data and Some Recent Developments in Stimulus-Response Theory," *op. cit.*, p. 2.

[33]Kenneth W. Spence, "The Relation of Learning Theory to the Technology of Education," *op. cit.*, p. 90.

However, he saw a great need for study of situations that involved different numbers and different delays of reinforcement, and those where a response tendency is weakened by nonreinforcement—extinction.

In what learning areas may research be developed?

Spence thought that psychologists eventually should design experiments which would result in studies revealing lawful relationships in at least six major areas of human activity.[34] These areas are classical and instrumental conditioning; spatial, nonspatial, and verbal selective learning; rote and maze serial learning; perceptual and motor skills learning; symbolic learning in the form of thinking and reasoning; and social learning in the form of attitudes and interests. He felt that adequate research in these areas ultimately would produce the knowledge needed for teachers effectually to direct the learning of students.

As to whether theories developed from laboratory experiments, when sufficiently elaborated, would enable explanation and control of behavior in real-life situations, Spence could only point to the success that such a type of theory has had in the physical sciences and assume that the same development would occur in psychology. In laboratory investigations of human behavior, psychologists have developed their objective methods of quantifying properties of behavior and its effects similar to the procedures ". . . in the other biological and physical sciences."[35]

How is language related to learning?

The fact that human beings talk to themselves and to others must be given careful consideration in a study of human learning. When principles developed through study of the behavior of lower animals are extended to man, language becomes an important factor. Indeed, Spence thought that study and analysis of language behavior of human beings was the key to investigations of complex motives, human adjustment, conflict and anxiety, attitudes and interests, and problem solving and reasoning. He also thought that psychologists have made only the barest beginning in these areas and that they should attempt to study all of the areas by objective techniques before they decide that some are not susceptible to empirical investigation. Spence

[34]*Ibid.*, p. 92.
[35]Spence, *Behavior Theory and Learning, op. cit.*, p. 76.

granted that perhaps some aspects of human activity, such as selfhood and conscience, cannot be studied objectively, but he also thought that we should attempt their study before decreeing that it cannot be done.[36]

Although Spence did not attempt to devise a theory of language, as such, he did think that words could act as stimuli and responses in the same way as do nonverbal physical objects. Hence, words may be viewed as a type of human stimulus and response, but they differ somewhat from simple, pure stimulus acts or cue producing responses. Let us examine how a quantitative S-R theorist like Spence sees language entering behavior situations.[37]

1. *Words are stimuli.* Words may constitute or modify a stimulus complex or pattern and elicit those classical or instrumental responses that previously have been conditioned to those words. A person comes to respond to "snake" as if a snake were present.

2. *Words are responses.* Like other behaviors, verbalizations have different habit strengths of association with different stimulus words. In middle-class American culture the habit strength of "sex" and "sin" is stronger than is the habit strength of "food" and "sin."

3. *Conditioning may be a verbal process.* A human organism may gain additional habit strength by performing stimulus-response-reinforcement sequences verbally. Symbols may be both stimuli and responses, and their connections may be reinforced by a symbolic stimulus. A teacher says—stimulates the child with —"dog"; the child says—responds with—"D-O-G"; the teacher says—provides the reinforcement—"Good." The effect of this verbal conditioning process depends upon the correspondence between the actual situation and the implicitly—verbally—practiced relationship.

4. *Words become secondary drive objects.* A secondary drive object induces an aroused state of an organism because it is associated with a need which activates the organism. A word may be conditioned as a secondary drive stimulus; in turn its occurrence will affect the organism's motivation as a secondary drive object. The word "dentist" is neutral to a child the first time he hears it. However, with a few visits to a dentist, it soon becomes closely associated with evocation and rapid increase of drive-produced stimuli—pain. "Dentist" comes to be something to be escaped or

[36]*Ibid.,* p. 80.
[37]See Frank A. Logan, "The Hull-Spence Approach," in Sigmund Koch, ed., *Psychology: A Study of a Science:* New York: McGraw-Hill, 1959, p. 302.

avoided; it is a secondary drive object. It has acquired a tendency to bring about painful drive stimuli.

5. *Incentive motivation can be affected by verbal cues.* Words can be used as secondary reinforcers. Secondary reinforcement occurs when an originally neutral or impotent stimulus becomes associated with some primary reinforcing stimulus and thereby itself becomes effective in reducing a need.[38] To span a long delay of actual reinforcement, an individual says, "I'll get paid for this tomorrow," and he proceeds to perform a task for which there is no immediate reward other than his talking to himself. Or, a previous stimulus-response sequence can be reinstated verbally immediately preceding a reinforcement: one says, "I'm getting paid for what I did yesterday."

What was Spence's attitude toward programmed learning?

Although Spence's own interests were confined to basic, pure research, he did endorse programmed learning and the use of teaching machines as advocated by Skinner. The essential requirement of programmed learning is that the response one desires to strengthen be made to occur and then be followed *immediately* by occurrence of a reinforcer. Programming requires a student to compose an answer to a question and then, if he is correct, provides him immediately with reinforcement. Programming keeps high the probability that responses will be appropriate, and this insures frequency of reinforcement.

According to Spence, application of the law of effect—reinforcement—is the primary principle behind the use of programmed learning and teaching machines. He stated that the law of effect is the

. . . one law that seems to me to have held consistently in all of our experimental studies of learning, no matter what the complexity of the situation . . . responses accompanied or followed by certain kinds of events (called reinforcers) are more likely to occur on subsequent occasions, whereas responses not followed by this class of events subsequently show a lessened probability of occurrence.[39]

Thus, programmed learning is to be based on the law of effect.

Spence predicted that a change in the function of teachers would result from the advancement of programmed learning and

---

[38]See Chapter 4, p. 94, for a description of secondary reinforcement.

[39]Kenneth W. Spence, "The Relation of Learning Theory to the Technology of Education," *op. cit.*, p. 93.

the use of teaching machines. A primary duty of teachers will be that of inculcating interests and goals in students; these will serve both as secondary reinforcers and incentive motivators. He further stated that acquisition of secondary reinforcing and incentive motivational properties by stimulus events is a fairly simple kind of classical conditioning about which we possess a considerable amount of knowledge.[40]

BIBLIOGRAPHY

CHAPLIN, JAMES P., and T. S. KRAWIEC, *Systems and Theories of Psychology*, 2nd ed., New York: Holt, Rinehart and Winston, 1968, pp. 291–296.
A briefer interpretation of Spencian learning theory.

HILGARD, ERNEST R., *Theories of Learning*, 2nd ed., New York: Appleton-Century-Crofts, 1956.
See pp. 414–420 for Spence's interpretation of reinforcement; pp. 434–445 for Spence's approach to discrimination learning.

LOGAN, FRANK A., "The Hull-Spence Approach," in Sigmund Koch, ed., *Psychology: A Study of a Science*, Study I, Vol. 2, *General Systematic Formulations, Learning, and Special Processes*, New York: McGraw-Hill, 1959, pp. 293–358.
An excellent, brief presentation of the Hullian-Spencian approach to learning. Spence's position *per se* is summarized on pp. 311–314.

SPENCE, KENNETH W., *Behavior Theory and Conditioning*, New Haven Conn.: Yale University Press, 1956.
A series of lectures which present major aspects of Spence's psychology.

SPENCE, KENNETH W., *Behavior Theory and Learning*, Englewood Cliffs, N.J.: Prentice-Hall, 1960.
A collection of Spence's research papers, most of which had been published previously in periodicals, etc. Provides the research basis for his learning theory.

SPENCE, KENNETH W., "Current Interpretations of Learning Data and Some Recent Developments in Stimulus-Response Theory," in Donald K. Adams *et al.*, *Learning Theory, Personality Theory," and Clinical Research*, New York: John Wiley, 1954, pp. 1–21.
The opening address in a 1953 symposium. Spence summarizes data investigated in learning experiments and the resultant theories, then presents recent developments in his own position.

SPENCE, KENNETH W., "The Empirical Basis and Theoretical Structure of Psychology," *Philosophy of Science*, April 1957, pp. 97–108.
A semihistorical approach to the aspects of the philosophy of science—logical empiricism—as they bear on experimental psychology. Pages 107–108 present Spence's operational scheme.

[40]*Ibid.*, p. 95.

SPENCE, KENNETH W., "The Relation of Learning Theory to the Technology of Education," *Harvard Educational Review*, Spring 1959. One of three papers in a symposium on the relation of a science of psychology and a technology of education. Appraisal of current state of learning theory with emphasis upon need for precise, basic research. Other two papers of symposium also are recommended.

SPENCE, KENNETH W., "Theoretical Interpretations of Learning," in S. S. Stevens, ed., *Handbook of Experimental Psychology*, New York: Wiley, 1951, pp. 690–729. An excellent, brief presentation of learning theories and their implications.

SEVEN

What Is
Field
Psychology?

In Chapter 2 readers are introduced to *mental discipline, natural unfoldment,* and *apperception.* These three outlooks toward learning, although now seldom promoted in teacher-education institutions, continue to be reflected in many present-day school practices. In Chapters 3 and 4, the two major contemporary families of learning theory, stimulus-response conditioning theory and Gestalt-field theory, are described in a general way. Then, Chapters 5 and 6 present two systematic examples of the behavioristic S-R conditioning family, Skinner's operant conditioning and Spence's quantitative S-R theory.

The next chapter presents a current representative of the Gestalt-field family, the cognitive-field psychology of learning. However, since cognitive-field theorists rely heavily upon Lewinian field psychology for many basic psychological concepts, a study of field psychology, as such, is an essential precursor to an understanding of cognitive-field learning theory. Accordingly, the present chapter is devoted to an examination of field psychology as it was developed by the late Kurt Lewin. Then, Chapter 8 builds upon the concepts of Lewin, along with those of a number of other psychologists to depict a cognitive-field theory of learning. Some of the others who have made worthy contributions to cognitive-field theory are Gordon W. Allport, Adelbert Ames, Jr., Roger G. Barker, Ernest E. Bayles, Boyd H. Bode, Jerome S. Bruner, Hadley Cantril, Arthur W. Combs, Morton Deutsch, John Dewey, Sigmund Koch, Rollo May, Donald Snygg, Edward C. Tolman and Herbert F. Wright.

Kurt Lewin (1890–1947), a native of Germany, received his doctorate at the University of Berlin where he was later professor of psychology and philosophy. In 1932 he came to the United States. He taught at Stanford, Cornell, and Iowa, and in 1944 became director of the Research Center for Group Dynamics at the Massachusetts Institute of Technology.[1] (It was at this time that he Americanized the pronunciation of his name from La-veen to Lewin.)

WHAT ARE THE BASIC FEATURES OF FIELD PSYCHOLOGY?

Lewin was interested primarily in a study of human motivation. Consequently, his field theory was developed not as a theory of learning, but as a theory of motivation and perception. However, he was concerned with the application of his theory to learning situations, and he did some writing in this vein.[2] Lewin thought that the net effect of simultaneous psychological forces operating in a psychological field or life space of an individual brings about a reorganization of that field and thereby provides the basis for psychological behavior. Thus, his basic, comprehensive concept was *life space*. Consequently, *life space* has become a model or paradigm for relativistic psychological thinking. It includes everything that one needs to know about a person in order to understand his concrete behavior in a specific psychological environment at a given time. Accordingly, it encompasses the *person* under consideration and his psychological environment. Its use implies that we cannot understand why an individual behaves as he does merely by knowing the characteristics of either a person or his environment; instead, we must know both.

Since Lewin considered psychology a science closely related to everyday life, he wanted most of all to study the various problems of the social sciences involving minority groups, po-

[1]See Alfred J. Marrow, *The Practical Theorist: The Life and Work of Kurt Lewin*, New York: Basic Books, 1969.
[2]See Kurt Lewin, "Field Theory and Learning," in Nelson B. Henry, ed., *The Psychology of Learning*, Part II, *The Forty-first Yearbook of the National Society for the Study of Education*, Chicago: University of Chicago Press, pp. 215–242.

litical organizations, and international and intercultural relations. In the course of applying his psychological theory to problems in these areas he became interested in "teaching" and "learning." In keeping with his interests, he developed some new problems for psychology and was highly creative in his methods for solving them. He thought that actual experiments with groups could be performed under precisely controlled conditions. Hence, he became a pioneer leader in development of methods for conducting group dynamics, action research, and sensitivity training.

His study of the effects of various social climates on youth is an example of his experiments. This study was conducted with groups of boys in a boys' club. By means of the relationship of a leader to his respective group, he experimentally developed anarchic, autocratic, and democratic social climates. Careful note was made of the behaviors of the boys in each social climate. The process required to change the social climate of a group from one form to another also was studied.[3] In many circles, action research has become an accepted method of scientific procedure. In action research, group studies are so performed that key individuals in the social situation being investigated actively participate in conducting the study through their serving as recorders, observers, and analyzers. Through this method, teachers may systematically study the student-teacher relationships that exist in their own schools.

The psychological studies sponsored by Lewin centered on five different types of problems: (1) recall of unfinished tasks, (2) development of levels of aspiration, (3) substitution of actions to release tensions, (4) development of satiation in regard to performance of tasks, and (5) the development of anger. All these studies involved changes in psychological tensions, and Lewin equated the development of tensions with the development of intensions or purposes.

The center of Lewin's psychological interest was in the motivating conditions of person-environment situations, and he was extremely interested in democratic principles and practices. Consequently, it is no accident that his psychological system provides a foundation for a psychology of learning germane to American democratic society. Although field theory is applicable to all fields of psychology, it is particularly useful in social, personality, and educational psychology.

Lewin thought that during its development psychology some-

[3]See Kurt Lewin, *Resolving Social Conflicts*, New York: Harper & Row, 1948, pp. 71–83 and Ralph K. White and Ronald Lippitt, *Autocracy and Democracy: An Experimental Inquiry*, New York: Harper & Row, 1960.

how had missed much of what was at the heart of scientific modes of thought. Furthermore, he was convinced that the various S-R conditioning theories represented an inadequate approach to the study of psychology. Consequently, he developed his "field psychology" in such way as to make it fundamentally different from the various behaviorisms. Whereas behaviorists study psychology as a series of events, the very term *field* of field psychology implies that, psychologically interpreted, everything happens at once.

Lewin's goal was to make the concepts of field psychology of sufficient scope to be applicable to all kinds of behavior and yet specific enough to permit representation of a definite person in a concrete situation. He observed that conventional laws of behavioristic psychology are based on statistical predictions, and that statistical predictions may apply to the average of children or to the typical behavior of an age group, but they do not anticipate what a given person will do in a specific situation. Therefore, he thought that objectivity in psychology demanded representing the field adequately and accurately as it exists for an individual at a particular time. Accordingly, to be objective in psychology one must be subjective; one must observe situations as the person being studied views them.[4]

Lewin's contributions have made a great impact on contemporary psychology. In 1958 Gardner Murphy wrote, "For it was the genius of Kurt Lewin that gave us the most appropriate tools for analyzing this problem of the diversity of human natures and the correlative problem of the flexibility, the range, the potentialities of human natures, both as they may take place in the world of today and as future human societies may know them."[5]

What is the method of field psychology?

Lewin's field psychology more precisely is called *topological and vector* psychology. In developing his psychology he borrowed ideas and concepts from other disciplines, especially geometry and physics. The key concepts that he borrowed were "topology" from geometry and "vector" from physics. However, in using these and related concepts, he did not adhere rigidly to the definitions of their mother sciences, but construed them in a manner most useful to his system of psychology.

[4]See Chapter 8, p. 238.
[5]Gardner Murphy, *Human Potentialities*, New York: Basic Books, 1958, p. 302.

Some scientists have criticized Lewin for giving these terms a somewhat different meaning from what they have had in other areas of knowledge. Lewin has answered their criticism by stating that scientists in any area should use any concepts in the way that lend themselves most effectually to pursuit of their problems. Relativists encourage cooperation among all scientific endeavors, but they do not insist that any area of science be restricted by the specific laws, principles, concepts, and definitions of a sister science.

Through use of topological and vector concepts, Lewin pictured psychological reality in terms of field relationships of a person and his psychological environment. In so doing he applied the method of field theory as it had been developed in the physical sciences. However, since the specific concepts of the physical sciences did not lend themselves to a science of psychology, he did not use the same concepts and facts as did field theorists in sister sciences.

What is the role of theories and laws in field psychology?

In contrast to the professed practices of many behaviorists, including Skinner, Lewin made much use of theories and hypotheses. To him, theories fulfilled two coordinate functions; they accounted for what is known and thereby also pointed the way to new knowledge. Hence, scientific method included not only the processes of observation and classification of data, but also formulating and testing hypotheses. Letting the facts speak for themselves was not enough. He wanted to develop considered hunches and see whether they would check out. Consequently, he deemed mere collection and classification of behavioral facts an inadequate process for answering questions involving conditions and causes of psychological events. Lewin agreed with behaviorists that research should begin with careful observation. However, since he emphasized the importance of inferring the motives of people being studied, his observation was done in a different way and for a different purpose. Thus, he wrote:

> Only with the help of theories can one determine causal interrelationships. A science without theory is blind because it lacks that element which alone is able to organize facts and to give direction to research. Even from a practical point of view the mere gathering of facts has limited value. It cannot give an answer to the question that is most important for practical purposes—namely, what must one do to obtain a desired effect in given concrete

184 Learning Theories for Teachers

cases? To answer this question it is necessary to have a theory, but a theory which is empirical and not speculative. This means that theory and fact must be closely related to each other.[6]

Lewin's purpose was to formulate laws—relationships—predictive of behavior of individual persons in their specific life spaces. He was convinced that, in order to understand and predict behavior, one must consider a person and his environment a pattern of interdependent facts and functions. Furthermore, he regarded as lawful all events that occur in a person's life space, even those happening only once. Thus, instead of placing emphasis on a mathematical average of as many different cases as possible, he centered attention on careful, full descriptions of particular person-environmental situations. Accordingly, he wrote, "The general laws of psychology are statements of the empirical relations between these constructive elements or certain properties of them. It is possible to construct an infinite number of constellations [life spaces] in line with these laws; each of these constellations corresponds to an individual case at a given time."[7]

WHAT ARE THE KEY CONCEPTS OF FIELD,
OR TOPOLOGICAL AND VECTOR, PSYCHOLOGY?

Readers will find this section, which explains why field psychology is more specifically named "topological and vector psychology," somewhat technical and perhaps difficult. However, should they seek sharper insights into the deeper implications of field theory, this section will greatly enhance their understanding.

Lewin, in development of field psychology, made much use of constructs. A construct is an invented idea. It points to the fact that the concept under consideration is not perceived directly, yet it is a notion that describes, or accounts for, phenomena which we may perceive. In the same way that the concepts *atom* and *gene* are nonpsychological constructs, *life space*, *person*, and *valence* are examples of psychological ones. In a sense, science largely is a matter of invention, development, refinement, and testing of constructs. Lewinians speak of observable data as *phenotypes* and unobservable constructural representations as *genotypes*.

[6]Kurt Lewin, *Principles of Topological Psychology*, New York: McGraw-Hill, 1936, p. 4.
[7]Kurt Lewin, *Field Theory in Social Science*, New York: Harper & Row, 1951, p. 61.

Lewin said, "Topological and vectorial concepts combine power of analysis, conceptual precision, usefulness for derivation and fitness for the total range of psychological problems in a way which, in my opinion, make them superior to any other known conceptual tool in psychology."[8] He thought topological and vector, or field, psychology was characterized by a set of concepts or constructs which permitted representation of psychological reality in a highly adequate fashion. He wanted concepts broad enough to be applicable to all kinds of behavior and at the same time specific enough to represent a definite person in a concrete situation. Lewin's field psychology implements a person's being represented as separated from, yet enclosed within, a larger totality—his life space. Thus, it enables one to represent adequately a psychological situation, which includes a person, his environment, his needs, his goals, the barriers to his goals, and their dynamic interrelations.

For one to grasp fully the ideas of a relativistic, field psychology, it is essential that its key concepts be defined precisely as they are used in this frame of reference. In studying these concepts, readers should keep in mind the essential idea of field psychology, that is, the *meanings of all its constructs are mutually interdependent.* Each depends for its meaning upon the meanings of all the others. Thus, there are no independent and dependent variables as in S-R conditioning theories, instead, all *psychological variables are interdependent.*

Furthermore, it should be remembered that a diagram of a life space is figurative. It is difficult, perhaps impossible, to show everything at once. A complete and accurate image of a life space would show all of the psychological facts and constructs in a total situation represented by a differentiated person and a differentiated psychological environment. A differentiated person or environment is one structured, i.e., functionally divided into various aspects as perceived by the one being studied. Some differentiated aspects of a person are friends, ambitions, self-aggrandizement, and needs and abilities to know about various matters and to carry out activities of different kinds. A differentiated psychological environment contains everything perceived by the person at the time under study.

Also, we should guard against reifying or making physical things of the psychological constructs whose purpose is to symbolize relationships primarily functional in nature. For example, we should at no time think of a psychological person as

[8]Lewin, *The Psychology of Learning, op. cit.,* p. 219.

being synonymous with a biological organism or of a psychological and a physical environment as being the same concept.

We may divide the key constructs—invented ideas—of field psychology into three pivotal concepts—*life space, topology,* and *vector*—and a number of auxiliary concepts. Life space is Lewin's principal construct; it represents a contemporaneous situation. His other pivotal concepts, *topological* and *vector,* are used to identify the pivotal characteristics of a life space. His auxiliary concepts are employed to describe the dynamic functioning of a person and his environment. We describe each of the three pivotal concepts in some detail after which we provide brief definitions of the auxiliary concepts. We conclude the chapter with an explanation of the meaning of the term *behavior* within field psychology and a summary of the changes that Lewin thought constitute learning.

What is a life space?

Life space is a scientific formulation of a series of nonrecurring but overlapping situations, each replete with its unique propensities and relationships. It is developed for the purpose of (1) expressing what is possible and impossible in the life of a person and (2) anticipating what is likely to occur. It represents the total pattern of factors or influences that affect an individual's behavior at a certain moment, or longer juncture of time. Within field psychology, behavior is any change in a life space that is psychological, that is, in accordance with a growing intelligence (see pp. 193–195 for a field definition of behavior).

A person's life space is his psychological world or contemporaneous situation. It includes the *person* and his *psychological environment*—that part of his physical and social environment with which he is psychologically engaged at a juncture of a moment, or longer duration, because it is relevant to his purposes at that juncture.

A psychological environment, then, consists of perceived objects and events; not an undifferentiated medium into which a person is immersed. A person, psychologically construed, is a consciously behaving self.

A life space represents not physical objects as such, but functional and symbolic relationships. Hence, it includes not only presently perceived objects but also memories, language, myths, art, anticipation, and religion. A continuous series of overlapping life spaces represents the total psychological world in which a person lives. This psychological world may include the person's precepts, knowledge, and beliefs; his forward and backward time perspective; and abstract ideas as well as concrete objects.

A life space consists of functional regions, each having a positive or negative valence. (Regions and valences are explained in some detail on pp. 190–191.) A life space is surrounded by a non-psychological *foreign hull*—the aspects of the physical and social environment which to the person at the juncture under study are not psychological. The foreign hull of a life space consists of all the merely potential perceptions as contrasted with the actual functional perceptions of a person's unique field.

A person, his psychological environment, and the foreign hull of his life space are represented by concentric figures. A person is within his psychological environment and both are within the foreign hull. Nonpsychological factors observed only by an outsider can at the next moment become psychological ones for the person being studied. There can be movement both ways through the boundary of a person or a life space or through any of their regions. For an aspect of the physical-social world to influence the intelligent behavior of a person, it must be moved from a foreign hull into his life space through his interaction with it.

A person may be represented as a differentiated region of a life space (see Figure 7.1). The field of a newborn baby is something like "one big blooming buzzing confusion." Then, as one lives his life, although he may not think of it in these specific terms, his total situation is structured as his *self* or *person* and his *psychological environment*. Some aspects of experience involve the central core of a person; they are very near and dear to him. Others are of a less vital, peripheral sort. Hence,

Figure 7.1
A structured person in a life space.

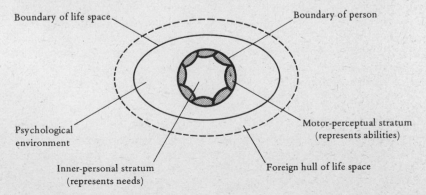

Boundary of life space

Boundary of person

Psychological environment

Motor-perceptual stratum (represents abilities)

Inner-personal stratum (represents needs)

Foreign hull of life space

we may think of a person as structured into outer and inner layers. Some experiences involve only the more peripheral areas, whereas others embrace the most central regions of a psychological person.

Psychologically, a person is composed of (1) a motor-perceptual stratum or region and (2) an inner-personal stratum or region. The motor-perceptual stratum has the position of a boundary zone between the inner-personal region and the psychological environment. It represents the knowing and manipulative abilities of a person. *Motor-perceptual system* denotes the phenomenon that a mechanist would see simply as body or organism. A mechanist, that is, would set his pattern of thinking in a biological rather than psychological frame of reference. In a sense, the motor-perceptual system is the tool of the inner-personal system. Like regions of the psychological environment, it provides opportunity and limits opportunity. However, it is more closely identified with the self than with the environment.

Whereas abilities are centered in the motor-perceptual system, needs are centered in the inner-personal system. A *need* is a state of a person that has a part in determining behavior toward any goal that may exist in relation to that state; it corresponds to a personal tension. Since the motor-perceptual region is functionally located between the inner-personal region and the environment, it performs functions of both person and environment. This means that a person acts in relation to his psychological environment and simultaneously realizes the consequences of so doing.

The form that the development of selfhood takes depends upon the interaction of a person and his psychological environment. An organism, in a sense, is an aspect of each—person and environment. Furthermore, whether something belongs to the self or to the environment depends, among other things, upon present needs and other factors of the inner-personal region. "Needs or other states of the inner-personal regions can influence the environment only by way of a bodily expression or a bodily action, that is, by way of a region which one can call the motor region."[9]

What is topology?

Topological ideas or terms—constructs—when applied to psychology, illustrate the position of a person in reference to his

9Lewin, *Principles of Topological Psychology, op. cit.,* p. 177.

functional goals and the barriers to their achievement. Thus, topology shows the various possibilities for psychological behavior or locomotion.

Topology is a nonmetrical geometry, which encompasses concepts such as inside, outside, and boundary, but has no dealings with length, breadth, or thickness. No distances are defined. Rather, topology is concerned with the relative position of the geometric figures being considered. "Topologically there is no difference between a circle, an ellipse, a regular or irregular polygon with any number of sides. . . . A drop of water and the earth are, from a topological point of view, fully equivalent."[10] It is helpful to think of a topological plane figure as being made of a perfectly elastic sheet of rubber; we may stretch, twist, pull, and bend it at pleasure, but the relationships it represents remain the same.

Two basic concepts that topological space denotes are connectedness and part-whole relationships. Topologically, things may be next to, inside, or outside one another. Size or shape has no significance in a topological figure. "Two figures are *topologically equivalent* if [and only if] one figure can be made to coincide with the other by an elastic motion."[11] The life spaces in Figure 7.2 are topologically equal. Each is a completely bounded area within a larger bounded area.

Topological concepts are used to represent the structure of a life space in such a way as to define the range of possible perceptions and actions. This is accomplished by showing the arrangement of the functional parts of a life space. The parts are shown as various regions and their boundaries. When an individual structures, i.e., makes sense of his life space, he divides it into regions. Boundaries of the major parts of a life space and their respective regions are either quite firm or more or less porous and permeable.

In addition to the person whose life space is being studied, regions represent activities like eating, going to the movies, and making decisions; more passive incidents like being fired or being rewarded; and social entities such as family, church, school, and gang. If the region "going to the movies" is located in a person's life space, the person is either engaging in or thinking about engaging in that activity. If "being fired" is in his life space, he is perceiving that incident and its conse-

[10]Lewin, *Principles of Topological Psychology, op. cit.*, p. 88.
[11]Bradford H. Arnold, *Intuitive Concepts in Elementary Topology*, Englewood Cliffs, N.J.: Prentice-Hall, 1962, p. 24.

Figure 7.2
Topology of life space—three equal figures.

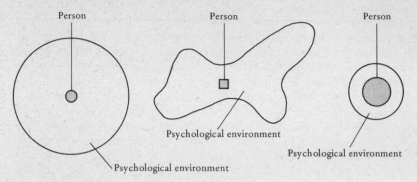

quences. "Church" in a life space involves what one makes out of what "church" means to him.[12]

What does vector mean?

The concept *vector* is borrowed from a system used in mechanics to represent direction and strength as two of the three properties of a force. The third property is its point of application. In psychology a vector represents a force that is influencing psychological movement toward or away from a goal (see Figure 7.3). A force is a tendency to act in a certain way or direction. A vector is a concept equivalent to, and descriptive of, a psychological force. If there is only one vector—force—there is locomotion in the direction toward which the vector points. However, if two or more vectors are pointing in several different ways, movement is in the direction of the resultant force.

Vectors indicate the moving forces within a topological structure; they picture what is happening or likely to happen. Hence, vectors indicate the valences of respective environmental regions —functional parts—of a life space. Valences are the attracting or repelling powers of regions; they may be either positive or negative. When an environmental object or event has positive valence for a person it is attractive to him, i.e., it supports fulfillment of a psychological need. When an object or event has negative valence it is repulsive, i.e., it threatens, impedes, or prevents the fulfillment of a need. Goal regions have either

---

[12]See Dorwin Cartwright, "Lewinian Theory as a Contemporary Systematic Framework," in Sigmund Koch, ed., *Psychology: A Study of a Science*, New York: McGraw-Hill, 1959, p. 25.

Figure 7.3
 A vector.

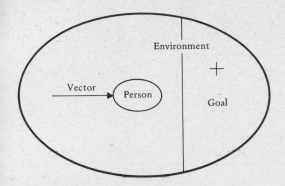

positive or negative valences; barrier regions have only negative
ones. Each vector, then, represents a force, which correlates
with the valence of a region of the life space; it is drawn as
an arrow which shows the respective force's direction, strength,
and point of application.

Whereas topological concepts are used to illustrate structurally
what is possible, vectorial concepts describe the dynamics of a
situation—what is happening or is likely to happen. Thus, vectors
deal with the tendencies of a life space to change or resist
change. In an illustration of what is happening or likely to
happen, a vector may represent either a driving or a restraining
force. A driving force is a tendency to change or move. A restraining force is a barrier or obstacle to psychological locomotion
which opposes some driving force. Both driving and restraining
forces may arise from the needs and abilities of the person being
studied, from actions of another person, or from the impersonal
aspects of a situation.[13]

What are the key auxiliary concepts of field psychology?

The pivotal concepts—life space, topology, and vector—and the
constructs that are auxiliary to the basic formula—$B = f\,(P, E)$
—are illustrated in Figure 7.4. The latter are described in the
following glossary of key auxiliary concepts of field psychology.
These constructs represent usable ideas, not "objective" self-
evident phenomena.

An analysis of the structure and dynamics of the life space

[13]See pp. 320–322 for an application of vectorial concepts to teaching.

Figure 7.4
Life space of an individual.

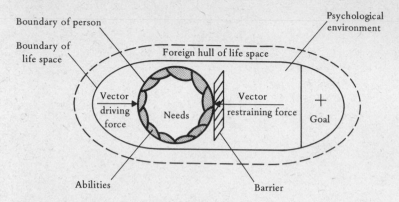

of a student in school will reveal numerous interdependent aspects of the situation, such as the person's relationships with his teacher and other students, the social pressures arising from his family, and even the consequences of his family's relations with other families. All of these various factors of a situation may be expressed through the use of the key pivotal and auxiliary concepts of field psychology.

Key auxiliary concepts of field psychology

Person.   A consciously behaving self. Center of abilities and needs. That which a child means when he says "I" or "me."

Psychological environment.   Everything in which, toward which, or away from which a person can make psychological movement—do anything about. Person and psychological environment are mutually interdependent upon one another.

Foreign hull of life space.   Complex of all nonpsychological facts that surround a life space. That part of a person's physical and social environment which, at a particular juncture, is not included in his psychological environment. Physical and social raw materials. Foreign hull limits behavioral possibilities.

Regions.   Psychologically significant conditions, places, things, and activities defined functionally as parts of a life space. They have positive or negative valences.

Valences.   Positive or negative imperative environmental facts. Properties that regions of a life space have if an individual is drawn toward them or away from them. A region that possesses a positive valence is one of such nature that forces correlated with the valence of that region tend to move the person in the direction of that region. A negative valence means that forces tend to move the person away from that region.

Needs. (person-centered) States of a person which, if they exist in relation to a goal, have a part in determining behavior toward that goal. Correspond to a tension system of the inner-personal region of a person.

Abilities. (person-centered) Cognitive—capacity to know environment. Manipulative—capacity to affect environment.

Tension. Very closely related to, and descriptive of, psychological needs. The state of one system relative to the state of surrounding systems. Either created as a result of opposed forces, or induced by internal physiological changes or external stimuli. The rise of tension is an intention. Release of tension may be achieved either through reaching a goal or through restructuring the life space. The release of tension corresponds to the satisfaction of a need.

Goal. A region of valence toward, or away from, which forces within a life space point. Region of life space toward, or away from, which a person is psychologically drawn.

Barrier. Dynamic part of an environment which resists motion through it. That which stands in the way of a person's reaching his goal.

Force. Immediate determinant of the locomotions of a person. The tendency to act in a certain direction. Its properties are strength, direction, and point of application. It is represented by a vector. The strength of a force is related to, but not identical with, the strength of a valence. The combination of forces acting at the same point at a given time is a resultant force. Force is analogous to, but not identical with, *drive* or *excitatory tendency* as used in behaviorism. (*Drive*, behavioristically defined, is a strong, persistent stimulus that demands an adjustive response.)

Cognitive structure. An environment, including a person, as known by the person. Synonyms are *insight* or *understanding*. Has one dimension—clarity.

WHAT IS BEHAVIOR?

In field psychology, the term *behavior*, when used, is interpreted quite differently from the way that behaviorists commonly define it. The latter, in harmony with their interpretation of psychology as a study of the relationships of biological organisms and their physical and social environments, think of behavior as some kind and degree of measurable, and publicly observable, muscular or glandular movement. The movement may be only incipient or covert or it may be overt; nevertheless, its being behavior means that it is physical movement. Were adequate devices available, it supposedly could be observed and measured. Field psychologists do not accept this definition of behavior. For them, psychological behavior involves purpose and intelligence; hence, it is not correlated one-to-one with physical movement. Furthermore, it is not directly observable but must be inferred through study of observable behavior.

In speaking of behavior, field psychologists imply psychological locomotion but not necessarily any sort of physiological movement. One may "come closer" to another person, yet exhibit no physical evidence of locomotion. Behavior takes place in a life space, rather than in observable space. Psychological behavior is more or less conscious—verbal or symbolic—and may be equated with experience. Every specific instance of behavior must be viewed as the result of interaction of several pertinent features of a concrete situation. Then, broadly defined, behavior means any change in a life space that is subject to psychological laws. Thus, behavior may be a change of the relative location of a person and his environment, a cognitive reorganization of his environment, or a restructuring of his person. It also includes any change in valence of any part of his life space.

Psychological behavior and *locomotion* are analogous concepts. *Behavior* describes the simultaneous functional changes within a life space of an individual. *Locomotion* refers to the relative positions of respective regions of a person's *temporally continuous* life spaces. When we concentrate study upon a person and his current environmental situation, *behavior* adequately denotes changes that occur in a life space. However, when we consider a time element, a person appears to occupy a series of overlapping life spaces. The life spaces usually manifest a continuity; they are similar but not identical. Change in subsequent life spaces is locomotion. Consequently, depending upon whether we are centering our study upon the person-environment interactivity or the psychological continuity of a person's life spaces, we may interpret any psychological change in terms of either behavior or locomotion; behavior centers upon how one sizes things up, locomotion on what one does about it as he moves into new life spaces. So, psychological behavior may be

(1) an overt purposive act, (2) an attitudinal shift, (3) a change in the perceived value of an object or activity, or (4) a new relationship established between two or more events.

WHAT KINDS OF CHANGES CONSTITUTE LEARNING?

Lewin considered learning to consist of four kinds of change, namely, *change in cognitive structure; change in motivation; change in group belongingness or ideology;* and *gain in voluntary control and dexterity of musculature*. He distinguished between the first two rather sharply. Thus, he tended to separate cognitive and motivational problems. To him, change in cognitive structure meant development of perceptual knowledge. It was centered in the topological—structural—aspects of a situation. Change in motivation, in contrast, meant learning to like or dislike certain regions—aspects—of a life space. However, he recognized that even changes in motivation arise from changes in cognitive structure; for a child to change the valence of an activity he must change the cognitive structure of his life space in regard to it.

Growing into a culture through one's change in group belongingness and ideology and one's development of skills also involves primarily perceptions of oneself and the people and objects around him. Thus, these two types of change, too, are principally a process of change in the cognitive structure. Consequently, in treating learning, Lewin's pivotal concept was change in cognitive structure. In 1945 he wrote, "A change in action ideology, a real acceptance of a changed set of facts and values, a change in the perceived social world—all three are but different expressions of the same process."[14]

BIBLIOGRAPHY

ADAMS, DONALD K., *The Anatomy of Personality*, New York: Random House, 1954.
A short treatise which applies field theory to personality development.
ARNOLD, BRADFORD H., *Intuitive Concepts in Elementary Topology*, Englewood Cliffs, N.J.: Prentice-Hall, 1962.
A readable explanation of topology—the "rubber sheet geometry"—from an intuitive viewpoint. Chapter 1 is especially helpful.
BIGGE, MORRIS L., "The Harmonies and Conflicts of Principles of Topological and Vector Psychology with the Tenets of Three Educational

[14]Lewin, *Resolving Social Conflicts, op. cit.,* p. 64.

Philosophies," unpublished doctoral dissertation, University of Kansas, 1951.

Comparison of Lewin's principles of topological and vector—field—psychology with the tenets of idealism, realism, and pragmatism. They harmonize most closely with pragmatism; however, there are realistic overtones.

HILGARD, ERNEST R., *Theories of Learning*, 2nd ed., New York: Appleton-Century-Crofts, 1956.

Chapter 8 contains an interpretation of learning within Lewin's field psychology.

LEEPER, ROBERT W., *Lewin's Topological and Vector Psychology, a Digest and Critique*, Eugene: University of Oregon, 1943.

Presentation and criticism of Lewin's topological and vector psychology. Also an attempt at revision of Lewin's statements on some points. Leeper recognizes Lewin as a trailblazer but thinks some re-examination is in order.

LEWIN, KURT, *A Dynamic Theory of Personality*, Adams and Zener, trans., New York: McGraw-Hill, 1935.

A collection of articles which Lewin had written prior to 1935 and a new survey chapter. This book shows Lewin's earlier thinking as his topological and vector psychology was emerging.

LEWIN, KURT, "Environmental Forces" in Carl Murchison, ed., *A Handbook of Child Psychology*, 2nd ed. rev., Worcester, Mass.: Clark University Press, 1933, pp. 590–625.

One of the earliest English translations of Lewin's position, stated while he still was a professor at the University of Berlin. Describes many aspects of field psychology most incisively.

LEWIN, KURT, *Field Theory in Social Science*, New York: Harper & Row, 1951.

A collection of Kurt Lewin's papers. The first three and last chapters develop guiding principles and constructs of field psychology. The remaining six chapters demonstrate application of field psychological principles to study of learning, development and regression, ecology, group dynamics, and social psychology.

LEWIN, KURT, *Principles of Topological Psychology*, Fritz and Grace M. Heider, trans., New York: McGraw-Hill, 1936.

One of the two basic books written by Lewin in German and translated into English. It contains practically all of the structure of his field psychology but is more difficult to read than are his later works. The latter pages contain a valuable glossary of field concepts.

MARROW, ALFRED J., *The Practical Theorist: The Life and Work of Kurt Lewin*, New York: Basic Books, 1969.

Develops the three areas of action that shaped Lewin's career: (1) his independent style of life, his constant involvement in cooperative enterprises and his continued collaboration with former students, (2) his persistent integration of theory and practical action, his exposure of theory to ingenious experimentation, and his close coordination of seemingly abstruse hypotheses with affairs of everyday life, and (3) his successful combination of scientific concerns with personal and civic ones.

TOLMAN, EDWARD C., *Collected Papers in Psychology*, Berkeley: University of California Press, 1951.

Also published in 1958 under the title *Behavior and Psychological Man.* Papers reflecting Tolman's unit of psychological study as molar behavior purposively organized. Tolman's ideas bridged S-R associationism and Lewin's field theory. He accepted many field concepts, such as purpose and insight, but remained a behaviorist. He was critical of S-R connectionistic theories.

TOLMAN, EDWARD C., "Kurt Lewin," *The Psychological Review*, January 1948, pp. 1–4.

A tribute to Lewin shortly after his death. A good, very brief professional appraisal of his work.

WOLMAN, BENJAMIN B., *Contemporary Theories and Systems in Psychology*, New York: Harper & Row, 1960.

Chapter 13, "Field Theory," an excellent overview of Lewin's field theory as an approach to general psychology. Develops historical background as well as basic concepts of the theory.

EIGHT

What Is the Cognitive-Field Theory of Learning?

The cognitive-field psychology of learning has been formulated in an attempt to construct scientific principles of learning highly applicable to classroom situations. Its advocates rest its validity upon educational results, scientifically ascertained. They are convinced that, in light of the present stage of scientific development, this theory of learning is more likely than any other of which they are cognizant to lead to the most productive results in classroom procedures.

A cognitive-field theory of learning describes how a person gains understanding of himself and his world in a situation where his self and his environment compose a totality of mutually interdependent, coexisting events. It involves the kind of generalizations about learning that may be applied to actual persons in school situations, and it is associated with the knowing and understanding functions that give meaning to situations. It is built around the purposes underlying behavior, the goals involved in behavior, and persons' means and processes of understanding themselves and their environments as they function in relation to their goals. Factors of a psychological environment acquire meaning as a person formulates his goals and develops insights into ways of achieving them.

Within cognitive-field theory, learning, briefly defined, is an interactional process within which a person attains new insights or cognitive structures or changes old ones. In no sense is it a mechanistic, associationistic process of connecting stimuli, which impinge upon, and responses, which are evoked or emitted from, a biological organism.

HOW MIGHT WE TEACH INSIGHTFULLY?

Now, let us examine how we might teach a school subject insightfully. Our illustration is taken from the subject of arithmetic, specifically the teaching of the multiplication combinations involving the 9s. We use the 9s because these combinations generally are considered the most difficult. Furthermore, we use arithmetic because many teachers feel that, however one might teach other subjects, arithmetic must be taught by rote.

This arithmetic lesson, as it develops, reflects the teacher's conviction that learning is an insightful process. The teacher is attempting to aid students in improving their understandings or insights in regard to multiplying by 9 and is doing it in such a way as to heighten their abilities to achieve new insights independently; *he is not merely giving students a gimmick.*

Let us assume that we are in a fourth-grade class and are ready to attack the 9s. We already have learned the 2s, 3s, 5s, 10s, and 11s, and we have learned them in such way as to have developed insight into the relationships involved in these tables. We can anticipate a kind of dialogue between students and teacher, which might go somewhat as follows:

The teacher reminds students of the combinations they know already and has them review these until it is clear that they know them well. The review process might appear on the surface as drill in the old-fashioned sense, but there is a fundamental difference. The teacher makes certain that students understand the relationships involved, that is, relationships of the same general type as those they are about to learn in connection with the 9s. After the review, the teacher suggests that the class advance to the 9s. (Some students are likely to protest that the 9s are more difficult than any of the others.)

The teacher begins writing the 9s table on the chalkboard, at the same time asking members of the class to supply answers which they already will have learned from their earlier study of the other tables. A "side trip" may be necessary to help students grasp, or perhaps only review, the insight that the product of 9 × 2 is the same as that of 2 × 9 (the commutative property). What appears on the chalkboard is something like this.

9 × 1 = 09	9 × 7 =
9 × 2 = 18	9 × 8 =
9 × 3 = 27	9 × 9 =
9 × 4 =	9 × 10 = 90
9 × 5 = 45	9 × 11 = 99
9 × 6 =	9 × 12 =

To this point, the answers supplied are based on students' prior learning of the 2s, 3s, 5s, 10s, and 11s. Let us now envisage the following dialogue:

Teacher: How do we know the answers to 9 × 1, 9 × 2, and 9 × 3?
Class: Because we know the 1s, 2s, and 3s.
Teacher: And what about 9 × 5, and 9 × 11?
Class: We know these because we know the 5s, 10s, and 11s.
Teacher: The ones that are left are the hard ones, aren't they? What is the answer to 9 × 7, Jimmie? Tell me without looking at the tables in your book. (Within instruction procedure, when the teacher addresses Jimmie or any other pupil, he anticipates that at least most members of the class are thinking along with the student spokesman.)

Jimmie probably will say nothing but will stare at the teacher, baffled. The teacher may then ask various other members of the class the answer to 9 × 6, 9 × 8, and 9 × 4. After the class begins to demonstrate a certain amount of bafflement (perhaps approaching the point of mild frustration), the teacher may entice them in this manner: "Would you like to gain enough understanding of the rest of the 9s so that after today you will know the answers to all of them?" The class is likely to respond in the affirmative with considerable enthusiasm.

Teacher: All right, let's work at this thing together. June, go to the board and write the 10s up to 10 × 5 right beside the 9s. (The class now will have before it the following combinations.)

10 × 1 = 10	9 × 1 = 09
10 × 2 = 20	9 × 2 = 18
10 × 3 = 30	9 × 3 = 27
10 × 4 = 40	9 × 4 =
10 × 5 = 50	9 × 5 = 45

Teacher: When we compare the 9s that we have answered to

the 10s, what difference do we see in the answers? What happens in the case of the 9s which did not happen in the 10s?

Class: Each step we move up in the 9s, one is lost.

Teacher: How do you mean?

Class: 9×1 is one fewer than 10×1, 9×2, is two fewer than 10×2, and 9×3 is three fewer than 10×3. That is why we get the answers 09, 18, and 27.

Of course, finding this principle may not come as easily as the foregoing dialogue might suggest. The teacher might need to do quite a lot more "fishing," by rephrasing the question and perhaps even offering some hints. The speed with which a class comes to see for itself principles which are new to it depends much upon what atmosphere has been established, and, of course, on the brightness of the students.

The teacher next helps students see that as in the 10s, the first digit goes up one each time, 09, 18, 27. By this time, the stage should be set for supplying the missing answers.

Teacher: Now think carefully about what we have learned. Since $9 \times 2 = 18$ and $9 \times 3 = 27$, Gary, what is the answer to 9×4?

Gary: 36.

Teacher: Why?

Gary: Well, if the first number increases by one for each larger table, and if we lose one in the last number of each table upward, it would have to be 36.

Teacher: You already know the answer to 9×5. Judy, does it check with the idea which we have learned?

Judy: Sure, the first number will be one larger, and we will have lost five numbers from the second number. That makes 45.

The reader should not be misled by the foregoing hypothetical dialogue. In order to economize on space, students have been pictured as saying the right thing the first time. In an actual classroom situation there would be more hesitancy, more fumbling, more tries on the part of students and teacher. But the process would remain essentially the same.

The class now is ready to deepen its insights in relation to the multiplication process.

Teacher: Look again at the first digit of each answer. (Teacher points to the 9s through 9×5.) Look at each of these digits in relation to the multipliers, 1, 2, 3, 4, and 5. Do you see anything interesting?

Gary: Why, the first digit of the answer is always just one number smaller than the multiplier.

Teacher: Why do you think this is so?

Gary: Would this be caused by losing a number each time—I mean, losing a number as compared with the 10s?

The teacher has succeeded in evoking the insight (at least in Gary) that when one multiplies by 9 rather than 10, there is a loss of one at each step, including the first. The answers "never catch up," so to speak. They keep falling behind, but according to a definite and predictable pattern.

Still another relationship may be taught the class:

Teacher: Look carefully at the answers which we have so far. (The teacher points to 09, 18, 27, 36, and 45.) Add the two digits of each answer and see what happens.

Class: The sum of the digits is the same in each answer. The sum is always 9.

Teacher: Yes. $0 + 9 = 9$; $1 + 8 = 9$; $2 + 7 = 9$. Why is this so?

Class: $9 \times 1 = 9$, then the first digit always increases by one, and the second digit decreases by one. They kind of balance each other, so the sum remains the same.

By this time the stage has been set for teaching the remaining combinations involving the 9s. When asked the answer to 9×7, students should reason that the first digit of the answer will be 6 $(7 - 1)$ and that the second digit should be 3 $(9 - 6)$. The class now should be able to complete the combinations through 9×10 easily. At 9×11, the first digit of the answer becomes two less than the multiplier. (Why?) Furthermore, the sum of the two digits of the answer does not equal 9, as it did in each preceding step. (Again, why?) Students will know the answer is 99. The problem is, why? Answer: $9 \times 10 = 90$; at 9×11 "we start around again"—$90 + 9 = 99$. At 9×11 the first digit of the answer has lost two from the multiplier: $11 - 2 = 9$, so in 9×12 the first part of the answer is $12 - 2$ or 10. For the sum of the digits to add to 9, the last digit is 8. Thus, $12 \times 9 = 108$. This can be extended into a game.

$$13 \times 9 = 117$$
$$14 \times 9 = 126$$
$$15 \times 9 = 135$$

The class members now are ready to test their new insights to see whether they will work. The teacher may suggest to his better students that they put into words the insights they have learned. However, it should be borne in mind that it is not always necessary for one to put an insight into words in order to use it.

In what specific ways does this lesson in arithmetic differ from traditional procedures used in teaching the multiplication tables? The answer to this question will express the significance of cognitive-field psychology for learning and teaching.

WHY IS COGNITIVE-FIELD THEORY CONTRASTED WITH S-R CONDITIONING THEORIES?

Since cognitive-field theorists are convinced that psychological activity depends upon energy related to psychological tension systems, to them no mere coupling or conditioning principle can adequately explain psychic activity. They challenge forcefully the principle of adhesion, the attachment of one thing to another so that revival of the first brings forth the second. Furthermore, they think that "reward" and "punishment" do not stamp in and stamp out learnings. In contrast with the practices of behaviorists, they stress the importance of our viewing the changes in the valences—values—of parts of the psychological environment and in the tension systems of the person in relation to his environment as crucial to description of the learning process.

Whereas behavioristic psychologies are biological-organism centered, cognitive-field psychology is psychological-person centered. "Organism" suggests a mechanism and human passivity; "person," in contrast, suggests purposiveness and interactivity. Consequently, whereas behavioristic educational psychologies have emphasized overt behavior, cognitive-field psychology has concerned itself with outward behavior only insofar as it may provide clues to what is transpiring psychologically or perceptually. ("Psychological," in the sense it is used here, refers to personal involvement, see p. 213.) Cognitive-field psychologists do not deny the validity, for certain purposes, of the study of the physiological behavior of man, but they think that physiological and psychological types of study represent different scientific dimensions, each with its own uses. Since these psychologists consider the teaching function to be most closely associated with psychological or cognitive processes, they confine their emphasis to a study of how the cognitive structure of psychological fields is achieved or changed, that is, how insight is developed.

Cognitive-field psychologists establish order, but they go about it in a different way than do behaviorists. Along with benefiting from the experimentation done under other banners, they develop their own unique type of scientific research. Experimentation within cognitive-field psychology involves the study of such matters as cognitive processes, the recall of uncompleted tasks, the relationship of levels of achievement and levels of aspiration, psychological ecology, group dynamics, action research, concepts of self, personality rigidity, individual and social perception, and reflective teaching.

HOW DOES COGNITIVE-FIELD THEORY WORK?

It is in the process of development of an *emergent synthesis* from the two horns of the active-passive or subjective-objective dilemma that cognitive-field learning theory has emerged (see pages 69–70 for an explanation of the meaning of an emergent synthesis). Within this psychology, learning is not equated with unfoldment and sheer expression of inner urges. Nor is it a conditioning process, which comes from the environment's impinging upon a biological organism from without. Instead, cognitive-field psychologists find the clue to the meaning of learning in the aspects of a situation within which a person and his psychological environment come together in a psychological field or life space.

The purpose of cognitive-field psychology is to formulate tested relationships that are predictive of the behavior of individual persons in their specific life spaces. In order to understand and predict such behavior, one must consider a person and his psychological environment as a pattern of interdependent facts and functions. Cognitive-field psychology is an interpersonal, social psychology that constitutes an effective vehicle for characterization of man. It integrates biological and social factors and treats respective persons as interacting with them. In the interactive process a person and his psychological environment are construed as interdependent variables. Thus, a person is neither dependent upon, nor independent of, his environment. Likewise, a person's environment is neither made by him nor independent of him.

Within cognitive-field psychology, one starts with a model of a person and the world around him as it is pertinent to that person. Learning is a modification of, that is, development of insight into the nature of, the person's world as represented by the model. Life space—the psychological model—contains the person himself, his psychological environment, the goals he is seeking, the negative "goals" he is attempting to avoid, the barriers between himself and his goals, which restrict his psychological movement toward them, and the potential and actual paths to his goals. (Psychological paths are ways of achieving goals.) The purpose of the life space model is to enhance the prediction of psychological behavior—that which is related to goals. As our knowledge of a child's or youth's life spaces increases, our ability to predict his behavior accurately also increases.

Why the terms cognitive and field?

The cognitive-field theory of learning is closely related to, and derived from, *cognitive* and *field* psychological theories.[1] The term *cognitive* is derived from the Latin verb *cognoscere*, which means "to know." The *cognitive* aspect of cognitive-field theory deals with the problem of how people gain an understanding of themselves and their environments and how, using their cognitions, they act in relation to their environments. The *field* aspect consists of the concurrent interrelationships of a person and his psychological environment in any one situation. Hence, field theory in psychology centers on the idea that all psychological activity of a person, at a given juncture, is a function of a totality of coexisting factors, which are mutually interdependent.

A field situation is perceived in such a way that any change in the field depends upon the nature of the field at that time. An astronomer uses "field" to describe the universe and predict the orbits of stars. A biologist relates the function of cells to their location in a growth "field." A physicist uses "field" in his study of the structure of an atom. Similarly, a psychologist uses "field" to mean the total psychological world in which a person lives at a given time. It includes a psychological past, present, and future, also a concrete and imaginative reality— all interpreted as simultaneous aspects of a current situation. An individual's understanding of his field—his learning—is his *insight* into, or *cognitive structure* of, his life space.

What is insight or cognitive structure?

Insight, concisely defined, is a basic sense of, or feeling for, relationships. Thus, it is either a particularized or generalized meaning or discernment. A generalized insight is an understanding.

Although there is nothing about the term *insight* that requires it to be right in any absolutistic sense, it is a grasp of a situation that often does go deeper than words. Thus, it is a realizing sense of a matter. So, insight into a situation is its meaning.

[1]See Gardner Lindzey and Elliott Aronson, *Handbook of Social Psychology*, 2nd ed., Vol. 1, Reading, Mass.: Addison-Wesley, 1968, Chapters 5 and 6.

Meaning, so used, denotes that to which an object or idea points or what it signifies. The insights of a person are not equated with his consciousness or awareness or his ability to describe them verbally; instead, their essence is a sense of, or feeling for, pattern in a life situation.

Development of insight means getting the feel of, grasping the idea of, catching on to, or seeing through a situation. An insight is acquired through one's actually or symbolically doing something and seeing what happens. The focus of the learning is on the seeing, not, as has been assumed by behaviorists, on the doing. Seeing, here, is broadly defined to mean catching the point or getting the idea. Any or all of the senses, however many these may be, may be involved, and the sensory action may be pronounced, or it may be so rudimentary that the person involved may not realize it is occurring. Thus, he may think he is learning through his "mind's eye."

A person may gain an insight through experiencing only one case. However, the most valuable insights are those confirmed by enough similar cases to be generalized into an understanding. A generalized insight or an understanding is a meaning or discernment that one may apply to several or even many similar, but not necessarily identical, situations or processes. In other words, it is an expectation or recognized rule.

A person's insights collectively constitute the cognitive structure of his life space. However, the term *insight* sometimes also is used in a generic sense. Thus, the two expressions *insight* and *cognitive structure* may be considered synonyms. *Cognitive structure* means the way a person perceives the psychological aspects of the personal, physical, and social world. Such a world includes a person and all of his facts, concepts, beliefs, memory traces, and expectations. Consequently, changes in the cognitive structure of life spaces prevail in the development of language, emotions, attitudes, actions, and social interrelations. Now, let us review an episode of insightful learning as observed by the author.

During World War II, the author watched a group of noncommissioned officers teaching recruits in basic training to fire army rifles (the author was one of these recruits). Army rifles have a powerful recoil or kick. A soldier is supposed to squeeze the trigger gradually and smoothly until the rifle fires. Recruits usually anticipate the recoil and jump before the shell explodes; thus, their aim is completely spoiled. The problem for a noncom was to teach his "pupil" not to make the anticipatory jump. Recruits were convinced that they really did not jump until after the explosion, and thus hours of pointed verbal comment had little, if any, effect. Corporal Jones helped his "pupil" gain an insight: He "scolded" him several times for jumping, with no avail. Then while his pupil's attention was diverted to a fellow sufferer, the corporal slipped a fired cartridge into the firing chamber. The recruit aimed, started to squeeze, and again jumped, thereby gaining an insight. He was jumping before his rifle fired and thus ruining his aim. His jumping before the rifle had fired soon ceased.

WHAT ARE SOME ESSENTIAL FEATURES OF COGNITIVE-FIELD PSYCHOLOGY?

There are some features of cognitive-field psychology that make it distinctly different from any of the mechanistic psychologies. The foremost of these features is its relativistic approach to the study of perception and reality. Other important characteristics are interpretation of intelligent behavior as purposive, emphasis upon psychological functions rather than objects, a situational point of view, and stress upon the principle of contemporaneity. We expand each of these points in the following sections.

Perception and reality defined relativistically

Cognitive-field psychologists think that, when a person perceives a thing, he is not indifferent toward it. For him, it is to some degree valent or he would not be perceiving it. Furthermore, perception of an object involves not only what one senses and feels about it but also what one is inclined to do about it. Accordingly cognitive-field theory represents a *relativistic*, as opposed to an absolutistic, mechanistic, way of viewing man and the learning process. Readers are warned that should they attempt to understand its concepts mechanistically, they will not grasp this theory.

A mechanist attempts to explain all the fullness and variety of a universe in terms of machinelike objects and movements. Thus, a mechanist in psychology considers a person an organism which is a product of its unique history of stimulus-response patterns. Consequently, he reduces all human activities to movements, usually in terms of stimuli and responses. Just as an automobile is built by workmen who assemble its respective parts, a person is educated by teachers who feed into his physiological make-up the various aspects of environment which supposedly make him what mechanistic teachers want him to be.

The basic principle of *relativism* or *interactionism* is that nothing is perceivable or conceivable as a thing-in-itself. Rather, everything is perceived or conceived in relation to other things. That is, a thing is perceived as a figure against a background, experienced from a given angle or direction of envisionment. Furthermore, how a person perceives his environment depends upon the degree of his maturity, his knowledge, and his goals. Consequently, relativism means that psychological reality is defined, not in "objective," physical terms, but in psychological, perceptual ones. So defined, reality consists of what one makes of that which one gains through one's senses or otherwise.

See if you can get the point of the following story. What is the significance of the third umpire's statement? What makes a ball a ball and a strike a strike? "The story concerns three base-ball umpires who were discussing the problems of their pro-fession. The first umpire said, 'Some's balls and some's strikes and I calls 'em as they is.' The second umpire said, 'Some's balls and some's strikes and I calls 'em as I sees 'em.' While the third umpire said, [I sees 'em comin' and] 'some's balls and some's strikes but they ain't nothin' till I calls 'em.' "[2]

According to the cognitive-field position, the only reality a man can ever know, or work with, is his own interpretation of what is real. Thus, for an individual, reality is what he gains through his five-plus senses and his manner of sizing it up. Consequently, the field or life space that influences an individual is described, not in "objective," physical terms, but in the way it exists for that person at that time. Thus, there is no attempt to relate behavior to a biological organism and its physical or geographical environment as such; in field psychology, the psychological con-cept *person* is much broader than is the biological concept *or-ganism*. A life space or psychological field consists of the content of an individual's perception. Neither the organism nor the en-vironment alone is the one main factor. Rather, a person and his environment are simultaneously interacting and participating in perception; they constitute an SMI (simultaneous mutual in-teraction).

Perception, here, is interpreted in its broadest possible sense. *It does not mean mere consciousness.* There is evidence from observation of human and animal behavior that one cannot use consciousness as the sole criterion of what is a part of a life space. A child playing in his yard behaves differently when his mother is home than when she is out, yet he probably at no

[2]Hadley Cantril, "Perception and Interpersonal Relations," *American Journal of Psychiatry*, August, 1957, p. 126.

time verbalizes—is specifically conscious of—her being home or away. Children in a schoolroom with teacher A conduct themselves quite differently from when they are with teacher B. Yet they may at no time consciously formulate the two patterns of behavior. Likewise, dogs and other animals size up situations and do the best they can for themselves; however, there is little if any evidence that in so doing they carry on a conscious process. Perception, then, must be construed to cover all the different ways one has of getting to know his environment.

In *apparently* the same situation, a person at different times may perceive quite different aspects of a situation and behave accordingly. Furthermore, provision of opportunity for one to perceive certain aspects of a physical or social environment in a certain way by no means guarantees that that particular perception will occur or that the perception that does occur will have anything like a one-to-one relationship to the objective environment as it appears to someone else. Adelbert Ames, E. Engel, and Hadley Cantril have performed experiments at the Institute for Associated Research, Hanover, New Hampshire, which show that in perception nothing is absolutely fixed. Rather, one interprets everything in terms of the situation as a whole. What one perceives—one's reality—consists of what one makes of what seems to be oneself and one's environment. Depending on the habits—insights or understandings—a person brings to a particular occasion, he seems to give meaning and order to things in terms of his own needs, abilities and purposes.[3]

A description of two experiments performed at the Hanover Institute will give some idea of the nature and significance of these studies. Engel was curious to see what would happen when a person viewed two different pictures through a stereoscope. One set of his "stereograms" consisted of pairs of small photographs of football players, one to be viewed by the right eye, the other by the left. There was enough similarity in the pairs of pictures for a subject to get binocular fusion. However, when a person looked into the stereoscope and described the face he saw, it was neither of the faces represented by the photographs. Instead, he described a new and different face, usually made up of the dominant features of the two faces that he was viewing with separate eyes.

Cantril reports experiments with a pair of stereograms. Each stereogram was a photograph of a statue in the Louvre; one the

---

[3]These experiments are summarized in Alfred Kuenzli, *The Phenomenological Problem*, New York: Harper & Row, 1959, Chapter 8.

Madonna with Child, the other a lovely young female nude. A typical viewing of the pair of stereograms proceeded as follows: The subject first saw only a Madonna with Child, then a few seconds later exclaimed, "But my—she is undressing." She had somehow lost the baby she was holding and her robe had slipped from her shoulders. Then in a few more seconds she lost her robe completely and became the young nude. Sometimes the process is reversed. Other people never see the nude and others never see the Madonna. Apparently, what a person "sees" in a situation depends upon his needs, abilities, purposes, and insights, as well as upon what is "out there."

Since reality, relativistically defined, consists of what one gains through his five-plus senses and his manner of sizing it up, one's person is what he makes of himself, and his environment consists of what he makes of that which surrounds him. In keeping with his relativistic outlook, a field psychologist shuns the use of concepts implying fixed traits or rigid habits of personalities. He recognizes the difficulty of man's ever getting outside himself sufficiently to make final statements about what is absolutely real or true. Since he regards truth as tentative and instrumental (not final), he shies away from making dogmatic statements about the nature of man and the universe. Rather, a statement is considered true because of its accuracy in prediction and the consensus of people competent in its area in regard to the possible consequences of acting on it—its usefulness. It should be emphasized here that a relativistic definition of truth in no way discounts the value of truths. Rather, it supposedly defines truth in a more discerning manner.

Purposiveness of behavior

Cognitive-field psychology is a purposive psychology; it assumes that a person, at his level of understanding, does the best that he knows how for whatever he thinks he is. Hence, intellectual processes are deeply affected by an individual's goals, and learning activity, including habit formation, is goal directed. Accordingly, goal or purpose is central to cognitive-field learning theory. This contrasts sharply with S-R conditioning theories, which either ignore goal or purpose completely or make it only peripheral and incidental. Behaviorists have tended to consider any concept of goal direction or purposiveness to be teleological. To them, "teleological" means deriving present behavior from the future. Consequently it sounds mystical and superstitious. Thus, they have placed emphasis upon past events as the cause of present behavior. They have seemed to overlook the possibility of the "presentness" of causes of behavior. Since field psychology is goal centered, cognitive-field theorists inveigh against use of such mechanistic terms as "reflex arc," "connectionism," "conditioning," "associationism," and "reinforcement" by psychologists in dealing with learning.

Whereas mental disciplinarians generally have held that man is endowed with *free will* and logical empiricistic behaviorists have adhered to *determinism*—the opposite of free will, positive relativistic cognitive-field theorists emphasize *situational choice*. This means that, at any juncture of a person's continuous, overlapping life spaces, he, to some extent, may choose which way he is going to turn next. So, cognitive-field theorists, postulate that men exercise choice, but they neither assert nor imply identification with either side of the metaphysical free will—determinism antinomy. Instead, they simply mean, to quote Dewey, that "Every intelligent act involves selection of certain things as means to other things as their consequences."[4] At a choice point or in a situation, a person does decide which way to go. But, his exercise of choice does not, of necessity, imply the operation of a supernaturally oriented free will even though the choice is not the product of preceding determining factors. Rather, human intelligent action is taken to be *immanently purposive*, and it is interpreted in the light of the goals it is designed to achieve. *Immanent* means remaining within the situation at hand. So, one's being immanently purposive means that one's goals arise within one's world of experience.

The *purposiveness* of cognitive-field psychology, then, is immanent in—operating within—not transcendental to—extending beyond—the world of experience; it prevails in workaday life situations. That is, careful study of children and youth (as well as of other animate beings) in life situations indicates that if they are active at all they are trying to do something, and that, it is only through our anticipating what they are trying to do, that we can predict most accurately what they are going to do. Whether there is transcendental—supernatural—purpose in the universe is another problem, which is related only indirectly to the concept "purposive" as developed in field psychology. Relativistic purposiveness is immanent.

Within cognitive-field psychology, "purposive" is virtually a synonym for "intelligent;" it signifies an intentionality that need

4John Dewey, *Logic: The Theory of Inquiry*, New York: Holt, Rinehart and Winston, 1938, p. 460.

not be conscious. A unique characteristic of human beings is their capacity to pursue long-sighted, as well as short-sighted, self-interests. Cognitive-field psychologists recognize the significance of this fact. When a child or youth is behaving purposively, he is pursuing his goals in light of the insights he has available; he is behaving intelligently. The goal or goals toward which the individual strives psychologically exist in his present life space. The phenomenon of goal is such that expectation—not actual realization—is its essence. Although the content of a goal may be in the future or may not occur at all, the goal as a psychological fact necessarily lies in the present life space. For example, a student's goal to become a teacher is a goal toward teaching as he now sees it. However, this goal may be a far cry from teaching as it eventually is experienced.

The purposiveness of cognitive-field psychology simply means that an individual acts in such a way as to achieve his goal or goals—satisfy his wants or desires—in the quickest and easiest way that he comprehends or senses as possible under existing conditions. When one is motivated toward doing something, his description of the matter is that he wants or desires to do it. So, one's activity is carried forward to a goal by a process of one's constantly searching out the conditions for the next step all along the way.

Emphasis upon psychological function

A third feature of cognitive-field psychology is its emphasis upon psychological functions or events as contrasted with physical objects or movements. A fallacy of behaviorists, noted by relativistic cognitive-field theorists, has been their tendency to describe the character of an activity by its physical aspects only and to neglect the great effect of the psychological setting. For example, experiments on satiation clearly indicate that fatigue often is largely a matter of psychological boredom, not physical tiredness. Moving one's arm in an identical way while making certain lines may have different psychological and physiological effects, according to the meaning of this activity to one. The act of repeatedly making a pattern of four lines may have become disintegrated and the arm fatigued as a result of oversatiation. Then a change of the same movements to making a different pattern of lines or a picture from these lines suffices to bring a reorganization of the activity and erase the bodily symptoms of fatigue. If the meaning of an activity is changed by imbedding it in a different context, bodily symptoms of fatigue tend to disappear.

Psychological is interpreted to mean in accordance with the logic of a growing mind or intelligence. So, to be psychological in his pursuits, a cognitive-field psychologist must look at the world through the eyes of the learner. To describe a situation psychologically, he must, to the best of his ability, describe the situation that confronts the individual under study. Such a situation is viewed as a pattern of person-environmental relationships that provides and limits opportunities. Once the person-environmental structure is established, the problem is to use psychological constructs and methods adequate to deal with the underlying dynamics of behavior and to do this in a scientifically sound manner.

A "psychological" interpretation of life opens the way for extensive use of systematic constructs. Whereas a behaviorist supposedly restricts his generalizations to those based on the use of "objective" data, a cognitive-field psychologist knowingly uses constructs that go beyond the observable data. His employment of such constructs provides a means of bridging the gap between general laws, which cannot be observed, and the functions of individual persons, which can be gathered as data. Thus, through the use of a few constructs the essence of an individual case can be adequately represented.

A *construct* is an invented idea. It is a generalized concept not directly observable but formed from data that are observed. Its purpose is to correlate a broad range of data having some basic functional similarity, despite their marked superficial differences. A need, psychologically defined, is an example of a construct. Since it has no length, breadth, thickness, or mass, it cannot be observed. Yet it is a crucial, functional concept in studying human activity. The *meaning of all the constructs of cognitive-field psychology are mutually interdependent.* Each depends for its meaning upon the meanings of all the others. Thus, there are no independent, dependent, and intervening variables, as in the behaviorisms. Instead, *all the variable or constructs of cognitive-field psychology are interdependent.*

Advocates of cognitive-field psychology do not deny the existence of some kind of couplings within the nervous system. Furthermore, they are interested in the results of recent research in neurophysiological functions.[5] But, they do challenge the need to understand the nature of neural couplings in order to develop an adequate picture of the learning process.

In 1958 K. S. Lashley (1890–1958), who had devoted a lifetime

---

[5]See Ernest R. Hilgard and Gordon H. Bower, *Theories of Learning*, 3rd ed., New York: Appleton-Century-Crofts, 1966, Chapter 13.

to the study of nervous function, stated: "I cannot pretend to have formulated a complete and satisfactory account of how the brain thinks. I recognize gaps and inconsistencies in my formulation of the problems, and the hypotheses that I have suggested will probably collapse under the weight of additional evidence."[6] More recently Hilgard and Bower have stated, ". . . both the nervous system and its behavior are complicated and neither will be understood with any completeness for a long time."[7] But, for cognitive-field theorists, this does not mean that it is impossible to develop an adequate and harmonious conception of learning.

Situational emphasis

A fourth definitive characteristic of cognitive-field learning theory is that a study always begins with a description of a situation as a whole—the psychological field or life space—and proceeds to specific detailed analyses of various aspects of the situation; this is implicit in the SMI concept. At no time are aspects of a field viewed as isolated elements. In the study of a life space with its various constructs, the idea constantly is kept to the forefront that no two constructs or concepts are mutually exclusive, but that everything to some degree and in some sense is dependent upon everything else. Readers again are cautioned that, should they slip into giving the constructs independent physical or biological existence, they will be attempting to understand a relativistic psychology in a mechanistic fashion.

Principle of contemporaneity

The fifth essential feature of cognitive-field psychology is the one most often misunderstood. Contemporaneity literally means all at one time. A psychological field or life space is a construct of such nature that it contains everything psychological that is taking place in relation to a specific person at a given time. The unit of time, microscopically viewed, is a moment; however, macroscopically considered, it may cover hours or even weeks. Whatever the length of time, everything is going on at once— that is the meaning of "field." Readers are urged neither to reject the concept of contemporaneity summarily nor to give it an oversimplified interpretation.

[6]Karl Spencer Lashley, *Selected Papers of the Neuropsychology of Lashley*, Frank A. Beach, D. O. Hebb, C. T. Morgan, and H. W. Nissen, eds., New York: McGraw-Hill, 1960, pp. 541–542.
[7]Hilgard and Bower, *op. cit.*, p. 427.

Use of the concept *psychological field* implies that everything which affects behavior at a given time should be represented in the field existing at that time, and that only those facts that are part of a present field can affect behavior. In order to understand a person's present personality structure, it often is convenient and perhaps necessary to inquire into the individual's personal history. But such inquiry is merely a means of knowing the present structure of his life space. A person's psychological field that exists at a given time contains, as well as the environment of the present, the views of that individual about his future and his past. But, it should be emphasized that any psychological past or psychological future is a simultaneous part of a psychological field existing at a given time. Psychologically, there is no past or future except as it enters into the present. Present situations are influenced by past or future ones if, and only if, the past or future ones, as viewed in the present, make the present appear differently than it otherwise would. It is the contemporary meaning of events that influences our behavior in relation to them.

The idea of the contemporaneity of a psychological field has been developing for some time. Some 40 years ago, George H. Mead wrote, "We live always in a present whose past and whose future are the extension of the field within which its undertakings may be carried out."[8] Kurt Lewin, the founder of field psychology, also emphasized that behavior depends on neither the future nor the past but on the present field. To quote him, "Since neither the [physical] past nor the [physical] future exists at the present moment it can not have [immediate] effects at the present."[9] "In 1947 Edward C. Tolman spoke of Lewin's emphasis on the ahistorical, contemporaneous, systematic determiners of behavior as an expression of a new and tremendously fruitful intellectual insight."[10] Then, more recently, as eminent social psychologist, Gordon W. Allport, has stated:

My own position, which goes under the designation *functional autonomy of motives*, holds that motivation may be—and in healthy people usually is—autonomy of its [historical] origins. Its function is to animate and steer a life toward goals that are

[8]George H. Mead, *The Philosophy of the Present*, La Salle, Ill.: Open Court, 1932, p. 90.

[9]Kurt Lewin, *Principles of Topological Psychology*, New York: McGraw-Hill, 1936, p. 35.

[10]See Alfred J. Marrow, *The Practical Theorist: The Life and Work of Kurt Lewin*, New York: Basic Books, 1969, p. 228.

in keeping with *present* structure, *present* aspirations and *present* conditions.[11]

The principle of contemporaneity means that psychological events are determined by conditions at the time behavior occurs. One cannot derive behavior from either the future or the past as such. Both behaviorists and cognitive-field psychologists see little basis for supposing a future cause of present events. However, cognitive-field psychologists differ sharply from behaviorists in their insistence that any attempts at derivation of behavior from the past is equally metaphysical, that is, beyond the realm of science. Since past events do not now exist, they cannot as such have any effect on the present. Thus, influence of a future can only be anticipatory, and effects of a past can only be indirect. Nevertheless, through the continuity of life spaces, past psychological fields do have their "trace" or residue in a present field, which influences a person's behavior. *Trace* is a region or condition of a present life space that has similarity to a characteristic of earlier life spaces. In other words, "trace" means that there is some similarity between regions of succeeding life spaces. This is the psychological basis of memory. When, in solving a current problem, a person uses an insight acquired earlier, the insight is an example of trace.

In order to understand a person's present personality structure, it is often convenient and perhaps necessary to inquire into the individual's personal history. But such inquiry is merely a means of knowing the present structure of his life space. A person's psychological field that exists at a given time contains, as well as the environment of the present, the views of that individual about his future and his past. It should be emphasized that any psychological past or psychological future is a simultaneous part of a psychological field existing at a given time. Psychologically, there is no past or future except as it enters into the present.

An individual's views about the past, as about the rest of the physical and social world, are often incorrect; nevertheless, they constitute a significant psychological past in his own life space. Furthermore, the goals of an individual as a psychological fact lie in the present, and they too constitute an essential part of his life space. The contents of the goals may lie in the future, and they may never occur; but the nature of an expectation is not dependent upon the event's coming to pass. If an Indian

---

[11]Gordon W. Allport, *Personality and Social Encounter*, Boston: Beacon Press, 1960. p, 29.

warrior were brave in order that in the future he would go to the happy hunting ground, whether or not a future happy hunting ground actually existed, would have no bearing on his being brave. His happy hunting ground is a part—a goal region—of his contemporaneous life space.

The principle of contemporaneity has definite implications for education. When through continuity the past enters into the present, knowledge of the past and its heritage is of great value and significance. However, the practice of making records and remains of the past *in themselves* the central materials of education cuts the vital connection of present and past. Thus, it tends to make the past a rival of the present and the present a more or less futile imitation of a past, which can never be known in its absolutely exact form.

HOW DO COGNITIVE-FIELD THEORISTS USE THE LIFE SPACE CONCEPT?

The basic concept of cognitive-field psychology is life space. Life space is a model of psychological reality or functional relationships developed for the purpose of describing what is possible and what is impossible for the person being studied, and of anticipating or predicting what he is likely to be thinking and doing now as well as what his subsequent thoughts and actions will be. Notice that the concept *life space* does not refer to the physical entities as such. Hence, the life space metaphor provides a pattern for thinking as contrasted with a picture of any absolute existence. It cuts below the splitting of man into *body* and *mind* and deals with him in terms of his distinguishing characteristics as a *person*.

Cognitive-field theorists, then, use *life space* as a model, paradigm, or root metaphor that enables them to take into consideration the total contemporaneous life situation of an individual. The object of study, when applied to man, is a unit that can best be described as a-discerning-person-in-interaction-with-his-psychological environment; this is a life space. *Interaction*, as herein used, characterizes the nature of perception. *It is a cognitive experiential process within which a person, psychologically, simultaneously reaches out to his environment, makes something of it, acts in relation to it, and sees the consequences of his action.*

As a person develops, he lives through a more or less continuous and overlapping series of life spaces. Each life space, consisting of a juncture of a moment's or longer period's duration, contains a person and his psychological environment of that juncture; it is characterized by the interaction of the two. All psychological events such as acting, thinking, learning, hoping, and dreaming are functions, not of isolated properties of either an individual or his environment, but of the mutual relations of a totality of coexisting facts that constitute a life space.

The concept *life space* constitutes an instrument whereby one may be objective in studying human activity by being, to some degree, subjective. A teacher may conjecture, "What would I be thinking if I were a student and were acting that way?" or "If I were in his situation, why would I be acting the way he is?" The meaning of life space was developed in Chapter 7, pp. 186–187. We herein explain the use of this uniquely psychological concept as the pivotal construct in a cognitive-field theory of learning.

The two principal aspects of a life space are a person and his psychological environment. The two are not mutually exclusive. However, they function as subwholes of a person's psychological field or life space. Both are surrounded by a *nonpsychological foreign hull*. A person is a consciously-behaving functional self, which is evidenced through expression of the individual's abilities and needs. A person's psychological environment consists of everything in which, toward which, or away from which he can make psychological movement—do anything about.

The foreign hull of a life space is composed of those aspects of a person's physical-social environment that are observable by the one who is studying the particular person but which, at the juncture under consideration, have no significance for the person being studied. So, they are not included in his psychological environment (the foreign hull concept is discussed in some detail on pp. 223–224).

What is the origin and nature of a person?

Cognitive-field psychologists place one's *person* at the center of his psychological field. A person is that body or configuration of matters with which an individual becomes identified, of which he takes care, and to which he gives his allegiance. So defined, it is not a fixed quantity or static thing. It is *achieved*, as contrasted with being inherently possessed. So, briefly stated, a self or person consists of everything an individual takes care of.

Under no circumstances is a psychological person considered identical with an organism. Nor is it limited either to a substantive mind alone or to a combination of a substantive mind and a physical body. Rather, a person is a *purposive behaving self*. It is the center of abilities and needs, and it is what a child, and later an adult, means when he says "I" or "me." The concept *person* may be considered synonymous with *self*. Whereas teachers more often think of Billy Smith and Sally Anderson as persons, Billy and Sally, when thinking of themselves, are more likely to use the term "self."

In its widest possible sense, a child's self is the total configuration of all that he calls or thinks of as *his*. This can include his body, his speech, his thoughts, his clothes, his home, his parents, his grandparents, his brothers and sisters, his reputation in various groups, his personal property, and his attitudes toward all these and the institutions for their realization. A person adjusts to his social and physical environment by identifying himself with many of the activities or concerns that comprise it. Therefore, *self*, *person*, and *interests* are names for the same psychological phenomenon.

The content of self is taken to consist of one's cherished ideals and interests. Consequently, the kind and amount of interest actively taken in affairs is a measure of the quality of one's selfhood or personhood. To say that a child is interested or concerned is a brief way of saying that he is interactively engaging his person with his psychological world. Throughout his waking hours, as a baby, later as a child, and then as a youth he learns by trying various acts and seeing what happens. Thus, through his purposively living in a human environment, he develops as a person or self.

A normal process of development produces self-involvement with objects, people, groups, and social organizations in a physical and social environment. In a negative sense, a human organism growing up in complete isolation probably would not develop a self-concept or appear to others as a personality. It seems reasonable to assume that he would have no basis for distinguishing between right and wrong, he would have no developed aesthetic sense, and he would have no use of language or symbols. Consequently, he would be incapable of abstract thinking. Only by his living in a human world and having a biological organism of a unique type does a biological man emerge as a psychological person or self. The form that the development of selfhood takes depends upon the learning that results from the purposive interaction of the person and his psychological environment.

How does a child construct his self?

A young child, to a greater extent than an adult, is a dynamic unity. When he cries, he cries all over; when he is hungry, all of him is hungry; and when he is frightened, he is startled completely. Later, he comes to perceive his self only as he distinguishes it from his environment and various aspects of it from one another. The rather sharp distinction between one's person and one's psychological environment is something that grows in an individual's thinking, as the "I" or "self" is gradually formed. However, one's person grows so that soon the central feature of his social and personal motivation becomes the maintenance and furtherance of the welfare of that self. Hence, it may be said. that the paramount human need is for preservation and enhancement of this emergent self or person. One even owns a "loyal" dog in order to enhance and give constancy to his psychological person.

A child's awareness of his self is manifested in at least four different ways: (1) he reaches certain results by his own efforts and comes to feel responsible for his acts, priding himself on his achievements and blaming himself for his failures; (2) his self, being embodied in values and goals, is realized in his transactions with other people; (3) as he evaluates his conduct over and against an ideal, an ideal self emerges (people often identify this ideal self with "conscience"); and (4) his self grows to a prominent place in his memories of a past and his anticipations of a future.[12]

How many selves does an individual have?

Selfhood, except as it has encased itself in a shell of routine, is always in the process of its making. Moreover, any self in process is capable of including a number of inconsistent selves or unharmonized dispositions. So, in a sense, an individual has as many different selves as there are distinct groups for whose opinion he has concern. Thus, Jimmy Jones at home is one self, in school another, on a date another, and on a football field still another. Every normal human being maintains a variety of interests or values in different situations, and so might be said to have a corresponding number of selves. However, although there is a different self in each successive life space of an individual, we can anticipate a continuity of selves of such nature that, in case of conflict, a deeper, continuous self pushes the others aside and becomes dominant. Consequently, each individual, if reasonably "normal," is a basic self or person made

[12]See Chapter 7, p. 187 for a Lewinian description of a structured person in a life space.

up of his major allegiances and commitments, among which there is some degree of harmony and continuity. Usually the psychological structure of a person is relatively constant over a long period of time, particularly as he advances in chronological age.

How is environment a part of life space?

A person's psychological environment contains that part of his physical and social environment with which he is psychologically engaged at a specific juncture of a moment's, or longer period's duration, because it is relevant to his purposes at that juncture. Such an environment is not an undifferentiated medium into which a person is immersed. It consists of objects and events, not a sum total of optical, acoustical, and tactile sensations.

A psychological environment, then, is what a person "makes of" his physical-social environment. Thus, it consists of everything psychologically outside an individual person that means anything to him. It is made up of everything in which, toward which, or away from which a person can change his psychological position. It sometimes means the *momentary situation* of the child, at other times it means the *milieu,* in the sense of the chief characteristics of the permanent situation.

How does psychological environment differ from physical-social environment?

The physical environment of an object or person includes everything surrounding that object or person as seen by an unbiased observer. Likewise, social environment consists of the generalized social milieu or atmosphere around a person. It includes the attitudes, values, and beliefs of the community, region, or nation. Although the physical and social environment furnishes a setting for the psychological environments of individuals in a group, it is distinctly different from the psychological environment of any one member of the group. Hence, we should never consider a child's physical or social environment as it appears to others to be his psychological environment.

Whereas the physical environments of a group of students in a classroom are relatively the same, each of their psychological environments is unique. Let us visit Miss Smith's classroom of sixth-grade students at Carbondale Elementary School. At 10:30 Tuesday morning, what is happening in the room? Miss Smith is holding reading class. What are Alice, Frank, Helen, and John doing? Alice is so absorbed with her teacher and schoolwork

Figure 8.1
Life Spaces Involved in a Classroom.

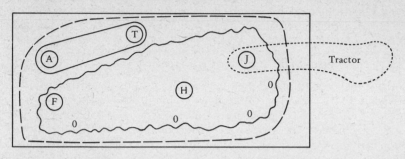

T   Miss Smith

A   Alice   ———————————— Boundary of Alice's life space

         — — — — — — — — Boundary of Frank's life space

F   Frank

         〜〜〜〜〜〜〜〜 Boundary of Helen's life space

H   Helen

         ------------------- Boundary of John's life space

J   John

0   Other children

that she is oblivious to everything else about her, including the other children. Frank is listening halfheartedly to the teacher but is concerned primarily with the other children in the room. Helen is a social butterfly; she wants the attention of most of the children in the classroom. She does give attention to the teacher from time to time, but right now she is concerned with other things. John's body is in the classroom, but "psychologically" John is riding a shiny new tractor which is being operated in the field adjoining the school.

This classroom is illustrated in Figure 8.1. Each small circle represents a person and has his initial on it. Each person has his respective environment, indicated by a larger figure which includes the person. Each person and his respective psychological environment constitute a life space. Practically everything within the four walls of the classroom, as well as much more, is included within either John's life space or his foreign hull. John's life space, drawn alone, would appear as in Figure 8.2.

Since a psychological environment, strictly speaking, is a momentary situation involving a specific person, such an environment and the person involved are constantly changing as

Figure 8.2
John's Life Space.

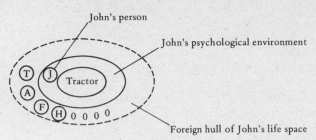

the person actively lives in relationship to that environment. What *appears to an observer* to constitute John's environment may include many elements not actually in John's psychological environment, and the observed environment may exclude some elements which, for John, psychologically are in it. For her to understand John, the teacher must study John in *his* own environment (John's psychological environment), not *the* physical environment.

Thus, to be objective in dealing with the child, the teacher must be subjective. She must see the world as John sees it. In order to predict John's behavior accurately, the teacher must understand the interactive nature of John's life space—his person and his environment—and she must be able to predict (anticipate) the boy's future life spaces. Then, for Miss Smith to be able to teach John in a significant way, it is imperative that there be some intersection of John's life space with hers and with the life spaces of other children in the room.

To repeat, the principal functional parts of a life space are the person and his psychological environment. However, a life space is always surrounded by a *foreign hull*. The foreign hull of a person's life space is the complex of all nonpsychological factors surrounding a life space. It is constituted of physical and social factors that, at the time, are not subject to the person's psychological interaction, but that may, at some future time, become aspects of his psychological field.

Since the content of a foreign hull has physical-social but not psychological reality, its physical and social conditions limit the variety of a person's possible life spaces. Anything that appears to be in a person's physical environment, but of which he is completely oblivious, is in the foreign hull of his life space. However, if he interacts with that thing in any way, either positively or negatively, it no longer is in his foreign hull but in his life space proper. So, a person can never experience any aspect of his own foreign hull; when he experiences a part of his previous foreign hull, it is no longer an aspect of his foreign hull, but belongs to his life space proper.

As succeeding nonpsychological physical and social environments—foreign hulls—are outside their respective psychological environments, they can have no immediate effect upon a person's intelligent behavior. However, through a person's interaction with the environment, parts of a present foreign hull can be transformed into goals, barrier, and other psychological factors of future life spaces. They then are no longer a part of the foreign hull. Factors so transformed become parts of subsequent psychological persons or environments. Thus, what a moment before constituted only a part of the foreign hull may at a succeeding moment be a central part of either the person or his psychological environment.

Although physical and social environments furnish a setting —matrix—for the psychological environments of individuals in a group, they are distinctly different from the psychological environment of any one member of the group. Hence, we should never consider a person's physical or social environment as it appears to others to be his psychological environment.

Since each person's perceptual environment is unique, obviously two persons may appear to be in the same location in space and time (or as nearly so as possible) and yet have very different psychological environments. Furthermore, the behaviors of two equally intelligent persons who are confronted with the same "objective facts" may differ drastically because each is different in his purposes and experiential background. Whenever a person has a new experience, he changes his environment and will never again be able to recapture the old environment in its identical form. The cognitive-field conception of environment helps explain why in a particular family one son may become a minister and another turn to crime; their interpretations of their world differ radically, even though to an outsider their social and physical environments would appear quite similar.

Continuity and interaction

The concepts that best characterize a life space are *continuity* and *interaction*. Usually, a series of a person's continuous, overlapping life spaces, each consisting of the person and the respective environment of the moment, are reasonably similar.

However, they are not identical. Each, to some degree, is different from the one that preceded it and the one that follows. Yet, a person's life spaces are not a series of discrete entities; there generally is a *continuity* from life space to life space of an individual. Since we can anticipate some degree of similarity and continuity of life spaces as the experiences of one moment shade into those of the next, for practical schoolroom procedures (depending upon the purposes being pursued), we may assume a fixity of life spaces for longer periods than a moment —perhaps a class period, a week, or a month.

In a life space, a person and his psychological environment are in simultaneous mutual interaction (SMI) and are mutually interdependent. Each depends upon the other for its nature and functions; it is impossible to treat one adequately without also treating the other. Accordingly, one's person is definitive of one's environment and likewise one's environment is definitive of oneself.

Within a series of overlapping life spaces, a person's life is a continuity of psychological tensions, locomotions, and new equilibriums. When there is an increase of tension in one part of a life space relative to the rest of the system, disequilibrium occurs. When a person finds himself in a state of disequilibrium and attempts to return to equilibrium, psychic energy is expended; he engages in psychological behavior or locomotion. Should tension throughout the system become completely equalized, output of energy would cease; the total system would come to rest.

Of course, throughout a life span this absolute balance is never achieved. Since a person is intelligent and purposive, he constantly expands and restructures his life space to some degree. Consequently, new disequilibriums continuously emerge. This process gives a dynamic nature to human living that makes it immensely interesting and challenging.

Nonpsychological factors observed only by an outsider can at the next moment become psychological ones for the person being studied. A prime characteristic of the parts of a life space and their regions is their permeability. There can be movement both ways through the boundary of a person or a life space or through the boundaries of any of their regions. Aspects of self may move into future environmental regions of the life space or even into foreign hull, and vice versa. Only the inner stratum of self—needs—remains relatively stable, although it too may change drastically over periods of time, as when a person changes his religious faith.

Figure 8.3
Relationship of a biological organism to a psychological person.

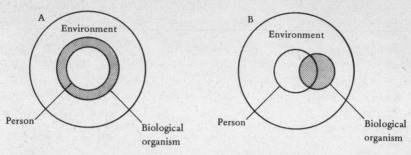

Is an organism considered person or environment?

In a relativistic sense, an organism is an aspect of both the person and his environment. A person usually closely identifies his biological organism with himself. But he also sees his organism in another light as an important aspect of his environment; it is part of that with which he must learn to live. A child's or youth's being crippled or abnormal in physical size or proportions may color everything he says or does. A 12-year-old girl who reaches the adolescent growth spurt early and becomes head and shoulders taller than any other student in her class may consider her physical stature a critical aspect of her psychological environment; she must live with what she "makes of" her physical stature.

We may illustrate the relation of a biological organism to a person in two different ways. The organism may be considered a boundary region of a person, which mediates between the person and his environment by providing cognitive and manipulative abilities (Figure 8.3A), or the functions of the organism may be pictured as a factor common to both a psychological person and his psychological environment (Figure 8.3B).

HOW IS LEARNING A CHANGE IN INSIGHT OR COGNITIVE STRUCTURE?

Learning is a dynamic process whereby, through interactive experience, insights or cognitive structures of life spaces are changed so as to become more serviceable for future guidance. Insights or cognitive structure are answers to questions concerning such mattters as how something is made up, what one belongs to, how one does something, of what good a thing or action is, and what one should be doing. They may be verbal, preverbal, or nonverbal. One may gain an insight before one has words to express it, one may have a complete and exact verbalization involving no or little insight, or the insight and the verbalization may be achieved simultaneously. There is evidence that even nonverbal animals solve mazes by formulating a series of cognitive structures and testing them, and that they solve their problems through gaining insight into their situations.[13] What occurs psychologically when by being given food, a dog is taught to "sit"; later when he wants a toy that he sees on a table, he goes to the table, assumes his "sitting" position, and barks?

Insights derive from an individual's best interpretations of what comes to him; they may be deeply discerning or they may be shallow. They may serve as dependable guides for action or they may prove ruinous. Chica, one of Köhler's apes, attempted to reach a banana by placing a box beneath it and jumping as high as possible from the box. After several failures, suddenly she held the box as high as possible, pressed it against the wall, and attempted to climb up on it. Chica had an insight, but not a true one.[14]

Human beings, when behaving intelligently, are assumed to be purposive, and their learning is related to their purposiveness. According to cognitive-field psychology, a child in a learning situation is not unfolding according to nature; neither is he being passively conditioned always to respond in a desired manner. Rather, at his level of maturity and comprehension, he is differentiating and restructuring himself and his environment; he is gaining or changing insights.

It is an insightful process when a ball player gets a feel for the correct swing of his bat, when a little child discovers how to dress himself, when a boy or girl learns to drive an automobile, when a child gets the idea of multiplication, perhaps through addition, or when a college student learns how to "read" Shakespeare.

It is in connection with goal-directed behavior that insightful learning occurs. One's direction or purposeful activity in his life space is dependent upon its cognitive structure. Remember that a life space contains a person (self) as well as his environment, and that through his gaining and changing insights the

[13]See Edward C. Tolman, "Cognitive Maps In Rats and Men," *Psychological Review*, July 1948, pp. 189–208.
[14]See Wolfgang Köhler, *The Mentality of Apes*, New York: Vintage Books, 1959, p. 139.

person cognitively structures both. A completely new situation would be cognitively unstructured; a person would have no knowledge of what would lead or point to what. Thus, at that moment his behavior would be completely random. (This is the position of a lower animal when it is first placed in a "problem box.") However, rarely, if ever, does a person function in a completely unstructured situation. More often we find students in situations that are inadequately or inharmoniously structured. This means that they have problems and need to extend their learning—change the cognitive structures of their life spaces.

A person's behavior in a relatively unstructured situation would appear exploratory, vacillating, and contradictory. An adolescent, for example, vacillates between a child's and an adult's world, neither of which to him is well structured. Newly acquired adult regions of his life space will not fit into a child's world, and some of the child's regions to which he clings will not fit in the adult world he is, at times, attempting to enter.

A person's behavior, to a very large degree, depends upon the cognitive structure of his life space. Learning results in building psychological traces, which contribute to the structure and dynamics of future life spaces and thus affect future performance. Memory processes refer to cognitively structured similarities between an individual's life spaces that exist at different times. It is because of the continuity of life spaces and their cognitive structures that learning is of value to a person.

Good insight into a present life space or situation tends to provide excellent foresight into the cognitive structure of future life spaces. Suppose a college student wishes to understand and appreciate principles of human development and learning and to prepare himself to apply them in future teaching situations. An excellent procedure would be for him to acquire a deep understanding of himself, his environment, and their relationships in his current series of life spaces.

Learning is a dynamic process within which a constantly expanding world of understanding is reaching out to encompass a constantly expanding psychological world. At birth, a child's psychological world is very small. But on his level he is trying to understand that small world. He is trying to understand how to get food. Soon he will be seeking warmth. Later he will seek means of getting attention. As he grows, in order more adequately to influence his own destiny, he will seek insights into his world as it affects him. Hence, to one with a cognitive-field approach, learning means development of a sense of direction or bearing which can be used, when occasion offers and if found desirable, as a guide for conduct. This all means that learning is enhancement of intelligence.

The cognitive structure of a life space corresponds to the meaningful knowledge of a person, knowledge being defined in the broadest sense possible. Thus, learning is discovery of meaning. A change of cognitive structure may occur in any part of a person's life space, including the psychological past, present, or future. By defining all learning as essentially a process of developing cognitive structure or insights, we escape the dangers of forming a dichotomy of knowledge and motivation. The formation of this dichotomy has led in the past to a rather sharp distinction between learning of facts and development of personality, character, and attitudes. Ideas involving emotional, motivational, and imaginative functions ultimately are as necessary in "factual" mathematical, scientific, and historical pursuits as they are in literature and the fine arts.

HOW MAY THE COGNITIVE STRUCTURES OF LIFE SPACES CHANGE?

A person changes the cognitive structure of his life space through *differentiation, generalization,* and *restructurization* of its respective regions. A region—a distinguishable, functional part of a life space—is the psychological meaning of an object or activity. The object or activity may be either a remembered, a contemplated, or a presently existing one. Regions of a life space may include aspects of one's self, specific activities such as working and eating, states of being such as being frightened or feeling secure, and membership in groups and classes as well as the personalities, objects, and events that one perceives. The cognitive structure of one's life space includes not only the arrangement and conditions of existing regions but also an understanding of what movements may occur and what may be the consequences of such movements. The relation of the region in which a person's activity is centered in reference to the other regions of his life space delineates the qualities of his immediate surroundings, the kind of regions adjacent to other regions, that is, the possibilities for his next steps, and what steps mean actions toward and what ones mean actions away from goals.

What is cognitive or perceptual differentiation?

Differentiation is the process within which regions are subdivided into smaller regions. In differentiation, relatively vague and unstructured regions of a life space become cognitively structured and more specific. Differentiation, then, means discerning more and more specific aspects of one's environment and oneself. What once were "kitties" come to be "leopards," "tigers," "lions," and "cats." What once was "toast" comes to be "crackers," "donuts," and "bread." What once was "baby" comes to be "me," "my arms," or "my legs," and, later, "student," "member of club," "ball player," and "lady-killer."

Differentiation proceeds at different rates at different times, and during crisis periods such as adolescence its speed rapidly fluctuates. As a child grows he differentiates (1) himself or his person from his environment; (2) different aspects of his person and environment from each other; (3) a psychological past and future from the present; and (4) imaginative reality levels from the concrete reality level of his life space. Since the meanings of the latter two kinds of differentiation—differentiation of time perspective and differentiation of imaginative from concrete reality—are so often misunderstood, we explain them in some detail.

Differentiation in time perspective. During a person's development, an enlargement of his time perspective occurs; a psychological past and future become more significant. A small child lives very much in the present. His time perspective includes only an immediate past and an immediate future. However, as one's age increases, one's time perspective tends to expand. Thus, anticipations of more and more remote future events and growing memories of past events come to influence present behavior. These time-binding events occupy such a central part of many adult life spaces that it is often assumed that a past and a future actually exist in their own right. Careful thought, however, will bring the realization that the only past with which a person can deal is *what he thinks happened in the past*. Likewise, the only future that can influence a person *now* is his *anticipation* of a future that he thinks may, or is going to, eventuate.

A child's present life situation contains traces, or "memories," of past incidents, but all of these are in his present situation or life space. When a second child has appeared in a family at some time in the past, the important factor now, as far as the first child is concerned, is not whether his mother rejected him when the second child was born, but whether he interpreted the past situation as one of rejection and carried the rejection into his present life space. The "past" can be of present significance only through operation of factors in the present which are identified as "past." That which persists from prior experience so that it is a "past" in the present is *trace*.

Anticipation of a future also occurs in the present; it is how one envisions the future, not what will actually happen then, that counts in the present. If a child is good in school on Monday so that he will get a star on Friday, whether or not he actually receives a star on Friday has nothing to do with his being good on Monday. His *anticipation* of the star is his motivation for his goodness on Monday. Recognition of the "presentness" of any past and future in no way depreciates them; it merely places them in a contemporaneous frame of reference within which growth of time perspective is conceived in terms of memory traces and anticipations, which are functional parts of a present life space.

Differentiation of imaginative from concrete reality. Normal human development carries with it not only an enlargement of time perspective but also an increased differentiation of the concrete-imaginative dimensions of one's life space. As used in cognitive-field psychology, imaginative processes are wishing, dreaming, imagining, symbolic thinking, and kindred practices. To young children, their products are concretely real; then gradually they are distinguished more and more from actual physical reality.

A young child does not clearly distinguish imaginary objects from concrete facts, wishes from goals, or hopes from expectations. Thus, to him, Santa Claus and Satan may be as real as any concrete object. However, when a child realizes that there "really" is no Santa Claus but still continues to talk about him, he is differentiating an imaginative realm from that of concrete reality. Then, as he grows older, he tends to make an even sharper distinction between concrete and imaginative reality. Fantasy in the form of wishful thinking is also common in adults. However, they generally are better able to distinguish imaginative processes from concrete experience. Furthermore, mature adults should recognize the degree to which they are engaging in each.

How are concrete-imaginative levels related to time dimensions of a life space? The salient characteristics of a life space at any given juncture are (1) the level of concrete-imaginative reality at which the person is operating, and (2) the degree to which the individual's life space encompasses a psychological past and future. There is a direct relationship between the respective concrete-imaginative levels of reality and the degree of time-binding that pervades the life space of a person at a given time. At the level of concrete facts, immediate goals, and practical expectations, a life space contains only an incipient past and future; they are just beginning to be. Thus, concrete reality is to be found only in the momentary present. But, as a person's life space assumes more imaginative dimensions, his time-binding functions become increasingly extended and significant until, at an extremely imaginative level, his entire life space may be centered on either a psychological past or future. But, even then, the time and imaginative dimensions of a life space continue to be both contemporaneous and present.

We should not confuse the adjectives *imaginative* and *imaginary;* the two words have significantly different meanings. Whereas *imaginary* means purely fictitious or fanciful and existing only in the imagination, *imaginative* applies to that which arises through one's cognitively creating concepts or plans for action. Thus *imaginative* is a much more constructive term than is *imaginary*. In fact, a person's being imaginative is analogous to his being creative.

Imaginative levels of reality range from mere expectations and their means of fulfillment to hallucinations that give rise to extreme guilts and fears. Some levels between the two extremes, ranging from concrete reality to extremely imaginative reality, involve aspirations, wishes, imagination, symbolic thought, creativity, fancy, fantasy, dreams, and nightmares. In the psychological past, these take the form of memory, pride, innocence, error, fault, sin, and guilt. In the psychological future, they embrace goals, hopes, anticipations, conjectures, fabrications, visions, fears, and despair.

Figure 8.4 symbolically depicts the interrelationship of the concrete-imaginative dimension of a life space of a person and his time perspective. The figure should be interpreted to signify not merely two but several or even many levels of reality, which may range from life on a purely biological level to one of complete autism—absorption in fantasy. As a person functions on more imaginative levels, his psychological past and future also become more salient aspects of his life space. Thus, whereas on the level of concrete reality a psychological past and future hold only a relatively minor significance, as the person involved operates on more imaginative levels the time dimension of his life space becomes more and more important.

Now, how may an adult's understanding of the concrete-imaginative levels of life spaces contribute to his being a more effective teacher, especially when he is teaching boys and girls of a social class other than his own? For one to successfully teach a child or youth, he must meet him on the level of reality where his life space is focused at the time. Recognition of

Figure 8.4
Concrete-imaginative levels of a life space as related
to its psychological past and future.

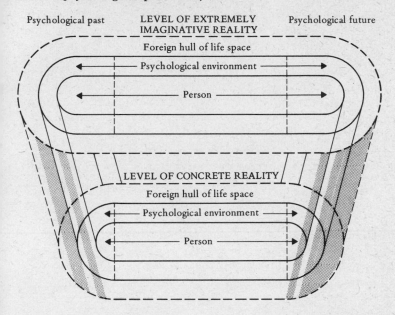

this key principle is highly essential, if a typical "middle-class" teacher is to reach and teach a child or youth from culturally-deprived homes.

In working for marginal wages and barely earning a living these boys and girls are likely to maintain their life spaces on a low, subsistence level of reality; their primary goals involve the acquisition of food, clothing, and shelter. However, from time to time, they leave this concrete level, and, when they do, they are most likely to jump to an extremely imaginative level of reality. This imaginative level, reflected in the persons' day-dreams and fantasy, is focused largely on a psychological future; it is a flight from routine drudgery and boredom.

Reserved, and dignified "middle-class" people generally do not pitch their psychological realities on either of the extremes that are characteristic of "lower-class" persons. Consequently, teachers, in their earlier contacts with boys and girls from the "lower class," should deliberately focus their interest, thoughts, and teaching on extreme levels of concrete or imaginative reality in order that their students will make the teacher's attitudes and ideas a part or region of their respective life spaces. Then, students' life spaces may be constructively reviewed and progressively improved through the joint inquiry of teacher and students.

What is cognitive generalization?

Cognitive generalization is a process whereby one formulates a generic idea or concept through his discerning some common characteristics of a number of individual cases and his identifying these as a class of ideas or objects. Thus, in cognitive-field terms, a generalization arises through a person's categorization of subregions into a unified region of his life space. When a child learns that vegetables, flowers, bushes, and trees are plants, or a student learns that his hopes, dreams, beliefs, and anticipations are all subregions of a "future" region in his contemporaneous life space, he is generalizing. A student of professional education, through differentiation of various instances of learning, may develop a generalized concept, learning, to cover any learning in any situation.

Although in common usage generalization is the opposite of differentiation, psychologically they are complementary. Generalization is the process whereby one groups a number of particular objects or functions under a single heading or in a single category. Thus, one generalizes when he forms a concept that includes previously differentiated aspects of himself or his environment. When a child learns that cats, dogs, horses, and birds are "animals" he is generalizing. Then, through a combination of differentiation and generalization, he may divide the physical world into vegetable, animal, and mineral.

What is cognitive restructurization?

Restructurization of one's life space means one's making more or different sense of oneself and one's world. A person not only differentiates and generalizes his life space into new regions but simultaneously restructures his life space; he changes the meanings of respective regions in relationship to himself and to one another. Within the process of restructurization, one defines or redefines directions in his life space; he learns what actions will lead to what results. He does this through perception of significant relationships of different functional regions of his life space. Restructurization, then, consists of separating certain regions that have been connected and connecting certain regions that have been separated. (Remember that regions are defined as functionally distinguishable parts of a life space.)

When we were quite young, most of us differentiated people from their environments. Later we differentiated people into various races, classes, and groups. Perhaps about the same time we generalized them into Republicans and Democrats, or Christians and non-Christians. As a person learns, he continues to differentiate and generalize himself and his environment, but he also restructures the differentiated and generalized regions of his life space so as to give them new meanings. In this way, a person becomes, or at least should become, an increasingly better thinker.

Restructurization includes, not only extensions of time perspectives and increased differentiation of imaginative from concrete levels of reality, but also changes in motivation and group identification and changes in bodily coordination. A person's change in motivation arises through his seeing regions or factors of his life space in a new light. To a 14-year-old boy, a girl, once something to be teased, comes to be a thing to be quite gently cuddled. A change in motivation is also closely related to changes in group identification. To a large degree it is the groups to which one belongs that are the source of his ideology and consequently of his motivation. One's person emerges through his becoming a member of a group and it develops as he changes his group allegiances. An adolescent's conformity to his peer group standards is a striking example of this developmental process.

A very noticeable evidence of a child's or youth's development is the change in control of his bodily muscular system—his bodily coordination. A small child gradually learns to handle himself quite well. Then comes the adolescent growth spurt. This entails such great changes in bodily size and proportions that a youth must almost start all over again in learning to control his musculature. This process ultimately becomes refined into development of the fine coordination of complex skills.

HOW IS INTELLIGENCE RELATED TO LEARNING?

Cognitive-field psychologists define intelligence as the ability to respond in present situations on the basis of anticipation of future possible consequences and with a view to controlling the consequences that ensue. One's intelligence so defined consists of the number and quality of one's insights—differentiations, generalizations, and structurizations of one's life space. Within

Figure 8.5
John's understanding of his life space at ages 4 and 8.

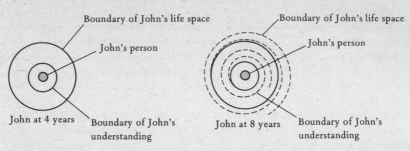

this frame of reference, successful behavior rightfully may be called intelligent only when a person might have done otherwise and his actions were premised upon his envisioning what he was doing and why. Learning is enhancement of one's intelligence. This means that all of its forms—development of logical organization, social insight, appreciation, information, and skills—have a common element. They all involve a change in the experiential situation of a person that gives him a basis for greater predictability and control in relation to his behavior; they enhance his intelligence.

To a large degree a person's intelligence is dependent upon the degree of his change in motivation, bodily coordination, and time perspective, his differentiation of aspects of his person from those of his environment, and his discernment of levels of concrete and imaginative reality. As a child develops by means of these processes, he learns increasingly to understand and control his environment. However, teachers have no reason to fear that a student will soon acquire complete understanding and will see no further need to learn. The only person who may think he knows everything is the one who knows practically nothing. Once a student launches a serious study of his environment, his life space accelerates its rate of expansion. As his understanding expands to encompass newly gained regions of his life space, his life space also grows to such a degree that his motivation for study actually multiplies. This is illustrated graphically in Figure 8.5.

How does intelligent behavior differ
from nonintelligent behavior?

Cognitive-field psychologists view an intelligently behaving person as one who acts as if he is pursuing a purpose and has some foresights as to how it is to be achieved. Nonintelligent behavior arises when a person is pushed or pulled about as an inert, nonliving object, just as a stone dislodged from a place of support falls to a lower lodgment. Let us picture a man straddling a pole and attempting to raise it from among a pile of similar poles. He is behaving intelligently. As the poles are moved, their position changes and suddenly a group of poles falls on the far end of the pole he is lifting; another group in the center serves as a fulcrum and the poles raise him into the air. When he is moved into the air, he displays nonintelligent behavior. He is behaving—moving—but there is no connection between this specific movement and his foresight of consequences. In intelligent behavior, an activity is carried forward to a goal through a process by which one constantly searches out the conditions for the next step all along the way. Intelligence, then, is largely a matter of foresight.

What is habit?

Learning is habit formation, but under cognitive-field psychology, habit comes to have a special definition. Habit is not an act that is repeated automatically simply because of its frequent repetition in the past. Neither is it a fixed sequence of acts that can be explained adequately as a system of preformed pathways in the nervous system. (Of course, some sort of concomitant neural action is not denied.) Rather, habit is fluid, effective, efficient action arising through a person's operating on the basis of the insights that he possesses.[15] When one operates in terms of the insights or cognitive structure he has, habit is manifested. Change in cognitive structure through differentiation, generalization, and restructurization means a change in meaning. When an event has meaning its psychological position and direction are determined; one knows what actions will lead to what results. This is the basis of habit.

Habits then, are goal-related—in fact, the essence of cognitive-field psychology is that all intelligent human endeavor is purposive. *A situation has meaning when it points to a course of action.* If a situation and its meaning are perceived simultaneously, then a person exhibits habit. Habit enables one to behave intelligently without thinking. Often there is not time to think; indeed, thinking then might be disastrous. What happens when your car is closely following a large truck and the truck stops abruptly?

[15]See Boyd H. Bode, *How We Learn*, Lexington, Mass.: Ratheon/Heath, 1940, pp. 249–250.

WHAT IS THE MEANING OF COGNITIVE-FIELD PSYCHOLOGY FOR TEACHING SITUATIONS?

To summarize a cognitive-field theory of learning, we may say that a person learns through differentiating, generalizing, and restructuring his person and his psychological environment in such way as to acquire new or changed insights, understandings, or meanings concerning them, and thereby achieves changes in motivation, group belongingness, time perspective, and ideology. In this way, he gains in control of himself and the world. So learning, concisely defined, is a process of one's gaining or changing his insights, outlook, expectations, or thought patterns. Now, how is this learning theory applicable to teaching theory and practice?

Within a cognitive-field approach to a school situation, each teacher and each student is considered a person-and-his-psychological-environment. A teacher's unique function is to implement the development of serviceable insights of students so as to help students become more adequate and harmonious personalities—that is, more intelligent. To accomplish this, a teacher needs a basic understanding of the structure and dynamics of life spaces. The structure of a life space is its topology; its dynamics are is vectors.

Topology of a life space shows the various possibilities for psychological movement or action; *vectors* show the moving forces within the topological structure. To understand the behavior of a child, one must determine the psychological position of the child's person in reference to the goal regions of his life space i.e., his topology. This entails knowing the child's social position within and outside various groups, his position in relation to various ideas and activities, and the role of physical objects in his life space. The relative region of a life space in which a child is located determines the qualities of his immediate surroundings, and it sets the possibilities for the child's next step in his psychological life. Vectors indicate what step or event means action toward and what step means action away from a person's goals. Thus, they represent psychological moving forces engendered by goals or barriers; they picture what is happening or likely to happen. The forces represented by vectors are equal to the valences—attracting and repelling powers—of respective regions of one's life space.

A student's life space on a given evening, topologically, may contain a television set, a book, and a movie. Vectorially, each object and activity has some degree of valence—alluring or repelling power. Should he go to the movie, this means that movie valence is greatest of all. When one behaves intelligently, he does what he wants most to do; if he does not want to do it more than he wants not to do it, he does not do it.

For a teacher to analyze a psychological situation, he should describe the structure of a person and his environment and ascertain their dynamic properties—what they have to do with the student's behavior. That is, he must see the relationships between the regions or parts of the student's life space, and he must establish the nature of the respective factors residing within, at, and outside its boundary. Furthermore, he must assess the degree of permeability of the boundaries of the various regions of his life space; how susceptible the student is to change.

Factors outside the boundary of a life space, the foreign hull, are those which may be perceived by others but at the moment have no place in the perceptual world of the person being studied. Knowing these facts helps a teacher determine what is possible and what is not, and what might happen and what might not. Then, to understand and accurately predict behavior, a teacher, in addition to understanding the structure of the student's field—the interpositional relationships beween the parts in his life space—must also ascertain the dynamic properties of the person's life space—the valences of, and the barriers to, his goals.

Now what does all this mean in a school situation? Let us return to the schoolroom described on pp. 221–223. "Alice is so absorbed with her teacher and schoolwork that she is oblivious to everything else about her, including the other children." The teacher is central in Alice's life space. Alice's schoolwork also is far within the border of her life space. The other children and everything else in the room that is not part of Alice's schoolwork are in the foreign hull of her life space. "Helen is a social butterfly; she wants the attention of most of the children in the classroom. She does give attention to the teacher from time to time, but right now she is concerned with other things." The other children are in Helen's life space; the teacher is at the margin, sometimes in and sometimes out. "John's body is in the classroom, but 'psychologically' John is riding a shiny new tractor which is being operated in the field adjoining the school." John's school environment and his psychological environment have little in common. Whereas little within the room is in his life space, the tractor is as central as it can be and its valence is very high.

For a teacher to teach a student in a significant way, it is imperative that there be an intersection of the student's life space with the teacher's and with the other life spaces in the room. Life spaces intersect when they have regions in common. To insure an adequate intersection of life spaces, a teacher must probe the various regions of the life spaces of his students.

The way to peripheral regions of a person is quite accessible in ordinary conversation. However, it is more difficult to reach more central regions, that is, those needs near and dear to him. To gain an understanding of each student and his cognitive world, a teacher has to develop a sort of disciplined naïveté. In order adequately to see Tom through he must *see through Tom*. He must see Tom's person and environment as Tom sees them. When a teacher gains rapport with a student—when he gains his confidence—his influence can extend to the student's central regions and he is in a position to speak of the student's needs. What a person needs depends primarily upon how he sizes up himself and his material and social environment.

Teachers should bear in mind that a self is in the making constantly as one develops new insights, or changes old ones, and forms new habits. Furthermore, a far-reaching change in structure of a self or person can occur through one's developing a significant educational insight. And, finally, acquiring a new educational insight can be as significant and far-reaching as a student's falling in love, becoming converted, or realizing a great change in his physical and social environment.

BIBLIOGRAPHY

BIGGE, MORRIS L., "A Relativistic Approach to the Learning Aspect of Educational Psychology," *Educational Theory*, July 1954, pp. 213–220. A proposed harmonization of the topological and vector psychology of Lewin with the pragmatic educational philosophy of John Dewey and Boyd H. Bode. It suggests that a relativistic approach to learning is highly predictive of individual behavior.

BIGGE, MORRIS L., "A Relativistic Definition of Stimulus-Response," *Journal of Educational Psychology*, December 1955, pp. 457–464. Implications of situational psychology for relativism. *Stimulus* and *response* gained their currency within mechanistic approaches to learning. If they are to be retained within relativism, they should be redefined. Stimulus does not occur first, followed by response; nor vice versa. Rather, the two operate simultaneously. Stimulus is environment-centered and response is person-centered.

BODE, BOYD H., *How we Learn*, Lexington, Mass.: Raytheon/Heath, 1940.

A classic in learning theory. Bode's views in Chapters XIV–XVII provide a precursor of present-day cognitive-field learning theory.

BRUNER, JEROME S., *et al., A Study of Thinking*, New York: John Wiley, 1956.
A study based on research carried on at the Institute for Advanced Study (Princeton) and at Harvard University. Focuses on the formation and use of concepts. Technical, but an average student can read the introduction with profit.

BUGENTAL, JAMES F. T., ed., *Challenges of Humanistic Psychology*, New York: McGraw-Hill, 1967.
Chapters 1, 2, 3, 8, 9, 18, 30, and 34 contribute to an understanding of cognitive-field psychology.

CANTRIL, HADLEY, ed., *The Morning Notes of Adelbert Ames, Jr.*, New Brunswick, N.J.: Rutgers University Press, 1960.
Ruminations of Ames in regard to his activities and thoughts. Notes that, whereas the *assumptive* world is a common one, a perceptual world is an individual one. Develops interdependencies of perceptions, purposes, and actions.

COMBS, ARTHUR W., *The Professional Education of Teachers*, Boston: Allyn and Bacon, 1965.
Application of a perceptual view of students and teacher to effective teaching. *Perceptual* as used here is analogous to *interactive*. Shifts emphasis from a mechanistic to a personal view of teacher-student relations.

COMBS, ARTHUR W., and DONALD SNYGG, *Individual Behavior*, rev. ed., New York: Harper & Row, 1959.
A perceptual approach to psychology which supports the SMI position. Study centers upon perceived selves and their needs, goals, and purposes.

DEWEY, JOHN, *Human Nature and Conduct,* New York: Holt, Rinehart and Winston, 1922.
Dewey's "psychology." It describes human nature in relativistic terms. Difficult but extremely rewarding for superior students.

GIBSON, JAMES J., "The Concept of the Stimulus in Psychology," *American Psychologist*, 1960, Vol. 15, pp. 694–703.
Thesis: When psychologists pick the variables of physics as they appear in physics textbooks, they choose the wrong variables. Whether a potential stimulus becomes effective depends upon the individual's perception of it.

KUENZLI, ALFRED E., *The Phenomenological Problem*, New York: Harper & Row, 1959.
A collection of technical papers clarifying the phenomenological—perceptual—approach in modern psychology which harmonizes with the SMI outlook.

LEWIN, KURT, "Field Theory and Learning," in Nelson B. Henry, ed., *The Psychology of Learning*, Part II, *The Forty-first Yearbook of the National Society for the Study of Education,* Chicago: University of Chicago Press, 1942, pp. 215–242.

Probably Lewin's best brief presentation of the learning theory that is implicit in his field psychology.

LINDZEY, GARDNER, and ELLIOT ARONSON, eds., *The Handbook of Social Psychology*, 2nd. ed., Vol. 1, *Historical Introduction and Systematic Positions*, Reading, Mass.: Addison-Wesley, 1968.

In Chapter 6: an excellent description by Morton Deutsch of field theory as it has been developed by Lewin and his students. Chapter 5 on cognitive theory and Chapter 7 on role theory contribute to understanding of the cognitive-field position.

MAY, ROLLO, *Psychology and the Human Dilemma*, New York: Van Nostrand Reinhold, 1967.

The human dilemma results from man's capacity to experience himself as both subject and object simultaneously. Man's being purely free or purely determined is not the way out.

NINE

How Does Learning Transfer to New Situations?

A predominant purpose of formal education in schools is to facilitate learning outside them. It would be difficult to justify any achievement of school learning that had no bearing upon students' future learning in life situations. Nevertheless, often what is learned in school contributes very little, if anything, to children's and youth's solving their future problems. Thus, there appears to be much room for improvement in our teaching procedures so that transfer of school learning to other situations will be enhanced to a much greater degree than at present.

Transfer of learning occurs when a person's learning in one situation influences his learning and performance in other situations. If there were no transfer at all, students would need to be taught specifically every act that they ever were to perform in any situation. Although, when we think of transfer, we usually consider how one learning experience *strengthens* another, we should remember that there also is a negative transfer process within which one learning experience interferes with, i.e., *weakens*, another. However, generally speaking, what we learn in one situation tends to facilitate or help our learning in others. But the opposite effect, interference, can also occur. For example, a person's study of foreign language or philosophy can make him a slower reader of English literature, or his becoming committed to certain dogmas or absolutes can interfere with his future creative, reflective thought.

In its broadest sense, *transfer of learning is basic to the whole notion of schooling.* People who support, as well as those who conduct, our schools assume that matters being taught today will have some learning value in later times in different situations. Accordingly, the assumption which underlies our entire educational system is that learnings gained in school not only will be available in the future but also will be applied in some degree to the solution of new problems as they arise in oncoming school and life situations. For instance, we assume that today's lesson in arithmetic will help with tomorrow's problems in the same subject and that it also will help in dealing with algebra, geometry, and the physical sciences.

The effectiveness of a school depends, in a large measure, upon the amount and quality of transfer potential of the materials that students learn. Thus, transfer of learning is a cornerstone upon which education should ultimately rest. Unless students learn in school those matters which help them in meeting situations more effectively further along the academic sequence and later in life, they essentially are wasting their time.

We suggest that you reflect briefly upon the learning that you achieved while you were in high school. You studied, and apparently mastered, a number of different courses. These courses contained factual detail, generalizations, and techniques. Periodically, you showed on an examination that you had learned fairly well the content of each course. How much of your high school learning do you now retain in such a way as to be able to use it in contemporary situations? What dealing did the United States have with Napoleon? How does a participle differ from a gerund? If the school house is 1½ miles north and 2 miles east of a boy's home, what is the shortest distance from his home to school? What is the basic difference between the structure of San Francisco Bay and the Strait of Georgia? If you do not do very well with questions such as these, you need not be completely chagrined. Studies such as the Regents' Inquiry of the State of New York found such inability to be typical among students.[1]

[1]See Morris L. Bigge and Maurice P. Hunt, *Psychological Foundations of Education*, 2nd ed., New York: Harper & Row, 1968, Chapter 1, pp. 2–3, for a summary of the findings of this study.

HOW IS TRANSFER A PROBLEM?

The basic problem of transfer is: In what way and to what extent will acquisition of skills, knowledge, understanding, and attitudes in one subject or learning situation influence performance or learning in other subjects or situations? Knowing the answer to this and some subordinate problems will enable us to teach for maximum, effective transfer of learning.

Some subordinate transfer problems are: (1) how does a person's current learning assist him in meeting future learning situations? (2) how does what youngsters learn in school affect what they learn and what they do outside school? and (3) does school learning have as much effect as it should and how can it be made more effectual?

More specifically, in what manner and how much does the learning of a given material, say, memorizing the names of all the states and their capitals, aid, hinder, or have no effect upon subsequent learning, for example, learning the content of a textbook? To what extent and in what way does the study of Latin enhance English vocabulary and grammar, aid in learning French or German, or contribute to knowledge of ancient history? How does a study of theories of learning contribute to one's knowledge of how to teach fourth-grade reading or high school physics? Will an individual carry over the arithmetic ability he learned in a classroom to the problems he actually encounters in business or in tasks about the house? Does practice in memorizing, reasoning, persevering, and willing improve the mental process in general? Can one improve his perception, retention, and imagination in all fields by practice in one?

The critical question in regard to transfer is not whether it takes place, but what conditions engender the greatest amount of it. Classroom teaching definitely can be conducted in such way as to achieve transfer. Furthermore, it is highly probable that teaching can be brought to achieve a much higher degree of transfer than it now does. However, in order that we may teach for maximum transfer, we need to understand how transfer occurs. Having done this, we need to help students learn how to learn in such a way that transfer will reach a maximum level.

Everyone seems to agree that we want maximum transfer of learning to new situations. But, when laymen and teachers discuss what and how the schools should teach, there is strong disagreement about the nature and likelihood of transfer. At one extreme, classical scholars advocate a strictly intellectual curriculum consisting of science, mathematics, classical languages, and history. At the other extreme, some educators maintain that learning which remains completely verbal or abstract has negligible effect on learning and acting in concrete life situations. The latter group thinks of learning and transfer as being highly specific. Thus, its members believe that we should prepare students step by step for personal, civic, and vocational adulthood.[2]

Although teaching for transfer is of prime importance, it can be overemphasized to the degree that it actually impedes learning. Consequently, though we should enthusiastically promote transfer of learning, we simultaneously should recognize the possible negative consequences of an overemphasis which may contribute to a "cold storage" concept of education. We might come to think that childhood is not worthwhile in itself and that we must always be preparing for adulthood. Thinking such as this can have disastrous consequences; "preparation," if overworked, can have a vicious connotation.

Then again, we should guard against defining transfer too narrowly. Although it was a tremendous jump, it was an example of transfer of learning when Newton shifted the concept of falling bodies from small objects to planets. Furthermore, when we say that our central aim in education is to increase students' abilities to think, we are discussing transfer.

WHAT QUESTIONS ARE BASIC TO A STUDY OF TRANSFER?

Each systematic theory of learning—mental discipline, natural unfoldment, apperception, S-R bond, conditioning, reinforcement, goal insight, and cognitive-field—implies a somewhat different theory of transfer. In fact, a description of the theory of transfer of a given learning theory has much in common with a description of the learning theory itself.[3] The transfer problem is so pervasive that any treatment of the position of adherents of a systematic learning theory in regard to transfer, of necessity, comprises a summary of the learning theory itself.

Adherents of each learning theory develop their respective position in regard to transfer through answering some specific questions, such as: (1) How is learning best defined? (2) What exactly does transfer of learning mean? (3) How is transfer

2See Percival M. Symonds, "What Education Has to Learn From Psychology, Transfer and Formal Discipline," *Teachers College Record*, October 1959, pp. 30–45.

3See Table 1.1, p. 10.

promoted most effectively? In the remaining sections of the chapter we review the various answers that adherents of different theories provide for these questions. Although question 1 on learning is not centered on transfer as such, we must first review it in order to establish a background for consideration of the transfer problem proper, which is represented by questions 2 and 3 on transfer of learning and its promotion.

In our examination of the various outlooks in regard to transfer of learning, we concentrate in turn upon natural unfoldment, mental discipline, apperception, S-R bond theory or connectionism, operant conditioning, generalizations, and cognitive-field approaches. Six of these also are names for theories of learning. Only *generalizations* is uniquely a theory of transfer. As such, it is an aspect of several learning theories. The generalizations theory of transfer emerged as a protest against the atomistic specificity of earlier associationistic psychologies. It may be considered a connecting link, although sometimes a confusing one, between the associationistic transfer theories of apperception, connectionism, and conditioning and the insight transfer theories of the Gestalt-field family.

Since, by its very nature, natural unfoldment has few, if any, positive implications for transfer, we deal with it here only briefly. Exponents of natural unfoldment regard intellectual development as something that "just naturally happens." To be consistent with their overall outlook, they would reject any kind of formal teaching for the purpose of stimulating development of intelligence. Instead, they would stress student-planned activities including highly permissive types of projects as the means for releasing or developing latent intellectual performance. In a laissez-faire classroom students would exercise unlimited freedom.[4]

Since Skinner is highly optimistic in regard to the application of his theory to practical schoolroom situations, we use his ideas on transfer as a contemporary representative of the S-R conditioning family. Each of the representatives of this, as well as the other psychological outlooks, has its own theory of transfer; however, there tends to be a similarity between the theories of transfer of the various members of each family of learning theory.

Because of the similarity in the theories of transfer of various members of the Gestalt-field family, we present only the cognitive-field theorists' treatment of transfer as a representative of this group.

[4]See Chapter 11, pp. 300–301.

HOW DOES MENTAL DISCIPLINE
IMPLY GENERAL TRANSFER?

The conception of education as mental (formal) discipline seems to go far back in recorded history. Furthermore, prior to the nineteenth century, general transfer of training through mental discipline was widely accepted in educational circles of the Western world.[5] Consequently, from its earliest beginning until the end of the nineteenth century, American formal education was dominated by the doctrine of mental discipline. During this period education was regarded as necessarily unpleasant. School room atmospheres were at least austere and sometimes harsh. Teachers usually were dictators, sometimes benevolent, but sometimes even spiteful. Children were expected to be respectful and obedient and to accept at face value whatever teachers told them. Curriculums were relatively fixed with an almost exclusive emphasis in elementary schools on the fundamental skill subjects, and in secondary schools on such "disciplinary" subjects as Latin, history, and mathematics.

In 1865, James B. Wickersham, State Superintendent of Public Instruction of Pennsylvania, wrote as follows in a book entitled *Methods of Instruction:* "The intellectual faculties can receive culture only by judicious exercise. . . . No means are known whereby the faculties of the mind can be developed but by exercising them. By the potent spell of the magic word Exercise, is evoked all human power."[6] Here we see an able scholar even as late as the middle of the nineteenth century definitely committing himself to a doctrine of mental discipline and more specifically, faculty psychology.

The two most influential groups in the United States who continue to favor a disciplinary approach to education are some leaders in parochial education and those liberal arts professors who are under the influence of faculty psychology and the classical tradition. In addition to these there are many thousands of other persons, including some public school teachers, who gravitate toward a theory of mental discipline.

How do mental disciplinarians define learning?

The central idea in mental discipline is that the mind—envisioned as a substance—or its faculties lie dormant until they are

[5]See Chapter 2, pp. 20–31, for a more detailed treatment of mental discipline.

[6]Taken from Ernest E. Bayles, *The Theory and Practice of Teaching*, New York: Harper & Row, 1950, p. 87.

exercised. Faculties such as memory, will, reason, and perseverance are the "muscles of the mind"; like physiological muscles, they are strengthened through exercise and subsequently operate automatically. Thus, learning is a matter of strengthening, or disciplining, the faculties of the mind which combine to produce intelligent behavior.

Adherents of mental discipline think that the primary value of history or any other disciplinary subject is the training effect it has on the minds of students. They are convinced that this effect will remain after the "learned" material has been forgotten. Furthermore, they consider the highest value of education to be its liberalizing effect. Education that is truly liberalizing, supposedly, prepared us not only to live in the world, but more important, to live with ourselves. In 1959 James D. Koerner, a contemporary exponent of mental discipline, wrote, ". . . *the purpose of [liberalizing] education is the harmonious development of the mind, the will, and the conscience of each individual so that he may use to the full his intrinsic powers and shoulder the responsibilities of citizenship."*[7]

How do mental disciplinarians define transfer?

According to mental discipline, germs of the various faculties supposedly are in each individual from birth, and learning is a process of developing these germinal, undeveloped faculties into powers or capacities. When a teacher is asked concerning the value of studying his particular subject and replies, "It sharpens the mind and improves the memory," or "it cultivates the reasoning faculty," he is thinking of learning as mental discipline and of that which is transferred as being generally exercised germinal capacity. Thus, he thinks that he is building in his students a great power reservoir that automatically goes into operation in any kind of subsequent mental activity.

The various faculties supposedly can be developed through training and become capable of effective performance in all areas in which they are involved. Thus, the training of the faculty of memory through memorizing nonsense syllables presumably improves one's memory for names, for meaningful material, and in fact for anything which calls for memory. Likewise, it is assumed that after training in reasoning through a study of geometry, a person can reason effectively in realms of philosophy, mathe-

[7]James D. Koerner, ed., *The Case for Basic Education*, Boston: Little, Brown, 1959, p. v.

matics, social issues, and housekeeping. Accordingly, education largely is a matter of training or disciplining minds with vigorous mental exercise in the classics, grammar, logic, mathematics, and pure science on the assumption that such training makes a person equally effective in all areas where a given faculty is employed.

Since, within mental discipline theory, transfer is assumed to be automatic, once a faculty has developed it supposedly goes into operation whenever its use is appropriate. Notice that, within mental discipline, *psychological processes* such as thinking, attending, remembering, and persevering became reified into mental objects or faculties—thought, attention, memory, and perseverance.

How do mental disciplinarians promote transfer?

Educational practice based on the theory of mental discipline stresses the necessity for developing the "sinews of the mind" by rigorous exercise. Mental disciplinarians have little desire to make school work pleasant or interesting. In fact, more discipline is engendered if the tasks are unpleasant and burdensome; the harder the exercise, the more the faculties are disciplined. Thus, the more difficult the school work, the more effective it is thought to be. Since subjects such as Latin, mathematics, and science taught mechanically seem particularly arduous, these subjects have been enthusiastically taught in the schools for their disciplinary value.

To a mental disciplinarian the direct utility of a subject is of little consequence; exercise of the mental faculties is what is important. The material or content upon which the exercise is expended makes little difference, except that it must be of such nature as to require strenuous exertion. Certain mental powers or faculties such as tenacity and logicality, exercised and developed in the study of, say, botany, supposedly carry over automatically to all aspects of life wherein the same mental powers are required.

Since mental disciplinarians are not interested in anything like life-adjustment education, they work to stretch, not relax, the minds of their students. They are convinced that a teacher should be not an amateur psychiatrist, social worker, and baby-sitter, but a scholarly educator. Since faculties supposedly are strengthened through mental practice much as muscles are strengthened through physical exercise, the most difficult subjects are the most desirable for stretching the mind. Furthermore, long, difficult assignments supposedly develop the faculties of will power and attention.

Mental discipline as an educational doctrine was first seriously challenged by William James, who found no improvement in his ability to commit poetry to memory resulting from a month's practice in memorizing Hugo's *Satyr*. Thorndike and Woodworth[8] reported similar findings in regard to possible development of mental faculties through exercise. However, even in the face of James's, Thorndike's and Woodworth's research in this area, many scholars continue to endow certain subjects, particularly the more abstract ones, with immensely superior transfer power.

Students who have mastered difficult subjects usually do have above-average proficiency in whatever areas of study and thinking they happen to pursue. Although it doesn't necessarily follow, it is easy to assign credit for this proficiency to the nature of the specific subjects that have been studied; it often is overlooked that people who elect or survive difficult subjects perhaps had more ability when they started them. This is an example of the *post hoc ergo propter hoc*—after this, therefore on account of it —fallacy; instructors and others may fallaciously reason that after taking certain courses youth are good students, therefore, the courses made them into good students.[9] We should recognize, however, that, even though mental disciplinarians' reasoning may be fallacious in this regard, their procedure becomes a screening device, whether or not it is an educating one. A school may "maintain high standards" through teaching for mental discipline and grading so rigorously that a high percentage of students fail and drop out. By so doing, it can raise the quality of its students; but the increased quality of students, so gained, is no indication of improved quality of instruction.

Today the concept "mental discipline" is unpopular with most psychologists and professional educators. Experimental evidence indicates that memory as a general function is not improved by strenuous memorization of poetry. Likewise, reasoning in fields other than mathematics is not automatically improved by studying algebra and geometry. However, there still are scholars, parents, and other school patrons who are convinced that Latin, science, and mathematics should be included in the school curriculum because they are "good for the students' minds."

In light of current psychological knowledge, it is difficult to

[8]See Chapter 2, pp. 29–30.
[9]See Chapter 2, p. 29.

justify school subjects purely in terms of improving students' minds through exercise. Evidently there is transfer of learning, but not the general transfer implied in mental discipline. Methods of solving arithmetic problems can be transferred to the solution of problems in algebra. The learning of Latin may, and often does, facilitate the learning of English grammar. However, if experimental research is to be trusted, transfer is not automatic, and it is not a matter of disciplining minds.

Herbartian apperception, S-R conditioning, and Gestalt-field theories of learning, while disagreeing on many points, all agree in their opposition to mental discipline. Their strongest weapon has been systematic research that tests the results of different teaching and learning procedures. During the first half of the twentieth century, it seemed that Thorndike, Woodworth, and James had rendered a killing blow to mental discipline, and that it no longer would be seriously promulgated in our public schools. However, during the 1950s and 1960s, many scholars in the arts and sciences and others following in their wake have seriously and vehemently advocated this theory of learning and transfer, divorced from experimental evidence and support.

As we study outlooks on transfer that have arisen to challenge mental discipline, perhaps we can crystallize on a point of view that is more adequate than mental discipline itself or any of the competing theories that immediately followed and challenged it.

HOW IS APPERCEPTION RELATED TO TRANSFER?

There are two broad types of associationisms: (1) early mentalistic associationisms, which focused upon the association of ideas in a mind, and (2) more modern physicalistic S-R associationisms, which concern themselves with formation of connections between cells in a brain and peripheral nervous system or between organic responses and environmental stimuli.

Herbartian apperception has been the leading example of the first type of associationism. Although Herbart's associationist psychology was built on fundamentally different premises from the natural unfoldment theory of followers of Rousseau, it was equally incompatible with mental discipline. Hence, Herbartian teaching, like Roussellian permissiveness, can be considered a counterinfluence to mental discipline. However, the formal, rigid approach of Herbartians, coupled with what seemed to be emphasis upon rote learning, made their teaching appear on the surface to be much like the kind of education practiced by the mental disciplinarians.

Herbart's prescription for good teaching, as implemented by his followers, became highly mechanical. Furthermore, apperception like mental discipline made teachers central and dominant in the educational process.[10]

How do apperceptionists define learning?

Apperception is a process of relating new ideas or mental states to a store of old ones. Memories stored in the subconscious and brought into the conscious enable one to interpret experiences of the moment. New ideas are learned through their being related to what already is in an apperceptive mass. Thus, apperception consists of becoming consciously aware of an idea and assimilating it with other, already acquired ideas. A student's mentality is made up of the world of ideas which is presented to him from without.

Learning, then, is not a matter of developing or training a mind, but rather one of formation of an apperceptive mass. Education is a process of teacher's causing present, specified experiences of students to combine with appropriate backgrounds. Consequently, apperceptionists emphasize implantation in the minds of students of a great mass of facts and ideas that have been organized by someone other than the learner—usually the author of a text or a teacher.

How do apperceptionists explicitly define transfer?

According to apperception theory, a student's "subconscious mind" contains a quantity of mental states that have been accumulated during his experiences. Any one of these elements of the apperceptive mass stands ready to spring back into consciousness when the appropriate occasion occurs; it is ready to join other mental elements with which it has an affinity.

By use of textbooks and lectures, apperceptionists "cover" their subject. Students learn the material, retain much of it in their apperceptive masses, and carry it over to meet future situations in and out of school. This information supposedly will be used whenever a situation arises in which it is needed. Appropriateness, however, is determined by the nature of the mental states or ideas, not by the person.

Mental states (sometimes called presentations) are stored in the form of sense impressions, copies of previous sense impres-

[10]See Chapter 2, pp. 33–46, for a detailed treatment of apperception.

sions or images, and affective elements such as pleasure or pain. Such mental states provide the total source of mental activity. Feelings and willings are secondary factors which are derived from original mental states. Consequently, volition or willing has its roots in thought; right thinking supposedly produces right action.

How do apperceptionists promote transfer?

Fundamentally, apperceptionists promote transfer by building up the apperceptive masses of their students. The Herbartian principles of association and frequency are the heart of apperception. The association principle is that, when a number of ideas form a mass, the combined powers of the mass determine the new ideas that will enter consciousness. The coordinate principle of frequency is that the more often an idea has been brought into consciousness, the easier it is for it to return. Application of these two laws leads teachers to emphasize frequent presentation of the *proper* ideas to students. Teachers are convinced that transfer is best when a goodly supply of facts and principles are stored for later use. If people know facts and principles pertinent to a given area of learning or living, they automatically will use them as appropriate occasions occur.

Apperceptive teaching, in order to maximize transfer, continues to follow the Herbartian five steps—preparation, presentation, comparison, generalization, and application. This entails careful preparation and rigid employment of detailed lesson plans that outline and prescribe a fixed order of teaching and learning.[11]

Apperception, as a theory of transfer, has been a vital force in attacking its predecessor—mental discipline. However, the jump from the assumption that people innately are either bad and active or neutral and active to the assumption that they are inertly passive was not all to the good. John Locke's *tabula rasa* theory of mind upon which apperception is based is perhaps as vulnerable as is mental discipline. *Within apperception, transfer becomes completely a matter of mechanistic storage of ideas in a mind which is composed only of those ideas.* As such it implies that teaching is an indoctrination procedure. Thus, it throws schools out of harmony with the democratic structure of American society.

Some specific charges can be leveled against apperceptive principles and procedures in today's schools and the outlook on

[11]See Chapter 2, pp. 41–42, for a description of these steps.

transfer which they imply. Since students completely depend upon the teacher, who provides all of the leadership in learning, critical thinking is discouraged and students tend to be docile. Facts are acquired for test purposes, then rapidly forgotten; their transfer value tends to be very low. Furthermore, problem-centered teaching is largely disregarded.

We should recognize, however, that, regardless of their shortcomings, apperceptionists have told us much about experience which otherwise might escape our attention. They have realized that when a person has a new experience there is a "reception committee" of background ideas that helps him interpret it. Furthermore, they have noted that experiences, in some way, abide after they have been undergone, and that they have considerable influence in determining the nature of subsequent experiences.

Apperception was a connecting link that led the way for development of both mechanistic and purposive contemporary psychologies. We examine these next to see how they have treated the problem of transfer.

WHY DOES CONNECTIONISM EMPHASIZE IDENTICAL ELEMENTS?

The S-R bond or connectionistic theory of learning was developed by Edward L. Thorndike and his followers. Its basic thesis is that, through conditioning, specific response patterns come to be connected with specific stimuli. The theory of transfer that accompanies connectionism is transfer of *identical elements*.[12]

The identical elements theory of transfer means that learning is facilitated in a second situation to the extent that it contains identical factors or elements which occurred in an earlier learning situation. "Chief amongst such identical elements of practical importance in education are associations including ideas about aims and ideas of method and general principles, and associations involving elementary facts of experience such as length, color, and number, which are repeated again and again in differing combinations."[13] Identical elements may take the form of like contents, procedures, facts, actions, attitudes, techniques, or principles.

The identical elements theory implies that a school should list the aspects of situations that are important out of school or in

---

[12]See Chapter 3, pp. 53–55, for a description of connectionism.
[13]Edward L. Thorndike, *The Psychology of Learning*, New York: Teachers College Press, Columbia University, 1913, p. 359.

later courses and teach the pupil to cope with each specific one. Accordingly, lists of spelling words are drawn from articles, letters, and documents written by adults. Likewise, reading vocabulary lists contain words that adults read in newspapers and magazines.

How do connectionists define learning?

Connectionism is "the doctrine that all mental processes consist of the functioning of native and acquired connections between situations and responses (Thorndike)."[14] The acquired connections, supposedly, are formed through random, not purposive, trial and error; they constitute learning. Since S-R bonds or connections are, in some way, the product of physiological changes in a nervous system, learning is associated with neurological changes.

Three major laws of learning and five minor ones supposedly operate whenever acquired connections occur. Thorndike's major laws of learning are *effect, exercise or frequency*, and *readiness*.[15] His minor laws are *multiple response, attitude or set, partial activity, assimilation or analogy*, and *associative shifting*. More recently, in addition to the eight laws of learning, *belongingness, impressiveness, polarity, identifiability, availability*, and *mental system* also have appeared as special learning concepts in the vocabularies of connectionists.[16] Thus, connectionists have developed some fifteen mechanistic laws or principles to encompass learning phenomena and pertinent research.

How do connectionists define transfer of learning?

Connectionists regard human activities of all sorts as responses made by human organisms to stimuli or stimulus situations. A stimulus or stimulus situation is any event that influences a person. A response includes all components of any unified, organic behavior.

When identical elements occur in two learning situations,

---

[14]From Howard C. Warren, ed., *Dictionary of Psychology*. Boston: Houghton Mifflin, 1934, p. 56.

[15]See Chapter 3, p. 54, for a description of Thorndike's major laws of learning.

[16]For a detailed treatment of both the major and the minor laws see Nelson B. Henry, ed., *The Psychology of Learning*, Part II, *The Forty-first Yearbook of the National Society for the Study of Education*, Chicago: University of Chicago Press, 1942, pp. 111–128.

transfer from the first to the second supposedly is automatic. Since, for connectionists, what one learns basically is a group of reactions to a complex situation, reactions are the elements that are transferred to new situations. However, for transfer to occur, learning situations must be of such nature that they contain some of the same reactions. For example, transfer from a study of Latin to English depends upon the extent to which there are identical elements or reactions in the two learning procedures.

In 1912 Thorndike stated, "When any response has been connected with many different situations alike in the presence of one element and different in other respects, the response is thereby bound to that element so that when that element appears, even in a very different total situation, it will tend to evoke that response."[17] The following year, he wrote, "A change in one function alters another only insofar as the two functions have as factors identical elements."[18] According to Thorndike's view as expressed in these quotations, transfer takes place from one learning situation to another only to the extent that there are identical aspects in the two. This means that transfer supposedly takes place from playing a piano to typing to the extent that such skills as eye-finger coordination are identical to both operations. However, elements of similarity between two situations are not necessarily restricted to skills. They might take the form of information, principles, procedures, or attitudes. Furthermore, identity of elements can be in either subject matter or procedures; thus learning is facilitated in a second situation to the extent in which it includes any factors of elements that occurred in the first.

Thorndike's colleagues and followers have recognized that stimulus and response generalization are basic processes in transfer. However, they have limited the generalization concept to characterization of stimuli and responses, and made very little, if anything, of teaching for generalizations as such. Accordingly, they have noted that, if an animal learns to respond to a given stimulus, it will tend to reach likewise to related stimuli. For example, when a dog learns to salivate at one tone, he also will salivate in response to similar tones. *Response generalization* occurs when a person learns to perform an act with one part of his organism and then is able to perform the same act, perhaps not so proficiently, with another segment of his organism.

[17]Edward L. Thorndike, *Education*, New York: Macmillan, 1912, p. 99.
[18]Edward L. Thorndike, *The Psychology of Learning*, New York: Teachers College Press, Columbia University, 1913, p. 358.

258 *Learning Theories for Teachers*

For example, in bilateral transfer, a skill acquired with one hand, foot, or eye is transferred to the other.

How do connectionists promote transfer of learning?

Since, according to connectionism, each person is limited by his inborn neural structure, the most that education can do is to take advantage of what capacity a child or youth has for forming dependable S-R linkages. A person's capacity for intelligent behavior depends upon how many links can be formed and retained. Hence, the best—in fact, the only—way education can serve humanity is to condition students efficiently.

Thorndike's studies had convinced him that the specific methods used in guiding a pupil's learning activities had great effect upon the degree of transferability of his learning. Hence, he thought that teaching specifically for transfer is the only method of teaching that is worthwhile. He was convinced that knowledge should consist of well-ordered groups of connections that are related to each other in useful ways and whose inner relationships correspond to those of the real world. Furthermore, he thought that, the more clearly the crucial elements or facts or principles in a situation are brought to the pupil's attention, the more readily the same element, fact, or, principle may be identified in another situation.[19]

The identical elements principle, when applied to curriculum matters, means *specific objectivism*. Schools are encouraged to decide exactly what students should be taught and to teach these directly, not through some roundabout means. Consequently, if a student is to learn English grammar, the most effective way of his doing this is to learn English grammar, not to attack English grammar by way of Latin or some other foreign language.

According to the theory of identical elements, although study of Latin does not discipline either mental faculties or a generalized mind, it does contribute to transfer to the degree that there are identical elements in Latin and English vocabularies. The "port" of Latin *portare* (to carry) supposedly does transfer to the "port" of English *transport*. Consequently, in accordance with identical elements, if Latin is taught at all, emphasis should be placed upon the roots or segments that are identical with those in English. However, even then the study of Latin

[19]See Edward L. Thorndike and Arthur I. Gates, *Elementary Princples of Education*, New York: Macmillan, 1929, p. 104.

roots of English words as they apply to English is more economical in learning English than is the study of Latin as a language.

If one bases a school program on the identical elements conception of transfer, his only choice is to incorporate in the curriculum as many learning tasks as possible which, when reproduced outside of school, will contribute to the effectiveness of living. An entire generation of curriculum makers in the 1920s and 1930s, led by Franklin Bobbitt and W. W. Charters, did, in fact, adopt this approach. They studied American community life much as an efficiency expert would conduct time-and-motion studies in a factory. They then tried to list the specific verbal and motor responses which are needed in daily life and to teach these, with only minor modification, in school.

This approach to education poses many difficulties, not the least of which is that there are so many kinds of situations in life to be faced that a school cannot possibly teach them all, even in the twelve or thirteen years of required attendance. Thus, curriculums tend to become cluttered with too many specific objectives, many of which conflict with one another.

Much research has been devoted to evaluation of the identical elements theory of transfer. In 1941, Pedro T. Orata, who has concentrated his professional study upon transfer of learning, wrote, "The evidence which tends to disprove Thorndike's theory of identical elements continues to cumulate. . . ." He continued,

> Not a simple succession of elements is transferred, but rather an attitude of response or a way of seeing the same kind of solution for different problems. Whereas senseless learning does not transfer, meaningful learning does. The process of learning for transfer becomes one of organization and reorganization of experience.[20]

Orata also lists some conclusions that have developed from his studies. He notes that, although transfer is found in approximately 80 percent of studies, it is not an automatic process that may be taken for granted, and the amount of transfer is influenced by many factors. Factors centered in the learner are age, mental ability, personality, stability attained by a learned pattern, knowledge of direction, attitude toward the learning situation, efficient use of past experience, accuracy of learning, and acceptance of methods, procedures, principles, sentiments, and ideals. Factors centered in the learning situation are meaning-

[20]Pedro T. Orata, "Recent Research Studies of Transfer of Training with Implications for the Curriculum, Guidance, and Personal Work," *Journal of Educational Research*, October 1941, p. 83.

fulness of the learning situation, suitable organization of subject matter presentation, and provision for continuous reconstruction of experience.

The identical elements theory affirms that transfer occurs, but may not adequately explain how. Some critics of the identical elements theory interpret it as really a fragmented faculty psychology; elements in learning may be construed as "small faculties." In discussing the identical elements theory of transfer, Bayles points out, "After all, such a theory is fundamentally the same as the faculty theory because all one needs to do is to divide faculties into sufficiently small units and, behold, one will have identical elements."[21]

WHAT DOES SKINNER'S OPERANT CONDITIONING IMPLY ABOUT TRANSFER OF LEARNING?

Skinner's operant conditioning theory of learning carries with it definite implications in regard to the nature of transfer and its role in teaching and learning. Since the transfer theories of most contemporary S-R conditioning theorists are much like Skinner's, we may consider his position representative of modern S-R conditioning theories or behaviorisms.

Since Skinner questions the reality of the inner qualities and faculties to which human achievements in the past often have been attributed, in his study of learning and transfer he turns from ill-defined and remote explanations of behavior to the study of observable and manipulatable behavior. For Skinner, the basic object of psychological study is the probability of observable behavior, which "is accounted for by appeal to the genetic endowment of the organism and its past and present environment, described wholly in the language of physics and biology."[22] Accordingly, he feels that there is nothing to be lost by applying Newtonian mechanistic science to education and moral discourse, and that any resistance to this movement is only an expression of culture lag.

How does Skinner define learning?

Operant conditioning is the learning process within which a response or operant is brought to be more probable or frequent

[21]Ernest E. Bayles, *The Theory and Practice of Teaching*, New York: Harper & Row, 1950, pp. 91–92.

[22]B. F. Skinner, "The Design of Cultures," Roger Ulrich, Thomas Stachnik, and John Mabry, eds., *Control of Human Behavior*, Glenview, Ill.: Scott, Foresman, 1966, p. 333.

through being reinforced by a change in an organism's environment after the operant or response occurs.[23] In this process there is no necessary connection of stimuli and responses; reinforcement simply increases the probability of a response or class of responses; a reinforcing stimulus is a differentiating not a connecting one.

In keeping with his physicalistic commitment (a physicalist is one who holds human thoughts and actions to be determined by physical laws), Professor Skinner states, "I do not see any distinction between predicting what an individual is going to do and predicting what, let us say, a sailboat is going to do."[24] "Operant conditioning shapes behavior as the sculptor shapes a lump of clay."[25]

Through receiving reinforcement of slightly varied instances of his behavior, a child supposedly learns to raise himself, walk, grasp objects, and move them about. Later on, through the same process, he learns to talk, sing, dance, and play games—in short, to exhibit the enormous repertoire characteristic of a normal adult. Furthermore, in a world in which ethical training is widespread, most men are reinforced by succeeding in reinforcing others. Thus, personal gratitude is a powerful *generalized reinforcer* (see pp. 264–265).

A list of values actually is a list of reinforcers. "People behave in ways which, as we say conform to ethical, governmental, or religious patterns because they are reinforced for doing so."[26] An organism can be reinforced by (that is, it can be made to "choose") almost any given state of affairs. Literature, art, and entertainment are contrived reinforcers. Whether a person buys a book, a ticket to a performance, or a work of art depends upon whether it is reinforcing to him, and usually it is reinforcing to him if he had been reinforced when he previously purchased such an article.

For Skinner, any innate behavior is in the form of unlearned reflexes. A reflex has been called such on the theory that, in its operation, the disturbance caused by a stimulus passes to the central nervous system and is reflected back to the muscles or glands. Although Skinner does not give reflexes the dominant position in his behavioral theory, he definitely recognizes both innate and conditioned ones. However, he notes that if we were

---

[23]See Chapter 5 for a more extensive treatment of operant conditioning.
[24] B. F. Skinner, *Cumulative Record*, New York: Appleton-Century-Crofts, 1961, p. 201.
[25]B. F. Skinner, *Science and Human Behavior*, New York: Macmillan, 1953, p. 91.
[26]Skinner, *Cumulative Record, op. cit.*, p. 34.

to assemble all the behavior that falls into the pattern of the simple reflexes we would have only a very small fraction of the total behavior of an organism.

Innate or hereditary reflexes primarily activate the internal economy of an organism where glands and smooth muscles are operative. When dust blows into an organism's eyes, he reflexively washes it out with a profuse secretion of tears, or when food enters the stomach, peristaltic action is stimulated. However, in addition to the internal reflexes, there are also some external innate reflexes, such as the startle reflex at the sound of a loud noise.

Skinner notes that reflexes, particularly innate ones, are of little importance when we study overt behavior. However, he believes that responsible behavior is determined by environmental stimuli just as are the reflexes. He states, "We do not hold people responsible for their reflexes—for example, for coughing in church. We hold them responsible for their operant behavior—for example, for whispering in church or remaining in church while coughing. But there are variables which are responsible for whispering as well as for coughing, and they may be just as inexorable. When we recognize this, we are likely to drop the notion of responsibility altogether and with it the doctrine of free will as the inner causal agent."[27]

What is transfer in operant conditioning?

Since within operant conditioning learning simply is a change in the probability of a response, transfer likewise is an increased probability of responses of a certain class occurring in the future. Remember that a reinforcer is any stimulus whose presentation or removal increases the probability of a response; there are both positive and negative reinforcers.[28] Because a single instance of a response or operant may be strengthened by being followed by a reinforcing event and the effect survive for a long time even though the same consequence never recurs, operant reinforcement provides a strong theoretical basis for transfer.

Skinner thinks that nearly all human behavior is the product of operant reinforcement and that most reinforcement improves the efficiency of behavior through continuously reshaping it. He writes, "While we are awake, we act upon the environment constantly, and many of the consequences of our actions are rein-

[27]Skinner, *Science and Human Behavior, op. cit.*, pp. 115–116.
[28]See Chapter 5, p. 135.

forcing. Through operant conditioning the environment builds a basic repertoire with which we keep our balance, walk, play games, handle instruments and tools, talk, write, sail a boat, drive a car, or fly a plane. A change in the environment—a new car, a new friend, a new field of interest, a new job, a new location—may find us unprepared, but our behavior usually adjusts quickly as we acquire new responses and discard old."[29] Thus, to Skinner's way of thinking, one's repertoire of conditioned operants is the basis for transfer of one's learning.

The two key concepts in understanding the meaning of transfer within operant conditioning are *conditioned reinforcement* and *induction*.

Conditioned reinforcement. In *conditioned reinforcement,* a new stimulus becomes a conditioned reinforcer, that is, a new reinforcer (stimulus B) is conditioned through its occurrence along with an originally adequate reinforcing stimulus (stimulus A). Thus, stimulus B comes to reinforce an act operantly in the same way as would the originally adequate reinforcing stimulus (stimulus A).

An example of conditioned reinforcement is that, if each time we give food to a hungry pigeon to reinforce an act which we are teaching him we turn on a light, the light eventually will become a conditioned reinforcer; it may be used to reinforce the act or some other operant just as food formerly was used.[30] "If we have frequently presented a dish of food to a hungry organism, the empty dish will elicit the animal's salivation. To some extent the empty dish will also reinforce an operant."[31] Thus, through conditioned reinforcement, other things may acquire the reinforcing power that food, water, and sexual contact originally had.

A characteristic of human behavior is that primary—originally adequate—reinforcers may be effective even after long delays. This presumably is only because in intervening events other objects such as symbols become conditioned reinforcers. In education, techniques are deliberately designed to create appropriate conditioned reinforcers and thereby transfer is promoted. When a student performs properly, the teacher gives him a smile and an A. An A thereby comes to be a conditioned reinforcer; it will "reward" the student for many kinds of activity —operants.

[29]Skinner, *Science and Human Behavior, op. cit.,* p. 66.
[30]See "How To Teach Animals," in B. F. Skinner, *Cumulative Record, op. cit.,* pp. 412–419.
[31]Skinner, *Science and Human Behavior, op. cit.,* p. 76.

Induction. Skinner prefers the term *induction* for what more commonly is called stimulus or response *generalization.* Thus, induction occurs in regard to both stimuli and responses; that is, there is both stimulus induction and response induction.[32]

Stimulus induction is a process through which a stimulus acquires or loses the capacity to elicit a response, control a discriminative response, or set up an emotional "state," because of its similarity to a stimulus which has acquired or lost such a capacity through direct conditioning. If a red light is established as a discriminative stimulus, an orange (or even yellow) light may be found to share the same function, perhaps in a lesser degree.

Response induction is a process through which a response changes its probability or rate because it shares properties with another response which has changed its probability or rate through reinforcement. When a dog has been trained to roll over by being rewarded and he is "told" to "roll over," he may make a twisting motion while remaining on his feet.

For us to understand Skinner's induction theory, we must remember that reinforcement does not strengthen the response which preceded it; it increases the probability of a class of responses, and the class is represented by certain specific responses which occur in the future. Furthermore, we must keep in mind that a class of responses consists of those responses containing the same elements. Thus, Skinner's basic measure of behavior is a response element rather than a response itself. A response element ". . . is a sort of behavioral atom, which may never appear by itself upon any single occasion but is the essential ingredient or component of all observed instances. The reinforcement of a response increases the probability [of occurrence] of all responses containing the same elements."[33]

A large complex of words—an idiom, a phrase, or a memorized passage—may be under the control of a single variable and thus constitute a functional unit.[34] Functional units of behavior, however, consist of a number of basic *behavioral atoms* or elements. Behavioral atoms, as contrasted with functional units, are at least as small as separate speech sounds. We must recognize these small behavioral atoms in order to account for distorted verbal responses such as spoonerisms and other verbal slips (a spoonerism is an accidental transposition of sounds—saying

[32]See B. F. Skinner, *Schedules of Reinforcement,* New York: Appleton-Century-Crofts, 1957, p. 728.

[33]Skinner, *Science and Human Behavior, op. cit.,* p. 94.

[34]*Ibid.,* pp. 94–95.

"blushing crow" for "crushing blow"). These "atoms" also are evident in the stylistic devices of alliteration, rhyme, and rhythm. When we identify elements rather than responses as units of behavior, we then say ". . . the *elements* [atoms] *are* strengthened wherever they occur."[35]

In the life of each organism, through the process of stimulus and response induction, there is constant movement from primary to generalized reinforcement. Usually, in this process, a conditioned reinforcer is being generalized.

Conditioned, generalized reinforcement. Conditioned reinforcement and induction or generalization combine to give conditioned generalized reinforcement. A stimulus that is a conditioned reinforcer is generalized when, in the process of its becoming a conditioned reinforcer, it is paired with more than one primary reinforcer. ". . . if a conditioned reinforcer has been paired with reinforcers appropriate to many conditions, at least one appropriate state of deprivation is more likely to prevail upon a later occasion."[36] Thus, a response is more likely to occur. For example, when we reinforce behavior with money, our subsequent control of the behavior of an individual is relatively independent of any momentary deprivation. Money becomes a conditioned, generalized reinforcer because, from time to time, money occurs along with many primary reinforcers. Thus, it acquires the capacity to reinforce many behaviors.

Skinner observes that a token such as money is a conditioned generalized reinforcer distinguished by its physical specifications. He further notes that money is not the only token that is a conditioned generalized reinforcer. In education an individual behaves as he does, in part, because of the marks, grades, and diplomas which he previously has received. These are not as readily exchanged for primary reinforcement as money, but the possibility of exchange is there. Educational tokens form a series in which one token may be exchanged for the next, and the commercial or prestige value of the final token, the diploma, is usually quite clear.

How is transfer promoted in operant conditioning?

For Skinner, "Education is the establishing of behavior which will be of advantage to the individual and to others at some future time."[37] Thus, the teacher is the architect and builder

35*Ibid.*, p. 94.
36*Ibid.*, p. 77.
37*Ibid.*, p. 402.

of behaviors. Within the building process a teacher is to supply arbitrary and sometimes spurious consequences for the sake of feedback—reinforcement.

Skinner's criticism of many of today's teaching procedures is not that there are no reinforcers operating, but that the ones that do operate mostly reinforce merely going to school and gaining a diploma or a degree. There is a woefully inadequate number of reinforcers for the subject matter elements themselves.

As stated in Chapter 5, the first task of a teacher, according to Skinner, is to shape proper responses in children, such as pronouncing and writing correctly. However, the principal task of the teacher is to bring these correct behaviors under many sorts of stimulus control. Thus, in the education of a child for future constructive behavior, four basic questions must be faced: what behavior is to be set up, what reinforcers are at hand, what responses are available in embarking upon a program of progressive approximation that will lead to the final form of the behavior, and how can reinforcement be most efficiently scheduled to maintain the behavior in strength? The last question states the problem of enhancement of transfer as it is understood by operant conditioning theorists.

The maintenance of behavior in strength after it has been acquired is as much a function of reinforcement as is the original learning. After an organism has learned how to do something, that is, after it has acquired behavior, further reinforcements are necessary to maintain the behavior in strength. In this process, various schedules of reinforcement are of special importance.[38]

HOW DID GENERALIZATIONS BECOME THE KEY IDEA IN TRANSFER?

Let us review an experiment which was performed in 1924 and see if we can discern the *learning elements* that were involved. Frederick B. Knight gave two groups of children of equal ability and equally ready for the topic the same amount of instruction in addition of fractions. Group A practiced on fractions that had as denominators 2, 3, 4, 5, 6, 7, 8, 9, 10, 12, 14, 15, 16, 18, 21, 24, 28, and 30. Group B practiced only on fractions having as denominators 2, 4, 6, 8, 12, and 24. The experimenter depended upon transfer for the learning of the addition of fractions with the other denominators. After their period of instruction the two groups were tested for their ability to add fractions with denominators of 3, 5, 7, 9, 14, 15, 18, 21, 28, and 30. These were the fractions which were taught to Group A but not to Group B. On their test, Group A scored only slightly better than Group B. Group B's score indicated that the group achieved almost complete transfer from mastery of the specifically taught fractions to mastery of the fractions which were not specifically practiced. Do the results of this experiment support or weaken the positions of connectionism, operant conditioning, and other atomistic, or mechanistic psychologies?[39]

Between 1915 and 1920, two of the most eminent educational psychologists of the time, Edward L. Thorndike and Charles H. Judd, carried on a running debate in regard to the nature of transfer. Whereas Professor Thorndike continued to champion his identical elements theory, Professor Judd insisted that generalizations, not identical elements, were transferred to new situations. Thus, the basic educational issue in this period was identical elements vs. generalization-of-experience. This issue centered upon the nature of transfer of learning, and it has persisted through the years past the middle of the twentieth century. Followers of Judd are convinced that the degree of transfer of learning that occurs depends upon the extent to which the products of learning are consolidated into generalizations. A generalization is a characteristic common to many situations.

How are generalizations learned?

Judd recognized two possible kinds or levels of learning: rote memorization with little, if any, meaning and generalized knowledge with many intellectual associations. He placed very little value on the first level and a high premium upon the second. He was convinced that knowledge always should be in the form that makes generalizations possible; that is, it should have many intellectual associations and many possibilities of new associations. He even emphasized his generalizations theory when discussing the teaching of basic skills. Thus, he stated, ". . . when new skills are cultivated by an individual, the muscles are brought into coordinated action through elaborately organized patterns developed in the nervous system."[40] Furthermore, ". . . generali-

[39]Frederick B. Knight, "Transfer Within a Narrow Mental Function," *Elementary School Journal,* June 1924, pp. 780–788.

[40]Charles H. Judd, *Educational Psychology,* Boston: Houghton Mifflin, 1939, p. 496.

zations which epitomize great numbers of experiences are the highest products of racial and individual intellectual effort.[41]

What is the generalization theory of transfer?

A generalization is a statement or understanding of relationships. It may also be called a principle, rule, or law. "Generalization is another name for the relating of experiences in such a way that what is gained at one point will redound to the advantage of the individual in many spheres of thought and action."[42]

For Judd and contemporary generalization theorists, transfer is the sensed relationship between the elements of a situation. Judd like Herbart, Thorndike, and the mental disciplinarians, and unlike Gestalt-field theorists, considered transfer to be automatic. He expected a generalization to spring into action whenever the environment set the stage for its occurrence. Thus, we should recognize that both Thorndike's emphasis upon the *commonness of elements* and Judd's emphasis on the *appropriateness of generalization* make the environment the determining agency in transfer.

Judd's dart-throwing experiment to test the value of generalizations has become something of a classic. Success in hitting a target under water requires readjustment of one's ordinary habit of throwing a dart. Since the light coming from the target is refracted as it leaves the water, there is an apparent displacement of the target. Judd selected two groups of boys comparable in those variables that seemed relevant. One group, the experimental one, was instructed in the principle of—generalization in regard to—the refraction of light; the other, the control group, was not. Both groups of boys were then asked to throw darts in such a way as to hit underwater objects with them. At the beginning of the experiment, none of the boys had any skill in throwing darts.

Both groups of boys were instructed to hit targets placed 12 inches under water. The boys who had had theoretical training in the principles of refraction did as poorly at this first task as did the control group; they had to learn to throw darts before their theoretical training could help. Once this was accomplished the target was moved to a position 4 inches under water. Immediately the experimental group showed a conspicuous superiority over the control group. Their understanding of the

[41]*Ibid.*, p. 514.
[42]*Ibid.*, p. 514.

nature of refraction had given them cues as to where to aim the darts in order to hit underwater objects which are not where they appear to be. Judd's experiment and his interpretation of it is related in detail in his various books.[43]

More recent research supports Judd's position. In 1957, Kittell measured the relative effects of three amounts of direction on sixth graders' discovery of established principles on transfer to differing situations and on their retention of learned principles.[44] He concluded that, "Evidence from this experiment in conjunction with that of similar experiments indicates that furnishing learners with information in the form of underlying principles promotes transfer and retention of learning principles and may provide the background enabling future discovery of new principles."[45]

How are generalizations promoted?

Since, for Judd, ". . . the most effective use of knowledge is assured not through the acquisition of any particular item of experience but only through the establishment of associations which illuminate and expand an item of experience so that it has general value,"[46] students should be taught the advantages of generalization by every possible device. "The preventive for the narrowness of school teaching and for lack of transfer is to be sought in the organization of instruction in such a way that the learner will constantly be made to see the broad relations of items of experience."[47]

Judd's position paralleled similar, but not identical, findings of the early Gestalt psychologists. Köhler, Koffka, Wheeler, Perkins, and other Gestalt psychologists[48] all insisted that what lower animals and human beings tend to learn in any meaningful learning situation is relationships. However, Gestalt psychologists imputed a purposiveness to behavior which Judd could not see. Statements of relationships also are theories, generalizations, principles, rules, or laws which, as Judd said, are ". . . a kind of summary of many experiences. It [generalization] makes

[43]*Ibid.*, pp. 507 ff.

[44]Jack E. Kittell, "An Experimental Study of the Effect of External Direction During Learning on Transfer of Retention of Principles," *Journal of Educational Psychology*, November 1957, pp. 391–405.

[45]*Ibid.*, p. 404.

[46]Charles H. Judd, *Educational Psychology*, Boston: Houghton Mifflin, 1939, p. 500.

[47]*Ibid.*, p. 514.

[48]See Chapter 3, pp. 299–301, for an account of the work of these men.

possible the proper interrelating and interpreting of a whole body of varied experiences."[49]

Since accumulated experimentation has shown that attempts to base transfer on identical elements theory leads to more problems than it solves, and since the generalization theory of Judd and the Gestalt psychologists seems highly productive as a basis for transfer, many educational psychologists today prefer some form of the generalization theory. However, we should recognize the sharp differences which exist among adherents of the generalization theory. *The position of Judd and his followers was decidedly different from that of contemporary cognitive-field psychologists. This difference is epitomized by the statement that whereas Judd adhered to a mechanistic concept of transfer, cognitive-field psychologists see transfer of learning always in the frame of reference of purposive intellectual pursuits.*

Some Gestalt psychologists and all cognitive-field theorists feel that Judd and most other investigators of the generalization hypothesis stopped short of a fully adequate statement of the conditions of transfer. It is increasingly apparent that the achievement of a generalization by a student does not in itself guarantee that transfer will take place automatically. For transfer to occur, a student must desire to use the understandings or insights which he has acquired.

In his discourse on the promotion of transfer, Judd emphasized that the effects of school instruction depend on the way in which the minds of pupils operate rather than upon the subject matter which they study, and that the same content of knowledge may have very different values because of the way in which the content is acquired by different individuals. Nevertheless, he never quite crossed over into seeing that an essential ingredient in transfer is the person's desire to use an insight that he already has gained. He recognized that human intelligence brings to the solution of each problem encountered by an individual a vast body of personal and social experience in the form of generalizations, but he seemed to fail to see that use of "human intelligence" involves a desire to use it.

HOW DO COGNITIVE-FIELD PSYCHOLOGISTS VIEW TRANSFER?

There are only minor differences among the transfer theories of Gestalt psychology, Bayles' goal-insight theory, and cognitive-

[49]*Ibid.,* p. 509.

field psychology. Consequently, we present the cognitive-field position on transfer as a representative of the Gestalt-field family.

Cognitive-field psychologists think that transfer of learning occurs because of perceptual similarities between situations, and that it is in the form of generalizations, concepts, or insights that are developed in one learning situation and are usable in others. However, to cognitive-field psychologists, it seems as futile to expect a generalization to spring into action whenever the environment sets the stage as to expect such of a faculty or of an identical element. For teachers to promote transfer in a dependable way, something more than commonness of elements or appropriateness of generalizations is necessary.

Experience shows that in actual practice transfer of a generalization will not always occur even when a person understands a principle thoroughly and has applied it often. A natural scientist repeatedly can be scientific in dealing with problems of natural science and simultaneously resort to folklore and superstition in dealing with problems of the social sciences and humanities. He either may not recognize that scientific method is applicable to problems in the social sciences and humanities, or he may recognize such applicability but have no desire to use it in the other areas of endeavor.

How do cognitive-field psychologists define learning?

Cognitive-field theorists think of four psychological movements transpiring simultaneously in the life of a person. It is within the course of these "psychological locomotions" that learning occurs. These movements are (1) continuity of successive life spaces (see page 224), (2) interaction within each life space (see page 74), (3) change in levels of concrete-imaginative reality (see page 231), and (4) differentiation in the person's time perspective (see page 230).

For cognitive-field psychologists, learning is a change or reorganization of the insights into, or the cognitive structure of, a contemporaneous life space or situation.[50] That is, it is a change in knowledge, skills, attitudes, values, or beliefs, and it may or may not be closely related to some change in overt behavior. One does not "learn by doing" except insofar as one's doing contributes to one's change in cognitive structure. For learning to occur, the doing must be accompanied by realization of con-

[50]See Chapter 8 for an expanded treatment of cognitive-field learning theory.

sequences. Thus, learning occurs through, and as a result of, experience. Learning, then, involves the catching, and generalization, of insights, which often are first caught on a nonverbal level—the level of "feel"; they may be verbalized at the time of their catching, at some later time, or not at all.

In learning, our tendency is to "generalize" our insights—to hypothesize, or get a hunch that they will work in other instances where conditions are similar. We test the validity of these generalizations by trying them in active experiences. If they have no predictive value, they tend to drop by the wayside. If they do have predictive value, they become a part of our intellectual make-up and contribute to intelligent behavior until they are changed or discarded.

How does cognitive-field psychology define transfer of learning?

For cognitive-field theorists, continuity of life spaces is the pivotal concept in their theory of transfer of learning. Along with the perceptual interaction, which occurs in each life space of a person, there is a continuity of cognitive structures of succeeding life spaces. Although in the most technical sense a life space is of a moment's duration, for actual schoolroom purposes it is generally taken to extend over a juncture of some time. Furthermore, succeeding life spaces are not completely different from each other; rather, there is a continuity of a person's life spaces, and it is within this continuity that transfer of learning occurs. The cognitive structure of each life space overlaps, and shades into, that of the life space that succeeds it.

Since both behaviorism and cognitive-field theory are scientific psychologies, they both project their findings into the future in the form of anticipations or predictions. However, in developing their findings, the focuses of their study contrast sharply. Whereas behaviorists center their study on the past stimulus-response reactions of organisms, cognitive-field psychologists focus their study on person's present situations. Accordingly, learning that is transferred consists of the cognitive structure of a present life space that is extended to future life spaces of an individual. Cognitive-field psychologists note that when transfer of learning occurs, it is in the form of generalizations, concepts, or insights that are developed in one learning situation being employed in others; this process is called *transposition*. Transposition of insights may also be described in terms of habits, but under cognitive-field psychology, habit has a special definition. A habit is a skillfully executed application of a principle in a situation wherein application of that principle will apparently help a person achieve a goal. Nevertheless, even habits are not blind, automatic behaviors. Rather, they are products of tested insights used in new situations. They are, therefore, precise adjustments to situations that call for them. One may operate on habit, and transfer may occur with little or no reflection. Or transfer may occur in a highly reflective situation. In either case, transfer is not automatic.

A person is in the best frame of mind for transfer to occur when he is aware of acquiring meanings and abilities that are widely applicable in learning and living. However, important as this is for cognitive-field psychologists, it is not enough. A person must also want to solve new problems, or approach new situations, in the light of the insights gained through previous experience. For transfer to occur, individuals must generalize—perceive common factors in different situations; they must comprehend them as applicable and appropriate to both, and thereby understand how the generalization can be used; and they must desire to benefit by the sensed commonality. Ernest E. Bayles tells us that any insight susceptible of generalized application *"will transfer if and when—and only if and when—(1) opportunity offers, (2) a trained individual sees or senses it as an opportunity; and (3) he is disposed to take advantage of the opportunity."*[51]

Cognitive-field theorists are committed to the proposition that transfer of learning to new tasks will be better if, in learning, the learner can discover relationships for himself, and if he has opportunities to apply his learning to a variety of tasks. Consequently, they think that, for transfer to occur at its highest level, we must help students understand many widely useful relationships, principles, or generalizations; we must foster sensitivity to the presence of opportunities for transfer so that likelihood of recognition is high; and we must encourage students to embrace goals, attitudes, and ideals that support the conviction that progressive refinement of outlooks on life is possible and commendable.

Gertrude Hendrix' new clue to transfer of training is that ". . . it is the intermediate flash of unverbalized awareness that actually counts for the transfer power. . . ."[52] She found that

[51]Ernest E. Bayles, *Democratic Educational Theory,* New York: Harper & Row, 1960, p. 58.

[52]Gertrude Hendrix, "A New Clue to Transfer of Training," *Elementary School Journal,* December 1947, p. 200.

the way a person learns a generalization affects the probability of his recognition of an opportunity to use it. In method I (a conventional method) a generalization was first stated, then illustrated, then applied to new problems. In method II, the generalization was not stated, but "drawn out of" the learners by asking questions; teaching was for unverbalized awareness.

In teaching for unverbalized awareness, the stage was set in such a way that as soon as the generalization dawned on the learner he would begin to apply it. Students were asked to find the sum of the first two odd numbers, the sum of the first three odd numbers, the sum of the first four odd numbers, etc. As soon as the subject knew the relationship between these sums and the number of odd numbers to be added, he started to gasp a little, or smile, or grew tense. That is, he showed in some way that something had happened to him. (The answer: the sum of the first n odd numbers is n^2.) Furthermore, he began to give succeeding answers rapidly, getting them by the learned short-cut method rather than by the laborious process of addition; by transfer behavior based on a generalization he revealed possession of the generalization.

In method III, students were taught as in method II except that subjects were asked to state the rule they had discovered. Arrival at a correct verbalization (method III) took about twice as long as discovery of a generalization on an unverbalized level (method II). In every case included in two experiments, the highest transfer effects were achieved in the group taught by the unverbalized awareness procedure. The lowest transfer effects came from the group taught by the method in which the generalization was stated first, then illustrated, then applied to new problems. (What theory of transfer did this procedure represent?) Groups that learned by verbalizing the discovered generalization showed up somewhere between the other two groups. Hypotheses emerging from the data are as follows:

1. For generation of transfer power, the unverbalized awareness method of learning a generalization is better than a method in which an authoritative statement of the generalization comes first.
2. Verbalizing a generalization immediately after discovery does not increase transfer power.
3. Verbalizing a generalization immediately after discovery may actually decrease transfer power.[53]

The crucial points of cognitive-field psychology in regard to

[53] *Ibid.,* p. 198.

transfer of learning and its promotion now may be summarized in seven points:

1. Opportunity for transfer may occur in many situations. It is not inherent in any subject but is possible from any field of knowledge.
2. Transfer is not dependent upon mental exercise with disciplinary school subjects.
3. Transfer is dependent upon methods of teaching and learning that use lifelike situations. It is facilitated by teaching for large generalizations that have transfer value.
4. Transfer is not automatic; opportunities for transfer must be recognized, and the person concerned must want to use them.
5. Transfer varies according to difficulty of generalization of subject matter and the intellectual ability of individuals.
6. Insights need not be put into words for their transfer to occur.
7. The amount of intraproblem insightful learning, not the number of trials as such, determines the amount of interproblem transfer.[54]

Chapter 11 extends our inquiry to consideration of the implications of the various outlooks on learning and transfer for methods of learning and teaching. But first let us peruse some common principles of learning that are generally accepted by adherents of the various "schools"; this is the subject of Chapter 10.

BIBLIOGRAPHY

BAYLES, ERNEST E., *Democratic Educational Theory*, New York: Harper & Row, 1960.
 Chapter 3, "Learning and Transfer," pp. 45–62, develops a goal-insight theory of learning which is closely related to cognitive-field theory, then states four conditions necessary to transfer of learning.
BAYLES, ERNEST E., *The Theory and Practice of Teaching*, New York: Harper & Row, 1950.
 Chapter 6, "The Transfer of Training," pp. 85–98, a historical summary of outlooks on transfer. Probably the best brief treatment of transfer available.
CRONBACH, LEE J., *Educational Psychology*, 2nd ed., New York: Harcourt Brace Jovanovich, 1963.
 Chapter 10, "Intellectual Development as Transfer of Learning," pp. 314–348, treats transfer in terms of transfer of response. Eclectically develops conditions favorable to transfer.

[54]See Harry F. Harlow, "Learning Sets and Error Factor Theory," in Sigmund Koch, ed., *Psychology: A Study of a Science*, New York: McGraw-Hill, 1959, p. 502.

GAGE, N. L., ed., *Handbook Of Research On Teaching*, Chicago: Rand McNally, 1963.
Pages 1014–1021 review research on consequences of teaching secondary school mathematics by tell-and-do methods as compared with heuristic—discovery—methods.

GROSE, ROBERT F. and ROBERT C. BIRNEY, *Transfer of Learning*, New York: Van Nostrand Reinhold, 1963.
A book of well-selected original writings on transfer of learning. Traces historical growth of the concept up to the present time.

HARLOW, HARRY F., "The Formation of Learning Sets," *Psychological Review*, January 1949, pp. 51–65.
Based on research with animals, Harlow emphasizes the importance of learning how to learn—learning sets. Emphasizes problems as contrasted with trials in learning .

HASLERUD, GEORGE M., and SHIRLEY MEYERS, "The Transfer Value of Given and Individually Derived Principles," *Journal of Educational Psychology*, December 1958, pp. 293–298.
Compares retention and transfer value of direct teaching and independent discovery and finds independent discovery method more effective.

HILGARD, ERNEST R., ROBERT P. IRVINE, and JAMES E. WHIPPLE, "Rote Memorization, Understanding, and Transfer: An Extension of Katona's Card-Trick Experiments," *Journal of Experimental Psychology*, October 1953, pp. 288–292.
A review of Katona's card-trick experiments and finding and report of further research to check the findings. Supports teaching for understanding as compared with rote learning, especially when transfer of learning to new problem-solving situations is involved.

JUDD, CHARLES H., *Educational Psychology*, Boston: Houghton Mifflin, 1939.
Reflects Judd's generalizations principle and its implications for learning, intelligence, and transfer.

KNELLER, GEORGE F., "Automation and Learning Theory," *The School Review*, Summer 1962, pp. 220–232.
Analyzes the nature of automation and its relation to learning. Points up that Skinner's teaching machines are effective only if the teacher accepts Skinner's special interpretation of behaviorism within which learning is considered to be always additive.

SKINNER, B. F., *Schedules of Reinforcement*, New York: Appleton-Century-Crofts, 1957.
Pages 728–730 develop Skinner's meaning of stimulus and response induction—generalization.

STEPHENS, JOHN M., "Transfer of Learning," *Encyclopedia Of Educational Research*, New York: Macmillan, 1960.
Pages 1535–1543, excellent summary of research pertinent to transfer of learning. Treats definition, characteristics, and conditions affecting the amount of transfer.

SYMONDS, PERCIVAL M., "What Education Has To Learn From Psychology, VII Transfer and Formal Discipline," *Teachers College Record*, October 1959, pp. 30–45.

A good historical summary of the transfer problem and pertinent research. Emphasizes transfer through application of general principles.

THORNDIKE, EDWARD L., *The Psychology of Learning*, New York: Teachers College Press, Columbia University, 1913.

Thorndike's early presentation of results of his psychological studies for students' use. Expands and explains his laws of learning. Chapter II, pp. 350–433, treats transfer of learning.

TEN

What Principles of Learning Are Commonly Accepted by Psychologists?

In previous chapters we have viewed several systematic theories of learning, and we have seen how much in contrast are the chief tenets of the two major families of contemporary learning theory. Now we review some principles of learning that are commonly accepted by modern psychologists, regardless of the schools of psychology with which they identify themselves.

This chapter focuses upon principles of learning that are not usually clearly attached to either S-R conditioning or Gestalt-field outlooks as such. Thus, they are widely stated in textbooks on educational psychology, irrespective of the overall orientation of the authors. Although the manner in which these principles are interpreted and used is influenced by whether one is an exponent of S-R conditioning or of Gestalt-field psychology, in the main they lead to somewhat similar classroom results.

The principles presented in this chapter are close to classroom practice in the sense that they provide rather specific directives to teachers. In this respect, the present chapter is a bridge between the relatively abstract nature of preceding chapters on learning theory and the largely "how-to-do-it" emphasis of educational methods courses.

Before moving into an elaboration of these widely accepted

principles of learning, we should make it clear that many psychologists, particularly those with the widest reputations, are interested as much as ever in "system building," that is, in constructing a body of theory that is cohesive and internally consistent and within which all elements, even minor ones, harmonize with the central premises. Examples of such persons on the side of Gestalt-field psychology are Donald K. Adams, Roger G. Barker, Ernest E. Bayles, Dorwin Cartwright, Arthur W. Combs, Morton Deutsch, Fritz Heider, Sigmund Koch, Ronald Lippitt, A. A. Lumsdaine, Robert MacLeod, Gardner Murphy, and Herbert F. Wright. On the side of the S-R conditioning emphasis are John P. De Cecco, W. K. Estes, A. I. Gates, Robert Glasser, Harry F. Harlow, Donald O. Hebb, Neal E. Miller, B. F. Skinner, John M. Stephens and Robert M. W. Travers.

These persons, like prominent figures in all the other social and natural sciences, recognize that scientific progress has thrived on systematizations of thought, such as the theory of relativity in physics. But most scientists also recognize a different level of principle—what we might call "working principle" because of its immediate applicability in practice. The chief condition a working principle must meet is that it not be inconsistent with the major system to which its practitioners are committed. However, it may be equally consistent with several competing systems.

The principles herein described have been selected from a wide range of literature. They are presented not as an all-inclusive listing of "working principles" of learning but as a sampling of some of the more useful, generalized statements that are supported by the research and conclusions of reputable psychologists.

HOW MAY WE IMPROVE MOTIVATION FOR LEARNING?

When a person develops a state of tension resulting from unsatisfied need, we say that he is motivated. Motivation may spring from a variety of needs, ranging from those that are largely physiological in origin to those that are primarily psychological, such as that engendered by a conflict in religious belief. A motive may appear as a generalized need for achievement or it may be specifically associated with a need to obtain a particular reward. The person's aim becomes the reduction of tension, which can occur only as the need is wholly or partially satisfied.

Obviously, motivation plays a central role in learning. Students who are motivated work purposefully and energetically. They display few if any "discipline" problems. Consequently, a teacher who can keep his students well-motivated has won more than half the battle.

The role of personal involvement

Where possible, through the medium of a democratic classroom climate, a teacher's task is to help induce personal involvement. Personal involvement at its best is perplexity just short of frustration. Because of the interactive character of the most productive classroom situations, both students and teacher eventually should test their attitudes, values, skills, and knowledge at the same bar of reflective examination.

We would be unrealistic if we failed to concede that such an accomplishment is easier to describe than to achieve in practice. In virtually every school subject, a few students will appear well-motivated toward solution of real problems. A few others will appear to have no motivation toward learning and, despite a teacher's best efforts, will seem to remain that way. Another group, which usually contains a majority of the class members, will respond more or less well to the teacher's efforts to engender involvement and promote motivation. It is in working with this middle group that teachers feel their greatest sense of either accomplishment or frustration.

Intrinsic vs. extrinsic motivation

Intrinsic motivation is that tendency to activity which arises when the resolution of tension is to be found in mastering the learning task itself; the material learned provides its own reward. If a job is done because doing it is somehow satisfying, if the job carries its own reward, if it is done for its own sake, then we say that motivation is intrinsic. If Johnny washes his neck not because of outside pressures but because he likes the feel of a clean neck, or if he studies the construction of model airplanes diligently so that he can make his own model, he is experiencing intrinsic motivation.

Extrinsic motivation occurs when a person pursues a learning task, but for reasons which lie outside it. If a boy studies model airplanes because he thinks it will please his father, an ex-pilot, rather than because of a personal interest in model planes, he is moved by extrinsic motivation. When a learning goal is extrinsic, it is obvious that once the goal is met there ceases to be any point in remembering the learned material. If certain facts about a gasoline motor are learned only for the purpose of passing a test, as soon as the test is passed the reason for knowing the facts no longer exists. When motivation is wholly extrinsic, no matter how hard the study, we may expect that retention, understanding, and transfer will be much less than when material is learned for the sake of the learner.

After making the distinction between intrinsic and extrinsic motivation, it is necessary to point out that in most situations motivation cannot be categorized so neatly. It is a function of the total situation and hinges on some blend of personal concern for the work itself and some concern for extrinsic factors. As a practicable working principle, motivation is probably always a function of an interactive situation.

Obviously, both emphases on motivation *work*, in the sense that each leads to learning. However, since the material learned through extrinsic motivation does not in itself serve any purpose of the learner, educational psychologists consider this type of motivation less desirable because the learner tends to forget what he has learned as soon as his extrinsic purpose is met. Furthermore, in addition to poor retention of material learned, extrinsic motivation usually leads to careless, inaccurate learning. The learning task is hurried through as quickly as possible so that the reward may be obtained. If Johnny tries for a B in arithmetic because his father promises him a one-dollar reward, Johnny is not likely to care how he gets the B—copying someone else's answers is as good a way as any. Usage of extrinsic motivation appears to represent the operation of Thorndike's law of effect. However, it is incompatible not only with the tenets of cognitive-field psychology but also with what usually is recognized in the literature as the best of modern school practice.

In spite of the undesirability, on psychological grounds, of an emphasis on extrinsic motivation, in some situations many teachers feel they have no choice but to employ it. "In the hurly-burly of teaching you may not always be able to lay your hands on an appropriate intrinsic motive. Here it would be better to use some safe and suitable extrinsic motive than to do nothing."[1] Furthermore, it always is possible that a learning activity, such as reading, promoted by an extrinsic motive may later become energized as an intrinsic motive or interest in its own right.

[1]John M. Stephens, *The Psychology of Classroom Learning*, New York: Holt, Rinehart and Winston, 1965, p. 92.

The role of success

Although occasional failure, including in some cases even pun-ished failure, is not inimical to the progress of learning, fairly regular success is a must. As Pressey and his associates put it, "Learning feeds on success."[2] Unless motivation is extraordinar-ily high, a continuous succession of failures discourages stu-dents to the point where frustration blocks further effort.

However, too much can be made of the role of success. An uninterrupted series of successes may be as bad for the cause of learning as an uninterrupted series of failures. It is healthful for students to make a certain number of mistakes—provided they are mistakes that contribute to their learning.

Related to the question of success *vs.* failure as a contributor to motivation is the question of whether students, at all times, should be kept informed of their progress. The answer seems to be that a knowledge of progress usually spurs students on to additional effort. However, this is not the case when the goals are too easy and students find themselves on the verge of success with much extra time and energy left. Moreover, for success to be experienced as such, there must be a possibility of failure.[3]

A number of studies, in the Thorndike tradition, have been conducted in an attempt to determine whether it is more effec-tive to praise students for what they learn or blame them for what they do not learn. After reviewing these studies, Stephens decides that the evidence is so conflicting that no definite con-clusion can be drawn. The only conclusion that seems warranted is that either praise or blame is usually more effective in pro-moting learning than a policy of ignoring the achievement or lack of achievement of students.[4]

Demotivation caused by "pat" answers

We experience our strongest motivation in situations that are puzzling. If we completely solve the problem facing us, all sense of tension disappears; we cease to be interested because there is nothing to be interested in. Some misled teachers feel that each unit of work, or each class period, should end with a full

[2]Sidney L. Pressey, Francis P. Robinson, and John E. Horrocks, *Psychol-ogy in Education*, 3rd ed., New York: Harper & Row, 1959, p. 355.

[3]See Morris L. Bigge and Maurice P. Hunt, *Psychological Foundations of Education* 2nd ed., New York: Harper & Row, 1968, pp. 180–181, for a sum-mary of research that supports this statement.

[4]Stephens, *op. cit.*, p. 89.

resolution of whatever issue was under study. They sometimes feel that it is better for a teacher to tell students the "right answers" than to let them leave the class "unsatisfied." No policy could be more effectively calculated to destroy sustained motivation. A truly skilled teacher will see to it that each day students, to a safe degree, will leave the class with unanswered questions. Such a teacher knows that there is a direct relation between the ages of students and the length of time they should be expected to cope with a problem. Even after an entire semester's work in a subject, high school and college students should be left with some of its problems still to be further explored.

Tests as sources of motivation

Some teachers feel that in order to keep students working it is necessary to give them frequent tests, both announced and unannounced. But Stephens surveys a number of relevant studies and draws a different conclusion.[5] At the college level, the research evidence suggests that tests given once or twice a term produce just as much motivation as frequent tests. In high school the results differ, in that tests spaced about two weeks apart seem efficacious. *Daily tests, however, produce less motivation than no tests at all.* Furthermore, studies indicate that students learn less in courses in which they are given surprise tests than in courses in which test dates and coverage are announced ahead of time.

Of course, tests employed as motivating devices function primarily as extrinsic motivators. A student's primary goal in such a situation is not to learn the subject content for his own enlightenment but to pass the test. Generally speaking, the frequent and widespread use of tests for other than diagnostic purposes indicates a teacher's commitment to either a mechanistic or a disciplinary psychology.

Self-imposed goals vs. teacher-imposed goals

It is a well-known fact among psychologists that when a person develops goals which he sees as personal to himself, although they also involve others whom he cares about, he tends to set ambitious goals. The tendency actually is for most students to set goals that are difficult to the point of being unrealistic. For

[5]Stephens, *op. cit.*, pp. 85–86.

instance, students who have great difficulty with mathematics sometimes choose engineering as their career. Consequently, in most school subjects it is not feasible for students to operate as completely free agents in setting their goals in the course. Conversely, although an experienced teacher has a good idea of what an average student can and will achieve, it makes for better motivation to discuss the objectives of the course with students. Through such discussion, both the students and the teacher may come to feel more personal involvement in the course objectives.

HOW WE MAY MAKE LEARNING MORE EFFICIENT?

Improving the efficiency of learning means establishing situations in which maximum change of insight or behavior may occur in a given time. In the learning process, active participation of learners is highly advantageous over passive reception. Effective, active participation is promoted through observance of some rather specific principles.

Readiness and learning

A young person is ready to learn something when he has achieved sufficient physiological maturation and experiential background that he not only can but also wants to learn it. For example, it is physiologically impossible for a child of 3 months to learn to walk. Furthermore, for all except an occasional prodigy it appears impossible for a child of 2 to learn to read; not only is his neuromuscular system insufficiently developed, but he doesn't want to read. A youth of 12 normally is not ready to study subjects such as calculus, advanced economic theory, or Shakespeare. However, his lack of readiness probably is more attributable to absence of suitable experiential background than to inadequate development of physiological structures. But, until a person is fully matured physically, it is usually difficult to say to what extent incomplete development of physical structure is a hampering agent, particularly in the case of primarily "intellectual" learning tasks. There is mounting evidence that certain school subjects can be taught successfully much earlier than was once supposed—algebra is a case in point.

Much of the research on readiness has pertained to the teaching of reading and arithmetic. When is a youngster old enough to learn to read or to do long division? Although specific figures are frequently given (for example, a child often is said to be ready to read at the age of 6½ years), they can be highly misleading. There is great individual variation among children. Some are ready to read at the age of 3; others might as well wait until they are 8.

Serious problems may result from taking data on readiness literally, particularly when virtually all formal education in most countries is *mass* education. It is a matter of administrative convenience to require all children to begin school at about the same age. If Mary, who is ready to read at 3, has been taught by her parents to read, and is reading at, say, a fourth-grade level when she enters the first grade, she is bound to find the school's reading program insufferably dull. She may become a highly bored and frustrated child and consequently frustrate both teachers and parents. If Johnny is incapable of learning to read at 6½, when we normally begin reading in this country, he may face a year or two of failure and eventually develop a mind-set against reading, which will make it difficult for him to learn to read at any age.

Similar problems occur at all age levels. Some persons are never ready for certain learning tasks that are assigned regularly in school. For example, a person might be required to take a succession of physical education activity courses while in high school or college for which he may *never* be ready. A combination of poor coordination, poor vision, lack of previous experience, and negative mind-set could make it impossible for him to achieve, even at the minimum standards set by the instructors.

In considering readiness for learning, it is impossible to isolate those factors that are innate from those that are a product of learning. We can only assume that when a person is ready for a new learning, it is because he has developed his ability and interest to the point that he sees the new learning as the next step for him to make.

We do not even have conclusive data on the possible degree to which strong motivation may speed physiological maturation and readiness. An average youngster may achieve the necessary coordination to perform a particular physical task at the age of 12. But those who are especially interested in learning the task, and thus begin trying it at an earlier age, may significantly accelerate the development of the necessary coordination so that they are able to perform the task at the age of 10.

The role of practice

Although some learning is of an "Aha!" character—that is, the learner gets the point in a flash and does not forget it—other learning requires lengthy practice. If a teacher is to help students make the most efficient use of practice, he must remember several important principles concerning its use.

First, repetition per se—doing exactly the same thing over and over again—does not teach. Thorndike's original "law of exercise" suggested that animals, and human beings, learn an act merely by repeating it enough times. But in the 1930s Thorndike himself decided that such a notion had no experimental support and retracted his earlier statement. When we use the term *practice*, we refer to trials which have an experimental character; that is, trials in which the action is varied, even though slightly, and each time the learner asks himself either verbally or nonverbally, "What does it feel like?" "What did I do wrong?" or "How can I do it better?" Pressey, Robinson, and Horrocks cite a study in which the conclusion was drawn that ". . . repetition that occurs in acquiring skill is not repetition of one set of identical elements, but the gradual development of structural features. Instead of doing the same thing over and over, the learner progresses to more advanced stages of performance."[6]

Old-fashioned teachers who kept Johnny after school until he could write 100 times on the blackboard, "It is wrong for boys to spill ink on little girls' hair," undoubtedly taught Johnny something, but assuredly not that it is wrong to spill ink on little girls' hair.

Practice may be massed or distributed. *Massed* practice means long practice periods. *Distributed* practice means a succession of shorter practice periods with rest or other forms of activity spaced between.[7] Virtually all of the research evidence seems to show that spaced is more efficacious than massed practice. With massed practice, both fatigue and boredom reduce attention and tend to cause practice to deteriorate into mere repetition.

In many instances, spacing actually speeds up the learning process. It is fairly common for persons to reach a plateau—a dead end—in learning, and to reestablish progress only after a waiting period. A certain person learned to swim "wrong." He never mastered the popular crawl stroke. He began learning this stroke in his 40s but was handicapped by poor coordination—he inhaled when his face was under water and exhaled when

[6]Pressey, Robinson, and Horrocks, *op. cit.,* p. 349.

[7]Cronbach's chapter on practice does a good job of summarizing and restating some of the more significant research concerning practice. See Lee J. Cronbach, *Educational Psychology,* 2nd ed., New York: Harcourt Brace Jovanovich, 1963, Chapter 9. Spacing is treated on pp. 295–296.

it was out. After a summer of near drownings and a winter's rest, the following June he again attempted the crawl stroke. Surprisingly, in the first trial he did much better. Although gains were slow that summer, the following year, after another winter's rest, he did better still.

One qualification needs to be made in connection with distributed practice as well as distributed study of any sort. Too much has been written about attention span. Some writers state with great specificity, in terms of number of minutes, the attention span of a person of a given age. Attention span refers to the length of time that a person can pursue a learning task without having his attention falter seriously. It obviously is a function of the level of motivation, and it is misleading to say, as some psychologists have, that the attention span of children increases with age. *It increases with motivation.*

We have seen small children work as persistently and diligently at a task as any adult would be likely to do. The difference between childhood and adulthood appears to be that adults are better able to subordinate short-run pleasures in the interest of longer-range ones; adults find it easier to "live for the future." Hence, they can more easily develop long-range motivation for a short-range learning task which requires massed practice over an extended period of time.

Provided sufficient motivation is present, physical fatigue does not interfere seriously with learning. However, this statement is true only within limits; exhaustion can become so intense that even the highest level of motivation flags. Conversely, in the absence of motivation, a rather simple learning task can produce marked feelings of boredom.

Part vs. whole learning

The issue of part *vs.* whole learning dates back to the 1920s, when connectionism was first being challenged by the Gestalt outlook. The standard connectionist approach had been "piecemeal" learning: one begins with individual elements and learns them one by one, eventually assembling them into a whole. It would be wrong to suggest that the connectionists originated an atomistic approach to teaching; such an approach dates back much farther than Thorndike. However, associationist thinking in psychology did provide a "scientific" rationale for the atomistic approach by giving it theoretical support.

The Gestaltist insisted that we learn best when we begin with the largest unit we can comprehend. In studying a poem, for example, instead of beginning with a word-by-word or line-by-line analysis, students should read the entire poem rather quickly and try to grasp its overall meaning. Once this is done, a Gestaltist would have no objection to an analytical approach; when a person has gained some "feel" for the entire poem, analysis plays a different role: each part is studied with respect to how it fits into the total picture or configuration.

The part *vs.* whole issue has plagued teachers of reading for almost half a century. Should a child learn to read by learning first the alphabet, then how to pronounce syllables, then words, then finally sentences, paragraphs, and themes? Or should he begin with simple themes and strive as rapidly as possible to envision word groups and later entire sentences or paragraphs as units? Under the latter approach (sight reading) students get a feel for pattern and, so the argument runs, learn to read more rapidly and fluently.

As Pressey points out, the experimental evidence to date does not favor conclusively either one view or the other.[8] Most educational psychologists today, even those with an associationist orientation, argue in favor of the "whole" method for all types of material susceptible to such an approach. Yet, as Pressey indicates, the relative superiority of one method over the other may hinge largely on ". . . the learner's motivation, his patience, and the extent to which he perceives the learning situation as being important and fulfilling a need."[9] Pressey also suggests that intellectual capacity is a significant factor, in that persons with higher-than-average IQs tend to learn better by wholes. The amount and quality of prior practice also enters the picture; practice in either approach seems to increase one's efficiency in utilizing that approach. Finally, some learning materials lend themselves better to part learning, some to whole learning.

People who begin a learning task by the "part method" tend at some point in its achivement to advance to the "whole method." When this transition is made, progress is likely to accelerate rapidly. A good example of this learning process is the mastery of typing. The traditional way of teaching typing was first to teach students the location of the letters on the keyboard and how to stroke each letter at will. The next step was to teach them to type syllables. Next came words, then phrases, then sentences. This was the "part method" with a vengeance. Students can learn to type this way. However, they usually hit a

---

[8]Pressey, Robinson, and Horrocks, *op. cit.*, pp. 353–355.
[9]*Ibid.*, p. 354.

plateau, a period of no progress in spite of diligent practice. Rather suddenly—often it comes with a rush in a matter of a few days—a student finds that he is no longer "spelling out" words on the typewriter. In fact, he is typing entire phrases or sentences without attention to individual letters or words. He has moved to "pattern typing." He has suddenly gained a feel for a stroking pattern appropriate to phrases, sentences, or groups of sentences. Now typing speed and accuracy tend to soar.

When a typist can no longer recall where individual letters are on the keyboard he has moved to a fundamentally different approach and apparently the only one whereby a high level of skill can be achieved.

HOW MAY WE IMPROVE RETENTION?

Most of the studies of retention have been made by connectionists and have been based on a learner's ability to reproduce at some later date a response which he could once make. Studies of recall have included both sensorimotor and verbal responses. Pressey has summed up a number of studies of the recall of verbal responses—the so-called "fact learning"—which is so commonly emphasized in schools. He concludes that "At the end of a course, students remember about three-fourths of the facts covered. One year following the conclusion of a course, students remember about one-half the facts covered. Two years following the conclusion of a course, students remember about one-fourth the facts covered."[10] These studies do not take us beyond two years after the learning occurred. There is every reason to suppose that the process of forgetting continues until, for most types of "fact courses," virtually all is lost. There is no research as yet that furnishes a basis for contradicting the opinion that many school courses might as well not be taken at all if their value is to be judged from any long-range results that we can measure. On the hopeful side, we know with little question that learning can be quite permanent; formal education is not necessarily doomed forever to be largely wasted.

Meaning and retention

Material that is meaningful to students is remembered much better than material that is not. Meaningfulness consists of *relations* between facts—generalizations, rules, principles—for which

[10]*Ibid.*, pp. 262–263.

students see some use. Solitary facts essentially are on the same level of meaninglessness as nonsense syllables, and approximately the same forgetting curves apply to both.

Making learning meaningful is a matter of selecting the right content—knowledge reducible to principles—and helping students see its applicability in situations which they are concerned about. However, as McDonald points out, the mere learning of *any kind* of organizing principle, in itself, contributes to retention of learned materials.[11]

The positive results of meaningful learning are quite apparent. Cronbach cites a study in which tests requiring the application of major generalizations to new problems were administered at the beginning of a course in zoology, at the end, and a year later. The respective scores were 35, 65, and 65. There was *no loss* of material learned. In another study, where zoology students were asked to draw conclusions, infer principles, from experiments not previously studied, the respective scores were 30, 57, and 64. Students did even better after an interval of a year![12]

Stephens sums up the situation very nicely when he says, "If the material is sufficiently meaningful, there may be no forgetting whatever. An important governing principle, like the old idea of the conservation of energy, may so help us organize the rest of our ideas that it stays with us for life. Content that is not so brilliantly structured, but which still has much meaning, will be remembered in proportion to its meaning. Nonsense material is headed for extinction before the last syllable is uttered."[13]

Possibly the whole point is that material that can be learned insightfully, particularly on the level of generalized insight, becomes a permanent part of one's personality structure. If teachers understood well enough the basic psychological principles involved all school learning *could* be of this nature.

Purpose in remembering and forgetting

Any rounded study of retention would need to include study of the extent to which our wishes govern memory. It is pleasant to be able to forget some things. We do not automatically remember effects of new experience according to the length or spacing of practice sessions or other mechanical formulas.

[11]Frederick J. MacDonald, *Educational Psychology*, 2nd ed., Belmont, Calif.: Wadsworth, 1965, pp. 231–233.

[12]Cronbach, *op. cit.*, p. 352.

[13]Stephens, *op. cit.*, p. 210.

Rather, we do a reasonably good job of remembering what we really want to remember and forgetting what we prefer to forget.

One professor we know makes no attempt to remember his automobile license number. "I have no reason to," he says, "because I have the number on a tag attached to my key chain. It is easier to refer to the tag than to try to keep the number in mind."

Some experiences are so painful that our mental health benefits by our either forgetting them or reconstructing them in memory so that what we recall in regard to them does not resemble closely what actually happened. On the other hand, some experiences are so pleasurable that we not only remember them in detail but even embellish them in our memory. The fish that we caught on our Canadian trip of 1951 become larger and more numerous every year.

With respect to learning in school, where controversial content is concerned, we tend to forget that with which we do not agree and to remember that with which we do. A frequently cited study was conducted by J. M. Levine and Gardner Murphy, in the early 1940s. Students were grouped according to whether they were procommunist or anticommunist in attitude. Both groups of students were given pro- and anticommunist reading references. In a later memory check, the anticommunist students remembered the anticommunist arguments much better than they did the procommunist ones, and vice versa.[14]

Purposive forgetting and remembering are examples of psychological homeostasis. Through these processes we preserve our self-organization in a reasonably adequate state. Thus, we employ forgetting and remembering to heal psychological wounds, to shore up self-respect, and to make better sense generally of our psychological world.

The final point of the foregoing sentence perhaps deserves a little elaboration. In Chapter 3 we discuss the Gestalt "law of Prägnanz" and related laws—all having to do with perception. It will be recalled that, according to these principles, when a person perceives fragmentary, incomplete, or asymmetrical objects he tends to see them as more complete, perfect, and balanced than they actually are. Probably every time we recall an experience we have a somewhat different perception, in the sense that we reinterpret what we recall in the interest of making a more pleasant pattern of it. Virtually all texts in educational psychology cite experimental evidence to support this view. One

[14]See McDonald, *op. cit.*, pp. 239–240.

of the better treatments is contained in the text by Frederick J. McDonald.[15] Perhaps the principal lesson to be had from these research results is that forgetting is an active and not a passive process, just as is any learning that has promise of retention.

The role of overlearning

A person can learn something well enough to make a perfect score on a test given immediately after the learning; he can then continue practice on the same material for an indefinite time, or at least until boredom poses an insurmountable barrier. It has been found that such overlearning does contribute to retention. Hence most books in educational psychology list overlearning as a means of improving retention. It should be noted, however, that when the material to be learned is sufficiently meaningful, over-learning is unnecessary. Overlearning is a counterpart to attempts to teach relatively meaningless subject matter.

Nevertheless, when a person is faced with a learning task such as acquiring the vocabulary of a foreign language, overlearning may be the sensible course to pursue. Overlearning is measured in terms of the percentage of additional pratice spent after initial mastery. According to one study, reported by McDonald[16] 50 percent of overlearning produced a gain in retention after an elapsed time of 28 days of approximately 50 percent; 100 percent of overlearning contributed only slightly more gain than this, possibly because boredom interfered with its effectiveness. Other studies do not produce the same percentages, but all seem to agree that overlearning contributes to retention.

Spaced review vs. cramming

Apparently retention is higher when study periods are spaced methodically over the course of an entire semester than when a student waits until a day or two before the final examination and then tries to assimilate the subject matter of a course all at once. However, results on a nonreflective type of final examination may be equally good with either study procedure; some students learn to cram quite effectively. Nevertheless, long-range results from cramming are likely to be meager.

The issue of spaced review *vs.* cramming is: In what temporal relationship to the initial learning should review occur; should

[15]See McDonald, *op. cit.*, pp. 228–231, 240.
[16]See McDonald, *op. cit.*, pp. 234–235.

Figure 10.1
A typical forgetting curve.

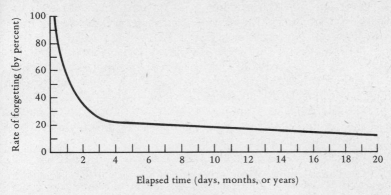

it be distributed or massed? The answer seems to be suggested by the nature of a typical forgetting curve, as shown in Figure 10.1. Since the rate of forgetting is much more rapid relatively soon after the initial learning, we may hypothesize that review periods should follow immediately after the initial learning and not be delayed. McDonald cites experimental evidence to suggest that spaced but frequent reviews immediately following initial learning, followed by widely spaced "brush-ups" during the period of desired retention, represent the most effective approach.[17]

Readers should remember that when we say "review" we are not referring to repetition; rather, we mean practice with an experimental cast, as described earlier. If the reviewer seeks to go beyond the initial learning by tying it in with new learning or interpreting it on a more sophisticated level, review is even more effective. Readers also should remember that the forgetting curve reproduced in Figure 10.1 and the present discussion of the role of practice in improving attention apply primarily to either complicated sensorimotor learning or verbal learning that is relatively low in meaningfulness and intrinsic motivation. Learning of the most desirable kind produces a rather flat forgetting curve and does not need to be practiced in order to be remembered.

Effects of intervening events

A great deal of writing is available on the general subject of how newly learned items of knowledge interfere with the recall

[17]McDonald, *op. cit.*, pp. 235–236.

294 Learning Theories for Teachers

of previous learnings and, conversely, how items previously learned interfere with the recall of those most recently learned. When a second set of learnings intrudes upon a first set, and prevents or distorts the recall of the first set, we say that *retroactive inhibition* has occurred. When a first set of learnings intrudes upon a second set, and prevents or distorts the recall of the second set, we say that *proactive inhibition* has occurred. Since there is a strong tendency for any two sets of related learnings to influence each other negatively as well as positively, some writers prefer not to make the above distinction, but rather to use the term *interactive inhibition* to describe any negative transfer effect of intervening events.[18]

Students who read the present book frequently report that, by the time they have completed the first three chapters, so many different points of view about key issues in psychology have been presented that they "can't remember any of it." They then go on to say that they could remember well enough through the first three or four positions, but after that, with the addition of still others, they "can't remember the first ones." This would seem to be a clear example of interactive inhibition. (Fortunately, several years of experience using the first edition of this book has demonstrated that most students can learn, by the end of a semester, to recall all of the major positions treated and to distinguish them sharply from one another. This suggests that sometimes a suitable antidote for interactive inhibition is simply more study.)

BIBLIOGRAPHY

COLADARCI, ARTHUR P., *Educational Psychology: A Book of Readings*, New York: Holt, Rinehart and Winston, 1955.
Carefully selected readings, many of them pertinent to the subject of learning. Reading 1 may help students tie together much of the present book. Also recommended are 2–4 and 23–33.
CRONBACH, LEE J., *Educational Psychology*, 2nd ed., New York: Harcourt Brace Jovanovich, 1963.
A popular general text in educational psychology. Eclectic in orientation. Treats most of the topics covered in the foregoing chapter.
FRANDSEN, ARDEN N., *Educational Psychology*, 2nd ed., New York: McGraw-Hill, 1967.
Chapter 3 on readiness and Chapters 11 and 12 on transfer, remembering, and forgetting are particularly germane to this chapter.
FULLAGAR, WILLIAM A., *et al.*, *Readings for Educational Psychology*, New York: Thomas Y. Crowell, 1964.

---

[18]See, for example, Arden N. Frandsen, *Educational Psychology*, 2nd ed., New York: McGraw-Hill, 1967, pp. 449–451, 487–490.

One of the best compilations of readings. Part I is "must" reading for all students of the present text.

HENRY, NELSON B., ed., *The Psychology of Learning*, Part II, *The Forty-first Yearbook of the National Society for the Study of Education*, Public School Publishing Co., 1942.

Explanations of the major schools of thought, by their respective exponents. In Chapter VII, T. R. McConnell attempts a reconciliation of competing theories. Section II (pp. 289 ff.) is steadily relevant to the foregoing chapter.

KRECH, DAVID, RICHARD S. CRUTCHFIELD, and NORMAN LIVSON, *Elements of Psychology*, 2nd ed., New York: Knopf, 1969.

A massive volume with several sections bearing on the previous chapter. See especially Part III, "Adaptive Behavior."

LEE, J. MURRAY, and DORIS MAY LEE, *The Child and His Development*, New York: Appleton-Century-Crofts, 1958.

Part III pertains to the foregoing chapter. See annotation at end of Chapter 6.

McDONALD, FREDERICK J., *Educational Psychology*, 2nd ed., Belmont, Cal.: Wadsworth, 1965.

A first-rate general text in psychological foundations. To supplement the foregoing chapter, concentrate on Part II.

MORSE, WILLIAM C., and G. MAX WINGO, *Psychology and Teaching*, 3rd ed., Glenview, Ill.: Scott, Foresman, 1969.

A basic text that emphasizes the role of experience in learning.

PRESSEY, SIDNEY L., *et al.*, *Psychology in Education*, 3rd ed., New York: Harper & Row, 1959.

A general text in educational psychology which has become something of a classic. Eclectic in view, highly readable and useful at the classroom level. Rather steadily relevant to material in the foregoing chapter. See especially Part II.

REMMERS, H. H., *et al.*, *Growth, Teaching and Learning, a Book of Readings*, New York: Harper & Row, 1957.

In Part I several readings which are relevant to the foregoing chapter. See especially those by Kramer, Trow, Tiedman, Ryans, Woodruff, Tuttle, and Blair.

STEPHENS, JOHN M., *The Psychology of Classroom Learning*, New York: Holt, Rinehart and Winston, 1965.

A first-rate text written within a connectionist framework. Part Two may help students understand better the various positions treated in the present text.

TILTON, J. W., *An Educational Psychology of Learning*, New York: Macmillan, 1951.

One of the most sophisticated books yet written in the area. Tilton leans toward field theory but makes a serious attempt to integrate opposing positions with it. An original book, worth anyone's study. Entire book is relevant to the preceding chapters.

WHEELER, RAYMOND, and FRANCIS T. PERKINS, *Principles of Mental Development; A Textbook in Educational Psychology*, New York: Thomas Y. Crowell, 1934.

A book intended to refute atomism and mechanistic preconceptions based upon absolutistic methods of thinking. It derives from Gestalt thinking in psychology and organismic thinking in biology. If nothing else, students should read the preface.

WOLMAN, BENJAMIN B., *Contemporary Theories and Systems in Psychology*, New York: Harper & Row, 1960.

An exceptionally good comparative psychology which treats all the major scientific systems. The author makes a case for eclecticism. This type of book may be used as a capstone for all the preceding chapters of the present volume. Not for beginning students.

ELEVEN

How Is Learning Related To Teaching?

In earlier chapters of the book we consider various learning theories that teachers might adopt. We now are ready to examine how the respective theories are related to teaching principles and procedures. But first, a necessary preface to inquiry into the relationship of learning theory to teaching practice is an examination of the unique role of teachers in our culture.

WHAT IS THE ROLE OF TEACHERS IN MODERN AMERICA?

When we consider the role of teachers in modern America we should study both of its aspects, namely, teachers' relationship to the culture and their relationship to their students. A *culture* is the established way of life or social heritage of a people. It is constituted of all those *socially transmitted* results of human experience through which a group of people carries on its way of life. It includes language, customs, morals, tools, institutions, knowledge, ideals, and standards.

What are the possible relationships of teachers to the culture?

Most persons would probably agree that one of the principal functions of teaching is to preserve, by transmitting to the young, that part of the culture that is regarded by most people as good. However, performance of this task alone makes education a highly conservative force. Teaching that does no more than merely conserve a culture is appropriate to a static, but not to a dynamic, rapidly changing culture such as ours. Hence teaching, in a fast-moving culture, must operate in relationship to change in such a way as to keep cultural innovations socially beneficial. Although there is general support for this twofold function of teaching, that is, cultural conservation and cultural improvement, it is difficult to get agreement on just how the two tasks are to be performed simultaneously.

A teacher may hold any one of three basically different attitudes in regard to his proper function in preserving and improving the culture. He may envision himself as (1) a cultural architect, (2) a conservator of the culture, or (3) a democratic leader in developing insights pertinent to amending the culture (to amend a culture is to modify it in some way for the better). Let us explore each of these attitudes briefly.

A teacher as a cultural architect.   A teacher who adopts this view sees himself as a radical innovator. In his thinking he designs the specifications of an ideal culture. He then teaches the attitudes, values, and knowledge that will cause new generations to move in the direction of his ideal. He is likely to promote ideas toward which resistance will develop, and he is not reluctant to indoctrinate and propagandize in order to achieve his purpose. Since a teacher who sees himself as a cultural architect is discontented with affairs as they are and wants to introduce a new cultural design, his point of view has been called "social reconstructionism."

A teacher as a conservator of the culture.   A teacher who accepts this role sees himself as a preserver of traditional attitudes, values, beliefs, and knowledge. To the best of his ability he analyzes the present culture and attempts to transmit this, intact, to new generations. He recognizes that accidents of history will induce cultural changes, and that if these changes contribute to the welfare of people they will be perpetuated. However, he never sees himself as an active agent of cultural change. Teachers who operate within this framework are called "conservatives." Since unorthodoxy bothers conservatives, they are likely to try to suppress any unconventional thinking on the part of students. In a manner very much like that of a social reconstructionist, who also has specific objectives in mind, a conservative teacher often indoctrinates his students and propagandizes his objectives into their thinking and behavior.

But, regardless of the degree to which teachers may be dedicated to conservation of their culture, their task is becoming impossible to perform. With the loss of the old sense of community and the accompanying decay of the cohesive and relatively consistent value pattern that accompanied it, there is no longer a harmonious structure of attitudes, values, and beliefs for teachers to promote. Confronted with a culture filled with confusion and contradictions, which elements is a conservative teacher to select and teach? Is it not reasonable that teaching today should help students examine as objectively as possible their disjointed culture in the hope that as they live their lives they will be able to work some integration into it? But this is a job for neither an impetuous seeker of change nor a conservative who is frightened of change.

A teacher as a democratic leader in developing insights pertinent to amending the culture. In contrast with both positions of the adherents to the two extreme, that is, reconstructionist and conservative positions, a teacher may visualize himself as functioning much as a head scientist in a laboratory. When the subject matter under investigation is the culture, the primary purpose of investigation is neither to change nor to preserve it, but to appraise it and strengthen its tenability. Accordingly, an attempt is made to uncover contradictions and conflicts in a culture and to determine possible ways of resolving them, or at least preventing them from causing serious trouble. The ultimate hope of a democratic teacher is that the culture will be progressively refined by a citizenry that has learned the habit of studying problems in a reflective and democratic manner. This kind of teacher fosters social change, but strives to keep it orderly and constructive. A teacher, as a democratic leader, does not discard his personal preferences. Like either a social reconstructionist or a conservator of culture, he too holds certain ideas in preference to others. However, his method of teaching, unlike that of either a social reconstructionist or a conservator of culture, is the method of democracy. In a very real sense, he and his students, together, are gaining more adequate insights for building their culture.

A teacher who functions as a democratic leader believes that, since man is a cultural being there need not be assumed any ceiling or limit to the possibilities of human nature. When human nature is assumed neither to be tied to a natural unfoldment process nor to be static or inert, it encompasses all the institutional achievements of dynamic society. With sufficient application of human intelligence, a society can continue growth in the direction of more adequate and harmonious living for all individuals involved. If teachers are to aid substantially in cultural progress, they must encourage students to study the culture of their own and other societies, but always with a view toward progressive refinement of those cultures.

What are the possible relationships of teachers to their students?

We may visualize three broad types of relationships between a teacher and his students: (1) authoritarian, (2) laissez-faire, and (3) democratic. Each form of relationship produces a distinctive type of situation within a classroom, characterized by more or less predictable results and carrying with it definite implications concerning the teacher's commitment to how he thinks students learn. Furthermore, a particular type of relation of a teacher to his students presupposes the teacher's correlative relationship to the culture. Whereas an authoritarian teacher considers himself either a cultural architect or conservator, a democratic one sees his cultural role as that of a leader in developing insights for the culture's amendment. A laissez-faire teacher views the culture as a necessary evil, outside nature, which should be ignored or neutralized as far as possible.

An authoritarian teacher. An authoritarian teacher exercises firm, centralized control. He closely directs the actions of his students. He does all the planning for the class and issues all the directions. Furthermore, he tells students what to think as well as what to do. In an authoritarian classroom, a teacher regards himself as the sole active agent and considers students passive receivers of instructions and information.

In the experiments with group climates conducted by Lippitt and White, it was found that boys in authoritarian groups tended to be apathetic and dependent and to demonstrate little capacity for initiating group action. When the leader left the room, they accomplished very little. Although they did not seem to resent authoritarian leadership strongly, they occasionally showed evidences of hostility, as expressed in aggressive acts toward fellow group members.[1]

A laissez-faire teacher. A laissez-faire teacher goes to the opposite extreme. He does not really lead at all. He is present, he

[1]See Ralph K. White and Ronald Lippitt, *Autocracy and Democracy: An Experimental Inquiry*, New York: Harper & Row, 1960, pp. 51–55, 66–80.

may answer questions, but essentially he lets students follow their own initiative. Students decide what they want to do and how they will do it.

In the Lippitt-White experiments, boys in the laissez-faire group got along together much better than those in the authoritarian group; they showed less tendency to direct resentments at fellow students. They did get some work done. However, they acted insecure; for example, they repeatedly asked for help and, after the experiment was completed, expressed dissatisfaction with its leadership.[2]

A democratic teacher. In a democratic teaching-learning situation the teacher fulfills the role of a democratic group leader. His chief purpose is to lead his students in the study of significant problems in the area in which he is teaching. Such study presupposes interchange of evidence and insights, give-and-take, and respect for one another's ideas. In a democratic classroom the teacher's ideas are subject to both student and teacher criticism just as are those of students. In this way both the students and the teacher learn together. Although the teacher may be an authority on his subject (and to teach it best he should be), the situation is arranged so that students are encouraged to think for themselves. Accordingly, a democratic teacher is most likely to hold an outlook on learning that emphasizes purposiveness in human experience and behavior.

In the Lippitt-White experiments, democratic groups evidenced a more friendly and confiding atmosphere than did authoritarian groups. Members seemed as able to extend mutual recognition to each other as did members of the laissez-faire groups. However, they worked on a higher level of efficiency and were much less dependent on the leader than were the laissez-faire groups. Furthermore, they showed more initiative and worked much more effectively in the absence of a leader than did the authoritarian groups.[3]

The traditional relationship between teacher and student has been authoritarian. Until the twentieth century, teachers tended to be despots—often benevolent, but despots nevertheless. During this century, despotism in the classroom has begun to disappear, but when this has happened, laissez-faire frequently has taken its place. Or, perhaps more often, teachers have come to alternate between a friendly despotism and situations close to

[2]*Ibid.*, pp. 55–58, 61–64.
[3]*Ibid.*, pp. 58–65.

laissez-faire. There are some good reasons why consistently democratic relations could well be substituted for both autocratic and laissez-faire modes of operation. It ill behooves a nation that is straining in democratic directions to maintain in its schoolrooms nondemocratic relationships between teachers and students. Furthermore, evidence now available indicates that students probably learn more effectively in a democratic than in either an authoritarian or a highly permissive classroom. Democratic learning situations seem to produce more retention and more transfer. Thus, even if there were no other reason for democratic relations between teacher and students, the general adoption of such relations would at least permit taxpayers who support education to receive more for their money.

In recent years and in many places, the idea of democratic schools and classrooms has fallen into ill repute. There are two basic, but unfortunate, reasons for this. (1) *Laissez-faire situations often have been mistaken by the wooly-minded for democratic situations.* Truly democratic teachers, however, hold no brief whatsoever for laissez-faire classrooms, and feel that it is tragic for an educator to call an uncontrolled and undirected classroom "democratic." (2) *The meanings of the terms democracy and democratic have become perverted.* As applied to teaching, they often have come to mean "easy," "soft," or "undisciplined." Yet, in fact, making allowances for the maturity and capabilities of students, a democratic group may work at the maximum level that health permits, and its manner of operation may be fully as rigorous as that of any scientific investigation.

There is a close connection between the respective types of relationships of teachers to students and the relative amount of usage of each of four different levels of learning and teaching. These *levels* are the subject of the remaining part of the chapter.

WHAT ARE THE LEVELS OF LEARNING AND TEACHING?

Teaching-learning situations may be classified according to where they fall on a continuum which ranges from "thoughtless" to "thoughtful" modes of operation. However, it is convenient to divide their total range into four broad classifications: memory-level, understanding-level, autonomous development-level, and reflection-level. Memory-level is most "thoughtless," reflection-level most "thoughtful," and understanding-level is between the two. But the autonomous development-level is difficult to classify on the basis of the thoughtfulness that it entails. Since, on this level, each student's feelings constitute the final authority for his truth, teaching consists merely of promoting each student's heightened intuitive awareness of himself and the artistic expression of his self-actualization.

So, within the autonomous development of psychedelic humanism, the teacher's function in education is more negative than positive in the sense that there is little or no leadership, direction, coercion, prescription, or imposition of student thoughts or behaviors. Intellectual development is something that "just naturally happens." Hence, there is no need for any kind of formal teaching. Instead, student-planned, permissive types of projects are promoted for the purpose of releasing latent talents. Students, as much as possible, are permitted, even encouraged, to live close to nature so that they may indulge freely their natural impulses and feelings. Inasmuch as creativity is an inherent characteristic of children and youth, it should be left to unfold in the highly permissive atmosphere of a child-centered school. Either Nature or the Creator has *enfolded* certain ideas, talents, and purposes into each child, and these should be permitted to *unfold* as he proceeds in school. Accordingly, each student should be permitted to choose his successive activities throughout the school day. (See Table 12.1, pp. 342–343, for a summary of the four levels of teaching and learning.)

Products of both the understanding- and the reflection-level are understandings or insights, but those of the reflection-level are understandings or insights *plus* increased ability of the learner to achieve further understandings or insights through thinking. Because of the nature of the process and products of reflection-level teaching and learning, this level harmonizes best with a teacher's or school's commitment to democratic teacher–student relationships.

WHAT IS MEMORY-LEVEL
LEARNING AND TEACHING?

Memory-level learning is that kind of learning which supposedly embraces committing factual materials to memory and nothing else. We all know how this can be done; it is possible for a person to memorize virtually any type of material, including that which seems quite nonsensical. The more meaningful the material to be learned, the easier it is to memorize. Furthermore, the more meaningful the learned material, the longer it tends to be retained. A collection of "nonsense" syllables might conceivably be remembered for a lifetime if a person had sufficient reason for retaining it. However, when one develops a reason for retaining something, it is no longer nonsensical.

At first glance, rote-memory learning seems to exemplify either a mental discipline or an S-R conditioning theory of learning; either a substantive mind is trained or simple relations are formed between stimuli and responses with no particular thought or purpose involved. But a cognitive-field psychologist denies that either is the case. Instead he insists that, if anything is learned at all, insight of a sort is always present. What characterizes rote learning, to a cognitive-field theorist, is that the insights acquired usually have no significant relationship to the material being studied. However, the learned material is *patterned* by the learner during the process of his learning it. Even "nonsense syllables," when learned, are not completely unpatterned.[4]

Capacity to memorize and retain material probably bears no positive relationship to capacity for intelligent behavior. Geniuses are notoriously forgetful, although not usually in their areas of major interest. Conversely, a mentally defective person may be highly proficient in memorization. Polly was a 13-year-old girl with the mental capacity of an imbecile. She had a quite brilliant memory of the "shotgun" variety. That is, she memorized indiscriminately anything she heard, and often could repeat verbatim an overheard conversation or a radio newscast. After hearing it once, she could recite faultlessly the words of every popular song being broadcast at the time. Nevertheless, Polly's "thought power" was so impaired that, if asked to close an outside door of the house, she could not decide on which side of the door to stand to avoid shutting herself out.

Every experienced teacher can recall numerous students who developed a considerable capacity to memorize standard curricular materials in most or all school subjects. Such students usually make high marks. However, when placed in situations requiring reflection, they may be at a loss. If, occasionally, they take a course with a teacher who employs problem-centered teaching, they may become extremely frustrated and do very poor work. Conversely, an experienced teacher also can recall students whose marks were spotty but who achieved magnificently once they got out of school. There is a fairly good chance that in such cases poor achievement in school is a result of rebellion against required rote memorization.

Memory-level teaching may, of course, contribute indirectly to

4See George Katona, *Organizing and Memorizing*, New York: Columbia University Press, 1940.

intelligent behavior. If memorized facts become pertinent on an occasion when a problem requires solution, they contribute to usable background and hence to the effectiveness of problem solving. However, memorized facts usually contribute little to effective student growth. One reason is that, as already suggested, they tend to be forgotten quickly. Another is that a large proportion of the facts memorized in school are irrelevant to future thought needs. In summarizing the value of rote-memory teaching we might even say that the best way to make sure that a student will *not* remember many facts is to place the whole emphasis upon teaching him facts.

It no longer is a matter for speculation that not much in the way of durable or useful results can be expected from memory-level instruction. Its contribution to intelligent behavior is too unpredictable and undependable for us to set much store by it as a favored instructional procedure. Yet there is no reason to suppose that most teachers are dedicated to some other approach. No matter how much talk is raised against straight memory-level instruction, there are numerous pressures placed on teachers to confine teaching to this level. Furthermore, many teachers may have little vision of anything different.

Despite all the legitimate criticisms we may make of rote memorization, it would be unrealistic to suppose that a teacher can always avoid it. In any ordinary school situation, on occasions even the most imaginative teacher will have no better approach than memory-level teaching. This may occur on days when lack of time has prevented planning anything else. Or it may happen when the teacher does not know how else to handle the material to be covered.

One might ask, Can the fundamental skills, such as spelling, be taught otherwise than through a process of straight memorization, using drill procedures? Generally speaking, they *can* be taught more efficiently through other procedures. However, much more study will be required to develop procedures for teaching all the fundamental skill subjects in ways that will free us entirely from rote memorization.

WHAT IS UNDERSTANDING-LEVEL LEARNING AND TEACHING?

The term *understanding* has been used so ambiguously by psychologists and educators that teachers are likely to use it rather glibly, without being able to define it clearly. For example a teacher may ask his students, "Are you sure you understand this?" and himself not know the meaning of his question. One may be fairly sure his students do not know either.

The *American College Dictionary* includes the following definitions of the verb *understand:* "1. to perceive the meaning of; grasp the idea of; comprehend. 2. to be thoroughly familiar with; apprehend clearly the character or nature of. 3. to comprehend by knowing the meaning of the words employed, as a language. 4. to grasp clearly as a fact, or realize."[5]

A serious student of educational psychology will be dissatisfied with definitions of this kind. Although helpful to a degree, they are not sufficiently operational. That is, they do not show what a person does, i.e., what psychological action he takes, when he comes to understand something. In the sections to follow, we present two key definitions of understanding, then show how they may be combined into one.

Understanding as seeing relationships

This definition of understanding is implied in the first category of dictionary definitions. One meaning for *comprehend* is "to take in or embrace"; the Latin root is *comprehendere,* meaning "to seize." In other words, we have here the idea of reaching out and gathering in individual items. As they are pulled together, they are understood. However, the definition implies still more; it involves inclusion or embracement of a group of particulars under a single overarching idea. If this definition seems too abstruse, perhaps the following illustration will help.

John M. is a beginning teacher. He has had little experience working with children and none with a group as diverse as his sixth-grade class. He notices that some of his students steal and others seem scrupulously honest. Some come to school dirty and unkempt, others are always well washed and well groomed. Some speak ungrammatically, others consistently use "school-teachers' English." Some use "dirty language," while others seem to use only language which would be approved in a Sunday school class.

For a long time, these differences in students puzzle John. But as a result of back-to-school nights, occasional contacts in the community with parents, and information received from other teachers, he finds that the habits of his students are very much like those of their parents, or, if not that, like the prevailing pattern of behavior within the socioeconomic group

[5]The American College Dictionary, New York: Random House Inc., 1964, p. 1321.

to which the parents belong. John gradually begins to form some generalizations—understandings—to explain the individual Marys and Jimmys in the class; he restructures his life space.

One of these generalizations is that "Much in the behavior of children can be explained by the nature of the social class in which they live." A number of corollary generalizations, of which the following three are illustrative, also are helpful: "Almost without exception, 'lower-class' children use 'rough' language." " 'Middle-class' children do not reveal as great an overt interest in sex as do 'lower-class' children." "On the average, 'middle-class' children get better marks than 'lower-class' children."

Note how John M. has changed the way in which he perceives his students. He has come to group or classify them in a more meaningful manner. He understands little Mary better because she is a member of a general classification: lower-middle class, Suburbia, U.S.A. There are other little Marys who exhibit the same habits and who can be placed in the same classification. Because of certain traits they have in common, John M. has grouped these students into a "class"; he has "pulled them together." As is illustrated in the foregoing paragraph, he sees each individual child in relation to appropriate generalizations or understandings.

Seeing solitary facts in relation to a general principle is the essence of understanding implied by our first definition of the term. Although we are about to suggest that there is significantly more to understanding, teaching probably would be more effective than it now is if all teachers grasped even this limited definition. Too few teachers realize that any item of factual knowledge is quite meaningless unless students see how it is embraced by a general principle. A fact must be seen as either supporting or casting doubt upon some principle or it means practically nothing. Yet entire textbooks have been written which contain little more than "descriptive facts." Teachers often labor away a professional lifetime without trying to teach students the generalizations that would be necessary for them to "pull together" the facts they are required to memorize.

One reason why Herbart, in retrospect, appears such a significant figure for his time is that his instructional steps, although described mechanistically, were designed to teach students how to move from individual facts to generalizations—principles—and to use these generalizations to interpret new facts. Herbart's insight concerning the crucial role of generalizations placed him far ahead of even many contemporary educators.

S-R conditioning psychology of learning, in actual practice, represents a combination of memory and understanding—as seeing relationships—levels of learning. Since this psychology centers upon behavior that is the result of forces exerted upon individuals, explanation for what persons do is sought in the circumstances which surround them, the pressures upon them, and the facts and principles they have learned. Consequently, a child or youth is something to be molded in the proper fashion; learning, primarily, is a process of amassing facts and principles; and teaching is a matter of setting objectives for students, and creating the proper environment to ensure their reaching these behavioral objectives. With these goals in mind, teachers strive to transmit facts and principles—rote memories and understandings—to students through telling, showing, guiding, rewarding, punishing, and, at times, forcing and coercing them.

Understanding as seeing the tool-use of a fact

This brings us to a second definition of understanding. We may say that a person understands any object, process, idea, or fact if he sees how it can be used to fulfill some goal. As soon as a person sees what something is for, he, to some degree, understands it. Of course, the degree of one's understanding is always relative. If a person knows that a camera takes pictures, he has begun to understand a camera. But if he is going to use a camera successfully, he also needs to know the details of its operation and the consequences of his using different types of lenses, film emulsions, lighting, and picture compositions.

Note that, according to this second definition, a person's *purpose* is involved in his understanding. The understander must have a goal, and he must see that which he seeks to understand in relation to that goal. Moreover, he must see how what he is trying to understand can be made to help in achieving the goal, or how it can be kept from hindering such achievement. It is as important to understand things that get in our way as it is to understand those that help us along. A rattlesnake may be understood as something to be avoided just as a good steak may be understood as something to add savor to life.

This second definition of understanding harmonizes well with the cognitive-field outlook. According to this outlook, each individual, when behaving intelligently, is trying to reconstruct his life space in terms of how its various functional regions— objects and activities—can better be made to serve his purposes. The chief of these purposes we labeled in an earlier chapter "maintenance and enhancement of one's self." This entails the progressive improvement of a person's ability to structure and use his psychological person and environment for his own purposes.

It is from experimentation that understanding grows. Within experimental experience, one tries first one course of action and then another, preserving only those that work best. Thus, through experience, the features of each person's environment progressively develop a "pointing quality"—dark clouds "point" to rain, Johnny's outthrust jaw and angry squint "point" to a poke in the jaw for Freddy. This pointing quality which we give to features of our environment permits us to behave intelligently— to act with foresight because these are signposts along the way. The pointing quality of things tells us the probable consequences of using them, which is to say, how to use them with maximum effectiveness.

Understanding as seeing both relationships and tool-use

It is important to realize that understanding as seeing the relation between particulars and generalizations and understanding as seeing the tool-use of things are complementary processes. Hence, in order to have a fully adequate definition of understanding, we need to consolidate the two definitions.

Because it ignores the role of purpose, understanding as merely seeing relationships is not an adequate concept. Suppose one sees the relationship of certain specific facts to the principle of flotation, as we portray in the example of a Herbartian lesson plan in Chapter 2 (pp. 41–42). A student reaction to a forced acquaintance with such relationships might simply be, "So what?" and no attempt would be made to delve deeply into the implications of the principle, to remember it for future use, or to transfer it to new situations. In other words, an understanding that is confined to seeing relationships between particulars and a general is a fragile and superficial achievement. But suppose a student is a boat hobbyist. He builds boat models and operates them upon a local lake. He is involved in developing a design and needs to know how much of the boat will be submerged when it is carrying four persons whose average weight is 130 pounds. To this student the principle of flotation, and the concrete facts subsumed under it, will seem of vital importance.

Thus, what we may label "true understanding," or, even better, "functional understanding" is much more likely to occur if a learner, in learning generalizations and the specific facts pertinent to them, sees how some purpose is served thereby. So, we should not divorce the problem of teaching for understanding from that of promoting student motivation.

If understanding is best achieved when we want to use that which is to be understood, it is equally true that, when motivation toward understanding is present, what is understood will inevitably consist primarily of principles derived from a pattern of specific facts. At this point, we must restate an assertion made in Chapter 4 to the effect that specific insights tend to be generalized. As soon as one achieves an insight, the thought occurs, "Possibly this idea will work in other—or all—similar situations." Accordingly, the insight's general value is tested through its repeated use in similar situations. If it fails to work, it will be discarded as having extremely limited worth. If it seems always to work, it will become a valued possession that will be added to the persons intelligence. Of course, most insights are valid in varying degrees of predictability; they fall somewhere between the two extremes just suggested.

We now have pushed our analysis to the point where we can offer a third definition of understanding. *Understanding occurs when we come to see how to use productively, in ways that we care about, a pattern of general ideas and supporting facts.* This is the definition that we use throughout the rest of the chapter. Furthermore, when we use the verb *mean* and the noun *meaning*, we intend them as equivalent to *understand* and *understanding*.

Understanding as a noun

So far we have been discussing what the verb *understand* means. In the literature of education, we also regularly encounter the noun *understanding* or *understandings*. The noun form refers to the *product* of acts of understanding. We go through an experimental process of trying to see how certain relationships may be put to use. We find a relationship between something done and the consequences of doing it. This is our *understanding*.

An understanding, then, is a generalized insight. Thus, it is the meaningfulness of a region of a life space. Often it may be put into words but not always. The understandings a person achieves about a golf swing, running the high hurdles, or casting a fly may lie, in part, in a "feel for the act" that would be difficult to verbalize. On the other hand, most persons who have thought about such achievements are able to make statements about the probable consequences of attempting them in alternative ways. Other names for understandings are *generalizations, theories, generalized insights, general ideas, concepts, principles, rules,* and *laws.*

A word of warning about the use of the word *generalization* is in order. Whenever we use the word in this book it is used synonymously with *generalized insight.* However, in other places generalization often refers to a statement based on inadequate evidence. For example, "You are only generalizing" sometimes means that we should not take the statement seriously. This is a very imprecise use of language which students should avoid. What people really mean by such statements is not that a person has "generalized" but rather that he has been vague or unclear. Since generalization is the only possible basis for intelligent behavior, the highest possible quality of generalization should be demanded in all situations.

Understanding-level teaching

Understanding-level teaching is teaching that seeks to acquaint students with the relationships between a generalization and the particulars—between principles and solitary facts—and that develops the uses to which the principles may be applied. When a teacher tries to teach students rules governing the use of, say, subjunctives, he is trying to keep his instruction on an understanding level. If he succeeds, his students will be able to identify cases in which a given rule applies and then use the rule as a guide. We are seeking the same kind of result when we teach rules of spelling, rules for dividing fractions, or rules for repairing a motor. We are likewise operating on the same level when we teach theories in physics, chemistry, or football. (A rule or principle, by definition, is a theoretical statement.)

A contrast may be drawn between understanding-level and memory-level teaching as follows: if understanding-level teaching is successful, students will know, in addition to facts, the principles by which the facts are related; memory-level teaching tends to ignore principles, or at best handles them on such a superficial level that they have little meaning.

Much of the inefficiency in education, which research has exposed, stems from the way most school subjects are organized and presented. Subjects often remain meaningless to students, not because of students' intellectual deficiencies, but because human mentalities work in such a way that the subjects, *as organized and taught,* have little meaning for them. Understanding-level teaching gives students a tool for more intelligent behavior. It equips them with generalized insights which can be applied in problematic situations both in and outside school. It provides them with a mental kit of rules. If the rules learned are the best that are known at the time by people in a position to have expert knowledge, students have at least gained something from their education.

By this time readers may have sensed that there is still something lacking. Understanding-level teaching, if it remains merely that, casts the student as a passive and the teacher as an active agent. The teacher tells, the student listens or the teacher stimulates and the student responds. Understanding-level teaching may be highly uncritical and authoritarian. Furthermore, the principles taught by the teacher may be wrong—and sometimes are. Consequently, understanding-level teaching may lead to more intelligent behavior on the part of a student, but it does not carry with it the quality of experience needed to enhance intelligence to its fullest potential.

WHAT IS REFLECTION-LEVEL LEARNING AND TEACHING?

When a person reflects, he turns his thoughts back upon an idea or article of knowledge which supposedly exists. Thus, reflection-level learning is careful, critical examination of an idea or supposed article of knowledge in light of the testable evidence that supports it and the further conclusions toward which it points.

Reflection-level learning also leads to understandings, but with reflection the search for understandings is pursued in a different fashion from that described in the preceding section. Instead of their being given a collection of facts and generalizations by a teacher, students are confronted with something that is problematic—either unclear or puzzling. A student's reflective learning may be based upon the inadequacies or disharmonies of the mental furniture that he brings with him to school—his own attitudes, values, and knowledge. Or it may begin with some observed inadequacy, inconsistency, incompleteness, or irrelevance in the subject matter. In any case, if reflective learning occurs, a problematic situation appears about which a student centers his thinking and research. In the reflective process, he examines existing facts and generalizations and seeks out new ones.

There are crucial differences between understanding- and reflection-level teaching. The latter requires, on the part of students, more active participation, more criticism of conventional thinking, and more imagination and creativeness. The classroom atmospheres associated with the two approaches differ markedly. Reflective teaching leads to the development of a classroom atmosphere that is more alive and exciting, more critical and penetrating, and more open to fresh and original thinking. Furthermore, the type of inquiry pursued by a reflective class tends to be more rigorous and "work producing" than that pursued in an understanding-level learning situation.

Since reflective teaching is problem-centered teaching, that which distinguishes reflective from nonreflective teaching and learning is the presence of genuine problems that students feel a need to solve. At the outset of a study, a real question develops for which students have no answer, or at least no adequate one. And, through the study, the students and teacher, working cooperatively, develop what is for them a new or more adequate solution.

When reflective teaching and learning are successful, students emerge with an enlarged store of tested insights of a generalized character and an enchanced ability to develop and solve problems on their own. The latter product is as important as the former. If only the first were accomplished, no claims could be made for reflection-level which could not also be made for understanding-level teaching. However, within genuine problem-centered teaching, students learn the very nature and techniques of problem-solving processes. And, if well taught, problem-solving approaches and procedures that are learned in school carry over to be applied to a wide range of problems both in and outside school.

An understanding of how to solve problems according to principles of scientific reflection is perhaps the most useful intellectual tool a person can possess. If the central goal of education is to foster intelligence, reflective teaching should be the basic approach used by teachers everywhere. Let us visit a college class in introductory psychology being taught *reflectively* and see whether we can discern what is unique to reflection-teaching procedures.

The problem of immediate concern to the class is, What is the nature of *mind?* Most of the students previously have adhered to a dualistic view of mind and body; they have held the idea that man is composed of two distinctly different kinds of substances—mental and physical. As mutual inquiry proceeds, the following discussion between the teacher and various class members ensues. When a student speaks, he probably is verbalizing the thoughts of most of his classmates. The teacher's goal is to help the students sharpen their insights in regard to the meaning of *mind*. The teacher speaks.

"Mr. J., do you have a mind?"

"Why yes, I think so."

"Then, possibly, you can tell us what is mind?"

"It is the thing with which we think."

"You have said that mind is a thing. But a chair and a table are things. You were not referring to this type of thing?"

"No! I really meant that we think with the mind."

"What about the use of gray matter? Don't we think with our brains?"

"Well, yes."

"Then, if we think with our minds and we also think with our brains, they must be the same thing."

"No, they are not the same."

"In that case we must arrive at the conclusion that the mind is not a thing and we do not think with the mind?"

The teacher continues. "Are we able to store ideas and knowledge in the mind or are they stored in the brain? We are able to use our memory and imagination. Aren't these two different phases of thinking?"

"Yes."

"We have just said that we think with our brain. Thus, our ideas seem to be stored in the brain and not in the mind. Besides, there are ideas and knowledge in your textbook. But certainly your textbook does not function in any way like a mind. Is the mind separate from the body?"

"Yes, it seems to be."

"What makes you think so?"

"Well, we always think of mind as one thing and body as another."

"But we agreed that mind is not a thing."

"It just makes common sense."

"Is common sense a valid method by which to judge truth?"

"No!"

"You know that it was once common sense to believe that the earth is flat and that it is the center of the universe. You said that the mind is separate from the body or that it seems that way. Have you ever said to yourself that you are going to raise your arm and your arm rises?"

"Yes."

"And you have seen the effect of physical illness upon mental processes. Then, how can the mind and body be considered as separate? Obviously, there must be some connection if we continue to hold this theory."

"Has anyone ever seen electricity?"

"No."

"Will electricity flow through a copper wire?"

"Yes."

"And you know other facts about electricity and what it will do. This description of what electricity can accomplish makes it possible to describe electricity. Let us see if we can apply this same technique to our problem of mind."

"You have said that you have a mind. What did you mean when you said that you have a mind? Did you mean that you act as if you have a mind?"

"Why, yes."

"How would you describe that action?"

"I act normally."

"In other words, the difference between the way you behave and the way someone behaves who we say has lost his mind is that you act in a sensible way. And how do you act if you are sensible?"

"I am reasonable."

"You say you act reasonably. But this does not completely describe your action. Therefore, let us look at your behavior from another angle. Imagine that you are looking at a tree. How do you know that the tree is a tree?"

"It looks like a tree and everyone agrees that it is a tree."

"Are you suggesting that such a simple object as the tree has a number of specific meanings?"

"Yes."

"For instance, you will know that a tree isn't metal, that it grows, that it has leaves in summer, and much other material of factual nature. In addition, you won't mistake a tree for anything else. Now, what does this tell you about the way you should behave with reference to a tree? What would you do with a tree?"

"I might cut it down for lumber."

"And you might use it for shade. But in any case, you will not try to eat a tree and you will avoid it if it stands in your path? If you understand the meanings which ordinarily are attached to the word tree and you act accordingly, it might be said that you are behaving intelligently. Couldn't this understanding of meaning be the function which we think of as mind?

"Thus, we have arrived at our definition that mind is a function. We take it to be the function which makes it possible for us to anticipate future consequences of present or proposed lines of action. What is meant by predicting future consequences? Don't we mean that we try to comprehend meaning and use foresight? Then, if we act on the basis of our predictions can we be said to act intelligently?"[6]

[6]Unit originally written by Leslie A. McKinnis quoted from Ernest E. Bayles, *The Theory and Practice of Teaching*, New York: Harper & Row, 1950, pp. 272–274. Reprinted by permission of Harper & Row, Publishers, Incorporated.

Because of space limitation the discussion between students and teacher is to some degree in outline form. In actual practice there would be more digressions, and many statements would be made that were not pertinent to the problem at hand. The latter part of the discussion particularly would be more involved and much longer than is reported.

Now, just what is there about this teacher-student reflective classroom procedure that makes it different from either memory- or understanding-level teaching? *Perhaps it could be summarized by describing the classroom atmosphere as one of teacher-student mutual inquiry within which genuine problems are developed and solved.*

Reflective teaching, then, involves problem raising and problem solving. In problem-centered or reflective classes, instruction begins with introduction of an "I don't know" or problematic situation—one in which students are faced with a question they cannot answer. The problem should be so compelling that students really want to study it, but not so overwhelming that they are prone to give up. Accordingly, it should generate an urge to analyze the possible obstacles and dilemmas in the situation, to understand them, and to devise means for resolving the difficulties. After aiding students in raising a problem, the teacher then helps them investigate it until the best possible answer is found. Problem solving consists of formulating hypotheses and testing them with all available pertinent evidence. Facts are gathered in profusion, but teachers make no attempt to encourage fact learning or fact recall *as such.* Problems which make for ideal classroom study involve situations that are difficult enough to be challenging, yet simple enough that most students in a class will be able to cast and test hypotheses leading to a solution.

WHEN IS A PROBLEM A PROBLEM?

Too many teachers who have attempted a problems approach to teaching have not adequately understood the psychology of learning as it relates to problem-centered study. Older psychologies—mental discipline, apperception, and behaviorism—had little to say about problem-centered study. Nor have neobehaviorists, with their more sophisticated S-R conditioning theories, contributed much understanding of reflective teaching. Prior to the twentieth century, Herbart probably came closer than any other psychologist or educator to formulating a problem-centered approach to teaching, but even Herbartian teaching was not problem-centered or reflective in any true sense.

Often "problem-centered teaching" has failed because what teachers have chosen as "problems" have not actually been problems in a psychological sense. Contributions of cognitive-field psychologists enable us to understand better what happens to a person psychologically when he has a problem. A learning problem is not just an objective issue to be resolved; it must involve *psychological tension in a learner*.

If a learning problem can be defined successfully in psychological terms, this should help resolve a common dilemma which arises in connection with a problems approach to teaching. The dilemma is this: students have a great variety of real problems, but often the "problems" that a teacher thinks students should study arouse no tension in his students; and if students do feel personally some of the problems posed by a teacher, they feel some much less intensely than others. Consequently, the motivation that should accompany problem study often does not develop; students remain cold and uninterested and their work tends to be lackadaisical. An analysis of pertinent psychological factors should help readers understand what lies behind this dilemma.

Some problems may be designated as *personal* in that students are personally involved and so experience tension, which is the essence of a true learning problem. While they are experienced, personal problems hold a dominant place in the life spaces of students. Problems of another category may be identified as *social* or *societal;* they represent social needs which some adults believe exist in a community, region, or nation. They constitute part of the social matrix and, as such, are at least in the foreign hulls of the life spaces of students. But often they constitute no part of their actual life spaces.

Societal problems are felt personally by someone or they never would have been identified as problems in the first place; but commonly they are perceived only by some adults, and sometimes only by experts in fields of knowledge relevant to specific questions. To students, societal problems often seem quite remote; the students' function of living does not bring them into play. Posed by a teacher, such problems, unless students feel themselves personally involved with them, are not real problems at all.

Students not motivated by "other persons'" problems

Reactions of students to the two types of problems—personal and societal—are likely to be quite different. A student can see the point of studying problems in which he is personally involved. The necessary emotional steam already exists; often all a teacher needs to do is to direct study so that it will be as mature as possible. But when students are asked to study problems that they do not accept as their own, they are likely to remain unresponsive. Furthermore, since no personally felt goals are involved, an inwardly motivated search for solutions is unlikely. Because of this detachment, relevant facts are seen not as data contributing toward a solution but only as lessons to be learned. Consequently, the quality of learning that results when students study someone else's problems is likely to be little different from that produced by conventional textbook-recitation teaching.

Textbook writers often include "problems" at the ends of chapters. But, these are tasks, not problems. There is little reason to suppose that, without skillful preliminary discussion led by a teacher, any of these "problems" as stated will induce any significant kind of psychological tensions in students. All too often textbook writers, authors of syllabi and courses of study, and classroom teachers themselves label as problems exercises which, no matter what their potential in the teaching-learning process, do not function per se as true psychological problems for students.

Since study of other people's problems results in learning that qualitatively is little different from traditional fact memorization, some writers have suggested that teachers exclude from study any problem in which students do not already feel involved, and confine instruction to problems that students, because of their life situations, spontaneously feel. Thus, they argue that the role of a teacher is to help students define carefully problems which, for them, already exist, and then to help them conduct whatever research and discussion seem to be appropriate in solving these problems. Although it should not be denied that in any school there is an important place for this kind of problem study, exclusive emphasis on it is highly reminiscent of the Roussellian natural unfoldment outlook. There is a strong flavor of "letting students do as they please." Of course, in the hands of a capable teacher, considerable freedom may be permitted students in *selection* of their problems and at the same time considerable rigor demanded in their study.

Need for classroom study of serious societal problems

One might defend confinement of problem-centered study to problems that students already feel on the ground that it teaches them methods of problem solving which will be useful all through life. However, there are a number of significant, persistent societal problems which, for the good of the community, state, and nation, students should come to understand and appreciate. Study of those problems, about which normally only specialists or other adults are concerned, may be of great importance in preparing students for intelligent citizenship. But how can we motivate students to study, in a serious and sustained way, problems that do not seem real to them? *In this question is the crux of problem-centered teaching.* Failure to give serious consideration to it is the reason why a problems approach so often bogs down, why students are uninterested, and why, after having tried "problem-centered teaching," teachers frequently return to "teaching the facts straight."

In recent years, teachers have tried to devise ways of interesting students in problems which intrinsically are not challenging to them. "Solutions" to the engima in which teachers find themselves have included suggestions that they explain to students just how the problems are bound to affect them eventually, that students be confronted face to face with the problems (as when we take a class to visit a slum), and that teachers use more eye-catching teaching materials (such as pictures).

But, as every practicing teacher knows, these "solutions" often fail to produce real intellectual involvement. Students still do not feel the problems as their own. Of course, some students always will do whatever work a teacher assigns, and seemingly do it with enthusiasm. But what seems to be intellectual involvement and a desire to study a genuine problem often is a desire to achieve other goals such as high marks, praise, and social status.

At this point, we should review the distinction between what psychologists often call *extrinsic* and *intrinsic motivation.* This difference is developed in Chapter 10, pp. 280–281.

Instead of striking out blindly and trying everything he can think of, willy-nilly, to motivate students to study seriously what does not seem to them any of their own concern, a teacher may try a drastically different approach; he may view his teaching problems in the light of a clear and adequate understanding of the learning process. Basic to such understanding is knowledge of what it means for a person to experience a problem as a felt tension, and formulation, based on this knowledge, of an approach to teaching that holds promise in many cases of effectively translating the "problems of others" into the problems of students.

Figure 11.1
Dewey's problematic situations.

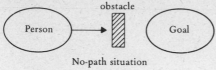

No-path situation
(obstacle appears insurmountable)

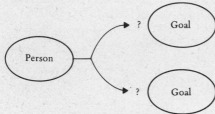

Forked-path situation A
(alternate, but equally attractive, goals)

Forked-path situation B
(single goal; alternate, but equally attractive, paths)

How is a problem a felt tension?

To have a problem, a person must have a goal or goals that he accepts as his own. A problem arises when he finds it impossible to proceed quickly and directly to the goal. When he cannot achieve his goal readily, it is either because he sees no open path to it or because he sees two or more competing paths, or two or more competing goals, and cannot decide which to pursue. These are the familiar "no-path" or "forked-path" situations described by John Dewey, and diagrammed in Figure 11.1.

Problematic situations defined in cognitive-field terms

Cognitive-field concepts and terminology also may be used to express the basic elements of a problematic situation. Either there is a goal region in a person's life space that has a positive

Figure 11.2
Field-conflict situations.

Barrier or no-path situation

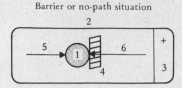

1. Person
2. Boundary of psychological environment
3. Goal; region of positive valence
4. Barrier
5. Vector of driving force toward goal
6. Vector of restraining force of barrier

Conflicting-goal situations

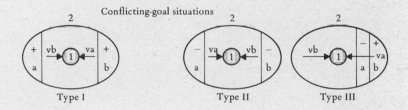

Type I Type II Type III

valence and a barrier between his person and the region of positive valence, or there are several conflicting goal regions toward which or away from which a person wants to make psychological movement. These two types of situations are barrier or no-path situations and conflicting goal situations and are shown in Figure 11.2.

Conflicting-goal situations lend themselves best to reflective or problem-centered teaching. In a Type I situation, a person has two conflicting goals or two psychologically opposite regions of his life space both with positive valences. (Positive goal regions being opposite means that both cannot be achieved at the same time.) In Type I illustration, vector vb represents a psychological force equal to the valence of region b, and vector va represents a force equal to the valence of region a. In a Type II situation, the person is faced with two psychologically opposite significant regions of his life space, each having a negative valence; he wants to escape both, and they are of such nature that this is impossible. In a Type III situation, a region of positive valence and a region of negative valence are in the same psychological direction from the person; they are functionally similar or perhaps identical. Movement toward or away from regions is determined by the relative strength of the pertinent psychological forces at the time of movement.

Superficially, Type I and Type II situations appear much alike; however, they are crucially different. A person in a Type II situation is like a ball being pushed from opposite directions by two sticks; once it gives a little, it flies off to the side out of the picture. A person in such a situation is trying to escape two opposite negative driving forces and is likely to become completely frustrated and, like the ball, leave the field—psychologically flee from the scene or become irrationally aggressive; this means that he suddenly moves from a relatively concrete level of his life space to an extremely imaginative level (see pp. 231–233). In contrast, a person in a Type I situation, like a ball being pulled in opposite directions, usually will stay in the field, i.e., remain engaged with the problem and try to resolve his conflict at the level of reality at which he meets it. He is influenced by two goals, both with positive valences. The goal toward which he moves is the one with the higher value or valence. (Should his two opposing goals be exactly equal, would he be like the donkey who starved to death while standing exactly halfway between two stacks of hay?)

Since Type II situations (two opposite negative goals) give rise to frustrations, they should be avoided in teaching procedures. Contrastedly, since Type I situations (two opposite positive goals) involve and perplex but do not frustrate students, they should be sought.

A Type III conflict situation develops when a person contemplates violating one of the basic mores of his society, especially if it is for the first time. He wants to perform the tabooed act and simultaneously he wants not to do it; thus it has both positive and negative valence. The person involved might perceive the taboo not as a negative goal region but as a barrier between him and the positive goal region. In this event, the barrier would have a negative valence which would need to be counteracted by the stronger positive valence of the act, if it is to be performed.

What level of tension is best?

A characteristic of a goal-centered situation is the presence of a certain amount of felt tension or discomfort. A person confronted with either a no-path or a conflicting-goal situation feels doubtful, puzzled, bewildered, and uncertain. How strongly he feels this way depends upon at least three factors: (1) desirability of the goal or respective goals; (2) apparent difficulty of the obstacle; and (3) his own personality make-up. Whether a person finds himself between opposite positive goals that he is trying to achieve or opposite negative aversions that he is trying to escape depends largely upon *how he construes himself and his psychological environment.*

In a sense a teacher must be a tightrope walker. He gets best results when he keeps his students in a state of full enthusiasm. When he has them involved to the point that, during discussions, they sit on the edges of their seats, arms waving and eyes glistening and all wanting to talk at once, he has a potentially fine teaching situation. However, there is a rather fine line between this type of situation and situations in which students either become so excited that their emotions are chaotic, feel despair because the problem posed is too difficult, or are bored because it is too easy.

Necessity for maintaining control of learning situations cannot be overemphasized. One of the difficulties that commonly arises when a teacher attempts reflective teaching is loss of control. When youngsters are either bored or highly excited, they are difficult to manage. A teacher following the reflective approach usually learns from experience when it is time to sidetrack a discussion that is producing too much heat.

HOW DOES PROBLEM RAISING PROCEED?

We have been considering when a problem is a problem, how a problem is a felt tension, and the level of psychological tension that is best. We now proceed to a study of the basic procedures that are involved in reflective teaching and learning. These include both problem-raising and problem-solving techniques. Problem raising is a process of persons' discovering and identifying inadequacies and disharmonies in their outlooks or the cognitive structures of their life spaces. Problem solving, in turn, is a process of reconstructing outlooks or cognitive structures so as to make them more adequate and harmonious. Problem raising is the first of the five aspects of reflective thinking; problem solving encompasses the other four (see pp. 331–337). Problem raising consists of both recognition and definition of a problem.

A problem arises in the thinking of a student whenever, by some means, he is induced to be either dissatisfied with, or doubtful concerning, some aspect of his present knowledge, attitudes, or values. The dissatisfaction or doubt represents a forked-path, blocked-path, or no-path condition within the student's life space that is characterized by conflicting goal regions. When a student has a real problem, he should be asking himself: "Is an existing insight, attitude, or value adequate, is it valid, or is an alternative to it more promising? In adherence to a given pattern of thought, is there a basic contradiction? What are the real issues in regard to the ideas that I hold? What are the available alternatives in thought and action?"

Whenever two or more competing alternative ideas, attitudes, or values are at stake, there is an *issue*. And since, by definition, all issues are controversial, *controversy is a fundamental aspect of any truly problem-centered teaching*. Controversy involves either interpersonal or intrapersonal conflict. *Interpersonal conflict* arises when respective individuals or groups hold ideas that are sharply opposed to those of other individuals or groups. We often refer to conflicts of this type as "controversial issues." Persons on each side of an interpersonal conflict or dispute may be quite consistent, each in his own outlook, even though the outlook is in sharp disagreement with that of the opposing party. In our culture such conflict may arise between social classes, between racial, religious, ethnic, or age groups, between capital and labor, and between the sexes.

When a student becomes aware of his own incompatibilities of outlook, the resulting internal struggle may be referred to as an *intrapersonal conflict*. The content of an intrapersonal conflict may be no different from that of an interpersonal one. Yet it tends to foment greater tension in the individual. Since *extreme* intrapersonal tension is hazardous to an individual's personality structure, this level should not be deliberately promoted. Nevertheless, for a reflective learning situation to exist at all, issues must come to be felt by students in such a way that each finds himself to some degree in controversy with himself. Hence, each individual must be attracted to some extent by two or more competing hypotheses and feel temporarily unable to make a choice between them; otherwise, for him, no problem exists. Accordingly, if teachers are to teach reflectively, they must help students expose contradictions and inadequacies in their thinking and action to their own critical examination.

How may teachers bring students to recognize contradictions and inadequacies in their thinking?

For a teacher to accomplish much in helping students see their inconsistencies, he needs a good idea of what kind of contradictions his students are likely to hold. This knowledge will enable a reasonably skillful teacher to pursue a line of discourse and questioning that will expose a student's ideological inconsistencies and inadequacies to himself. Some techniques for exposing contradictions and inadequacies and thereby raising problems in the thinking of students are the teacher's use of a *subject matter switch*, his introduction of *disturbing data*, his permitting students to *make mistakes*, and his helping students *convert some societal problems into personal ones.* The examples of these techniques that we give are hypothetical ones and, of course, are very much simplified. To make the contradictions and inadequacies explicit to most students in a class, much more discussion than is herein described would be necessary.

A subject matter switch. A subject matter switch is accomplished when a teacher helps a class generalize—reduce to a principle—a particular idea that is expressed by a student, then demonstrates how a further thought that is held by the same student is incompatible with the generalized principle and, consequently, with the first idea. For example, a student expresses the opinion that "Government price supports for cotton are ridiculous." The teacher then seeks agreement with the principle that "the federal government should not interfere with the economy." The teacher then places the principle in a different context, that is, gives it a different subject matter with a question like "Do you favor a protective tariff on cotton?" The student, who also adheres firmly to the principle that "a high protective tariff brings prosperity to a nation," is placed in a position that forces him to make some kind of revision of either one or both of his contradictory opinions, should he attempt to extricate himself from the contradiction. To achieve the desired result, the teacher must hold the student closely to the issue. If a student is permitted to qualify his opinions by introducing exceptions, he may extricate himself readily without having to do any serious thinking.

Teachers should realize that often, when a subject matter switch does not provoke thinking in the particular student who is trapped by it, it does motivate constructive thought in several other members of the class. The word *trapped* is used here advisedly; yet some rationale for its use is needed. A teacher who wishes to teach reflectively is probably justified in using almost any device that helps get reflection going. Some such devices may seem so teacher-centerd that the whole procedure may appear to be rigged in favor of the teacher's biases. But, this is only the beginning aspect of an inquiry. When it comes to casting and scrutinizing hypotheses and drawing conclusions there should be no rigging. Although the teacher performs key functions throughout the reflective process, the relationship between the students and the teacher is centered in mutual inquiry.

Introduction of disturbing data. Another means of inducing students to feel problems is to introduce them to data from outside their life spaces which have the effect of making them doubt some currently held item of knowledge, attitude, or value. The teacher may ask students to read a book, to watch a television program or motion picture, to go on a field trip, or to engage in some other activity that confronts them with facts contrary to those they have taken for granted. Of course, this approach, like any other, may not work. Students may refuse to admit the new facts into their life spaces. Unless they recognize the significance of the facts and truly come to doubt their existing ideas, no problem is created.

Permitting students to make mistakes. Teachers usually do not let students make enough mistakes. Making a mistake often encourages a student to reexamine something he had previously regarded as true. It is much more educative to let students do something their own way, experience the consequences, and see their mistakes than to tell them the "right way," which they then follow more or less blindly. Of course, some situations preclude this. A shop teacher might achieve maximum student motivation for study of safety practices by allowing a student to cut off a finger with a power saw, but he would not be morally justified in using such means to establish an efficient learning situation. However, a teacher has many opportunities to permit students to make "problem-raising" mistakes without endangering anyone.

Converting societal problems into personal problems. There are numerous areas of adult and societal concern about which students normally have some more or less superficial attitudes, evaluations, and knowledge. These include politics and government, international affairs, economics, business, labor and employment, pure and applied science, religion and morality, various arts, and personal relations. The ideas that students have acquired are often sketchy, disorganized, and poorly understood. Nevertheless children, and especially adolescents, do have attitudes, opinions, and some knowledge about most operations with which adults are concerned. This can be demonstrated by a reasonably free classroom discussion of any one of these subjects. Our question now is, How may a reflective approach to learning serve to build a psychological bridge between adult-societal problems and student-personal concerns?

When students appear in public school classrooms, the total knowledge, both true and untrue, that they have is usually more than teachers realize. With modern media of communication, frequent opportunities for travel, and continuously rising educational levels of parents, it seems likely that a great many youngsters have more factual knowledge than they can make much sense of. So, one of the major jobs of a modern school is to help students both verify and make sense of the welter of information that they acquire outside their schools.

Although students willingly make statements about matters in such areas as government, economics, international affairs, and the relationship of science and religion, the commitment that they feel toward such statements varies greatly. In some instances, a student's commitment is so slight that he will abandon a pet idea with little hesitation. At the other extreme, statements may represent convictions so highly cherished and strongly held that a student resists bringing them under any kind of critical scrutiny.

Ideas and attitudes that students hold concerning matters that are also of concern to adults constitute the psychological bridges between youth and adult interests. If a student feels enough personal attachment to a view to care, the moment the position becomes a subject of doubt he is likely to want to start thinking about it. At that point, if teaching is skillful, he can be led to want to study a subject about which he previously felt little or no curiosity. For example, if a considerable number of students in a class think that "most businessmen are dishonest," and the teacher can create sufficient doubt of this notion, students may want to make a study of general business practices. They may want to know what motivates businessmen, and what the consequences of such motivation are. There is no telling where critical analysis of such a problem might lead. Hopefully, it would spearhead inquiries into the most important aspects of our economy.

The point is that by using the challenge of students' attitudes, goals, and knowledge as a lure, teachers may arouse real interest in situations that otherwise would never have been felt by students to be in any way problematic. Consequently, in relation to areas in which students at first feel no personal goal or involvement, a learning problem can be created and thereby genuine student involvement can be achieved. Accordingly, students can be led to see that their problems involve the various subject matters of the social sciences, the natural sciences, and the humanities.

The essence of a problematic situation is that there is something in it that is unknown. The unknown can be uncovered only when right questions are asked. One of the best questions is also the simplest: "Why?" "*Why* did you say that?" "*Why* do you have the opinion you have stated?" Because of the demise of several fish in the classroom aquarium, a class of fourth-graders embarked upon an enthusiastic study of the biology and ecology of fish life. The students had been caring for the fish according to what they thought were "right principles." These included the assumption that fish need to eat as much in proportion to their size as do fourth-graders. The teacher, whether or not by design, allowed the children to make a mistake—to overfeed the fish. He then posed the question, "Why did the fish die?" and thereby launched a reflective study.

A reflective teaching-learning unit on race: its problem-raising aspect

The problem herein described was selected through the author's conversations with a number of high school students. The students had various definitions of the term *race*, they recognized that their definitions were cloudy, and they wanted to bring them into sharper focus. So, it was assumed that for most high school students of today the meaning of *race* probably constitutes a real problem. It also was assumed that this problem could emerge in a senior problems, social studies, history, psychology, sociology, or biology class on any one of the senior high school grade levels.

The problem and the aspects of its solution were developed by means of members of an undergraduate class in educational psychology playing the roles of high school students. Throughout the unit the teacher is designated by "T" and each of the participating students by "S." All members of the class participated to some degree, but respective students are not identified. Only the more incisive and significant statements are recorded; limited space precludes our including every detail of the class discussion. To repeat, problem raising consists of both *recognition* and *definition* of a problem. The class discussion proceeded as follows.

T: I noticed in our reading assignment for today that the term *race* appears several times. What does that word mean to most of you?

S: Why, there are three races—white, black, and yellow.

S: I don't think it is that easy, I know some white people who are called Negroes.

S: To me, *race* is a cultural word, the color of people's skin is not the real difference.

T: When you say there are three major races, are you stating the way things really *are* or are you merely classifying people for convenience? In other words, what is the basis for your distinction?

S: Biologists say that there are three races, maybe four.

S: That may be so, but cultural differences are also called racial features. For instance, people in the United States think of Jews as a race and in Germany Hitler talked about the Nordic race.

T: When people refer to the Jewish race, are they thinking of biological traits, social traits, or what?

S: They are thinking about the fact that Jews have been different down through history.

T: Oh! Then we identify them as a race because of their ancestors?

S: Partly because of their ancestors, but also because of things they do, such as make money.

S: We are getting clear away from our discussion; one's race depends upon his genes.

T: So, you think race is purely biological. How many of you think race is purely biological? (A show of hands indicated that about one-half of the class would answer this questions in the affirmative, but the other half definitely would not.)

T: So, according to biologists, there are three definite races plus a fourth that even the experts can't agree upon. Then this fourth could be almost any group, so the problem of race is wide open.

S: It is not quite that way. We can limit our definition of *race* to inherited physical characteristics that one group, and not others, has. It is the physical characteristics of a person and his ancestors.

T: For instance?

S: Color of skin and type of hair.

S: But, as I see it, everyone to some degree has a mixed blood.

T: Do you mean that everyone is some sort of a hybrid?

S: I think were making too much of this. Race is simply a biological variation of *Homo sapiens*—a subdivision of the species.

S: Then, according to you, it is very easy to place each of us in a certain race.

S: I'm beginning to think that we should just quit talking about races; we should do away with the idea.

S: We can't do that. *Race* means something to everybody; if they didn't have the word *race*, they would use some other word.

S: The trouble is that race started as a biological word, then people have added a lot of other meanings to it.

T: Let us be more specific in regard to our problem and the issues involved. Just what are we trying to decide?

S: What a race is.

T: O.K. How many of you want to pursue this question further and attempt to arrive at an answer? (Most of the class members favored this procedure.)

T: All right, now we may look at the meaning of the word *race* in at least two different ways. Do specific Races, each spelled with a capital R, exist in the very nature of things, the way gravity and the planets supposedly do, or is a race merely what people call it?

S: I'm not sure I understand the first meaning, but I am more concerned with the second.

T: You may recall that a few weeks ago we developed the difference between realism and nominalism in regard to the source of large concepts. The question that I am raising is, Do we want to find the *real* meaning of a concept Race, which transcends or extends beyond any and all existing races, or do we want to conceive of race as a name for an idea that men have developed?

S: I, too, am more concerned with the second type of meaning.

T: How many prefer to concentrate upon the meaning of the named idea *race* and leave any transcendental or absolutistic definition out of our discussion? (Most students agreed with the two who had expressed more interest in the nominalistic meaning.)

T: O.K. We shall assume that a word means what it means because of the meanings people give it, not because of its being derived from some basic transcendental source. Now, we must decide one more question. Are we concerned with what the word *race* does *mean*, what it *should* mean, or both?

S: When we discussed democratic and reflective procedures, we decided that we should study both how things are and how they should be.

T: Any other reaction or ideas?

S: How much are just *we* going to change things by thinking how *race* should be defined?

S: I get your point. But how much are we going to change things by merely studying how things are? I think we should figure out both what *race* means and what it should mean.

T: How many concur with this position? (About two-thirds concurred; the other third expressed the idea that their treatment would be too superficial to attempt any "oughts" in regard to the meaning of the word.)

The next step was to make a precise statement of the problem at hand through using the contributions of the students. The statement of the problem was then reworded until it was acceptable to all members of the class. The problem was: "What does the term *race* mean to all kinds of people, including experts, and what should it mean to us?"

At this point, we should remind ourselves of the fact that in any fertile group inquiry, two types of discussion are always in progress—one the public discussion that an observer can hear, the other a series of private discussions within which each interested student debates the issue with himself. Most of the questions and assertions that are uttered aloud emerge from, or are influenced by, the concurrent private, silent debates. The primary aim of vocal discussion is to help each individual in the classroom, including the teacher, push forward his private thinking. Hence, during the course of a single discussion. Mary may reach a conclusion that seems quite satisfactory to her, John may have his faith in a conclusion that he once held badly shaken, and Fred may merely formulate a hypothesis. In each case, the student may have thought the problem through to a further degree than at any previous time. Hence, in a discussion that appears rather chaotic to an observer, members of the group involved may actually achieve a considerable amount of pointed thinking.

HOW DOES PROBLEM SOLVING PROCEED?

Reflective teaching does not end with the inducement of psychological tension. Helping students see problems is just a beginning; it is only the first of five aspects of reflective teaching-learning. However, this aspect is very important in that it provides the motivation and direction for the problem-solving aspects of reflective inquiry. Once doubt or uncertainty has been induced, reflective teaching and learning enter the problem-solving phase.

Problem solving consists of formulating and testing hypotheses; it envelops the last four aspects of the reflective teaching-learning process. Formulation and testing of hypotheses should be conducted in an atmosphere which resembles as far as possible that of a scientific laboratory. The same open-minded and objective attitudes that characterize any scientific investigation should prevail. Hence, the teacher's role should be analogous to that of a head scientist in a laboratory; he should help students construct hypotheses, then assist them in testing them out.

Formulation of hypotheses
and deduction of their logical implications

Formulation of hypotheses—considered guesses or hunches—constitutes the second aspect of reflective learning. Deducing the logical implications of the hypotheses constitutes the third. Often, the two aspects are so intermingled that it is difficult to distinguish one from the other. In reflective teaching, students are encouraged to formulate as many hypotheses as possible in regard to what might resolve the discrepancies or inadequacies in thought that have been exposed. Simultaneously, a class is urged to deduce as many of the logical implications of each hypothesis as its members can muster. Within this aspect students think, "If this hypothesis holds, what checkable consequences should result from its operation?"

In the unit on the meaning of *race*, hypotheses are the various alternative definitions of the concept. We now proceed with the second and third aspects of the unit (the first aspect is delineated on pp. 328–331).

T: Let us restate our problem. It is, "What does *race* mean to all kinds of people, including experts, and what should it mean to us?" Now, let's see how many possible answers there are to this question.

S: The use of the word *race* does a lot of harm, and no good; let's drop it.

S: But, there are some racial characteristics.

T: For example?

S: Sickle cell anemia is characteristic of Negroes.

T: Is this a disease?

S: Yes, and its incidence is much higher in Negroes.

T: Could you say that a person who has sickle cell anemia is a Negro?

S: No, I couldn't do that.

T: If a person has three white grandparents and one black one, which race is he a member of? (This question opened up a great deal of discussion and disagreement.)

T: Can we say that, even though a person is much more "white" than "black," in the U.S.A. he is a "black?"

S: Are we concerned with the definition of the word in this country?

S: This should be our first concern.

S: If we even do this, we will be doing quite a lot.

S: Some minority groups think they can help their position by emphasizing their race.

S: But other racial groups have made themselves a part of the American culture. Chinatown has been pretty American.

S: A member of any minority group has things stacked against him.

T: This morning on the "Today Show" a Negro professor at a New York University appeared. New York public universities pay top salaries. Do you think this man still finds the cards stacked against him?

S: Yes, I do.

T: How many agree that he does? (About one-half of the class agreed.)

T: It now seems to be the time for us to "handicap" ourselves with some information. Let's all go to the library and find at least one article on the subject of race. Each of you be prepared to give us the high points of what you find out.

At the next class, students in turn contributed the ideas that they had gained through their reading. The teacher then asked each student to write out, in one short paragraph, the very best statement on, or definition of, race that he could devise.

Between classes the teacher and several class members summarized the contents of the statements. The summary in terms of the ideas stated and their frequency was as follows (ideas stated only once are not included).

1. Race primarily is a biological concept. (15 times)
2. In light of the improbability of there ever having been any pure races, the increasing miscegenation—cross-breeding—that is occurring, and the emotionality surrounding the term *race*, the concept of race has always been ambiguous and is now becoming archaic. (13 times)
3. The term should be either discarded or disregarded. (11 times)
4. The only term with which people should be concerned is the *human race*. (4 times)
5. A biological definition is inadequate. (3 times)
6. We can't ignore the term, so we should understand it. (3 times)
7. *Race* should be replaced with *ethnic groups*. (2 times)

This summary was dittoed and distributed in the next class. The various ideas were taken as hypotheses whose implications were to be tested through further reading and thought.

Testing hypotheses, the fourth aspect

In the fourth aspect of reflective thinking, teaching, and learning, *students are encouraged to examine the hypotheses in the light of all obtainable, pertinent evidence.* Provided the teacher promotes an atmosphere of mutual inquiry, problem-centered study in school may encompass a variety of evidence-seeking activities. It is likely to include the use of individual and group research, home study, field trips, and guest speakers. It may also include considerable explanation and illustration on the part of the teacher. An informal lecture can be a highly useful tool both for providing data for students' consideration and for instigating and promoting further reflection.

In the process of testing hypotheses, a teacher does not play the role of a softhearted baby-sitter. At times he must be quite tough-minded in his insistence that students examine and consider all pertinent available evidence. He also must guard against students' making hasty generalizations, arriving at snap conclusions, achieving premature closure, or taking other liberties that either impede or pervert the reflective process.

Testing hypotheses concerning the meaning of race

At this point in the study of the meaning of *race* the class reviewed the summary of hypothetical statements. The instructor next divided the areas and sources of inquiry among the students so that the investigation would be reasonably comprehensive. The entire class moved to the library during several class meetings to gather as much more pertinent information as possible in the time available. Then, the students returned to their classroom and continued their inquiry.

First, several students presented definitions that they had taken from dictionaries, encyclopedias, and other books. Next, other students presented some new ideas that they had gained from their reading. At this stage of the study several sharp disagreements arose. Samples of student expressions are as follows:

S: Why are we talking about race at all? We are just building up more prejudice and racism.

S: Each individual has his own definition, so let's let it go at that.

S: Cultural distinctions are not racial ones.

S: William A. Boyd and Isaac Reisman, in *Races and People,* say that physical features are useless criteria of race.

S: Although a biological definition is the most ideal, it is not the most practical. A word can mean many things to people.

S: The best we can do with the word is to try to understand what it really means in relation to the evolution of man, to separate fact from fiction, and to pass on our knowledge to others. Then, hopefully, as people learn to live together, the word will disappear from their vocabularies.

S: Ashley Montagu, in *The Concept of Race,* says that the term *race* has had a long and tortuous history. Biologists see it as the subdivision of a species, and laymen have an emotionally muddled interpretation of the word. But anthropologists see the term as facts forced into predetermined categories. The major idea he brings out is that the meaning of the term *race* is far from being a solved problem, and that man generally refuses to see this. The ethnic groups formed by virtue of community, language, religion, and social beliefs just add to the confusion. If *race* is to be a scientific term, it must have a genetic meaning; geographical, linguistic, and ethnic grouping then would be unnecessary. However, race is a trigger word because it is loaded with prejudice and misunderstanding.

S: If we are to form an operative definition of race, we should limit it to the inherited physical characteristics that are predominant in one group of people as opposed to another group. The prejudice implied in the word *race* should be limited to noticeable anatomical features so as not to confuse Jewish "race" and Negro race and consider both to be races.

S: Basically, there are physical differences in people. Therefore, people need some way of explaining or understanding this. The word *race* is an attempt to do this. It describes three (or possibly more) sets of physical characteristics, each set belonging to one of the races. It should be based only on these biological aspects, because within each race there are many cultures.

S: Race started out as a biological term, but society has taken the term and added other meanings to it. The easiest answer would be to do away with the word, but I think that it is here to stay for a long time yet, and if we're going to find answers to our problems today the change is going to have to come from within the people themselves. The older generations won't or can't change their feelings and ways of thinking, so it is up to the younger generations to accept changes in their society, and this takes time.

S: I think that defining *race* biologically is a complete waste of time and meaningless. *Race* does, however, imply or refer to characteristics that *exist* in some way or another, and quite obviously it causes much strife within our society. So, I think that we can't ignore the term.

Arriving at conclusions, the fifth aspect

The fifth aspect of reflective teaching-learning is *drawing conclusions*. This is perhaps the most difficult aspect of a teacher's endeavor to promote reflective learning through reflective teaching. However, the basic, guiding principle of reflective teaching and learning is that the teacher and students should strive to achieve at least a consensus on the conclusion, unanimity being the ideal. But even though a student may represent a minority of only one person, he should not be coerced in any way to swing his position to the conclusion of either the group consensus or the majority.

So, ideally, problem-centered study should culminate in at least a tentative conclusion about how the problem might be alleviated or solved. However, in many instances a definite conclusion will not be achieved. Furthermore, when a conclusion is reached, the teacher should emphasize its tentativeness and relativity. An irrevocable conclusion is like a locked door whose only key has been thrown in the sea. Students should be taught that the door to knowledge must always be left unlocked, or even ajar. Nevertheless, at the termination of an inquiry, a conclusion should be considered to be a warranted assertion; it should provide greater predictive accuracy than any alternative hypotheses that have beene entertained and examined.

A conclusion may involve either reacceptance of the idea that was originally brought under question, modification of the idea, or formulation of a substitute one. The important concern is that students push their thinking further than it had gone before. Reaffirmation of the same idea that the teacher had earlier induced students to doubt is quite acceptable, provided that in the course of their study the students come to understand the idea better and to have a better grasp of the evidence pertinent to it.

Conclusions of the study in regard to the meaning of race

The high school class had completed the first four aspects of reflective inquiry. It had stated the problem in definite terms; it had formulated some hypotheses and deduced their implications; and it had gathered much pertinent data and tested the various hypotheses. The culminating task was to formulate a tentative concluding statement in regard to the hypothesis or hypotheses that seemed most tenable.

In drawing the class's conclusions, the first step was for a committee to construct a carefully formulated summary which incorporated the statements earlier listed as hypotheses. The class then discussed each clause of the summary, and either made changes in it until a consensus would support it, or deleted it. The teacher reminded the students that their decision should rest upon what the data—pertinent information—supported, not personal whims. Out of a class of thirty, there were from none to three dissenting votes in regard to the final form of each clause. The class's concluding statement in regard to the meaning of the term *race* was as follows:

Since we cannot ignore the concept *race* in our American culture, we need an understanding of its meaning. Race is primarily a biological concept. But a biological definition, in itself, is inadequate; cultural aspects also enter into its meaning. Because (1) there is an improbability of there ever having been any pure races; because (2) miscegenation is increasing; because (3) the concept *race* serves little long-range beneficial personal-social purpose; because (4) it has been and continues to be ambiguous; and because (5) it is emotionally loaded, the term *race* now should either be discarded or considered archaic. So, we should move toward elimination of the concept *race* as such. The only race with which enlightened people should be concerned is the *human race*.

T: Does our conclusion imply that we should strive to build one unified culture to replace various racial cultures? If so, should the one culture be a pluralistic one; that is, should it be one that reflects a unity of peoples, but recognizes and accepts diversity within the unity? Or, should people attempt to blend themselves into one generalized race? Perhaps these questions involve problems for our further study.

The teacher then urged dissenting students to develop cooperatively an alternative statement that they would support and report it to the class. These students were allotted some class time to do this as a group. The teacher also reminded the class of the many insights or understandings that they had gained during their study. These ranged from simply learning some new words—for example, *miscegenation*—to gaining a more meaningful and effective grasp of the race problem. The class then moved ahead to a new problem or area of inquiry.

Throughout the study, the teacher had to make it clear that he preferred and expected serious thinking on the part of his students. His role had been to elicit compelling questions pertinent to the area of study and to lead the ensuing inquiry along lines of gathering pertinent evidence and doing logical thinking.

IN WHAT SUBJECT FIELDS IS REFLECTIVE TEACHING APPLICABLE?

Many teachers see reflective or problem-centered teaching as a possible approach to instruction in a very limited number of courses, such as social studies, literature, industrial arts, or home economics. These teachers are unable to imagine the use of problem-centered teaching in such subjects as mathematics, physics, music, physical education, and foreign language. However, such teachers have an inadequate conception of reflective teaching procedures.

With respect to subject areas, it appears that the essential characteristics of reflective teaching have enough flexibility to be employed in all school subjects, including those which seem on the surface to be rather cut-and-dried. Problem-centered teaching does not require development of elaborate unit plans. It emerges whenever a teacher, through adroit questioning and use of negative evidence, induces students to doubt that which they now accept, and then helps them analyze reflectively the issue which has arisen. In most conventional subjects, opportunities regularly appear for a teacher to operate in this manner. Passages in a textbook, assertions made by students, a news story, a motion picture or TV show—any of these may serve at times as a "springboard" for creation of problems. Problem-centered teaching seems to spring into existence in those situations where minds of teacher and students engage. *It grows more from a unique relationship between teacher and students than from any different nature of formal course materials.*

Of course, some courses and some types of course organization lend themselves more readily to reflective teaching than do others. A course construed broadly—that is, whose subject matter is not narrowly prescribed—is probably a better tool than is a more narrow course. Thus, as usually defined, general business is a better course for reflection-level teaching than is shorthand; problems of democracy better than economic geography; history and philosophy of mathematics better than algebra; world literature better than freshman composition. This difference, however, is not inherent in the nature of the subject matter as such but lies in the frame of reference within which it customarily is treated.

A course in which problem-centered teaching is used cannot be bound rigidly to a textbook. Real problems are psychological; data used in solving them are rarely organized in the same pattern as textbooks and courses of study. The "logical" organization of a book simply does not usually coincide with the logic of live thought. Hence, courses should be allowed to cut across subject matter lines whenever the cutting across makes sense in terms of the particular problem being studied. This perhaps is the most defensible rationale of a core curriculum.

Determination of which subjects, or which topics within a subject, should be handled as problems cannot be made without reference to a specific classroom situation. In each case, a teacher should reckon with the maturity and experiential background of students, community attitudes, his own preparation and skill, and anticipated consequences of having a class delve deeply into the subject.

BIBLIOGRAPHY

NOTE: References pertaining to Chapters 11 and 12 are at the end of Chapter 12. These two chapters should be studied as a unit.

TWELVE

How Is Testing
Related To
Teaching
and Learning?

Although there are many kinds of techniques and instruments that may be used for evaluating student progress, formalized testing continues to hold a very prominent position among them, especially in the minds of students. When students consider their teachers' evaluation of their achievements they usually, first of all, think of tests. Thus, they tend to gauge their levels of learning to the level of testing that their teachers employ; this is where the pay-off occurs. Hence, the nature of a teacher's system for evaluation of student learning has very great influence upon the quality of learning that actually develops.

A teacher's program of evaluation not only governs his students' study habits, their manner of interaction in class, and the number and quality of their learnings; it also greatly influences the teaching-learning level upon which their learning efforts proceed. For example, even though a teacher strives to teach on either an understanding or a reflection level, so long as he continues to give memory-level tests, most of the learning that ensues will be accomplished on a memory level. So, he should give careful consideration to the nature of his testing program and his other evaluational procedures. To quote Benjamin S. Bloom, "The point to be emphasized is that the type of mental process the student *expects* to be tested will determine his method of study and preparation."[1]

Testing, like teaching, may be conducted on any one of three levels—memory, understanding, or reflection. Autonomous development, because of its very assumed nature, cannot be evaluated by anyone other than the learner himself. Thus, student learning, when gauged to this level, can in no way be objectively measured by a teacher.

Table 12.1 summarizes the principal characteristics of the four levels of teaching and learning that are described in Chapter 11, and outlines the testing procedures that are appropriate to each level. In the rest of the chapter we discuss how the testing that harmonizes with each respective level relates to the teaching that is accomplished on that level.

WHAT TESTING PROCEDURES ARE APPROPRIATE TO MEMORY-LEVEL TEACHING AND LEARNING?

Memory-level teaching and learning may take the form of either a mentalistic-factual or a physicalistic-behavioral process. *Mentalistic-factual* teaching and learning are based upon either theistic or humanistic mental discipline both of which imply the existence of an ethereal *mind substance*, which actually does the learning. The emphasis in teaching is on exercising students' mental faculties and training their intrinsic mental powers. It is assumed that the learning of factual materials is the process that builds minds best. The results of mentalistic, memory-level learning are both disciplined minds or mental faculties and a mass of retained factual material. So, in the process of appropriate mentalistic testing, either factual essay or short-answer "objective" tests are employed to check for recall of memories that have been retained in the students' minds. Factual essay tests are in the form of "what are the four levels of teaching and learning?" Objective tests geared to this level in the form of "the four levels of teaching and learning are (1)_____, (2)_____, (3)_____, and (4)_____."

Physicalistic-behavioral teaching and learning depend upon the S-R conditioning theories of the behavioristic family for their psychological underpinning. In the process of learning memories are acquired, i.e., behaviors are either acquired or modified,

[1]Benjamin S. Bloom "Testing Cognitive Ability and Achievement" in N. L. Gage, ed., *Handbook of Research on Teaching*, Chicago: Rand McNally, 1963, p. 392.

Table 12.1
Levels of the Teaching-Learning Process
and the Testing Procedures Appropriate to Each Level

level of teaching-learning	underlying learning theory	attributes of the teaching-learning process
1. Memory a. Verbal-factual; mentalistic	Mental discipline theories of mind substance family; learners are active	Rote memory, mind training, repetitive drill, catechetical; teacher-centered
b. Behavioral; physicalistic or mechanomorphic	S-R conditioning theories of behavioristic family; learners are passive or reactive	Conditioning or behavior modification; formation of either S-R linkages or R-S reinforcements; reductionistic teacher-centered
2. Explanatory understanding	Apperception; learners are passive	Teacher explanation and student grasp of generalizations, relationships, rules, or principles; teaching facts in relation to principles and the tool use of generalizations and their supporting facts; teacher-centered
3. Autonomous development (Neo-Progressive Education)	Natural unfoldment theory of psychedelic humanism (delic= delight) or romantic naturalism; learners are autonomously proactive—forwardly active	Promotion of intuitive awareness of each self; artistic expression of self-actualization; negative education—no coercion, prescription, or imposition, one's feelings are the final authority for truth student-centered
4. Reflection or problem-centered; exploratory understanding; requires personal involvement, not merely interest; conflict or incompatibility of ideas is essential (not Progressive Education)	Cognitive-field theory; learners are situationally, perceptually interactive (SMI)	Purposive involvement and perplexity, problem raising and solving, and getting a "feel" for a principle, idea, or act teacher–student-centered cooperative inquiry and evaluation; goal is student perplexity just short of frustration and resultant learning

...ture of learnings	*nature of appropriate tests*	*basis for appropriateness of test items*	*method of test evaluation*
...sciplined minds or mental ...aculties and retained factual ...materials	Factual essay or short-answer true-false or completion	Recall of retained memories	Check students' answers against list prepared at time the test is made; teacher-centered
...ther proper responses or ...ncrease probability of desired responses	Sampling of responses	Manifestation of previous conditioning or reinforcement	Check students' responses against a prepared list; teacher-centered
...derstandings, insights, ...principles, relationships, ...concepts, generalizations, ...rules, theories, or laws	Factual and explanatory essay or short-answer true-false, selection, or completion	Recognition, explanation, or use of understandings, insights, principles, generalizations, rules, laws, or theories	Check students' answers against prepared list, but, on essay tests, credit a student for "right" answers even though he uses words other than the instructor's; teacher-centered
...elf-directed active unfoldments; expressed intuitive awarenesses; unfolded or developed natural needs or instincts and accompanying feelings	No testing; students alone evaluate their achievements according to their respective feelings		
...urposely acquired understandings, insights, principles relationships, concepts, generalizations, rules, theories, or laws *plus* enhanced scientific outlook and instrumental thinking	Reflective or problem-centered essay	Essay questions that are real, unanswered problems for the students and pertinent to the study having been pursued; real problems involve both generalization and tool-use of ideas as well as some degree of creativity	Check students' answers on basis of criteria agreed upon prior to the test—probably adequacy of pertinent data applied to the solution and harmony of the data, problem, and answer; teacher-student-centered

through either formation of S-R linkages or connections or occurrence of R-S reinforcements. Learnings take the form either of proper responses being acquired and retained in memory or of the probabilities of desired responses being increased.

Within behaviorism, testing like teaching centers upon behavioral modification or change. The desired behaviors of students are sampled in such a way as to measure the manifestations of previous conditioning. In testing for learned physicalistic behaviors, the teacher takes a sampling of the behavioral modifications that had been included in a statement of behavioral objectives that was developed prior to the beginning of the course. These modifications all are in the form of observable responses. Hence, a teacher who is teaching on this level would expect his students to be able to list or name the four levels of teaching and learning. Consequently, he would use test items much like those used in mentalistic memory testing.

HOW IS UNDERSTANDING-LEVEL LEARNING EVALUATED?

Within the understanding level of teaching and learning, teachers, along with other media, give understandings, insights, or discernments to their students. They may employ either apperception or Gestalt-insight learning theory to guide their teaching activities. Understandings, insights, principles, relationships, concepts, generalizations, rules, theories, or laws are taught through teachers explaining and describing them to their students. Teachers present understandings to students both through teaching related facts and the principles that may be drawn from them and through explaining the tool or instrumental use of the generalized principles.

Either factual and explanatory essay tests or short-answer true-false, selection, or completion tests are most appropriate for testing students' understandings that are learned on an understanding level. Through the use of these, students demonstrate how well they can either recognize, explain, or use the understandings or generalized insights that the teacher has expected them to acquire.

In testing on an understanding level, just as on both aspects of the memory level, the teacher checks students' answers against a prepared list of answers. However, the process differs somewhat from that of memory-level testing in that so long as the answers are correct the teacher credits students for "right" answers even though they may use wording somewhat different from that of the instructor. An appropriate understanding-level essay test question would be, "describe how the four levels of teaching and learning differ from one another." An appropriate objective test item might be as follows. "Select the word that completes the sentence best: When a teacher teaches on an understanding level he gives his students (1) advice, (2) insights, (3) thoughts, (4) memories."

Although mentalistic-memory, physicalistic-memory, and understanding levels of teaching and learning each has its unique characteristics, the three also have a common significant trait, namely, all three are teacher-centered processes. The teacher sets the objectives for the students and the teacher measures the relative achievement of those objectives. In some cases learners are considered to be active, in other cases they are assumed to be passive, and in still others they are taken to be intermittently active and passive. But, seldom, if ever, are they considered to be perceptually interactive as is the case in reflective teaching and learning.

If teachers assume that their students are active and if they pursue either memory or understanding-level teaching, they do so for the purpose of making sure that the students' active natures either are exercised or unfold in the proper manner. If teachers assume that their students are basically passive, and this is most often the case, they bring the proper stimuli or ideas to impinge upon the students and thereby inculcate the designed behaviors or understandings.

CAN AUTONOMOUS DEVELOPMENT BE TESTED?

Autonomous development, as an approach to teaching and learning, implies not only that students are active, but that they are forwardly so or proactive. Hence, it is student-centered as contrasted with both memory and understanding levels' being teacher-centered and reflective level's being teacher–student-centered.

An autonomous development approach to learning betokens a *negative* education within which not only is there no coercion, prescription, or imposition, but also there is no teacher leadership or student-teacher cooperative learning and evaluation. Each student's feelings are the final authority for truth. The educative function of teachers is to promote intuitive awareness of each student's self and artistic expression of his self-actualization.

School learnings are in the form of naturally unfolded or developed needs and accompanying feelings being actively expressed by self-directed active persons. Hence, there can be no valid systematic, teacher-developed testing program. Students alone can evaluate their respective achievements in accordance with their individual feelings.

WHAT IS UNIQUE
ABOUT REFLECTION-LEVEL EVALUATION?

The seminal concept that has provided the originative power for reflective teaching and learning has been *perceptual interaction*. To repeat again, perceptual interaction, i.e., simultaneous mutual interaction (SMI), is a cognitive experiential process within which a person, psychologically, simultaneously reaches out to his psychological environment, acts in relation to it, and realizes the consequences of his so doing. Perceptual interaction, so defined, is supported and amplified best by a cognitive-field psychology of learning.

The results of reflection-level teaching and learning, as is the case with the understanding level, include understandings, principles, rules, or laws, but not these alone. The reflective level implies that these results are *purposively acquired*. In addition, reflection-level learning enhances students' scientific outlook and experiential-instrumental thinking, and thereby points them toward doing further creative thinking on their own.

Since reflective teaching entails problem-centered, exploratory personal involvement, testing that is compatible with it will likewise be centered on genuine problems. When one is teaching on a reflective level he should be trying, in testing as well as in all other evaluational procedures, to ascertain whether the individual student is able to apply adequate information to the solution of a problem in such a way as to harmonize the problem, all available pertinent data or facts, and the answer. The most practicable instruments for the accomplishment of this purpose are problem-centered essay tests. A reflective-level essay test usually consists of four, three, or even fewer carefully constructed questions. Each question should be pertinent to the study that the students have been pursuing and should constitute a real problem for them. A sample reflective-level test question is as follows: "How is the listing of the behavioral objectives of a course related to the course's being taught reflectively?"

The best type of reflection-level question is one to which there is possibly more than one true answer. So, *answers cannot be written out at the time the test is constructed*. Each answer must be evaluated on its own merits. In an adequate answer many facts will be used, but the number of facts listed as such will not be the basis for evaluation. Instead, answers will be evaluated on the basis of some criteria—measuring sticks—that the teacher and students have agreed upon prior to the time of the test. These criteria probably will be *adequacy* of the pertinent data that are applied to the solution of the problem, harmony of the problem, data, and answer, and perhaps one or two others.

A teacher who is committed to reflective teaching would neither test his students on a memory level nor use so-called true-false tests. He would prefer to use essay tests, and he would strive to make his questions truly reflective ones. At times he might use selection tests, but he would realize that in so doing he would be drawing his student away from reflective thinking.

Since programmed learning and machine teaching now are so much in the limelight, readers may wonder what levels of teaching and evaluation are served through this medium. Briefly stated, linear programming as advocated by B. F. Skinner is geared to memory-level, but it may possibly teach and test for understandings. Intrinsic or branched programming as advocated by Norman Crowder through the use of "scrambled textbooks" and by O. K. Moore through the use of "talking typewriters" can teach for understanding and perhaps for some reflection. However, since the conclusions are decided in advance of the studies, reflective learning and testing, in its richest sense, probably is not fostered.[2]

In concluding, we should remind ourselves that, regardless of the level of learning pursued, students need facts in order to understand anything. Furthermore, they need both facts and understandings in order to learn reflectively. However, teachers need not be reluctant to experiment with understanding- and reflection-level teaching and testing for fear that their students will not learn a sufficient number of facts. When students are taught and tested on the reflection level, they acquire many facts as well as understandings, and likewise when they are taught and tested on the understanding level they acquire much factual information. However, this process does not work in reverse; there is little about factual learning as such that contributes to understanding, and little about teaching for understanding in a nonreflective way that contributes to a student's reflective powers and habits.[3]

[2]See Morris L. Bigge and Maurice P. Hunt, *Psychological Foundations of Education*, 2nd ed., New York: Harper & Row, 1968, pp. 533–542.

[3]See Ernest E. Bayles, *Democratic Educational Theory* (New York: Harper & Row, 1960), especially Chapter 1, "Experiments with Reflective Teaching."

BIBLIOGRAPHY

ANDERSON, HAROLD H., ed., *Creativity and Its Cultivation*, New York: Harper & Row, 1959.
Addresses presented at the Interdisciplinary Symposia on Creativity, Michigan State University. Top authorities cover numerous facets of the subject. Excellent.

ASCHNER, MARY JANE, and CHARLES E. BISH, eds., *Productive Thinking In Education*, Washington, D.C.: The National Education Association and the Carnegie Corporation of New York, 1968.
A report on two conferences on productive thinking. Part Four: Education For Productive Thinking and Chapter 12, "Summary and Interpretation" are especially pertinent to these two chapters.

BAYLES, ERNEST E., *Pragmatism in Education*, New York: Harper & Row, 1966.
Pages 109–127 depict elementary school units for teaching spelling, arithmetic, art, nature study, and grammar reflectively. Pages 127–140 describe secondary units in literature, American history, and natural science.

BEVANS, WILLIAM, "Perceptual Learning: An Overview," *Journal of General Psychology*, January 1961, pp. 69–99.
Characterizes perceptual development as a process of progressive refinement, definition, and specificity rather than of building associate linkage.

BIGGE, MORRIS L., and MAURICE P. HUNT, *Psychological Foundations of Education*, 2d ed., New York: Harper & Row, 1968.
Pages 573–575 report an actual unit that was used in teaching a high school English class reflectively.

BLOOM, BENJAMIN S., *et al.*, *Taxonomy of Educational Objectives; Handbook I: Cognitive Domain*, London: Longmans, Green, 1956.
Develops six general areas of educational objectives and test exercises, namely, knowledge, comprehension, application, analysis, synthesis, and evaluation.

BONNER, HUBERT, *Group Dynamics*, New York: Ronald Press, 1959.
One of the best general texts in the field. Covers history of research on groups and present status of group work.

BRUNER, JEROME S., *The Process of Education*, Cambridge, Mass.: Harvard University Press, 1960.
The chairman's report of the major themes, principal conjectures, and most striking tentative conclusions of a 1959 conference of 35 natural scientists, psychologists, and educators on teaching science and mathematics in elementary and secondary schools. The report emphasizes teaching for understanding the *structure*—pertinent relationships—of a subject matter rather than for mastery of facts and techniques.

BRUNER, JEROME S., *et al.*, *Studies in Cognitive Growth*, New York: John Wiley, 1966.

Chapters 3–12 present research studies of cognitive growth of children. The studies are concerned with intellectual growth as it is affected by the way people gradually learn to represent their worlds through action, imagery, and symbolizations. Thus, the chapters describe children's solutions of problems and thereby provide patterns, but not specific details, for reflective teaching.

BRUNER, JEROME S., *Toward a Theory of Instruction*, Cambridge, Mass.: Harvard University Press, 1966.
Presents Bruner's conclusions concerning what should go into a theoretical basis for teaching procedure. Highly recommended to be read in connection with the section of Chapter 11 entitled "What Practical Suggestions Can Be Made for Improving Understanding-Level Teaching?" Bruner writes on a more theoretical level but his ideas are highly thought-provoking.

BURTON, WILLIAM H., *et al.*, *Education For Effective Thinking*, New York: Appleton-Century-Crofts, 1960.
A key reference, not only in connection with the foregoing chapters, but in connection with the entire book. The theoretical basis is laid down in Parts I and II. Part III discusses teaching to think in a number of specific school subjects.

CARTWRIGHT, DORWIN, and ALVIN ZANDER, eds., *Group Dynamics*, 3d ed., New York: Harper & Row, 1968.
A collection of readings, all of which are relevant to classroom procedures. Readers will detect a strong Lewinian influence. A very useful reference.

COLUMBIA ASSOCIATES IN PHILOSOPHY, *An Introduction to Reflective Thinking*, Boston: Houghton Mifflin, 1923.
Still one of the best books in its field. Chapter 1 defines reflection, and the remainder of the book presents "case studies" of reflection in action. Covers a number of different subject areas.

EBEL, ROBERT L., ed., *Encyclopedia of Educational Research*, 4th ed., New York: Macmillan, 1969.
Benjamin S. Bloom, "Higher Mental Processes," pp. 594–601, treats theories of learning, schools of psychology as related to teaching and learning, analysis of problem-solving processes, and education for improvement of thinking abilities. Margaret Ammons, "Objectives and Outcomes," pp. 908–912, summarizes historal approaches to educational objectives and their evaluation; discusses meaning of "behavioral objectives."

EISNER, ELLIOT W., "Educational Objectives: Help or Hindrance," *School Review*, 75 (1967), 250–282.
Reviews history of specific objective movement back through 1918. Develops case for and against the use of specific educational objectives.

ENGELMANN, SIEGFRIED, *Preventing Failure in the Primary Grades*, Chicago: Science Research Associates, 1969.
Chapter 4, "Reading for the Nonreader," explains how to teach

reading in order to help children *get the ideas* surrounding the use of words. Hence, it opens the way for a teacher to teach beginners how to read using reflective processes.

GAGNE, ROBERT M., *The Conditions of Learning,* 2nd ed., New York: Holt, Rinehart and Winston, 1970.
Views learning from vantage point of instruction. Describes eight classes of performance change and the conditions for learning associated with each.

GAGNE, ROBERT M., "Some New Views of Learning and Instruction," *Phi Delta Kappan, 51,* No. 9 (May 1970).
Some newer theories of teaching and some provocative experiments that support them.

GRIFFITHS, I. ACE, and MORRIS L. BIGGE, "Educational Guidance and Quality Education," *Education,* May 1963, pp. 556–559.
Relates guidance practices to classroom atmospheres and teaching procedures.

HILDRETH, GERTRUDE H., *Educating Gifted Children,* New York: Harper & Row, 1952.
An account of practices at Hunter College Elementary School. Chapter IV describes teaching methods. The emphasis is on reflective learning, and the approaches employed are applicable to all children and youth.

HULLFISH, H. GORDON, and PHILIP G. SMITH, *Reflective Thinking: The Method of Education,* New York: Dodd, Mead, 1961.
A noneclectic argument to the effect that unless education dedicates itself to teaching students to think, it dedicates itself to nothing at all. Highly recommended reading.

HUNT, MAURICE P., and LAWRENCE E. METCALF, *Teaching High School Social Studies,* 2nd ed., New York: Harper & Row, 1968.
Part One contains a general treatment of reflective teaching which applies equally to all subjects and grade levels.

LEWIN, KURT, *Resolving Social Conflicts,* New York: Harper & Row, 1948.
A fundamental reference. Lewin's experimental work paved the way for much that is now known about the dynamics of groups.

McBURNEY, JAMES H., and KENNETH HANCE, *The Principles and Methods of Discussion,* New York: Harper & Row, 1939.
One of the best treatments of "reflective discussion." The authors reject any discussion which is a mere pooling of ignorance.

MAGER, ROBERT F., *Preparing Instructional Objectives,* Palo Alto, Calif.: Fearon Publishers, 1962.
Instructional objectives are to be stated and measured in terms of observable terminal behaviors. Divides objectives into content and non-content ones. By implication, rules out reflective teaching.

MEYER, AGNES E., *Education for a New Morality,* New York: Macmillan, 1957.
A provocative little book with profound implications for what and how we teach. It suggests a philosophy of education which might

close the gap in our thinking between science and humanism.

MILES, MATTHEW B., *Learning to Work in Groups*, New York: Teachers College Press, Columbia University, 1959.
The contributions of many experimental and research studies of the nature of group dynamics brought together and focused on the process of helping people to learn to work in groups.

MILLER, GEORGE A., EUGENE GALANTER, and KARL H. PRIBRAM, *Plans and the Structure of Behavior*, New York: Holt, Rinehart and Winston, 1960.
A creative treatment of the psychology of the cognitive processes. Ideas developed in communication and computer theory are applied to psychology. A TOTE—Test-Operate-Test-Exit—unit based on "feedback" is conceived as an alternative to reflex arc theory. A challenging innovation in psychology.

ROGERS, CARL R., *Freedom To Learn*, Columbus Ohio: Charles E. Merrill, 1969.
A plan for self-directed procedures in education. Emphasizes openness, spontaneity, and learning how to learn. A contemporary presentation of autonomous development and psychedelic humanism.

SAETTLER, L. PAUL, *A History of Instructional Technology*, New York: McGraw-Hill, 1968.
Treats theories of learning in relation to technology of instruction, including programmed instruction. See especially Chapter 4.

TABER, JULIAN I., ROBERT GLASER, and HALMUTH M. SCHAEFFER, *Learning and Programmed Instruction*, Reading, Mass.: Addison-Wesley, 1965.
Probably one of the best-written and scholarly expositions of Skinner's linear programming. Includes a concise theoretical treatment of Skinner's concept of operant conditioning.

USHENKO, ANDREW, *The Field Theory of Meaning*, Ann Arbor: University of Michigan Press, 1958.
A highly technical discussion which attempts to harmonize the theory of meaning with field psychology. For advanced students.

WALKER, MARSHALL, *The Nature of Scientific Thought*, Englewood Cliffs, N.J.: Prentice-Hall, 1963.
Written by a physical scientist for general readers. Basic purpose of science is prediction; basic procedures are use of conceptual models.

WAYNE, JOHN P., *Theories of Education*, New York: Harper & Row, 1963.
A philosophical-historical treatment of educational theories. Describes principles, psychological approaches, methods, and practices implicit in each theory. Excellent background material for this volume.

INDEX